The Specter of Speciesism

Recent titles in
AMERICAN ACADEMY OF RELIGION
ACADEMY SERIES

SERIES EDITOR
Carole Myscofski, Illinois Wesleyan University
A Publication Series of
The American Academy of Religion
and
Oxford University Press

AMERICAN ACADEMY OF RELIGION

THE SPECTER OF SPECIESISM

Buddhist and Christian Views of Animals

PAUL WALDAU

OXFORD
UNIVERSITY PRESS

2002

OXFORD
UNIVERSITY PRESS

Oxford   New York

Athens   Auckland   Bangkok   Bogotá   Buenos Aires   Cape Town
Chennai   Dar es Salaam   Delhi   Florence   Hong Kong   Istanbul   Karachi
Kolkata   Kuala Lumpur   Madrid   Melbourne   Mexico City   Mumbai   Nairobi
Paris   São Paulo   Shanghai   Singapore   Taipei   Tokyo   Toronto   Warsaw

and associated companies in
Berlin   Ibadan

Copyright © 2002 by The American Academy of Religion

Published by Oxford University Press, Inc.,
198 Madison Avenue, New York, New York 10016

Library of Congress Cataloging-in-Publication Data
Waldau, Paul.
The specter of speciesism : Buddhist and Christian views of animals / Paul Waldau.
p. cm.—(American Academy of Religion academy series)
Includes bibliographical references and index.
ISBN 0-19-514571-2
1. Speciesism—Religious aspects—Buddhism.   2. Speciesism—Religious aspects.
3. Animal rights—Environmental aspects.   4. Animal welfare—Moral and ethical aspects.
I. Title   II. Series.
BQ4570.A53 W35 2001
291.5'963—dc21   00-051653

1 3 5 7 9 8 6 4 2

Printed in the United States of America
on acid-free paper

To a father,

who invited all of his children to explore the world,

and to a mother,

whose natural compassion gave her children

the ability to care about those

we have encountered in our own life journeys

Preface

The broad topic "religion and animals," though in important respects an ancient concern, remains an area that has not been worked out systematically by modern scholars. If one scours publications from the fields of religious studies, theology, anthropology, ethics, or any of the other fields increasingly dealing with one or both of the topics "religion" and "animals," one will not find a work that attempts to lay out the many issues that arise when one tries to assess the relationship of these two vast subjects. In such a circumstance, it is difficult to see many, let alone all, of the inevitable pitfalls awaiting that person who tries to say something general about the relationship of these important realms of human experience.

Such an attempt is, however, sorely needed for many reasons. For example, grappling with the constructed nature and ideological character of Buddhist and Christian views of nonhuman animals has great potential for contributing to contemporary projects of reconceptualizing Buddhist and Christian teachings and practices. This is true not only with regard to the views and treatment of nonhuman animals in the light of the new zoological knowledge but also with regard to ecological issues generally. Indeed, the very attempt to identify tendencies to construct value systems, worldviews, and lifeways that either intentionally or inadvertently marginalize "others," whether they be human or otherwise, is of momentous importance today. It has broad relevance to many contemporary exclusions, not the least of which are the exclusions that concern the contemporary social and environmental justice movements. As the antisexism and antiracism movements have often shown, identifying the underpinnings of one exclusion often enables us to see better the underpinnings of others.

Given the state of this developing field, the first attempts may well stumble or even wander aimlessly, for the terrain is both vast and daunting. Indeed, as is so often the case with human endeavors, mapping this terrain will likely be accomplished only collectively through the efforts of many, many people. This book begins the journey, taking a few of the preliminary steps encountered when one tries to assess the characteristics of Buddhist and Christian views of the living beings outside the human species. What follows is a slightly revised and updated version of a doctoral dissertation submitted by the author to the University of Oxford in September 1997 under the title "Speciesism in Christianity and Buddhism."

Acknowledgments

Completion of one's first book is a distinctive event, and certainly cause for reflection on the fact that, even if only one "author" is listed, so very many others inevitably contribute in obvious or subtle ways to a long publication or work of art. To remind oneself of this simple but crucial fact, as well as to alert those who read the book carefully and from cover to cover, it is the custom to honor the roles of those who were most significant.

Keith Ward, John Hick, and Andrew Linzey must be acknowledged first. Each in his own way has been a remarkable guide for me, as well as a personal friend.

Other friends such as Pascal Marland, Nat Greene, Louisa Vessey (now Greene), Laurie Claus, and Niles Pierce added the texture of daily support. Dan and Francine Robinson also provided much community and inspiration. Intellectual and other deep companionship came from Diana Butler-Bass and Kristin Aronson, two very special women indeed. Diana, for your remarkable support as I conceived and wrote the project, and Kristin, for your sensitive, informed reading of the official dissertation transcript, I will long be grateful. Harvard Divinity School's Tovis Page and Jonna Higgins-Freese also provided much special support, and the remarkable trio of Sarah Luick, Steve Wise, and Theo Capaldo of Boston constantly stimulated me to think about many different issues, but most especially the real-world animals whose lives are so affected by human actions.

The Spalding Trust's financial support, and the support of the Center for the Study of World Religions at Harvard during 1997, also must be acknowledged. In their quiet manner, these institutions support scholars in important and varied ways.

Contents

Abbreviations

The bibliography contains additional information regarding the editions and translations of the scriptural works listed here.

A.	*A"nguttara-Nikāya*
Abhi-P.	Abhidamma *Pi.taka*
A-S.	*Abhidhammatha-Sa"ngaha* (*Compendium of Philosophy*)
B.C.E.	Before the common era and equivalent to B.C. (before Christ), that is, before the year 0 in the Western calendar
Bv.	*Buddhava.msa*
C.E.	Of the common era and equivalent to A.D. (*anno Domini*), that is, after the year 0 in the Western calendar
Cp.	*Cariyāpi.taka*
D.	*Dīgha-Nikāya*
Dk.	*Dhātukathā*
Dpda.	*Dhammapada*
DPPN	*Dictionary of Pali Proper Names* by Mālālāsekera
Dsan.	*Dhammasa"nga.ni*
DW	Walshe's translation of *Dīgha-Nikāya*
HBD	*Harper's Bible Dictionary*
IB	*The Interpreter's Bible*
Itv.	*Itivuttaka*
J.	*Jātakas*
JB	*The Jerusalem Bible*
Khp.	*Khuddakapā.tha* translation by ~Nā.namoli
Khp2.	*Khuddakapā.tha* translation by Mrs. Rhys Davids
KhpA.	Buddhaghosa's commentary on Khp. known as *Paramatthajotikā*
KJV	*King James Version Bible*
Kv.	*Katthuvatthu*
LXX	*Septuaginta: Id est Vetus Testamentum Graece Iuxta LXX Interpretes*; occasionally "Septuagint" for stylistic reasons
M.	*Majjhima-Nikāya* translation by Horner
MA.	*Papan~ncasūdanī Majjhimannikāya.t.thakathā*
Mil.	*Milindapa~nha*
MNB	~Nā.namoli and Bodhi translation of the *Majjhima-Nikāya*
MSBB	Chalmers translation of the *Majjhima-Nikāya* in Sacred Books of the Buddhist Series
Mv.	*Mahāvastu*

NEB   *The New English Bible: The Old Testament*
NRSV   *The Holy Bible containing the Old and New Testaments with Apocryphal/Deuterocanonical Books, New Revised Standard Version*
OED   *Oxford English Dictionary*, 2d ed. (compact disc)
Pat.   *Pa.t.thāna*
PED   *Pali-English Dictionary*
Pm.   *Pa.tisambhidāmagga*
Pp.   *Puggalapa~n.~natti*
Pv.   *Petavatthu*
RSV   Revised Standard Version
Sam.   *Sa.myutta-Nikāya*
SBB   Sacred Books of the Buddhists Series
SBE   Sacred Books of the East Series
Sn.   *Suttanipāta*
SP   *Saddharma-Pu.n.darīka or The Lotus of the True Law*
Tag.   *Theragāthā*
Tig.   *Therīgāthā*
U.   *Udāna*
UA.   Dhammapāla's commentary on the *Udāna*
USBB   Woodward's translation of the *Udāna*
Vib.   *Vibha"nga*
VibPali   The romanized Pali text of *Vibha"nga*
Vv.   *Vimanavatthu*
VvA.   Dhamapāla's commentary on Vv.
Vin.   Vinaya *Pi.taka*
Vis.   *Visuddhimagga*
Vul   The Vulgate, and specifically, *Biblia Sacra: Iuxta Vulgatam Versionem*

The Specter of Speciesism

Introduction

This is a study of how other animals have been viewed in the Buddhist and Christian religious traditions. At first glance, providing an account of these traditions' views, or indeed of the larger subject "religion and animals," may seem a relatively simple task. Upon examination, however, the topic swells into a multitude of diverse issues, a number of which are extraordinarily complex.

Some of the complexities stem directly from the well-known fact that the Buddhist and Christian traditions are far from monolithic. It is a commonplace among scholars of comparative religion, for example, that each of these traditions is extraordinarily internally diverse. Upon even a cursory examination, one finds that, over the millennia of their existence, these traditions have provided an astonishing array of views and materials, some of which are in significant tension with each other. Since such diversity leads to challenging problems on virtually any subject that believers, scholars, and other interested parties might explore, it also affects significantly many issues that arise when one seeks to describe each tradition's views of animals.

A very different set of complexities arises from the fact that the category "animals" is also well described as "internally diverse." In other words, the living beings included when we use the generalization "animals," however it is defined, can be startlingly different from one another. Many are mentally, socially, and individually very simple, but others are so complicated and enigmatic mentally and socially that we may not have the ability to understand their lives well. Indeed, as pointed out in this study, at times various animals are so different from one another that failure to use some description other than the generalization "animals" risks crass oversimplification and profoundly inaccurate descriptions.

A third and equally decisive factor that complicates our approach to the awe-inspiring complexity and diversity of problems we collect under the rubric "religion and animals" is something altogether closer to home. This is the fact that our most familiar ways of talking about "animals," are, upon careful examination, coarse caricatures. As will be discussed later, these familiar patterns of speaking often mislead in the extreme because they are dramatic oversimplifications of the realities that we seek to describe and otherwise engage when inquiring about the "animals" side of "religion and animals" topics.

Given the difficulties that our everyday and even scholarly habits of discourse involve when we try to talk about religion and/or animals, some care is in order when considering just what we might say about the rich intersection of religious and animal issues. For example, though they will likely seem somewhat awkward at first, the terms "other animals" and "nonhuman animals" are frequently used in this work as a reminder that the prevailing uses of the term "animals" have some very unusual

features. "Animals" in contemporary English usage, as in many other familiar lan‑
guages, usually means, of course, only "all animals other than humans." What makes
this use peculiar, from one vantage point at least, is the fact that virtually every
speaker of English is also familiar with uses of "animals" that include humans. When‑
ever, for example, someone restates verbatim Aristotle's claim that "man is the only
animal who has the gift of speech,"[1] listeners are not surprised in the least by refer‑
ence to humans as animals.

The coexistence of these two conflicting senses of "animals" reflects our general
awareness of connections between all animals, human and otherwise, even as many
value systems, and certainly the dominant ones in the developed world, emphasize
the special role that human animals have so often accorded themselves on this planet.
Thus, even though use of the term "animals" for members of the human species is,
by and large, uncontroversial, reliance on phrases such as "human animals" and
"nonhuman animals" disturbs some readers because they perceive the recurring phrase
to signal an agenda, if you will. What is not noticed so readily is that the more com‑
mon use, as in the phrase "humans and animals," also advances an agenda or world‑
view. In fact, the phrase "humans and animals" is so commonly used that its under‑
lying agenda or metamessage—that humans are distinct from all other animals—is
not easily noticed even though the phrase is, logically, a problem (this is discussed
in chapter 5).

In order to get beyond the caricature, impoverishment, and stilted conceptuali‑
zation that reliance on any single discipline, vocabulary scheme, tradition of speak‑
ing, or, to use the phrase common in this study, "tradition of discourse" would
threaten, I use an interdisciplinary approach. This combination of different orienta‑
tions, concerns, and vocabularies is used to help identify and organize problems,
assisting the reader in a survey of the various kinds of limitations and issues involved
in assessing Buddhist and Christian views of other animals. Thus, certain words,
concepts, and perspectives developed outside of these two religious traditions, as well
as outside the academic fields that have been involved in the study of religious phe‑
nomena, are used to identify and then clarify features of the prevailing attitudes
toward animals.

In part I, "Religion and Speciesism," the cumulative and internally diverse na‑
ture of religious traditions, as it is relevant to an examination of views of nonhuman
animals, is addressed (chapter 1). In chapter 2, the concept "speciesism" is introduced
as an interpretive tool. Richard Ryder coined the word in 1970, and since then the
noun "speciesism" and the adjective "speciesist" have come to be used widely, though
by no means universally. Chapter 2 surveys the history of the concept by evaluating
various uses by philosophers and others who clearly value the term. An examina‑
tion of these various uses, however, shows that many different concepts have been
called "speciesism." Likewise, many facile, inadequate definitions of the term have
been offered.

After an examination of the context in which the term was originally used and
some of the purposes for which it was coined, I suggest a working definition to be
used as a tool in assessing early views found in the Buddhist and Christian tradi‑
tions. This definition has been designed to meet some of the objections to various

criticisms of the term's use. Interestingly, even though the term has received significant play in certain philosophical circles, the discussion has been inconsistent. A review of contexts in which the term appears, whether philosophical, journalistic, or theological, or the context of activism, shows that it has often been used without definition, and that even when definitions have been offered, they have not been rigorous or carefully tied to the term's origin as a challenge to a particular type of exclusion. Such facile uses of the word out of context have led some critics to assert that no valid concept called "speciesism" can be framed.

Chapter 3 examines the criticisms of several prominent philosophers in detail. An analysis of the limitations of the concept of speciesism reveals that it is not a panacea. It also reveals, however, that some features of the term's use are quite valuable, even if limited in scope. Of some note is the fact that various critics' ploy of holding poor definitions and overreaching uses of "speciesism" to be representative of the whole range of concepts and uses to which the term can be put is itself a rhetorical approach not justified by careful examination. Even if scrupulous examination of some uses of "speciesism" and "speciesist" reveals various shortcomings, then, there remain uniquely valuable uses for a carefully drawn definition of speciesism. In particular, Ryder's original critique of the exclusion of all nonhuman animals from centrally important moral protections, referred to later as the "anti-speciesism critique," is a valuable tool. It permits one to identify certain features of some common approaches to determining which living beings should matter to informed moral agents. Part I thus concludes that while some uses are inexcusably vague, there are valuable uses that make the term "speciesism" a helpful and valid tool for identifying and assessing the rationale for various claims made in the Buddhist and Christian traditions.

Part II takes a very different tack, turning first to what is known about specific, distinctive nonhuman animals. Chapter 4 is an examination of information about some other animals that has been developed in highly specialized biological sciences. Chapter 5 is an examination of certain reasoning and discourse habits that characterize statements found not only in the early Buddhist and Christian materials but also in contemporary societies of the developed world. Throughout this chapter, various features of more rigorous reasoning and careful discourse are proposed. The chapter also includes the argument that any attempt to address the substance and implications of the ways in which the Buddhist and Christian traditions engaged other animals cannot be successful if one focuses solely on views held about the general category "other animals." In addition, one needs to focus on what was said about certain specific nonhuman animals. Further, for the reasons stated in part II, the animals used as representatives of nonhuman animals' abilities must not be poor representatives but, rather, the more complicated, so to speak, of nonhuman animals. Thus, this study seeks to assess the ways in which early Buddhists and Christians saw or dealt with the more complicated biological individuals outside the human species, such as other great apes,[2] elephants, and whales and dolphins (called the "key animals" or "key species").

Parts III and IV are, respectively, reviews of Buddhist and Christian materials. Chapter 6 reviews those portions of the ancient collection of Buddhist texts known as the Pali canon. Focusing on the vocabulary used in these texts, chapter 6 argues that the manner of reference to nonhuman animals reveals both some important negative attitudes and a persistent refusal to investigate.

Chapter 7 evaluates the common view that the Buddhist tradition is sensitive to nonhuman animals and concludes that this claim is often overstated in a way that misleads. In fact, as shown in chapter 7, the tradition has a highly ambivalent view of existence as a nonhuman animal, one element of which is very derisive and dismissive of the realities of nonhuman animals. Part III concludes that a rigorous concept of speciesism is helpful in identifying certain important features of the early Buddhists' views of nonhuman animals. More specifically, the early Buddhists, and in important ways the entire tradition in reliance on the foundational insights appearing in early strata of the tradition, characteristically held mere membership in the human species to be an achievement of a moral nature. A corollary of this claim was that mere membership in the human species was such an elevated status that humans were rightfully entitled to benefit from practices that were obviously harmful to some other animals. Thus, uses of even the most complicated nonhuman animals, such as elephants, were deemed to be humans' prerogatives under the moral order even when such uses clearly harmed the nonhuman individuals.

Part IV focuses first on Old and New Testament views of other animals and then on those general views as they were worked out by major postbiblical theologians through Augustine (chapter 8). The method used here is an examination of the Hebrew terms found in texts of the Hebrew Bible that the Christians inherited as the Old Testament and of the Greek and Latin words used by Justin Martyr, Irenaeus of Lyons, Clement of Alexandria, Origen, and Augustine of Hippo, as well as various words found in the Septuagint and Vulgate.

Chapter 9 provides an assessment of early Christians' views, concentrating on the notions of dominion, sacrifice, and the narrowing of the rich and sometimes contradictory values regarding nonhuman animals that were part of the Hebrew view of the surrounding world inherited by the early Christians. In summary, the early tradition established a view regarding humans and other animals that still operates for many Christians today. This claim is that each and every member of the human species, by virtue of species membership alone, has a special ontological status relative to other animals. Further, this special status not only is unlike that of any other animal but also is qualitatively better. It is this last feature in particular that provides the foundation for the claim that it is eminently moral to assert that the interests of any human animal quite properly prevail in virtually any nontrivial circumstance over the interests of any other animal.

Both part III and part IV conclude with observations about problems and advantages of using "speciesism" as a concept that illuminates features of how these traditions have come to understand the place of other animals. Note, however, that even if one does conclude that either of these traditions, or any other religious or ethical tradition for that matter, has had attitudes illuminated by the definition of speciesism used in this study, such a conclusion is logically distinct from the very different claim that humans, either as individual moral agents or as members of a larger community, do not have special powers and/or responsibilities. Indeed, as noted in chapter 2, the view of morality implicit in the critique of alleged speciesism, at least as that critique is framed here, affirms in many respects the claim that humans have special abilities to care about "others," whether they be human or otherwise. Further, as noted in both parts III and IV, one can find approaches within both traditions that clearly do not fit the description "speciesist."[3]

The questions, then, that drive this study are these: (1) What are the prevailing attitudes about other animals in the Buddhist and Christian traditions? and (2) How helpful is the concept of speciesism in understanding such attitudes?

PART I

RELIGION AND SPECIESISM

Religious traditions, whatever else may be said of them, have unquestionably had profound impacts on countless humans' actions affecting the living beings amid which we live. Religion has often been the primary source for answers to questions such as What is my relationship to others? Who are the others in our community? Which living beings really should matter to me and my community?

The answers of the early Buddhists and early Christians to such questions have had, in their respective cultural milieus and beyond, great influence on how the living beings outside the human species have been understood and treated. For example, consider the possible implications of some early Christian questions about the ancient provision of Deuteronomy 25:4, "You shall not muzzle an ox when it is treading out the grain." The apostle Paul asks at 1 Corinthians 9:9–10, "Is it for oxen that God is concerned? Does he not speak entirely for our sake? It was written for our sake." As noted in chapter 9, Paul's assertion here need not imply that Paul thought his God did not care about oxen, since Paul may have only meant that God provided the Deuteronomy provision for human instruction. The passage has not, however, often been so generously read. Rather, it has had effects that were negative, at least from the standpoint of oxen, since some of the Christian tradition's leading lights, including Aquinas,[1] deduced from Paul's language that God was suggesting that humans had no direct duty to any animals outside of the human species. Consistent with this are some well-known statements regarding nonhuman animals by prominent and otherwise very morally inclined Christians, an example of which is Pius IX's comment that "humankind has no duties to the animals" (discussed in chapter 5).

On the Buddhist side, consider possible implications of the historical Buddha's observation: "Men are indeed a tangle, whereas animals are a simple matter."[2] Although this translation might be taken to suggest that nonhuman animals are not culpable in any morally significant way because they are "simple" (in the sense of "innocent"), the Buddhist tradition took such sweeping claims about all nonhuman animals in a different way. Rather, this statement reflects the general Buddhist view that all nonhuman animals are both intellectually *and* morally inferior to humans (this controversial conclusion is based on the arguments of part III). This view has had, like the interpretations of Paul's comments about oxen, real-world consequences. A leading Buddhist scholar comments regarding treatment of nonhuman animals in Buddhist societies, "[A]nimals are enslaved by man: used as vehicles, beaten and exploited" (Schmithausen 1991a, 15). There are, however, many scholars and adherents who argue the opposite view, claiming that Buddhists have, on the whole, been considerate of other animals.[3]

The aim of this study is to engage such generalizations about living beings and their interpretations within these traditions, especially as they shaped statements about and acts toward nonhuman animals. Part I, composed of three chapters, addresses several preliminary questions for such a study. Chapter 1 analyzes what it means to claim generally that an entire religious tradition is, across time and place, characterized by a "view of" or "claims about" nonhuman animals. It also addresses the issue of anachronistic imposition of modern constructs on ancient strata of these traditions. Chapter 2 then engages the notion of speciesism, asking whether it is a valuable interpretive tool that might help the interested party discern various features of general views about nonhuman animals. After laying out the historical and ideological origin of the term, chapter 2 provides an overview of many uses of the term "speciesism." At the end of the chapter, a working definition is proposed. In chapter 3, criticisms of the term stated by various philosophers are engaged, since these provide a test by which to assess limitations of the notion generally.

1

Animals and Religious Traditions

[I]n Buddhist texts animals are always treated with great sympathy and understanding.
　　　　　　—Story, *The Place of Animals in Buddhism*

The generalization in this claim by Story raises a specific set of problems that are an inevitable part of any attempt to generalize about the views of "Buddhism" and "Christianity" regarding nonhuman animals. Various problems in this set, namely, those arising out of the attempt to say something general about Buddhism or Christianity, are addressed in the opening two sections of this chapter through use of the concepts "religious tradition" and "dominant attitudes." As noted later, however, one must remain sensitive to the considerable risks of anachronistic imposition and cultural imperialism. The next two sections list the portions of, respectively, the Buddhist tradition and the Christian tradition to be used in assessing views of nonhuman animals. The last section turns briefly to the nature of claims being made in passages that mention other animals. More specifically, it addresses the differences between, on the one hand, use of specific passages from each tradition as if they were descriptions about other animals and, on the other hand, the important, *nondescriptive* uses many passages have even when they include words that literally mention other animals. Part II will address other problems that arise from the attempt to say something general about the subject we usually describe as "animals."

Religious Traditions

While the title of this book uses the nouns "Buddhism" and "Christianity," the argument relies on the far more flexible and sensitive concepts of the "Buddhist tradition" and the "Christian tradition." This approach is based on the insights of Wilfred Cantwell Smith, who described his proposal as follows: "[W]hat men have tended to conceive as religion and especially as a religion, can more rewardingly, more truly, be conceived in terms of two factors, different in kind, both dynamic: an historical 'cumulative tradition,' and the personal faith of men and women" (1962, 194).

"Religious tradition" here will refer to the first of Smith's two dynamic aspects, "cumulative tradition":

> By "cumulative tradition" I mean the entire mass of overt objective data that constitute the historical deposit, as it were, of the past religious life of the community in

question: temples, scriptures, theological systems, dance patterns, legal and other social institutions, conventions, moral codes, myths, and so on: anything that can be and is transmitted from one person, one generation, to another, and that an historian can observe. (1962, 156)

While the other dynamic factor ("personal faith") is, for Smith, perhaps the more important element in that he deals with it more extensively, this study relies solely on the "cumulative tradition" factor for three reasons.

First, the notion of cumulative tradition is historical and provides, to use Smith's words, "overt objective data" that can be readily identified, thus providing a source for views of other animals that can be attributed to the tradition.

Second, this concept is flexible enough to encompass the astonishing complexity of the traditions. Smith's own words cited here emphasize that it is not only the faith element that is dynamic; the cumulative tradition element is as well. Hughes, in his analysis of Smith's work, states the implications of this notion:

[R]eligions as cumulative traditions may be seen as constantly shifting processes. Doctrines, rituals, ecclesiastical institutions are all in movement. Even when certain elements of a tradition such as long-standing doctrines appear relatively stable, what they mean to the faithful shifts from generation to generation. (1986, 11)

Thus, as Hick has pointed out, the concept of "cumulative tradition" is capable of handling "the rich detailed variety . . . not only between traditions, but also within each tradition" (1978b, xvii).

Third, the notion of cumulative tradition is not reliant on any essentialist definitions of what it means to be "Christian" or "Buddhist," in the sense that there is no unchanging core required for purposes of identifying what is truly Christian and Buddhist. Smith reveals his antiessentialism in the following passage:

[A] Christian can come to an adequate understanding of his faith, or a Muslim of his, and indeed, either of them to an understanding of each other's, only if he extricate himself from a concern as to the essence or nature of Christianity or Islam, only if he shift his attention away from questions such as "What is true Christianity?", "What is real Islam?"[1]

Thus, cumulative "historical deposits" are identifiable, can be used by the historian, and are capable of reflecting the variety and diversity amid the continuity.

Smith's notion of cumulative tradition can be broken down into the distinguishable elements of (1) historical transmission from one person to another, across cultures and time, and (2) the mere accumulation of views. The process of accumulation over centuries of whatever views exist, whether received from predecessors or simply created without precedent, suggests the possibility, though by no means the inevitability, that some of the accumulated views will be inconsistent with others. The process of transmission is what creates the persistence of features within the tradition, whether they be marvelous insights *or* continuing, but unsupportable, prejudices. Hughes refers to "long-standing doctrines which appear relatively stable" (1986, 11). These provide the continuity by which one might conclude that a tradition has always had, and is thus characterized by, view(s) of a particular subject. For example, parts III and IV will argue that this kind of continuity is true of both traditions with regard to views of other animals. More specifically, it will be argued that (1) there are dominant views of other animals in each tradition; (2) these views of animals are persistent features that stem from the earliest strata of the traditions; and (3) even the vast majority of nonmainline interpretations reflect such valuations. Thus, despite the extraordinary complexity of these traditions, the notion of "cumulative tradition" works well on this particular issue because it permits one to include many materials that are not now central features of the tradition, but that nonetheless reflect the dominant attitude on this particular issue.

Dominant Attitudes

In parts III and IV, it will be argued that each of these traditions has its own particularly interesting and paradigmatic complex of ideas about other animals. These often are unstated, operating as "background" or "foundation" in ongoing debates. Further, even though there are variations in the ways in which the dominant view dictates the adherents' conceptualization of other animals, the recurrence of the basic view is so pronounced that it qualifies as a fundamental feature of the tradition. These dominant attitudes appeared even when various adherents of these traditions experienced different segments of the internally diverse group of living beings we traditionally call "animals." In other words, certain Buddhists experienced some animals, while other Buddhists experienced other, very different animals, yet the dominance of a single, paradigmatic complex of ideas about other animals resulted in all the adherents having the same notion, or at least functionally equivalent notions, of other animals. This is also true of the Christian tradition. There were, to be sure, some voices that might be construed on one issue or another to have been dissenting or nonconforming voices, but it will be argued that the traditions were, on the whole, monolithic in their view of other animals.

Ancient Concerns, Modern Constructs

Concerns for nonhuman animals have appeared in different ways in many cultures and have been a venerable, even if sometimes minor, portion of all major religious traditions and in some philosophical traditions.[2] Concern for other animals has been a prominent feature of many indigenous societies as well.[3] Such concerns came to limited prominence at the end of the eighteenth and nineteenth centuries in several countries in western Europe, although "it is only in the last twenty years that there has been what can accurately be described as a popular movement for social reform" (Gold 1995, 5).

In contemporary societies, the broad-based movement referred to variously as "animal protection," "animal liberation," and "animal rights" is, upon close inspection, many different things and movements, and these are by no means internally consistent phenomena. These many movements most characteristically rely on discourse taken from ethical reflection and scientific research that is "Western" and modern. Good examples of this are the many ongoing discussions regarding great apes (other than humans), which rely heavily on fields such as genetics, cognitive sciences, various fields of anthropology, and comparative developmental psychology (see, generally, the fourth section of chapter 4). Since present-day discussions are carried on in discourse that relies on modern constructs, an unqualified imposition of the post-eighteenth-century vocabulary and conceptuality on these two religious traditions would be anachronistic.

In order to assess how concerns expressed in a modern idiom might nonetheless have potential application to ancient traditions, it is instructive to consider Schmithausen's comments on the potentially anachronistic endeavor of seeking a Buddhist view of environmental ethics:

> [H]ow can we expect help from an old tradition for which [the contemporary problem of environmental destruction and pollution] did not exist and by which it was therefore not expressly addressed. But this is not entirely true. [Schmithausen then mentions environmental problems and species extinctions that confronted ancient humans, including Buddhists.] Hence, the question what old religious traditions may contribute to what we now reflectively call "environmental ethics" is not illegitimate, still less so when the tradition considered is still alive and a major force in a country like Japan. (1991a, 2–3)

Since concerns for, awareness of, and strong opinions about other animals have long been characteristic of both traditions in the ways discussed in parts III and IV, it is here assumed that asking about concerns for other animals generally, or inquiring whether adherents of a religious tradition have "seen" other animals on the basis of those other animals' realities, is not anachronistic.

It remains true, however, that to impose modern constructs without modification, or at least without subtlety, risks reductionism and caricature. In particular, the speciesism analysis used in this study threatens a violation of the cultural uniqueness of Buddhism. This risk is related to the fact that the vocabulary, range of concepts, and science-based claims that are part of what is defined in chapter 2 as the anti-speciesism critique were developed in the Western cultural sphere after, roughly, the sixteenth century. Further, even though the vocabulary used, namely, that of recent Western ethical reflection, has grown alongside and in some instances out of Christian viewpoints, this vocabulary is certainly not consistent with all things Christian. Thus, using this vocabulary and approach on either of these traditions is a sensitive matter, especially because the vocabulary and conceptualizations being used import concepts that are, at least to some extent, alien to the terms and conceptuality in which most Christians and Buddhists have expressed their experiences with other living beings.

Natural Histories in Cumulative Traditions

It is a given that the relevant materials of the cumulative traditions were never designed to be natural histories of either animals or the key species. "Natural histories" is used here in the sense of systematically organized views of other animals that describe the features of their bodies and lives for identification purposes. In fact, it can be persuasively argued that ancient writings from these two traditions had purposes entirely unrelated to inventory-like listings of other animals or reality-based descriptions of their lives. For example, Conze notes, "the statements of Buddhist writers are not meant to be descriptive propositions about features of reality, but advice on how to act, statements about modes of behaviour, and the experiences connected with them" (1975, 16). Conze drives the point home further with his observation, "If one, however, isolates the Buddha's statements from the task they intend to perform, then they become quite meaningless, and lose all their force" (17). Similarly, Lamotte confirms this soteriological bent: "The Word of the Buddha has only one flavour (*rasa*): that of deliverance. . . . It is not, properly speaking, an encyclopedia of religious knowledge but a way of deliverance discovered and proposed by the Buddha" (1991a, 46). Gombrich says this slightly differently, implying that Buddhist formulations and injunctions will at best have an indirect relationship to the particulars of nonhuman lives that one can discover by empirical investigation: "Buddhism as such is not about this world. Such spheres of human activity as the arts and sciences are not part of its concerns" (1991a, 10). Thus, the documents of the tradition that refer to other animals were undoubtedly heavily influenced by existing conventions of discourse and rarely, if ever, had as their principal purpose a description of the animals mentioned.

Nevertheless, the traditions do have definite views of other animals, and these are prominent features with significant consequences for other living beings. In parts III and IV, the materials listed in the next two sections as Buddhist and Christian sources will be analyzed in order to reveal how the two traditions have conceived of other animals. Much of the evidence will be indirect and circumstantial. Further, it will often be necessary to distinguish between purely symbolical references and those references that have, at least relatively, greater literal value. In some cases, failure to consider other animals is taken to be significant. This is not, of course, a simple matter, for the uses to which traditional language and art were put by later adherents were, and indeed now are, no doubt at times quite different from, perhaps even alien to, the uses we can only hypothesize their originators had in mind long ago. Through all this complexity, however, certain principal features do emerge.

The Buddhist Tradition

Of the items on Smith's inventory of the cumulative tradition (what he refers to as "the entire mass of overt objective data that constitute the historical deposit, as it were, of the past religious life of the community in question"), at least the following have potential relevance to what views of the key and other animals were held by Buddhists:

1. The "scriptures" contain references to these animals, and thereby indicate (a) their presence, (b) some of the information held about such animals, and (c) the attitude toward these creatures. The Buddhist scriptures are considerably longer than the Christian scriptures, and the circumstances and time frame of composition are dauntingly complex. Because of the central role of the Pali canon in reconstructing "original" Buddhism,[4] that collection will be used as the primary reference point

in part III. In addition, some references that appear in the vast *Mahāyāna* materials will also be considered.

2. The term "theological systems" has on its face more application to the Christian tradition given the nontheistic nature of Buddhist claims about ultimate reality, but systematic works do abound (such as the Abhidhamma). These contain references that reveal basic attitudes or claims about the key animals and animals in general.

3. "Legal and other social institutions, conventions, and moral codes," including the Vinaya, or monastic code, contain rules betraying foundational attitudes and claims held to be "knowledge" about other animals. In addition, "conventions" and "moral codes" may, if written, convey the conceptualization about other animals generally, and the key animals in particular.

4. "Myths" abound in the Buddhist scriptures, and references that appear in cosmogonic stories and especially stories of the past lives of Gotama will supply interesting material regarding the prevailing views and claims about the key animals.

References to the key animals that occur in the Buddhist tradition are extremely varied as to context. Because the references considered in chapter 6 are taken primarily from the Pali canon, they are drawn from a more homogeneous set of writings than are the Christian references considered in chapter 8. But, like the early Jewish and Christian references to natural phenomena, the references are found in writings that attempt to convey an overwhelming and defining religious experience founded on the spiritual accomplishments of an extraordinary individual. Thus, the references to the key animals that will be considered were written for purposes quite different than mere description of encounters with these animals. These writings, however, reflect convictions about the world and other animals. To be sure, there were classifications of other animals of a quasi-scientific nature that existed in the milieu, but adherents of the Buddhist tradition, like adherents of the early Christian tradition, did not pursue or develop these. Instead, Buddhists placed unquestioning reliance on folk taxonomies when using language about other animals; indeed, like the Christian tradition, the Buddhist tradition was not original in its valuation of all other animals. The views of animals in each tradition, then, reflect acceptance of a certain amount of cultural baggage drawn from the sociocultural complexes that gave birth to the founders of the traditions.

A recitation of the changes in Buddhism over its twenty-five hundred years would make the complexity of the tradition immediately apparent. That complexity might also lead one to conclude that current forms of the tradition ought to be diverse and layered as to the experiences and insights which the adherents have had regarding other animals. Interestingly, however, the tradition is dominated by a single, paradigmatic complex of ideas about humans versus other animals. As documented in part III, the early Buddhist tradition held *mere* membership in the human species to be a moral achievement. Further, this achievement was viewed as elevating members of the species to a status that entitled them to benefit from instrumental, obviously harmful uses of other animals. This special privilege, namely, the right to benefit from manifest harms to other sentient creatures, was deemed to be humans' prerogatives under the moral order.

The Christian Tradition

Of the items in Smith's list of "overt objective data," at least the following have potential relevance to Christian views of the key and other animals:

1. "Scriptures." These will provide the most significant references, as the Christian tradition is centered on claims about the central events of Jesus' life and death found in the New Testament. These claims are themselves heavily reliant on experiences described in the Hebrew Bible/Old Testament.[5] The documents considered "scriptures" for the purpose of this study are the original Hebrew texts,[6] the Septuagint, the New Testament in Greek,[7] the Vulgate, and the following English translations of the Bible: the King James Version, the Revised Standard Version, the New Revised Standard Version, the Jerusalem Bible, and the New English Bible.
2. "Theological systems." This is an inexact term for what will be examined, in that it is not only those works that constitute "systems" that will be examined. Rather, nonsystematic theological work containing references to the key animals will be included as well. The principal writers to be referred to include some of the church fathers through Augustine, since, on this issue, the dominant features of the tradition were set by the close of Augustine's life, and his successors' claims and arguments generally only varied the expression, but not the substance, of the theme of the absolute importance of members of the human species relative to all other animals.
3. "Legal and other social institutions, conventions, and moral codes" will include those codifications of rules, such as Roman Catholic canon law, that reveal attitudes and claims regarding other animals.
4. "Myths" will be deemed to include stories that use terms that are, or may be, relevant to the prevailing views and claims about the key animals or other animals generally. In most instances, these are scripturally based.

These references by Christians to the key and other animals occur over such an extended period and in such diverse sources that the context often differs dramatically from one reference to the next. Though the passage of time and the dramatic variety of contexts have led to a daunting complexity that makes the Christian tradition diverse and layered as to views regarding subjects other than nonhuman animals, the tradition is, it will be argued, dominated by a readily identified and remarkably consistent complex of ideas about humans versus other animals. In summary, the earliest strands of the Christian tradition held that each and every member of the human species, by virtue of mere species membership, had a special ontological status. This special status was held to be not only unlike that of any other animal but also qualitatively better in all ways relevant to moral considerations. The result was that Christians adamantly claimed then, and still do now in the mainline interpretations of the most influential and populous subtraditions, that the moral status and interests of any human animal should prevail over those of any other animal whenever a human would benefit from such a conclusion.

Religious Experience and Specific Claims about Animals

In the argument here regarding the non–natural history features of Buddhist and Christian accounts mentioning other animals, quotations from Conze, Lamotte, and

Gombrich were used to suggest that *core* Buddhist claims, though often in the guise of propositions that purport to describe features of the surrounding world, have rather different and more specific functions. A primary feature is, of course, these claims' soteriological function. The apparently factual content of various statements or other views implicit in various arts as they seem to be related to other animals may not be, then, propositional or descriptive regarding the phenomenal world.[8] Similarly, the broader interpretive features regarding the specifics of other animals' lives and the general conceptualization of nonhuman life may be more a claim about humans' special natures than an informed, reasoned, and non-ignorance-based judgment of humans' standing relative to all other animals.

The fact that work other than "propositional, descriptive" work is often being done by scriptural passages that mention other animals raises the question of the value of what appear to be, and what are often construed as, propositions about the nature of other animals or their value relative to members of the human species. It is possible that such statements, though not meant initially to be "propositional, descriptive," were taken by adherents as having such value. In other words, statements mentioning other animals, or even artistic portrayals of them in some way, may have been taken as accurate and even exhaustive descriptions of those natural world individuals referenced. If so, adherents might then think that such references provided factual knowledge or some other foundation upon which one could base actions and an understanding of one's position relative to other animals out in the world. For example, it has been claimed that the sea creature that swallowed Jonah was a particular kind of whale—one of the baleen or mysticete species known as the "right whale."[9] If a Christian chose to read scriptural passages as providing natural history of this kind (believing that the biblical description supports the view that some whales swallow humans), the scriptural passage has been used as a "propositional, descriptive" claim, even though it functions in other ways as well. One alternative, then, is to read various claims and images as if they were intended to have both "propositional, descriptive" and non–"propositional, descriptive" functions, either of which might properly be deemed important.

To be sure, it is now uncontroversial in many circles to assert that at least some claims found in the Buddhist and Christian traditions, including some that have the form of apparently specific claims about other animals, are not necessarily or automatically to be construed as "propositional, descriptive." This is often true even when the language is in the form of a specific and seemingly factual claim. Thus, even language that appears to be, and has been construed as, specifically factual and an exclusivist claim about humans (such as the claim that all and only members of the human species have been made in the image of God) might be read not as strictly true "propositional, descriptive" statements with implications for all other animals but as disclosures of, say, the divine presence in humans. Using the idiom of Western theological discourse, one could argue that the divine might disclose itself to believers in ways that are subject to *our* prejudices without in fact confirming those prejudices.[10] Thus, racist, sexist, *or even speciesist* exclusions in the scriptures of religious traditions do not necessarily imply a divine sanction of, respectively, racism, patriarchy, or the exclusive importance of humans, as so often has been the interpretation.

Nonetheless, whatever the intent of the originators of the paradigmatic Buddhist and Christian statements about other animals to be considered later, it is clear that on the whole they have regularly been taken as "propositional, descriptive," especially on the issue of the relative importance of members of the humans species and all other animals. This kind of interpretation is a principal, persistent feature of both cumulative traditions. These statements, then, even if they were not originally intended to work in precisely this way, have played a role in the development of these traditions' dominant views of other animals. It is for this reason that they can be treated as representative of the traditions' views on the issue of nonhuman animals.

2

Exclusion and the Concept of Speciesism

The term speciesism was invented . . . as a device to winkle out exclusively humanistic radicals from an inconsistent position. . . . Its most obvious use is to deny . . . the supposition that the species boundary not only makes a difference, but make the gigantic difference of setting the limits of morality, of deciding whether a given creature can matter to us at all.
—Midgley, *Animals and Why They Matter*

[T]he term is already used quite widely. . . . For some it equates with little more than cruelty to animals or, more tamely, with a nonbenevolent attitude toward other species.
—Wynne-Tyson, "The Subtleties of Speciesism"

Attention is now turned to the meaning of the modern term "speciesism." The opening section of this chapter addresses the broad critique out of which the word "speciesism" arose. The next two sections turn to the history of the word's use, and the last section proposes a definition as a tool for understanding attitudes toward animals.

The Anti-Speciesism Critique

The word "speciesism" was first used in 1970 by Richard Ryder in a privately funded pamphlet distributed in Oxford, England.[1] The pamphlet bears the title "Speciesism" and begins with a reference to Darwin's arguments that "there is no 'magical' essential difference between humans and other animals, biologically speaking." Ryder concludes that the attempt to justify "benefits for our own species" which are achieved through the "mistreatment of other species" occurring in biomedical experiments is "just 'speciesism' and as such a selfish emotional argument rather than a reasoned one" (1992a, 170–71).

Historically, the 1960s and 1970s were a time of both novel and increasingly intensive use of other animals. Biomedical experimentation was expanding rapidly, and methods used to create economic efficiencies in "factory farming" were increasingly being implemented. Such economics-driven changes were contentious from the standpoint of some existing ethical sensibilities because the conditions of the animals used for food were dictated solely by cost and handling efficiencies rather than the traditional welfare concerns that had been developed since the end of the eighteenth century.[2] The text of Ryder's pamphlet makes it clear that he intended the word "speciesism" to address attitudes supporting secular, science-based experiments that were, in his estimation, selfish, illogical, and yet sanctioned by society generally. The pamphlet conveys Ryder's conviction that a fully informed moral agent *should* challenge such practices.

There was also a larger target of Ryder's use of the term, namely, what he termed in the pamphlet the "present moral position," which was composed of the culturally pervasive attitudes that excluded all nonhuman animals generally from the kinds of morality-based protections offered members of the human species. This larger challenge addressed attitudes that have two essential components: (1) an emphasis on the status "human" (that is, species membership) as the rationale for inclusion, and (2) the position that all other animals are to be excluded from such protection.

This challenge to attitudes that have these two essential parts, that is, where inclusion of all humans is paired with exclusion of all nonhumans, will be referred to as the "anti-speciesism critique." It is this feature of Ryder's critique that is potentially relevant to a discussion of the Buddhist and Christian views of other animals. Of particular relevance is the sanctioning of humans' use of other animals as if they (the nonhuman animals) were either unimportant or radically less important than humans (this will be referred to as "instrumental" use).[3] Consider examples where the instrumental-use dimension is central:

> The king lives on the milk from one udder of a cow that has a calf, . . . his chief consort lives on the milk from the second udder, the brahman priest lives on the milk from the third udder, and the milk from the fourth udder they offer to the fire; the calf lives on what is over.[4]

> Brutes are as *things* in our regard: so far as they are useful for us, they exist for us, not for themselves; and we do right in using them unsparingly for our need and convenience, though not for our wantonness. (Rickaby 1888, 250)

"Interests"

What is being ranked in these two passages is often referred to as "interests." Defining "interests" is not an easy task, even though the term is widely used. In 1789, Bentham commented, "Interest is one of those words, which not having any superior *genus*, cannot in the ordinary way be defined" (Bentham 1970, 1 n. 1). Despite these difficulties, the term is used by a wide range of theorists. An example is Bentham's own argument:

> It is vain to talk of the interest of the community, without understanding what is the interest of the individual. A thing is said to promote the interest, or to be *for* the interest, of an individual, when it tends to add to the sum total of his pleasures: or, what comes to the same thing, to diminish the sum total of his pains.[5]

Singer, following in the utilitarian tradition, adds, "The capacity for suffering and enjoying things is a prerequisite for having interests at all" (1993b, 57). Rollin, arguing that plants are to be excluded because it is crucial to be able to impute some sort of conscious or mental life to that which is said to have the interest, says, "Very simply, 'interest' indicates that the need in question *matters* to the animal" (1992, 76). In this book, the term "interests" will designate the fact that lives can, from the standpoint of the individual, go better or worse.

Focusing on Exclusion of Interests

A recent Catholic pronouncement regarding other animals provides the opportunity to examine a nonsecular attitude to which Ryder's broader anti-speciesism critique might have applicability: "Animals, like plants and inanimate things, are by nature destined for the common good of past, present and future humanity" (Catholic Catechism 1994, paragraph 2415).

The specific features of this claim are examined here, and then again in chapter 9 in the discussion of the Christian notion of dominion. For the purpose of introducing the simple notion that underlying conceptualities and vocabulary choices guide the manner in which interests of other animals are excluded, only a few features of this claim need to be noted here. First, the authors use the term "animals" to mean all other animals (the implications of this linguistic habit are discussed in chapter 5). Second, paragraph 2415 sanctions the exclusion of other animals' interests through its assertion that other animals are destined for the common good of all members of the human species, signaled by the collective noun "humanity." Such an exclusion of interests, especially when it is associated with species membership as in this passage, is the central feature of the *secular* attitudes to which Ryder initially addressed the word "speciesism" in 1970.

Parts III and IV address prominent Buddhist and Christian claims that, beyond maintaining hierarchical rankings, assert confidently a profound divide between, on the one hand, all members of the human species and, on the other hand, all other animals. Historically, such claims have had the beneficial effect of elevating the category "member of the human species" to the highest level of what here will be called "moral considerability," a term that in this book is used in a very precise and limited sense.[6] Specifically, it will designate *only* the notion of moral agents holding a biological individual to deserve *three fundamental protections*, namely, *a right to life, freedom from captivity*, and *freedom from intentionally inflicted harm that is unnecessary*.[7] Importantly, limiting the meaning of "moral considerability" here to a narrow set of the most basic protections (and it is assumed that the *basicness* of each of these is a matter of consensus) *must* occur, because many other protections or opportunities commonly associated with "morality" are simply irrelevant to the lives and abilities of nonhuman animals. These three fundamental protections will be discussed further in the concluding section of this chapter when they are defined as "essential concerns."

Major and Minor Interests, and "Unnecessary" Exclusions

Consider as a paradigm the exclusion of interests that occurs when one human uses another as a slave. It can be said that in such cases the interests of the master override the interests of the slave. The master's interests, such as the added wealth or conveniences derived from the work of the slave, are, in a relative sense, not unfairly said to be minor or secondary when compared with the slave's major or primary interests, such as freedom from captivity or opportunity for self-determination, that are being overridden. Thus, the slave's interests that have been excluded are commonly said to be of greater importance than those interests of the master furthered by the institution of human slavery. Further, because the exclusion of the slave's interests does not occur for the purpose of the master's immediate biological survival, the practice is "unnecessary" in an important sense (the master can give it up and still have a healthy life), and this is what will be meant later when it is said that an exclusion is "unnecessary."

Some human uses of other animals may also fit this model (that is, minor interests overriding major interests in nonsurvival situations). An example used in parts II and III is the use of wild-caught elephants as vehicles for ceremonial purposes. What is at issue in this practice is not human survival but a kind of human *thriving* or *luxury* obtained by denying captive elephants the freedom to pursue their own interests. Such a practice will be unnecessary, in the sense defined earlier, since it has qualitative differences from the killing of other living things for self-defense or to obtain vitally needed protein not available from other sources.

Paragraph 2415's Exclusion of Interests

The treatment of interests in paragraph 2415 of the Catholic Catechism can be broken down into four principal features.

1. The exclusion of interests is based on membership in the *human* species.

The critical factor in determining which biological individuals will be included, as well as which will be excluded, is species membership. As a matter of first impression, the validity of this criterion may seem "obvious." It is, however, as discussed later, controversial for some. What is relevant to the discussion as it has so far progressed is that, using the senses of "minor," "major," and "unnecessary" referred to previously, the species membership criterion undergirding the prescriptions of paragraph 2415 allows minor interests of humans to override major interests of any biological individual that is not a member of the human species. Indeed, there is either no or relatively little inquiry as to whether the human needs to be met are necessary.[8]

2. The exclusion of interests has features that fit a narrow sense of the term "ideology."

The terms "ideology" and "ideological" will be used here to describe a feature of some claims regarding human superiority to all other animals. These words are, like the notion of moral considerability, used in a very particular *and* narrow sense. This narrow sense appears in the fourth definition of "ideology" given by the OED. That definition, adjusted here for the purposes of this book, is "A systematic scheme of ideas . . . regarded as justifying actions, especially one that is held implicitly or adopted as a whole and maintained *regardless of the course of events*." Some sense of the functioning of "ideology" in this narrow sense is evident when "ideological" is used as a term of abuse, as occurs when Midgley (1995, xvi) describes sociobiology as an ideology.

A recent comment makes clear the relevance of this sense of "ideology" to the interpretation of important textual references within religious traditions:

> [I]t is becoming painfully obvious that much modern interpretation of the NT has been consciously and unconsciously influenced by the prevalent ideology of the modern West which for two centuries or so has understood human history as emancipation from nature. . . . Once the prevalent modern ideology is questioned, as it must be today, we are freed to read the NT differently. (Bauckham 1994, 3–4)

Another use of "ideology" in this narrow sense illustrates the relevance to some other animals: "Every species is different from every other species: this much is plain biology. The ideology lies not in the search for differences, but in the unwavering belief that humanity is defined by attributes that have absolutely no precedent in the rest of the biological world" (Radner and Radner 1989, 8).

For claims of the kind addressed by this comment, logical criticism can seem almost irrelevant, because the formal arguments for the superiority of members of the human species are dominated by something more fundamental, namely, a deep, unreasoned, "before the fact" prescriptive judgment of some kind. It will be suggested later that the claim of paragraph 2415 that *all other* "[a]nimals . . . are by nature destined for the common good of past, present and future humanity" has these "ideological" qualities, since, on its face, it appears to be immune to the development of information that would exempt *any* other animals (such as the key animals described in part II) from the claim that they are *by nature* destined for human use.

3. The radical exclusions of all other animals' interests found in paragraph 2415 (as well as those found in at least some other religious traditions) are not unlike exclusions found in institutions that are nonreligious in nature and origin.

The widely discussed claim that "the roots of the ecological crisis" can be found in the Christian tradition sometimes has been taken to suggest that religion *alone* has been responsible for exclusivist attitudes leading to environmental destruction, but that view is surely wrong.[9] Apart from the science-based projects challenged by Ryder, exclusivist concerns can be found in many other secular realms. These include Roman law (discussed in chapter 5), certain behaviorist theories in psychology, many forms of atheism and humanism, and various other, secularized philosophical thinking mentioned in part II. This is not to say that religious attitudes have not been formative for nonreligious attitudes, since they often have been. The point is simply that exclusivist thinking occurs regularly outside explicitly religious contexts.

4. Such radical exclusions of interests have visible consequences.

Assertions that humans *should* use other animals are common features of contemporary ways of human life. Visible consequences of such exclusion may, however, extend beyond treatment of nonhuman animals. Thomas provides evidence that the domestication of nonhuman animals "generated a more authoritarian attitude" and "became the archetypal pattern for other kinds of social subordination," suggesting that the domination of other animals is related to the domination of other humans.[10]

Problematizing the Exclusion

The exclusion of nonhuman animals' most basic interests that is explicit in the secular practices that Ryder challenged and implicit in claims such as paragraph 2415 has taken place in an identifiable set of circumstances which has some features that are potentially troubling for the moral agent. For example, one can contrast (1) the sweeping nature of the generalizations that undergird the exclusion and (2) the actual knowledge held about other animals. As noted in part II, even a cursory review of modern biological sciences reveals a verifiable shortfall between (a) the knowledge of the lives of other animals claimed by those who hold the common view that only human animals matter and (b) the knowledge of other animals' lives actually held.

Second, in light of the modern emphasis on impartiality in moral judgments (discussed in chapter 3), a question can be raised about the self-interested features of the exclusivist claim that "only humans are morally considerable." Self-interest by no means necessarily invalidates such judgments, because moral agents will *always* be in the group that their judgments protect. Yet the fact that many contemporary moral views favor *all and only* members of the very species whose members make this judgment can be used to prompt questions about the criteria used in establishing who and what will be included and excluded from the protections offered by moral agents.

Third, problems might be raised by the inquiring moral agent in light of other, potentially relevant features that are part of the history of human valuing. Paley (referring to Aristotle's view of non-Greeks as slaves) noted at the end of the eighteenth century, "Nothing is so soon made as a maxim; and it appears from the example of Aristotle, that authority and convenience, education, prejudice, and general practice, have no small share in the making of them; and that the laws of custom are very apt to be mistaken for the order of nature" (1788, 32). There is a growing awareness that human history has been characterized by many prescriptions and proscriptions sounding in morality that could not withstand serious scrutiny, including illicit biological lines of demarcation (for example, race and sex). Awareness of this history challenges any moral agent's facile acceptance of the existing consensus as to what morality requires of him or her.

Fourth, problems can also arise from awareness that simple, logical errors have at times occurred in reasoning about the justifiability of culturally pervasive values or socially sanctioned exclusions. For example, the absence of evidence of grounds on which one could base the moral considerability of some other animals has at times been mistaken for evidence of absence of such grounds. Many examples of such fallacious reasoning can be drawn from human-human interactions, such as the prevalence in history of claims that "barbarian" races, African pygmies, or New World indigenous peoples were not in fact human. The simple fact that there was an absence of evidence of these humans' moral considerability was mistakenly taken as evidence that they lacked commonalities with those who were deemed "fully human."

Finally, what has been characterized as an anomaly or peculiarity arises when universalism (as to moral considerability) is asserted within the class "members of the human species." Some individuals of the human species differ quite significantly, in terms of basic abilities, from other members. Referring to the fact that less able members of the human species have been referred to as "marginal cases," Pluhar notes, "the term 'marginal' simply means 'not paradigmatic'; it in no way implies that 'marginal humans' fail to be human beings" (1995, 63). She lists as marginal cases "fetuses, children, brain damaged or congenitally retarded, those who suffer from insanity, and the senile" (62) and "infants, . . . autistic, the comatose" (64). The term is thus a reference to the fact that the "marginal" individuals do not possess what is considered either the normal set of traits of the human species, or the essential traits in sufficient degree. The possible relevance of this is that "marginal cases" may be less able than some other animals in every important capacity traditionally said to be the province of the human species alone (such as language ability, rationality, self-awareness, and moral agency). The "marginal cases argument" holds, then, that certain, "higher" nonhuman animals cannot fairly be denied basic moral rights if some humans, having less ability in crucial areas, are granted such rights.[11]

Can Only Humans Be Speciesist?

If speciesism turns out to be a viable concept, it will be important to consider an additional question. Should discriminations by *nonhuman* animals that appear to be species-membership related also be included within the definition of speciesism? One might argue that species-membership decisions occur whenever any animal prefers its own "kind" to some other kind, for this is a kind of discrimination, and it is clearly related to considerations that, if not *solely* species-membership related, are certainly somewhat similar. There are, however, reasons to limit the application of the term to humans alone. In chapter 3, a distinction is made between (1) loyalty to *some* members of one's own species and (2) loyalty to *all* members of one species. The latter concept clearly is a high-level abstraction, and animals *without* the ability to generalize at this level will, by virtue of their lacking the ability to use a species line concept as the principle of exclusion, be unable to be speciesists. That only humans (actually, only *some* humans)[12] have this ability is the prevailing assumption, and this accounts for the fact that many of the definitions analyzed here focus on humans *alone* being speciesists.

There is a second reason the word "speciesism" has been used as if *only* humans could be speciesists. Originally, the anti-speciesism critique was a challenge to human practices and attitudes that excluded, either explicitly or implicitly, all nonhuman animals. Attitudes that protected *some* nonhuman animals would *not* have been considered speciesist. This is true *even though* these less exclusivist attitudes manifested utilitarian attitudes toward the remainder of the animal world. Suppose, for example, a group accorded basic moral protections to all humans *and* members of only one other species (say, chimpanzees for religious reasons). Suppose also that this group had *exactly* the same attitude toward the rest of the animal kingdom as did those humans who favored only humans. This group's members would *not* have been deemed speciesists under the original anti-speciesism critique. One could argue that there is an anomaly here, because attitudes toward the vast majority of living beings remain exactly the same in the human exclusivists and the human-chimpanzee exclusivists. Of course, by definition there is one difference, namely, the protection of members of a second species, even though the remaining nonhuman and non-chimpanzee animals are, arguably, excluded *solely* on *mere species-membership grounds*, just as in standard speciesism, in that they lack membership in any of the *two* favored groups.

The point is that the accusation "speciesist" was originally used to challenge the view "only members of *one* species, namely, the very group doing the evaluating, will be protected." Inclusion of *any* nonhuman group would break that pattern, although, to be sure, some "ism" might still be being committed (indeed, the words "chimpocentrism" and "*pan*morphism" have been coined).[13] In other words, the "species" part of the charge "speciesism" as originally used was, in effect, the equivalent to "*human*-speciesism." Adding chimpanzees or some other protected animal destroys this particular form of exclusivism, because the determinative factor or principle of exclusion is no longer solely the failure to possess membership in the human species.

It will be pointed out later that some critiques of existing practices regarding other animals have at times been based on principles that contain the seeds for challenging exclusivisms as broad as "*human*-chimpanzee speciesism," but it remains the case that the word "speciesism" was not used in this way originally. The obvious reason for this was that, in the milieu in which the term was coined, "*human*-speciesism" was the norm and the source of the problems and attitudes that Ryder wished to challenge.

In this book, speciesism will be deemed to be an exclusively human phenomenon, based on the assumption that the kinds of abstract thinking required to conceive of an entire species is found only among humans. Second, it will be assumed that the best use of the word "speciesism" is the original use to describe what has been characterized previously as "*human*-speciesism."

The View of Morality Implicit in the Anti-Speciesism Critique

As a general matter, the anti-speciesism critique presupposes several general features of humans' tendencies to morality that are, in important respects, identical to those features of humans presupposed in many *theoretical defenses* of exclusivist practices. For example, both presuppose that humans can and should be moral agents. This is evident in the anti-speciesism critique's assumption that one could choose to protect the interests of some nonhuman animals, as humans plainly can and sometimes do. The anti-speciesism critique, then, is premised on an affirmation of the moral abilities found broadly in human cultures. This is equally true of many defenses of the propriety of allotting moral considerability to all and only members of the human species. Such defenses rely explicitly on the conclusion that universalism within the biological class of humans is demanded by moral principles, whether such principles be provided by revelation or other mechanisms (such as reason or sociobiological realities).

It could even be argued that the anti-speciesism critique is framed in terms of generalizations that are, in an important sense, broader than those generalizations necessary to reach universalism within the class of humans. These "broader" generalizations include the assertion that humans' moral sense demands respect for biological phenomena other than the features or potentials conferred only by membership in the human species. This generalization could be said to be "broader" because, while it includes the class of humans, it also looks beyond that class by virtue of its assumption that other animals are candidates for moral considerability. Such considerations are based upon very broad notions, such as sentience,[14] mental life of a certain complexity, the status of "fellow creature,"[15] or traits found in both humans *and* some other animals.

The Subsequent History of "Speciesism"

Ryder coined the word "speciesism" at a time when other movements had already provided wide-ranging critiques of existing value systems in influential European and North American cultures. These included well-known attempts to (1) abolish slavery, (2) provide voting rights to women and non-property-owning males, (3) recognize the rights of children and the handicapped, and (4) eliminate colonialism and other forms of cultural and economic imperialism. In addition, ecological and environmental awareness had become a prominent concern.[16] Anthropocentrism had been identified and banished in some human sciences (first in astronomy, then in physics, and finally in biology), but it remained, in the opinion of some, a dominant force in the fields of psychology and ethics.[17] In addition, in England a movement focusing on the domesticated and food mammals and birds was heir to similar movements that had had limited success at the end of the eighteenth and nineteenth centuries.[18]

These social justice critiques provided much material and many approaches for challenging traditional value systems, as is evident in Ryder's pivotal attempt to analogize speciesism to racism. The 1970 pamphlet made this association, and in 1975 Ryder explained this parallel more fully: "I use the word 'speciesism' to describe the widespread discrimination that is practised by man against other species, and to draw a parallel with racism. Speciesism and racism are both forms of prejudice that are based upon appearances—if the other individual looks different then he is rated as being beyond the moral pale."[19]

The racism-speciesism parallel has both substantive and tactical aspects. The similarities between race-based and species-based exclusions are analyzed in chapter 3, but beyond these the parallel had the tactical advantage of associating those practices that Ryder wished to condemn with widely repudiated attitudes of racial discrimination. In 1977, Ryder, together with Andrew Linzey, convened a conference in Cambridge during which "A Declaration against Speciesism" was signed by 150 of the attendees.[20] That declaration expanded the bases of objection beyond medical experimentation, stating, "We do not accept that a difference in species alone (any more than a difference in race) can justify wanton exploitation or oppression in the name of science or sport, or for food, commercial profit or other human gain." In this expanded usage addressing "human gain" from instrumental use of other animals in sport, food production, and other commercial endeavors, the word is again used for the purpose of advocating a particular kind of challenge to versions of morality focused solely on benefits to members of the human species. The term used in this way has both descriptive and evaluative purposes. Descriptively, it is a tool used to identify practices that benefit humans, exclude the interests of other animals, *and* involve infliction of suffering, often for minor needs that can be met otherwise. Evaluatively, it is used to characterize those practices as *abuses*.

Although Ryder has continued to use the term in descriptive and evaluative ways, a review of his works generally shows that he does not systematically explore the concepts involved in the implicit and explicit analogies.[21] In summary, he uses the term to charge that, under the guise of morality, membership in the human species, rather than the ability to suffer, has been sanctioned as a justification for instrumental use of biological individuals outside the human species.

Singer's Use of the Word

The history of the word was affected greatly when it appeared in Singer's *Animal Liberation* (1976), a book sometimes described as "the bible of the animal rights movement" (Blum 1994, 115). The title of the fifth chapter, "Man's Dominion . . . A Short History of Speciesism," reveals that Singer accepted the word as having valuable explanatory power regarding the history of humans with other animals. Singer defined "speciesism" in this way: "Speciesism . . . is a prejudice or attitude of bias toward the interests of members of one's own species and against those members of other species" (1976, 7). In explanation of what he meant by "prejudice" or "attitude of bias," Singer followed Ryder's lead in connecting speciesism with racism as an unjustifiable exclusion along biological lines. In addition, Singer made the association with sexism more prominent (Singer 1976, 7 n. 3).

Using as a basic moral axiom "the principle of equal consideration of interests,"[22] Singer argues that this principle is violated in similar ways by a racist, sexist, and speciesist:

> The racist violates the principle of equality by giving greater weight to the interests of members of his own race when there is a clash between their interests and the interests of those of another race. The sexist violates the principle of equality by favoring the interests of his own sex. Similarly, the speciesist allows the interests of his own species to override the greater interests of members of other species. (1976, 9)

The allegedly common elements are (1) the exclusion of interests and (2) the making of decisions as to which interests should prevail not on the basis of a comparison of the interests involved but on the ground of another's sharing membership with the moral agent in a limited biological group. Importantly, a background feature of the analysis is the belief that some of the excluded "others" *outside* the favored biological group can reasonably be said to have similar *or* even more important interests.

Singer has continued to use a notion of "speciesism" as a central feature in his work, offering varying formulations and descriptions. For example, he notes,

> Nor can we say that all human beings have rights just because they are members of the species *homo sapiens*—that is speciesism, a form of favouritism for our own that is as unjustifiable as racism. Thus if *all* humans have rights, it would have to be because of

some much more minimal characteristics, such as being living creatures. Any such
minimal characteristics would, of course, be possessed by nonhumans as well as by
human animals. (1987, 4)

The argument "if *all* humans have rights, it would have to be because of some much
more minimal characteristics" is an indirect reference to the marginal cases problem. Singer's reference here reflects the focus of the anti-speciesism critique on those
views of morality that exclude all other animals while protecting all members of the
human species. This line of argument, then, relies on an understanding that the
problem being addressed is the kind of "own species favoring" that earlier was called
"*human*-speciesism." This formulation also reflects a fairness criterion that looms large
in the anti-speciesism critique, as reflected in both (1) the concern for minor interests overriding major interests and (2) the issue of unnecessary harms caused to
nonhuman living beings.

Singer's use of "speciesism" has precipitated widespread use of the term, as well as
discussions among philosophers regarding the value of the overall concept and the
underlying critique (discussed further in chapter 3).

Others' Use of the Word

The "arrival" of the term at the popular level is signaled by the fact that it now appears in major dictionaries, although these definitions are often inconsistent and
incomplete.[23] For example, the OED definition is unaccountably narrow, confining
the discrimination to only "certain species": "Discrimination against or exploitation
of certain animal species by human beings, based on an assumption of mankind's
superiority." A broader, arguably more accurate definition emphasizing the exclusion of members of *all* other species occurs in *The Oxford Dictionary of Philosophy*:
"By analogy with racism and sexism, the improper stance of refusing respect to the
lives, dignity, rights or needs of animals of other than the human species" (Blackburn
1994, 358).

The primatologist McGrew uses the term in his description of problems associated with assessing whether "culture" occurs among chimpanzees. He does not explicitly define speciesism, saying only that it is an "error" by means of which "the
capacities of another species are underestimated on grounds of the presumed superiority of all things human" (1992, 215–16). The zoologist Dawkins, having stated
earlier that "the ethic of 'speciesism' . . . has no proper basis in evolutionary thinking" (1989, 10), uses speciesism in a clearly evaluative manner. He criticizes what
he describes as "the *automatic*, unthinking nature of the speciesist double standard"
(1993, 80). Dawkins does not define the term, and in several passages he associates
it with what he calls an "unthinking failure" to ask the kinds of questions about
humans that are asked about other animals (1993, 80–81, 87). Dawkins concludes
broadly that, "at present, society's moral attitudes rest almost entirely on the dis-
continuous, speciesist imperative" (1993, 86).

The appearance of "speciesism" in these and other contexts such as journalism
indicates several things.[24] First, the word is in ordinary use. Second, it is most typically used in a very negative way and as a condemnation (though not always, as noted

later). Third, it is sometimes dismissed as having validity for only one side in a polarized debate.

Theological Uses

The term is not a prominent feature of the contemporary theological landscape. Linzey (e.g., 1987, 24) uses it, but without definition, explanation, or discussion. As with many of the uses mentioned earlier, his use is that of a descriptive-evaluative tool. The process theologian McDaniel uses the word, juxtaposing the phenomenon of "speciesism," which he criticizes, with an "ecological" orientation, which he recommends (1994, 27). The process theologian Cobb uses the term for "an irrational prejudice against other species" in his wide-ranging discussion about the development of biological life (Birch and Cobb 1981, 157). His use is not explicitly tied to any theological discussion, however.

Pinches appropriates the term for positive uses, as can be seen in the title of his essay "Each According to Its Kind: A Defense of Theological Speciesism" (1993), which asserts the propriety of using the "species" category for purposes of moral assessment. Specifically, Pinches uses the species category in an essentialist manner, that is, he understands each biological species to be characterized by a privileged essence. He thus argues that each member of the human species shares a special essence that no members of other species have (this view and the notion "biological species" are discussed in chapter 5). Regarding the term "speciesism," Pinches states unequivocally, "I hope the term can be restored after Singer's plundering" (1993, 200). Pinches's use, however, does not engage the anti-speciesism critique in any detail. He suggests that acceptance of the anti-speciesism "diatribe" seeks "abandonment of species distinctions or even relegates them to the unimportant" and "has as its specific end the abandonment of species distinctions as in any way morally relevant" (200). It will be suggested later that this either is rhetorical overstatement or reflects a serious misunderstanding, for to argue that species membership should not be the sole or principal criterion of moral considerability is not to argue that it has no relevance whatsoever to such considerations.

While Pinches's use of "speciesism" is a plea to have species membership be considered "the primary category" (203) for moral assessments, his argument does not require any *exclusion* of other animals' interests. In fact, he suggests that the view of different species should be that of "separate but equal" (200) groups. His use of the term, then, is to mark species differences, not to emphasize the superior right of humans to advance their own interests to the complete exclusion of other animals' interests. Pinches is thus using the term in a way that does *not* conflict with the central thrust of the anti-speciesism critique.

Pinches's claim that the word can have positive associations is not unique in the literature. C. Cohen, defending biomedical experimentation on nonhuman animals and challenging the explicitly moral tone of the condemnations of the anti-speciesism critique, has argued, "I am a speciesist. Speciesism is not merely possible, it is essential for right conduct."[25] Bernard Williams's positive characterization "speciesism is humanism" is analyzed in chapter 3. Such uses are, however, atypical, since evaluative uses of a negative nature clearly predominate.

The term has also been used in a few discussions of religious traditions. Lal has said that the Hindu tradition "is open to a charge of speciesism" (1986, 209), and Chapple uses the term "non-speciesistic" (1993, 70) regarding the Jain religion. Yet, the term has not penetrated far into theological or religious studies circles, as is apparent from the fact that the 1996 database for *Theological and Religious Abstracts* has but one reference to speciesism, and that is from the journal *Environmental Ethics*. The term does appear in some general texts and collections, however.[26]

Comparable Terms

Numerous other terms have been proposed to do work similar to that which advocates of the antispeciesism critique want the term "speciesism" to do. The notion of anthropocentrism sometimes functions in this way,[27] but the logic of the term itself requires only that humans be self-centered. It need not imply negative views of the relative importance of the interests of other animals, any more than egotism implies an assertion of factual superiority to, or a lack of worth in, others. Lovejoy used the term "anthropocentric teleology" to describe and criticize the narrower claim that the physical world, including other animals, had been designed by a Creator to serve humanity, a view he called "one of the most curious monuments of human imbecility" (1960, 188, 186). Brumbaugh used the similar term "teleological anthropocentrism" for the same claim, and called it "preposterous" (1978, 8, 11).

To designate exclusivist attitudes centered on human species membership, some have advanced the notion of "human chauvinism" (Sagan 1977; Sapontzis 1987, 85; Routley and Routley 1995), and Kalechofsky and Pluhar have used the term "homocentrism."[28] W. Fox referred to "human imperialism" (1990, 21), while Jeffers spoke of "human solipsism" (cited at Devall and Sessions 1985, 101). Ehrenfeld used the notion of "humanism" in similar ways, calling modern, vague, and exclusivist humanism "the religion of humanity" (1981, 5) and challenging the exclusivist aspects of human-centered thinking. Grim described "the religious utilitarian position" as one that "understands material resources as simply given by the divine for human exploitation with little reflection on the relation of cosmology to resource exploitation" (1994, 51–52). Midgley uses the term "exclusive humanism" when arguing that there was a regressive series of narrowings as the Christian tradition developed.[29] Her influential *Animals and Why They Matter* opens with a discussion of the Western tradition's "absolute dismissal" of other animals, that is, the belief that only human beings matter.[30]

Importantly, none of the thinkers just mentioned as using comparable words is opposed to universalism among humans. Rather, they appear, in coining and explaining these somewhat similar terms, to be concerned with the *exclusions* of the interests of all other animals.

Uses by Academic Philosophers

The word "speciesism" appears in many contemporary works on ethics, although most philosophers use "speciesism" or "speciesist" as a descriptive term without significant discussion or analysis. For example, Glover does not give the concept itself much attention even though he explicitly rejects views he calls "speciesism" and gives definitions of several kinds. He defines speciesism in terms of both action ("human life being treated as having a special priority over animal life *simply* because it is human") and ideas (the "view according to which mere membership of our species, independent of any empirical properties carried with this membership, gives a privileged claim over members of other species") (1990, 50, 121). He challenges directly the exclusion of a biological being solely on the grounds of *non*membership in a species: "[I]t is not in itself sufficient argument for treating a creature less well to say simply that it is not a member of our species. An adequate justification must cite relevant differences between the species" (50–51).

Many other philosophers use the term in a way that suggests their acceptance of its value *but* without significant analysis of the underlying critique or concepts. Examples can be found in the works of Ferré (1986, 403–4), Raphael (1994, 127–29), Miller (1993, 235) and Häyry and Häyry (1993, 179), and Persson (1993, 191). Such uses are also found, not surprisingly, in the discourse of thinkers who can be described as "pro-animal," such as Regan,[31] the philosopher of psychology Robinson (1985, 165), Benton (1988), Sapontzis (1988), and Bekoff (1997, 16). Some environmental ethicists use "speciesism" as if it were a valid charge against certain reasoning.[32] This is true of some feminist philosophers as well. For example, C. J. Adams comments, "The speciesism of Homo sapiens is perhaps nowhere more pronounced than in the protestation about the fate of the human conceptus and zygote, while the sentiency of the other animals is declared morally irrelevant because they are not human beings" (1994a, 60). Adams also argues that some other feminists use arguments which presuppose a speciesist paradigm by arguing that women are, but should not be, treated like "animals" (145).[33]

Uses of the term without extensive consideration of the word's precise definition suggest indirectly that the underlying concept(s) are thought by these philosophers to have conceptual integrity.[34] Many of these uses are superficial, employing short descriptions of the underlying problem as definitions; the passage from Wynne-Tyson at the beginning of this chapter hints at such casual uses. The occurrence of too broad, even facile definitions suggests that what has been designated as "speciesism" by various parties, including some philosophers, has actually been many different things. Thus, views and actions previously described as "speciesist" may not, upon closer examination, fit under a fully worked out concept.[35]

Extended Analyses

Three analyses exhibit specific thinking about the term's possible value. LaFollette and Shanks (1996) use a definition of speciesism as a central notion in their analysis of a dilemma faced by researchers who advocate experimentation on other animals. This dilemma is described by Rachels, who refers to it as "a logical trap": "[I]n order to defend the usefulness of research [researchers] must emphasize the similarities between the animals and the humans, but in order to defend it ethically, they must emphasize the differences" (1990, 220). LaFollette and Shanks explore this dilemma with the aid of contemporary biological theory about the relation between causal mechanisms and organism-level functions of animals. They conclude that there is indeed an irreconcilable tension between scientific justifications and moral justifications:

> [I]f the cognitive abilities of humans and animals are so drastically different as to morally justify experimentation, then those differences will reflect and promote other biological differences which undercut inductions from animals to humans. On the other hand, if underlying biological mechanisms are sufficiently similar to justify scientific inferences from animals to humans, then the higher-order traits of the test subjects are sufficiently similar to human traits to make research morally problematic. (1996, 56)

This analysis relies heavily on the notion of speciesism. LaFollette and Shanks define the term simply, beginning with the general statement that "speciesists" are "people who unjustly discriminate against members of other species," and they specify two kinds of speciesism: "The *bare* speciesist claims that the *bare* difference in species is morally relevant. The indirect speciesist claims that although bare species differences are not morally relevant, there are morally relevant differences typically associated with differences in species" (41–42).

One benefit of differentiating the *bare* speciesist from the *indirect* speciesist is recognition that exclusivism occurs in degrees and can be based on fundamentally different notions, such as *mere* membership for the *bare* speciesist and empirically based claims of species-typical traits for the *indirect* speciesist. But one can also ask, who are the *bare* speciesists? Many who insist that *mere* membership in the human species supports the right to eclipse any interests of nonhuman animals state this claim in terms *other* than mere membership. A review of the many exclusivist claims noted so far suggests that it is rare for mere membership to be the *only* acknowledged basis for such a claim. Rather, membership in the human species is characteristically said to entail that individual species members possess a certain "essence," "nature," or set of potentials. According to most claims, it is these features (whatever they may be called) that justify the conclusions about the special status of *each and every member*. Sometimes the claim is extended to any *potential* human, as in the Catholic Church's claim that any human fetus is "an innocent human being," "absolutely equal to all others."[36]

Claims stated in terms of *features* of species membership, rather than mere membership itself, appear to fit LaFollette and Shanks's definition of indirect speciesism because they mention something beyond mere species membership, that is, something "typically associated with differences in species." Because these additional features are sometimes very general or even very vague, such as the potential to be rational or being "in the image of God," their occurrence may be simply the equivalent to mere membership. If so, this makes the "bare"-"indirect" distinction less than helpful. The distinction may be helpful, however, in identifying how people argue their case. Those who assert "it is mere membership in the human species that confers privileged status," *and* give no other argument, are *bare* speciesists. Those who make this assertion *and* add a reason, that is, argue additionally that species membership entails a valuable trait, will be the *indirect* speciesists.

Rachels's Analysis

Rachels's extensive discussion of speciesism is couched in his heavy emphasis on the realities of individuals as the locus of moral decisions and issues:

> The basic idea is that how an individual may be treated is to be determined, not by considering his group memberships, but by considering his own particular characteristics. If A is to be treated differently from B, the justification must be in terms of A's individual characteristics and B's individual characteristics. Treating them differently cannot be justified by pointing out that one or the other is a member of some preferred group, not even the "group" of human beings. (1991, 173–74)

This "moral individualism" (176) is an attempt to see and resolve issues by means of a "principle of equality" (182). Rachels's goal of having species-neutral rules of morality govern moral agents' treatment of other creatures is an attempt to work out the consensus view that impartiality is an important feature of moral thinking. Rachels's acceptance of the anti-speciesism critique, however, causes his analysis to sound very different than the parts of Kant's writings that focus on rational creatures being the universe of morally considerable individuals. Rachels concludes that a far wider range of biological individuals should be treated in the same way unless there is a relevant difference.

Rachels lists four categories of speciesism (these are not mutually exclusive, but rather overlapping). The first is "radical speciesism," which occurs when "[e]ven the trivial interests of humans take priority over the vital interests of non-humans" (182). Rachels contrasts this with "mild speciesism," an attitude not so wide "in extent" (182). In mild speciesism, while the trivial interests of humans do not prevail over the interests of nonspecies members, human interests do prevail when the competing interests are comparable or equal. Rachels rejects this principle of exclusion because it violates the principle of equality which "implies that the interests of nonhumans should receive the *same* consideration as the comparable interests of humans" (182).

"Unqualified speciesism" is distinguished from a qualified version. "Unqualified speciesism is the view that mere species alone is morally important" (183), while "qualified speciesism" is "the view that the interests of humans are morally more important, not simply because they are human, but because humans have morally significant characteristics that other animals lack" (194). Rachels dismisses unqualified speciesism as "implausible," but he notes that it is nonetheless defended by some contemporary philosophers.

Rachels examines four versions of "qualified speciesism," each of which relies on the claim that humans possess a "morally significant characteristic that other animals lack" (194). The versions are variously based on humans' unique possession of (1) rationality and its related autonomy, (2) language, (3) a contractual social arrangement, or (4) greater sensitivity to pain. Rachels provides detailed arguments to challenge each of these as a ground for favoring *all* humans over all other animals. A common feature of his rebuttals is that *none* of these four features of the lives of *some* humans is a feature of the lives of *all* humans, as similar genetic composition or lineage would be. Thus, each of these four arguments purporting to justify inclusion of *all and only humans* needs an additional argument by which to include those humans who do not have the allegedly central feature. This additional argument is, in turn, subject to the charge of inconsistency that is made by way of the marginal cases argument (addressed in the following discussion of Pluhar's views).

Pluhar's Analysis

Pluhar's book-length discussion of the marginal cases problem, published in 1995, contains a lengthy analysis in which the concept of speciesism plays a central role. She focuses particularly on the responses of philosophers to the problem occasioned by attempts to grant human marginal cases moral considerability while at the same time *excluding* all other animals. Pluhar notes that views which, like those of Kant, purport to grant only "persons" the highest level of moral significance have a problem including those humans who, for a variety of reasons, do not have the features of persons.[37] Whenever the interests of a marginal case are allowed to eclipse the interests of another animal that possesses equivalent or superior levels of morally relevant characteristics, there is a risk that something unfair has occurred. Requiring individuals to be treated in accordance with the *norm* for their species rather than their own characteristics, then, has at least the *appearance* of a violation of the influential moral principle that like cases be treated alike.[38]

Pluhar first examines the "frequently held" view she calls "homocentrism," defined as the view that "all and only human beings can be maximally morally significant" (1995, 10). Her discussion focuses on the arguments of P. Harrison and Carruthers, philosophers who contend that nonhuman animals cannot be said to suffer. Harrison (1991) argues that conscious pain is reasonably attributable only to rational agents. Carruthers (1989, 268–69) suggests that humans have a "moral imperative" to curtail sympathy for other animals, and that humans should believe that other animals are conscious only when this has no "morally significant" effect on humans.

Pluhar suggests this position has two crucial weaknesses. First, homocentrism is characterized by overt reliance on membership in the human species as morally relevant. Such membership is thought to imply the existence of, or potential for, intelligence, creativity, communication, autonomy, or any other feature alleged to be characteristic of the species. Pluhar (1995, 46) argues that this is flawed because it is a verifiable fact that many members of the species do not have these features. Second, the claim fails because it is error to claim that no nonmember of the human species can possess any of these traits in any degree (46). Thus, in that the homocentric view implies that being human is itself a morally significant characteristic, it is as objectionable as a claim that one's race or sex is, in and of itself, morally relevant.

Pluhar's chief concern, however, is the set of views that emphasize the importance of "persons" but that *also* find a basis for including all other members of the human species, but no members of other species, in the highest level of moral protection. She calls this "full-personhood speciesist" thinking and notes that it is a common view today. She also notes that these attempts at justifying the inclusion of "nonperson" humans while excluding all other animals use many different conceptual schemes.[39] She concludes that such arguments amount to making human species membership a morally relevant criterion. The basis for this conclusion is these arguments' inclusion of all human marginal cases, even though some other animals equal or exceed the marginal cases in their possession of any feature relevant to moral significance *other* than membership in the human species.[40] Pluhar objects on the ground of inconsistency, arguing that in any consistent full-personhood view *only* full persons would get maximum moral significance. Although she notes that the full-personhood view is not per se speciesist, because some other animals could be deemed "full persons," she objects to such views generally on the ground that they have "extremely disturbing implications" because such views must, on their own terms, exclude marginal cases. Pluhar, who urges that there are good, nonspeciesist reasons to include marginal cases,[41] concludes that "full-personhood view advocates who resist exploitation of marginal humans but see nothing wrong with the continued exploitation of nonhumans must become *speciesists* instead" (1995, 123).

Pluhar identifies two versions of the marginal cases argument. The first she calls the "categorical version," which has the following structure:

1. Like beings have equal moral significance;
2. some other animals are similar in all morally important respects to marginal humans;
3. marginal humans are maximally morally significant;
4. therefore such other animals are maximally morally significant. (63–64)

The second version is a "biconditional" argument:

1. Like beings have equal moral significance;
2. some other animals are similar in all morally important respects to marginal humans;
3. those other animals that are the equals or superiors of marginal humans have maximum moral significance,
4. *if and only if* marginal humans have maximum moral significance. (64–65)

Pluhar contends (120–21) that advocates of a full-personhood position must either accept the argument from marginal cases (and protect other animals) or deny protection to the human marginal cases.[42]

Pluhar's Definitions

Some of the "speciesism is . . ." statements in Pluhar's book-length treatment are narrowly focused on one or two elements of the underlying problem of excluding *all* nonhumans from the kind of very basic moral protections commonly said to be the birthright of *any* human. An example is, "Anyone who believes that species membership can itself, independently of the capacities of the individual, be a morally relevant characteristic, is a speciesist" (1995, 79). Arguably, then, if an animal rights activist ascribed "basic moral rights" to a bottlenose dolphin solely because it was a member of a cetacean species, the definition would hold this to be speciesist. Similarly, the description of "speciesists" as "believers in the justifiability of favoring members of one sentient species over another" (126) is a weak definition, since it does not stipulate that the issue involved must be a critical issue. Additionally, on its face this definition includes the kind of trivial favoring that has not been a concern of the anti-speciesism critique. Finally, the claim that a speciesist is one who claims that "membership in a species characterized by full personhood is sufficient for maximum moral significance" (125) is arguably too broad, because there could be *other* sufficient conditions that qualify other animals for this high level of moral protection.

As noted earlier with regard to her views on the inconsistencies of "full-personhood speciesist thinking," Pluhar emphasizes the tension between the inclusion of *all* humans and the exclusion of *all* other animals. This aspect of her analysis is consistent with the thrust of the anti-speciesism critique. Her claim that speciesism is the view that "*humanity* as such is necessary for maximum moral significance" (136) is more adequate than the definitions considered earlier because it implies that the crucial element of *exclusion* of other animals' central interests must be part of speciesist attitudes.

A Working Definition

The two obvious principal ideas of speciesism are the contrasting inclusion of all members of the human species and exclusion of all members of all other species from certain privileged considerations. Merely asserting the dignity of each and every human, without any related exclusion of nonhumans' interests, value, or moral considerability, would in no way be speciesist. An element of pervasive exclusion is a critical addition. Beyond these two components, the anti-speciesism critique also draws upon other distinct ideas that can be isolated for the purpose of understanding that critique. One of these additional ideas is the importance of open-minded, empirical investigation of other animals' lives rather than adherence to ideology-based exclusivist thinking. This is, in part, a corollary of the "fairness" emphasis noted earlier.

Another central idea is the irrelevance of *absolute* distinctions based on the dividing line between the human species and all other animals. Of course, to claim that this line is not absolute is logically distinct from claiming that there are no nontrivial differences between species. What Rachels calls the "complex pattern of similarities and differences" between humans, on the one hand, and some other animals, on the other hand, is addressed in part II. This complex pattern makes the species line something less than conclusively relevant when interests of biological individuals clash, although in important ways (as discussed in chapter 5), membership in a species will remain highly relevant to assessments of moral considerability.

These disparate elements of the anti-speciesism critique are found inconsistently in the definitions considered earlier. Here, a working definition is given so that a specific concept can be used to describe how the Buddhist and Christian traditions have understood other animals:

> Speciesism is the inclusion of all humans animals within, and the exclusion of all other animals from, the moral circle.

The components of this definition are (1) the inclusion-exclusion tension, (2) humans versus other animals, and (3) the moral circle (discussed in the next section). This definition focuses on species membership as crucial *only* insofar as *human* species membership is involved. Note also that the definition would not hold a moral agent to be a speciesist if he or she advocated inclusion of all humans and *any* other animals.

The Narrow Sense of "Moral Circle"

The notion "moral circle" is used very narrowly here in that it coincides with what was designated in the opening section as "moral considerability." Thus, an individual will be said to be "within the moral circle" if three fundamental interests (for ease of reference these are defined in the following as "essential concerns") are protected by whatever rules or principles exist to protect individuals. Correspondingly, an individual will be said to be "outside the moral circle" if such rules or principles neither recognize nor protect all three of these fundamental interests. The three fundamental interests, or "essential concerns," are the following three distinguishable interests or concerns of each living animal:

1. An opportunity for continued life. Negatively, this can be phrased as an obligation not to kill. An important qualification is that this interest can be terminated if there is an immediate and unreasonable danger to others.
2. Freedom from interruption of that life by captivity, enforced work, or any other form of harmful instrumental use. Importantly, not *all* instrumental uses of other beings are harmful. For example, use of a messenger is in some sense *instrumental* but rarely, if ever, harmful. In this study, however, the term "instrumental" is meant to include only *harmful* instrumental uses.
3. Freedom from direct, intentional infliction of negative consequences such as harm, pain, or suffering that is unnecessary (in the sense already defined) and not inflicted for the benefit of the biological individual receiving these consequences.

These three "essential concerns" do *not* constitute all of the bases on which moral sensibilities might focus. The features of sentience, for example, can also be grounds for moral significance of some kind, as occurs in many cultures' consensus ethic revolving around kindness and cruelty concerns. Other grounds of moral significance *not* included within this definition of essential concerns arise from the extraordinarily complex nature of the individuality and personality possessed by healthy humans, which generates very specific interests distinguishable from those interests defined here as essential concerns. The existence of these additional interests, in turn, creates realities (such as the need for honest communication, the right to know, and the right to fulfill abilities) that have moral dimensions and thus are of great importance. I argue throughout this book, however, that the occurrence of these special dimensions in any human does not *necessarily* eclipse the essential concerns of those humans and other biological creatures that do not have these additional abilities. Differences in abilities, and even hierarchy, to the extent they exist, do not *automatically* imply the propriety of dominance, let alone tyranny. This is an ancient insight that has come in many culturally distinct forms. As Clark, citing Porphyry, notes, "To argue that they [that is, any animal outside the human species] have no reason because men have more is like arguing that partridges cannot be said to fly, because hawks fly higher" (1977, 18).

3

Criticisms of Speciesism

*[The term "speciesism"] has been used for an attitude some regard as our ulti-
mate prejudice, that in favor of humanity. It is more revealingly called "humanism," and it is not a prejudice.*
—Williams, *Ethics and the Limits of Philosophy*

There are, as Bernard Williams's words suggest, prominent challenges to the concept of speciesism. The following section examines various attacks on the validity
of the prominent analogies to racism and sexism. The next section addresses
Williams's criticism in detail. Mary Midgley's challenge on the basis of a postulated
"species-bond" is then analyzed, and the final section assesses the conceptual challenge from Wittgenstein-inspired philosophers.

The Analogies to Racism and Sexism

Some have repudiated altogether attempts to analogize speciesism to racism and
sexism. Francis and Norman (1978, 527) argue that the analogy trivializes human
liberation movements. Cohen asserts, on the basis of his view that humans are of a
different natural kind than other animals, that the parallels are "utterly specious"
(1986, 867). Such repudiations raise the issue of whether conceptual problems arise
when analogies to other discriminations are used for the purpose of clarifying the
nature and utility of the concept of speciesism. To be sure, when an analogy is drawn
between any human discrimination against other humans and human discrimination against nonhumans, some dissimilarities are obvious. The targets of discrimination are, by definition, different in each case (the first is within the species line,
while the second is outside the species line). Historically, the exclusions of human
versus human discrimination have been argued to be problems primarily because they
are a negation of a certain essentialism that is the central idea of human-centered
normative ethics, namely, the notion that humans are important because each shares
with all other humans, but with no other animals, a special "essence" or "nature."

Such dissimilarities cause antiracism and antisexism arguments to be, in some
respects, different from anti-speciesism arguments. For example, it is possible to be
completely against racism and sexism while *fully* affirming the propriety of anthropocentrism in ethics. The theologian Cone opposed racism in Christian churches by
referring to any minister who backs racism as "inhuman. He is an animal. . . . We
need men who refuse to be animals and are resolved to pay the price, so that all men

40

can be something more than animals" (1969, 80). Similarly, some feminists argue that various feminist arguments have, "through metaphoric comparisons to treatment of animals—that a violent man treats a woman like a dog, or pornography treats a woman like meat, etc.—actually validate[d] the oppression of animals, implying that while these things should not be done to women, they *may* be done to animals."[1] In fact, as pointed in out in parts III and IV, such explicit and implicit disparagement of all other animals as a way of enhancing the status of all humans has been a common occurrence in the Buddhist and Christian traditions.

It is therefore not surprising that the structure and components of recent arguments challenging the exclusivist aspects of human-centered ethics differ from the structure and components of the arguments that were the most prominent historically in opposing racism and sexism. These differences, in turn, suggest that claims relying on simple and *complete* analogies between racism or sexism and speciesism will not work well.

Limited Value of the Analogies

Beyond these dissimilarities that make analogies of speciesism to racism and sexism potentially problematic and at best inevitably partial, Klug (1992) adds additional comments challenging what he considers facile analogies to racism and sexism.[2] Klug argues that, since "whatever life the word 'speciesism' possesses it borrows from the two words on which it has been consciously patterned: 'racism' and 'sexism'" (3), the whole approach is "mistaken" (2). Klug offers effective criticism of Ryder's claims of parallels and analogies, showing that Ryder's claim that both racism and speciesism "are based on appearance" "oversimplifies and distorts the nature of racism" (3) for at least two reasons. First, discrimination on the basis of appearance is not group- and ancestor-related in the way racism is; second, discrimination on racial grounds is not confined merely to those who appear different but is extended to biologically related entities no matter what their appearance. Klug thus argues that Ryder's claim that "[t]he illogicality in both [racist and speciesist] forms of prejudice is of an identical sort" (4) is misleading.[3]

This argument shows well that the analogies are not precise. Klug assumes, however, that if he can show that the charges "racism" and "speciesism" are not used in logically parallel ways, he has fatally undermined both use of the analogies and speciesism as a concept. The conclusion does not follow, however, because Klug fails both to consider the *limited* usefulness of the analogies and to explore any non-analogies-based concepts of speciesism.[4]

Consider one limited point of comparison. Diamond (1978, 467–68) has noted that there are legitimate analogies between the case of human relations to other animals and the case of a dominant group's relation to some other group of human beings that it exploits or treats unjustly in other ways; she adds, however, that such analogies are not straightforward, and it is not clear how far they go. In fact, Klug himself acknowledges the existence of partial analogies, for despite his stronger claim that the whole approach is mistaken, he states, "I do not mean to deny that there is analogy and overlap" (1996, 13). Arguably, analogical thinking is valuable precisely because it can show similarities while maintaining differences. McFague (1983), addressing the use of "as" (15–16) and "like" (37 ff.) comparisons, analyzes the views of Aristotle, I. A. Richards, Max Black, and Paul Ricoeur, all of which emphasize the necessary tension between similar and dissimilar aspects of what is being compared. Analogies do not require isomorphism to work; they require, instead, some similarities. *All* analogies, then, are to some extent limited.

LaFollette and Shanks argue that speciesism and racism are "sufficiently similar so that analogies between them cannot be blithely dismissed as category mistakes" (1996, 42). Analogies to racism and sexism are useful in a limited way for pointing out certain features such as the pervasiveness of systematic exploitation of "others," human and otherwise. They can also be used to highlight the fact that discrimination relying on biological criteria can be illicit if premised on morally irrelevant criteria such as race, sex, differences in appearance, or mere species membership. LaFollette and Shanks add that the comparison with racism is used "to focus our attention on the human tendency to unreflectively accept contemporary moral standards. We are fallible. Even our deeply held view may be wrong" (41). There are, then, limited but still valuable analogies between speciesism and other discriminations that can help call attention to features of how nonhuman animals are generally viewed and treated.

Bernard Williams: Prejudice, Persons, and Duties of Inquiry

Williams's comments about speciesism (1985, 118–19, 216 nn. 20, 21), the most poignant of which is found at the beginning of this chapter, amount to a dismissal. His observations have some force regarding the more *superficial* definitions of speciesism, such as those that focus only on inclusion, but they are inadequate for the fuller definitions and the more complex analyses addressing the exclusions that generated the anti-speciesism critique. Since Williams gives so little argument for this renaming (speciesism is merely humanism), it is possible that his equation is not a substantive proposition but, rather, a rhetorical device meant to convey his lack of resonance with the underlying critique. If one tries to address the substance of the renaming, it is impossible to know on which aspects of the diverse, sometimes contrary phenomena collected under the umbrella "humanism" Williams relies when associating the two so closely.[5] For example, it is unclear if Williams means to equate "an attitude . . . in favor of humanity" with the aspects of humanism recognizing the value or dignity of humans, or with the logically distinct aspect that sees humans as the raison d'être and measure of all things.[6]

Taking Williams's renaming as a challenge to the fuller definitions and analyses of the anti-speciesism critique, his argument is inadequate for several reasons.[7] A mere affirmation of humans, accurately called "an attitude . . . in favor of humanity," does not, in and of itself, amount to speciesism. It is the negative side of speciesism, the exclusion, that is the source of problems. Prejudices in favor of members of one's own species, and even a general prejudice in favor of *all* members of one's species, can theoretically exist without entailing harm to any other species, just as a kind of prejudice for one's own family members can exist without eclipsing the rights and interests of others outside the family circle. Thus, while there may be an important overlap between humanism and speciesism, namely, a preoccupation with and even favoring of humanity, there are significant conceptual differences, and it is conceivable that one could be a humanist without being a speciesist. Further, even the claim that humans are, or should be, the "measure of all things" does not, as a logical matter, entail the eclipse of others' interests. Parts III and IV mention some notions of the bodhisattva (both *Mahāyānist* and *Theravādin*) and Christological formulations that do not require such an exclusion.[8] In each of these cases, there is no cancellation of the interests of others but, rather, the possibility of an affirmation. Thus, humanist interpretations can be inclusive, whereas speciesist ones cannot.

Is Speciesism a Prejudice?

Williams states flatly that an attitude "in favor of humanity" is not a prejudice. Yet an examination of some exclusivist thinking about nonhuman animals reveals some very meaningful uses of the word "prejudice" that Williams does not countenance. For example, there is an important sense in which the traditional arguments for human superiority are "a judgement formed before due examination or consideration; a premature or hasty judgement; a prejudgement."[9] What was "pre-judged" in the traditional arguments was the exhaustiveness or finality of the arguments' conclusions, and therefore the morality of preferring human interests *completely* to the essential concerns of *all* other animals. Our human forebears often framed their opinions about other animals on the basis of uninformed assumptions and coarse generalizations about the behavior and lives of any biological individual outside the human species. Such views are evident in (1) the ancient view of the Indian subcontinent, inherited by the early Buddhists, that all other animals belong to the same *lower* level of the hierarchy of beings (discussed in part III); (2) crassly speculative ideas of the origins of other animals, such as their status as reincarnations of failed women who were, in turn, failed men;[10] (3) the folk taxonomies of the medieval bestiaries;[11] and (4) the Cartesian position that all other animals are "beast-machines."[12] Those who created and advanced traditional arguments were dramatically ignorant of much of nonhuman animal behavior. Instead of conducting empirical investigation, they often relied on unproven assumptions regarding what abilities all nonhuman animals had relative to an overdrawn image of what they considered paradigmatic examples of human existence (often that of males of the ruling class).

Without implying anachronistically that "*they* should have known better," it is possible to observe that the claims and supporting arguments *we* have inherited from our religious and philosophical traditions amount to prejudgments when *our* adherence to them remains unwavering in the face of our radical ignorance about many nonhumans' lives and the current availability of contrary evidence (such as that discussed in part II). Contemporary exclusivist views, then, are particularly subject to the characterization "prejudice."[13] Using these important senses of the word "prejudice," Williams can be challenged when he asserts that "favoring humanity" "is not a prejudice."[14]

At the root of Williams's perfunctory dismissal of speciesism is his assumption that the dichotomy "human and animal" works well as a serviceable distinction when assessing the practices that are questioned by the anti-speciesism critique. His analysis suggests that he has not probed general information available about complex behavior in some other animals, such as *their* self-awareness, communication, social lives, intelligence, individuality, cultural transmission, or even possible *personhood*.[15] Similarly, Williams does not use categories or distinctions that suggest familiarity with the history of diverse human relations with other animals. Rather, he is content to allow the universe of relevant issues to be determined along the lines of the "humans-animals" dualism characteristic of the tradition of anthropocentric ethics in which he stands. Importantly, however, humans have not always and everywhere been as ethically detached from nonhuman animals as is characteristic of the mainline Western philosophical tradition stemming from the Greek and Judeo-Christian sources. Ethnographic data reveal that humans have often seen other animals as ethical subjects and patients.[16] Exclusion has been the norm in urban societies for several hundred years, but, as Midgley notes,

> ethological investigation . . . has shown that Western urban thought was (not surprisingly) often even more ill-informed than local superstition on many such questions [regarding the capacities of nonhuman animals], and that it had consistently attributed to animals a vastly *less* complex set of thoughts and feelings, and a much smaller range of knowledge and power, than they actually possessed. (1984, 123)

Of course, concluding that there is a *profound* divide between all human animals and all other animals might well be a justifiable conclusion following a careful, close, and sympathetic examination of all other animals' lives, but such a proposition cannot be an unexamined assumption that in and of itself is the basis for refusing to countenance the possibility that other animals might have morally considerable dimensions.

Williams's critique thus goes forward without careful reflection upon some of the most basic and unjustifiable features of his own ethical tradition's claims about other animals. One of those features is a foundation of fundamental ignorance about many other animals. It is historical accident that the intellectual traditions relied on heavily by Williams were developed in environments separated from many large-brained, long-lived, socially complex animals. For example, other great apes were absent from the cradles of now-dominant ethical notions, while contacts with nonterrestrial whales and dolphins were minimal, in the sense that they live in a radically different environment that is inaccessible to humans. The elephants that were known were captives, respected for their intelligence, but ultimately used only instrumentally. These circumstances provide grounds for being concerned that the traditional ethical notions and vocabulary relied on by Williams when he thinks about and speaks of other animals might have been framed on the basis of misinformation or even in ignorance.

In summary, Williams's repudiation of the concept of speciesism does not reflect either a close engagement with the concept or its history or a concern to use any basis other than his own tradition's prejudgments of all other animals for assessing the possibilities of human-nonhuman relations.

Williams, Kant and "Persons": An Implied Duty of Inquiry

Williams's analysis relies on the widely accepted approach of treating "persons" differently than nonpersons, a view that draws much of its contemporary strength from Kant's division of "persons and things" (1993, 91). Kant's emphasis on rational beings as persons was related to his concern for impartiality in moral judgments; in his opinion, rational beings alone can conceive the idea of the law, which in turn is related to universalizability and thus impartiality.[17] The language and concepts of universalizability and impartiality have become an integral part of modern ethical discourse and thus of the tradition in which Williams finds himself. Statements such as "like cases should be treated alike" or "relevantly similar cases should be treated similarly" can be found in the work of both deontologists and utilitarians.[18] Such a general rule is, of course, by definition nonspeciesist, for it reaches beyond considerations of mere membership in a species to features that might be shared by biological individuals from different species.

While Kant's division of "persons and things" has been a very influential means of trying to say something about a kind of individuality, namely, the special, complex individuality of "rational beings," it has *also* been a dualism reliant upon anthropocentric notions of individuality and rationality. Kant, in spite of virtually no exposure to nonhuman complex individuals, argued confidently that *only* humans could be persons. Midgley notes that many contemporary discussions among bioethicists proceed by using "the word 'person' in a technical, Kantian sense, meaning one who merits respect" (1994b, 33). Midgley adds, however, in a critique of a suggested extension of "person" to other great apes, that "in ordinary life the word so plainly means 'human being' that it has little force when it is stretched to accommodate chimps, gorillas and orangutans" (33). Of course, using "person" as if it means *any* complex being, when in fact it is taken to mean "any *human* but no other animal," can be extremely problematic and obviously risks unfairness and partiality.

It is, however, notoriously difficult to apply the criteria of impartiality and "relevantly similar" in a world populated by other, nonhuman biological individuals who have both different sensory apparatus than do humans and radically different mental and social lives far more complex than Kant ever suspected (this is the subject matter of chapter 4). Outrageous violations of the rules "like cases should be treated alike" or "relevantly similar cases should be treated similarly" are easy to spot. For example, virtually every ethicist repudiates exclusions of interests that rely on obviously irrelevant features like big ears or blond hair in combination with blue eyes and absence of Jewish ancestry. Agreement on such examples is possible because the exclusions are *intraspecific* and focus on features that are, by consensus, unrelated to moral considerability. But these cases, although they exemplify the rule to be followed, are not always illuminating for the difficult cases that come up in real life.

Consider, for example, the complexities of a problem that has already been alluded to, namely, the issue of extending "personhood" status to any animal outside the human species. Ward notes, "Persons can build upon their experiences, forming an experience unique in shape and pattern, contributing distinctive personal actions to the world which manifest their nature and what they have made of it by their relatively free decisions" (1986, 63). It will be suggested in part II that this applies *fully* to at least some of the key animals whose day-to-day lives exhibit, upon careful examination, features that justify extending the moral principle or axiom that "a personal being should have the chance to realise its nature, at least to a reasonable degree" (Ward 1986, 63). To be sure, how one weighs the complexities of, say, dolphins, which have large brains but live in a different physical and thus social medium, is not so easily determined, but that difficulty alone cannot be the basis for dismissing the importance of their lives.

Particularly difficult cases are the instances of possibly analogous features or functional equivalents. As argued throughout part II, features of the lives of biological individuals do not occur in isolation, and thus context is critically important. Atomizing individualized features such as "intelligence," "cognitive mapping," and social ties is an analytical exercise where the participants are at high risk for bias and ignorance. Deciding which features will be accounted analogous or similar across species lines, or which similarities and dissimilarities will be weighted heavily and which ones ignored, is not an easy task. The notion of functional equivalents is also hard to apply for various reasons. First, the contextual manifestation of abilities can be radically different from one case to the next. Second, causal mechanisms producing an organism-level intelligence might differ radically from one species to the next. These and other factors make functional equivalents difficult to recognize on the basis of anything other than fully informed scrutiny over time.

Thus, arguing that one must treat "relevantly similar cases" in the same manner is only a first step. Subsequent inquiry into and appreciation of context are equally a part of the moral principle at issue, for it is only in context that traits will be manifested, and it is precisely the "in context" manifestations that are at issue as "relevantly similar." Just as the property of being human cannot be separated from the actual, in-context realities of human personhood, the realities of other biological beings cannot be separated from their contextual realizations. Similarly, just as "human persons are distinctive types of entity, and our moral response to them is precisely a response which is appropriate to the form of reality which they possess" (Ward 1986, 70), any entity when assessed for purposes of the moral agent's goal of "treating like alike" *must* be understood in terms of the form of reality which it possesses. To assert the validity of the principle "relevantly similar cases must be treated similarly" *without* at the same time committing to inquire into, and adjust for, the consequences of basic contextual differences, is to assert in concept what one implicitly denies in performance.

There are, then, no simple answers to how to treat "like cases alike" because cases to be compared are *not* alike in so many material respects. Simply assuming that the principal criterion for interpreting what "like" means is participation in the same language, race, sex, *or species* is arbitrary. There are many significant meanings of "this one case is like the other." Consider the meaning of "like" in these claims:

1. She is like me because she speaks the same language.
2. He is like me because he is a member of my race (or sex).
3. She is like me because she is a member of my species.

Examples of *broader* senses of the word "like" occur in the following two sentences:

4. This other animal is like me because it, too, as a complex individual suffers by virtue of the fact that it is removed from its community or family.
5. This other animal is like me because it maps the world with cognitive abilities which, though not identical to mine, function like my cognitive abilities.

In summary, given the diversity of circumstances in the lives of biological individuals, one cannot make the "treat like alike" claim in good faith without a corresponding openness to the variations in the lives of biological individuals. Further, since the relatively more complex individuals among animals (including humans) manifest their potential over time (rather than exhibiting all of their traits at any one particular moment), the inquiry should extend to their whole lifetime. Confining the inquiry to an uninformed caricature created in the face of unfamiliarity is not likely to produce the impartiality so often said to be the heart and soul of moral judgments. While it surely will be the case that, after such empirical inquiry "there is not going to be an articulation of the issues and an adjudication on the weight of the various principles involved, which will be agreed by all informed moralists,"[19] the *failure to inquire* will in and of itself reveal a critical weakness in any position. Such a failure is arguably a material consideration as to who can realistically be considered "an informed moralist." In essence, an impartial viewpoint requires inquiry and cannot be achieved without it. Williams, relying so heavily on the validity of the common dualism "humans and animals," ignores this fundamental requirement.

Midgley and Species Loyalty

Midgley (1984) concludes that the concept of speciesism does valuable work of a *limited, preliminary nature* but cannot do all the things asked of it (the positive features of her evaluation are evident in the passage at the beginning of chapter 2). Midgley concludes that some uses of the concept are "well-placed," "useful," and "fully justified" (98), and she even uses a slight variant in other works.[20] She notes, however, that there are problems in the way proponents have attempted to use the concept of speciesism, for "[t]he demolition of extreme positions [that is, absolute dismissal of all nonhuman animals] by no means gets rid of all unfair habits of thought" (Midgley 1984, 101).

The basis for Midgley's conclusion that speciesism involves "unfair habits of thought" is her analysis that the "surface likeness" of speciesism to racism is not sufficient, especially because racism is an "ill-informed, spineless, impenetrably obscure concept, scarcely capable of doing its own work" (99).[21] Midgley goes further, however, concluding that speciesism as a charge cannot stand because of a fundamental difference between species loyalty and race loyalty. She argues, "Race is not a significant grouping at all, but species in animals certainly is" (98).[22]

Is There a General Species-Wide Loyalty?

Midgley's principal reason for rejecting the term "speciesism" is her assertion that humans have a natural bond or loyalty to all other members of the species. This is a central issue, for if broad connections and loyalties to *all* other members of the human species occur, their existence may be relevant to attempts to justify the exclusivist attitudes challenged by the anti-speciesism critique.

Midgley states, "The question which people who want to use the notion of speciesism have to decide is, does the species barrier also give some ground for such a preference or not?" (1984, 102). The "preference" Midgley refers to in this question is the phenomenon of family and local community loyalty. While Midgley accepts that a preference for family and/or local community can fairly be characterized as "discriminatory" (102), she argues that such a "natural bond is not fairly called a prejudice" (101).

The validity of the bond that many biological creatures have to their kin and local community is not challenged by the anti-speciesism critique as immoral or otherwise wrong.[23] Such a bond is a particularly common feature in the lives of mammals. It answers an inevitable question arising from the fundamental limitations of each finite creature, namely, who are the candidates for my limited resources of time and allegiance? Thus, natural bonds with family and small, local communities do not merely function well; more significantly, they are *necessary* for many mammals because they create the means for survival in a world populated by many predators. To characterize a necessary condition of survival as a "prejudice" would be to make a peculiar argument, for it hardly constitutes a judgment or opinion formed prematurely or without due consideration of relevant issues. Generally, preferences for family have not been criticized as morally suspect. For example, it has been commented that kinship and reciprocity in a local social group are perhaps the only "claimants to the title of universally accepted moral principles" (Singer 1993a, 150).

The existence of such biologically based preferences leads to a broader question. Beyond the existence of a natural bond to relatives and local community members, is there *also* a natural bond to one's species *as a whole* or to *all* the members of one's species? Midgley answers affirmatively.

Problems with the Assertion of a Species Bond

To unpack Midgley's analysis, it will help to distinguish the notion "loyalty to nearby members of one's own species who constitute a community necessary for survival" from the distinct notion "loyalty to all members of one's species." Midgley relies heavily on the latter, which will be referred to as "general species-wide loyalty."

To establish her claim that there is a general species-wide loyalty, which she calls the "species-bond," Midgley argues, "There does seem to be a deep emotional tendency, in us as in other creatures, to attend first to those around us who are like those who brought us up, and to take much less notice of others" (1984, 106). There are at least five grounds on which to challenge Midgley's reasoning that this observation is relevant to questions about the existence of a general species-wide loyalty that can be called upon to justify the eclipse of nonmembers' interests.

First, Midgley seems to suggest that attending "first to those around us who are like those who brought us up" is something like general species-wide loyalty, especially when she argues, "Questions about the morality of species preference must certainly be put in the context of the other preferences which people give to those closest to them" (103). But this close linking of kin and local community loyalties with a broader, species-wide loyalty, as well as the common assumption that a general species-wide loyalty exists in humans or other animals, should be carefully scrutinized. Occurrence of loyalty to those who are truly "around us" cannot automatically be equated with general species-wide loyalty, since humans who are halfway around the globe are not "around us" in any meaningful sense. To make this equation is to beg the question of whether general species-wide loyalty is like the "natural bond" of family and local community loyalty. Cook, writing about Buddhist views of nature, argues, "[O]ur familiar world is one in which relationships are limited and special. . . . How am I related to an Eskimo in Alaska, except through the tenuous and really nonoperative relationship of species?" (1989, 215). It may be disputed that species is a more operative category than suggested by this passage, but Cook's point is forceful if understood as claiming that what is true of the undeniable family and local community bonds is simply not obviously true of general species-wide loyalty.

Second, Midgley's contention that this is a "deep emotional tendency" also begs clarification. It is unclear if Midgley intends to claim that this is a natural tendency, in the sense of "native" feature in humans, rather than a product of culture. It is possible that a preference for all humans is a manufactured, culturally relative artifact. Such artifacts can be taught in such a way as to create a "deep emotional attachment." In this way, attachment to the notion of species can come about precisely because exclusivist thinking is inculcated as the correct ("moral") way to understand the individual's relation to the rest of life. It can then function as "a deep emotional tendency" just as racism does in some humans. Thus, the mere fact that a preference functions as a "deep emotional tendency" is not conclusive as to either its occurrence as a natural phenomenon or its justifiability from the vantage point of the moral agent.

Similarly, Midgley's claim that this is a natural phenomenon, even if true, would hardly be conclusive as to the justifiability of the preference. Warfare and xenophobia are widespread phenomena among humans (and, as noted in part II, among some chimpanzees), but that fact alone does not justify them. Further, the phenomenon Midgley is addressing is essentially *relational*. Her argument is an appeal not to intrinsic features of our fellow species members ("conspecifics") but to our relationship with them. As Pluhar notes, an appeal to this phenomenon, whether natural or not, has a peculiar structure: "Instead of arguing that 'we prefer individual A to individual B because it is right to do so,' one is claiming that 'our preferring A to B makes it right to do so'" (1995, 171). This form of argument could be used to sanction the worst kinds of prejudice. Additionally, the claim is problematic given that many humans *in fact* have far greater emotional ties to their companion animals than to other humans.

Fourth, Midgley's assertion that such a tendency occurs "*in us as in other creatures*" must be challenged. If she means that general species-wide loyalty occurs in most or many other animals, she is wrong. This tendency is clearly *not* a product of evolution; Dawkins notes, "But now that we have eschewed the 'good of the species' view of evolution, there seems no logical reason to distinguish associations between members of different species as things apart from associations between members of the same species."[24]

Finally, Midgley seems to equate preference for one's own species with a justification for favoring the interests of the members of one's own species over the interests of those individuals outside the species. Biological individuals' preference for members of their own species is related to the fact that biological individuals can share more easily and fully with members of their own species. For example, communication and ease of recognition of similar and often complementary interests make possible joint efforts that enhance the fulfillment of all participants' interests.[25] This kind of preference does not equate to, or automatically justify, preference for *all* conspecifics' interests over the interests of members of other species in situations of conflict. It is possible to prefer the company of one's nearby conspecifics without preferring the interests of all conspecifics to the exclusion of the interests of all non-members of one's own species.

The Species-Bond as Cultural Artifact

The notion of loyalty to one's entire species is arguably better understood as a kind of fiction, though a culturally significant one at present.[26] As argued in chapter 5, it is a discursively created and supported set of beliefs, bound up in culturally relative forms with other, more fundamental beliefs about the importance of life, relationships with some other beings, and taking responsibility as a moral agent. Its tie to the more fundamental beliefs often gives it the features of a moral claim; that is, advancement of the exclusivist concerns here called speciesism is sometimes characterized as a moral necessity. But appealing to a general species-wide loyalty as a fundamental, "natural" feature of human lives in order to rebut the anti-speciesist critique is problematic in light of certain factual realities. Such a loyalty almost certainly was *not* a feature of the earliest humans, for even after the commencement of human culture and commerce "[r]elations between neighbouring tribes were marked by an uneasy shifting balance between trade and xenophobic hostility" (Diamond 1992, 199). That early humans did not exhibit a general species-wide loyalty suggests that such a phenomenon might not be naturally based, although this alone is not conclusive proof that Midgley is wrong in claiming that "the instinctive [species-wide] bond is a real one" (1984, 104). Additional circumstantial evidence of the questionable nature of the claim is the absence of this tendency in children and certain "primitive" societies. Freud noted, "There is a great deal of resemblance between the relations of children and of primitive men towards animals. Children show no trace of the arrogance which urges modern adult civilized men to draw a hard and fast line between their own nature and that of all other animals. Children have no scruples over allowing animals to rank as their full equals" (1913, 126).

Reasons for the absence of a biologically based general species-wide loyalty include the fact that biological competition, in the Darwinian sense, is overwhelmingly more common with conspecifics, a feature of life that is often thought to be a factor contributing to the health of the species.[27] This is not to say that there is no competition across species lines, for there surely is when members of different species compete for the same resources. But this kind of competition has very little, if any, bearing on the issue of the existence of a general species-wide loyalty.[28]

Spiro, when writing about Burmese Buddhism, notes that some human cultures produce "a characterological disposition" of "basic lack of concern for other people" (1971, 433; he had in mind the Burmese and certain Chinese Taoists). The existence of humans' great cultural abilities, then, can lead to an exacerbation of the natural fear of and competition with neighboring humans, since cultural distinctiveness and loyalties make recognition of a friendly or competitive conspecific relatively easier for humans. In this sense, some humans display very little of the supposed "natural" tendency to general species-wide loyalty.

Talk about general species-wide loyalty is a late cultural addition, a fact which suggests that it is not a natural tendency. Lecky noted regarding the development of European morals, "At one time the benevolent affections embrace merely the family, soon the circle expanding includes first a class, then a nation, then a coalition of nations, then all of humanity, and finally, its influence is felt in the dealings of man with the animal world."[29] General species-wide loyalty comes far along in the process, whereas family loyalty is first. Parts III and IV suggest that both the Buddhist and Christian traditions were important in generating cultural acceptance of inclusivist views that repudiated narrow, xenophobic values and practices. These achievements were necessary, however, precisely because no really effective respect existed for those humans who were not part of one's own group. As Clark notes, "The commonest moral distinction, historically speaking, is between those creatures that are part of our own community (whether strictly human or not) and those that are outsiders" (1995, 6).

Midgley might be taken as arguing that there is a "species-bond" *only* in cases in which there is conflict with members of *other* species. If so, one must ask, how could such a mechanism ever develop in nature? It is, by definition, radically different than family and local community loyalties, requiring loyalty to unseen, unmet, and unfathomed conspecifics who have different languages, customs, and values. If this is indeed the claim, it, too, seems to have no basis in fact, since there have been many other cultures that have not been fixated on a radical demarcation between members of the human species and all other animals.[30]

In summary, Midgley's postulated general species-wide loyalty is inconsistent with important factual realities. It possibly stems from an excessive reliance on the legitimacy of using the species notion as a frame of reference. This heavy reliance is apparent in Midgley's charge that "the tendency for human beings to regard their cultures as if they were actually separate species" makes one guilty of "pseudo-speciation" (1984, 109). As Pluhar notes, "The term 'pseudo-speciation' in this context implies that preferences along species lines are legitimate while others are not. Speciesists must *show* that their view is not merely another form of deep-seated prejudice" (1995, 175). Midgley does not carry this burden with regard to the existence of a general species-wide loyalty. Further, she fails to provide compelling arguments for why the loyalty stops at the species level on the following continuum: immediate family, extended family, local community group, ethnic group, nation, race, species, genus, taxonomic family, order, class, phylum, kingdom. If morality is the extension of sympathies to others, and we can, as Midgley argues, extend such sympathies to each and every species member (and in this sense to the species level), what is it that prevents extensions from going beyond the species line? Advocates of universalism within the human species have argued, in effect, that those who fail to go this far have committed the fallacy of misplaced community. What these same advocates must justify is why the community stops at the species level. It is possible that they, too, by relying so exclusively on the concept of species, commit the same error.

Midgley, of course, knows these facts, for she acknowledges the phenomena of human exclusion of other humans and coexistence with other species (1984, 109). Her insistence that a vague species-bond has some sort of natural basis can be accounted for by assessing what she thinks is at stake. Midgley argues, "I think it is important to stress in this way that species-bonds are real, because *unless* we take account of them, the frequent exclusive attitude of our own species is hard to understand" (106, emphasis added).

This approach, however, risks mistaking speciesist avowals for a description of reality, for one can take account of the "frequent exclusive attitude of our own species" without postulating that a general species-wide loyalty is naturally based. It can be understood as a cultural artifact, an interpretation that is not at odds with either the long history of excluding other humans or the common phenomenon of some humans valuing other animals as more than mere tools, pests, or lower beings.[31] Alternatively, one could at least as plausibly postulate that such a bond must be *unreal*, or at least inoperative, if one is to understand the phenomena of individual selfishness, xenophobia, or many humans' and cultures' recognition of other animals as possessors of morally considerable interests. The key should be what is happening broadly in the natural world, not what is needed to understand one facet of certain humans' behavior excluding other animals.

Wittgensteinians and "All That Natter about Speciesism"

C. Diamond offers a fundamentally different critique of the concept of speciesism.[32] Her argument begins by noting that arguments advanced on behalf of vegetarianism "often start with discussion of human rights" and focus on the ground of the rights attributed to individual humans. These arguments next ask if similar grounds might not also be found for some nonhumans. Diamond responds, "This is a totally wrong way of beginning the discussion, because it ignores quite central facts—facts which, if attended to, would make it quite clear that *rights* are not what is crucial" (1978, 467, emphasis in the original). For Diamond, "fundamental" (465) or "central" (467) aspects of human acting in the world are found in the fact that we do not eat dead humans even though we, including the vegetarians among us, do see dead nonhuman animals as something to eat (for example, those killed accidentally by lightning). Diamond's description suggests her impatience with those who use the speciesism arguments: "[B]eyond all that natter about speciesism and equality and the rest, there is a difference between human beings and animals which is being ignored" (468).

Regarding this "fundamental" difference, Diamond argues that our valuing of other humans is not based on their possession of particular interests, traits, features, or characteristics but instead is grounded in practices and actions that, in some foundational manner, are ways of living. It is not always easy to give conceptual descriptions of these, for they constitute a general background that is the foundation and continuing context of both language and learning to act in the world. At issue is much more than habit, for it is a form of life against and amid which practices and actions are measured and understood.[33]

Diamond points out specific "facts" that are missed by those who conceive of the problem as a matter of equal consideration of interests: "[T]here are some actions, like giving people names, that are part of the way we come to understand and indicate our recognition of *what* kind it is with which we are concerned" (469, emphasis in the original). Diamond again and again emphasizes that it is not a matter of our respect for identifiable, atomizable "interests" (469) that causes humans not to eat each other:

> Similarly with having duties to human beings. This is not a consequence of what human beings are: it is itself one of the things which go to build our notion of human beings. And so too—very much so—the idea of the difference between human beings and animals. We learn what a human being is in—among other ways—sitting at a table where *we* eat *them*. (470, emphasis in the original)

Diamond uses a key distinction as a way of understanding just how important the conventions of "human-to-human relations" are relative to the conventions of "human-to-nonhuman relations,"[34] and this functions well as the hallmark of her position:

> One source of confusion here is that we fail to distinguish between "the difference between animals and people" and "the differences between animals and people". . . . In the case of the difference between animals and people, it is clear that we form the idea of this difference, create the concept of difference, knowing perfectly well the overwhelmingly obvious similarities. (470)

Thus, Diamond contends that our special treatment of humans vis-à-vis other animals is *not*, despite what philosophers like Singer and Regan suggest, premised on an assessment of human beings' traits. For her, it is not relative differences that ground humans' preference for members of their own species. Instead, similarities possessed by other animals, whether biological or psychological, are not relevant to the differences in treatment. Such conclusions put her at odds with the philosophers who use speciesism as a term because they, according to Diamond, inquire only of similarities and differences and, thereby, miss *the difference*.[35] She argues that if one concedes a merits-based analysis of *the difference*, then one risks the very vitality of our forms of life, for "to argue as Singer and Regan do, is not to give a defence of animals; it is to attack significance in human life" (471).

Shortcomings of the Argument

While Diamond's repudiation of the traits-based analysis of the anti-speciesism critique relies on an understanding of ethical systems as conventionalist, her arguments are more profound than mere conventionalism, which does nothing more than accept the current ways of seeing the world. Her arguments rely heavily on the insights of Wittgenstein regarding how meaning (1) works, (2) is embedded in a community, and (3) has a "background" that is often hard to see. But Diamond's analysis remains subject to some of the standard objections to conventionalism. She states:

> The difference between human beings and animals is not to be discovered by studies of Washoe or the activities of dolphins. It is not that sort of study or ethology or evo-

lutionary theory that is going to tell us the difference between us and animals; the difference is, as I have suggested, a central concept for human life and it is more an object of contemplation than observation. (1978, 470)

Diamond is confident that the *central facts* are ongoing features of humans' treatment of each other and other animals. They are "central" because they constitute, in Diamond's view, the really distinct features of human life, namely, special treatment of members of the human species that goes to build our understanding of "*what kind it is with which we are concerned*" (469). This is why listing objective traits that other animals might share with humans amounts to "a totally wrong way of beginning the discussion" (467).

But these "facts," though clearly central in the way many humans understand themselves, are a very peculiar kind of fact. Recall that Diamond argues that "in the case of the difference between animals and people, it is clear that we form the idea of this difference, create the concept of difference, knowing perfectly well *the over-whelmingly obvious similarities*" (470, emphasis added). In effect, making the socially constructed creation of a self-image the "central fact" that tells us about our lives, rather than shared features of the broader world such as those revealed by "studies of Washoe or the activities of dolphins," loads the case against the possibilities of comparisons. It establishes as the measure (since it is "central") a standard by which humans will inevitably be measured as "different." But self-assessment and treatment according to vague, socially created, and sustained conventions, as relevant as these are, cannot be the *sole* measure of which *other* beings are morally considerable. To make it such is to countenance only those parts of reality that humans choose to call important.

The difference may, then, have very little relation to what other animals actually are in their world. It may be only *an assumed difference*, a symbol or convention reified into a "fact" by lifestyles. Diamond's appeal to "facts" is thus not a standard appeal to information about reality but an appeal to a special class of views premised on human ways of acting which in themselves create the reality she is describing. When examined, these have more the character of a lived-out prejudgment. In fact, this analysis could be used to justify any widespread practice. Thus, arguing in this way risks assuming precisely what is at issue, namely, the propriety of the challenged practice.

Challenging This Conventionalism

Consider several implications of Diamond's exclusive reliance on existing conventions revolving around a community of speakers.

1. It would be possible for one set of humans to eat members of another class of humans, speaking about and acting toward them in ways identical to those described in Diamond's argument. Diamond's argument leaves no room for challenging practices that eclipse the moral considerability of those outside the community of discourse.
2. One can imagine a community that is inclusivist with regard to at least some other animals. The discourse of such a community could be different than the formative practices relied on by Diamond (all of which take for granted the importance of the species line). Humans might still have a very important sense of *the difference*,

but one that is based on several species rather than just the human species. There is nothing that compels the sense of *the difference* to be confined to one species.

3. Similarly, if other communicators constructed a form of life that assumed *their* uniqueness, such that humans were excluded, Diamond's analysis offers no means of challenging the exclusion of humans. One species' shared construction of its own members' uniqueness simply has no bearing on the moral considerability of members of other species.

4. Diamond implicitly treats the category "human species" as the equivalent to the community of discourse, even though her analysis suggests that the operative concept should be the human linguistic community that shares ways of acting and speaking. Arguably, this is both counterfactual and oversimplified, since there are many communities of discourse on the issue of humans' relation to other animals, some of which have views dramatically different than those of the modern, developed world that Diamond assumes are the norm.

These problems make one wonder what resources Diamond's argument has for identifying and challenging moral schemes imposed by a dominant group. The traits-based arguments that she repudiates supply a means of challenging existing practices held in place by the force of tradition, and arguably were the bases for the now partially successful challenges to the once-dominant practices of racism, sexism, and slavery.

Synopsis of Observations

The challenges of these philosophers, while providing an important corrective to (1) excessive reliance on the analogies to racism and sexism, (2) polemical claims that humans are not different than other animals, and (3) the tendency to analyze traits rather than whole lives, fail to focus on the usefulness of the anti-speciesism critique as a descriptive tool for what has happened in history. In what follows, the term is used both as an analytical tool regarding operative definitions of the edge of the moral circle (the human species line) and as a descriptive tool for what Diamond has called the "awful and unshakable callousness and unrelentingness with which we most often confront the non-human world" (1978, 479).

PART II

ANIMALS AND RELIGION

Attention shifts in this part to animals, or, as will be discussed later, that group of living beings less prejudicially described as "other animals." Chapter 4 addresses certain information and perspectives that have been developed, largely in reliance on various biological sciences, regarding the key animals. Chapter 5 turns to problematic features that dominate the manner in which many humans speak about other animals.

4

Other Complex Animals: Missed Opportunities?

There is no prejudice to which we all are more accustomed from our earliest years than the belief that dumb animals think.
—Descartes, *Descartes: Philosophical Letters*

In this chapter the spotlight is cast, as much as possible, on some specific animals. The first section provides technical, "taxonomic" information about these animals, and the following section describes why these animals were chosen. The third section addresses two serious limits on our ability to know the lives of nonhuman animals generally (epistemology and sociology of knowledge), and the concluding three sections present brief sketches of, respectively, nonhuman great apes, elephants, and whales and dolphins (cetaceans).

Three Groups of Animals

The breakdown of the key animals into the standard groupings used here (apes, elephants, and cetaceans) is found in nonscientific, folk taxonomies that are, with only one exception on the specific animals considered in this study, generally consistent with contemporary scientific taxonomies. The exception is, of course, humans, who, though great apes, are not generally spoken of as such. This exception was also characteristic of early scientific taxonomies, although now "[s]ome taxonomies place human beings and the African apes in the same subfamily, the Homininae, a classification that would have been unthinkable a generation ago."[1]

The following discussion utilizes the terminology of contemporary scientific classification and thereby provides an example of how humans possess, from one vantage point, detailed technical knowledge of the key animals.[2]

The other great apes are members of four species:[3]

1. *Gorilla gorilla*. There are three known subspecies: *Gorilla gorilla gorilla* (the western lowland gorilla); *Gorilla gorilla graueri* (the eastern lowland gorilla); and *Gorilla gorilla beringei* (the highland or mountain gorilla).[4]
2. *Pan troglodytes* (chimpanzees or common chimpanzees). There are three known subspecies: *Pan troglodytes schweinfurthii*; *Pan troglodytes troglodytes*; and *Pan troglodytes verus* (McGrew 1992, 23–27).
3. *Pan paniscus* (bonobos or pygmy chimpanzees); and

4. *Pongo pygmaeus* (orangutans). The dominant view is that these animals comprise two subspecies: *Pongo pygmaeus pygmaeus* (the Borneo orangutan), and *Pongo pygmaeus abelii* (the Sumatran orangutan) (McGrew 1992, 42).

The genetic relationship of the other great apes to humans is quite close, such that Diamond has argued that, according to the principles of scientific taxonomy applied to all other animals, humans should be labeled "the third chimpanzee," along with chimpanzees and bonobos.[5]

Elephants are members of two species:

1. *Laxodonta africana* (African elephant), with possibly two subspecies: *Laxodonta africana africana*, the typical savanna and woodland elephant; and *Laxodonta africana cyclotis*, the forest elephant of central and western Africa.
2. *Elephas maximus* (Asian elephant), with perhaps three subspecies: *Elephas maximus maximus* of Sri Lanka, *Elephas maximus indicus* of India, and *Elephas maximus sumatranus* of Sumatra (Haynes 1993, 8).

Cetaceans are members of at least seventy-nine species.[6] These species divide into two major groups, the odontocetes (commonly called "toothed whales") and the mysticetes (etymologically, "moustached whales" because they have moustachelike filters known as baleen rather than teeth). There are eleven species of mysticetes, which include the largest whales (blue whales and fin whales). The generally smaller odontocetes total approximately sixty-eight species, which break down into nine distinct families, the largest of which is the family Delphinidae (which has approximately twenty species); there are, in addition, six species of porpoises and five species of freshwater dolphins (Reeves and Leatherwood 1994; Klinowska 1991, 7–9).

Why These Animals Provide an Important Focus

The key animals are members of about eighty-five different species and constitute a very small percentage of animals beyond the human species line.[7] They are, by consensus, among the more complicated of animals, and provide an opportunity to examine: 1. a constellation of general characteristics leading to rich social relationships among complex individuals; and 2. a unique set of problems related to ethical considerability.

A Constellation: Rich Social Relationships among Complex Individuals

The last three sections of this chapter argue that *some* members of the key species have in common the following general characteristics: large brains, communications between individuals, prolonged periods of development in complex familial and social envelopes, and levels of both social integration and individuality that humans can recognize.[8] These features combine to produce unique individuals with distinctive personalities, histories, and community membership. The term "complex individual" is used in the following to refer to biological individuals who possess some combination of these general characteristics.[9] "Complexity" as it is used here is a reference to features that occur at the level of the whole organism. There are admittedly other senses of the word "complexity" that might be used regarding certain intricate and complicated organic and inorganic systems (such as the genetic code of a particular virus or the solar system). But in this book when the term "complex individual" is used, the adjective "complex" is meant to address and characterize the occurrence of mental organization of the world and distinctive personalities of individual biological organisms, as exemplified by the following descriptions of the key animals.

Unique Sets of Problems

Attempts to learn about the key animals create an interesting set of problems. For example, assessing the mental lives of these animals has some features in common with the classic problems of knowing other human "minds."[10] There are, however, additional problems, since the mental lives of the key animals are dramatically less accessible and obviously radically different from the mental lives of humans.

More specifically, the other great apes provide an opportunity to ask about a group of animals that are by far the most closely related to humans. For example, humans are probably genetically more closely related to chimpanzees than chimpanzees are to gorillas (Parker 1990a, 32). One aspect of the similarity between humans and other great apes, based on common evolutionary history, can be quantified by DNA comparisons.[11] It was discovered in the mid-1980s that humans and chimpanzees are extraordinarily similar in terms of genetic material.[12] The figures usually given are 98.4 percent for human-chimpanzee similarity and 97.7 percent for human-gorilla similarity. Such a high degree of genetic similarity means that many of the physical features of members of the closely related species are identical,[13] but it does not mean that the appearance (morphology) must be so. The identity is, so to speak, more than skin-deep. For example, chimpanzees and humans, though different in appearance, are closer genetically than are the two species of elephants (Fouts 1997, 94–95). The genetic similarity also results in nonhuman great apes sharing many *psychological* features in common with humans (described in a later section).

Elephants provide an opportunity to ask about another group of terrestrial animals with a genetic endowment radically different from that of humans. These animals have had a remarkable history with humans:

> An object of worship, a target of hunters, a beast of burden, a burden to the people, gentle in captivity, dangerous in the wild, the pride of kings, the companion of mahouts, a machine of war, an envoy of peace, loved, feared, hated, the elephant has had a glorious and an infamous association with man in Asia. For its sheer contrast and splendour, this association is unequalled by any other interaction between animal and man in the world. (Sukamar 1989, 1)

The ambivalence evident in Sukamar's description is related to the fact that these animals compete with humans for the use of vast tracts of land, and the physical prowess of the animals alone makes them formidable competitors for the finite space of many ecosystems. That same prowess, together with obvious cognitive abilities, has made them a coveted tool used by humans for many purposes.

Cetaceans provide the chance to ask radically different questions, namely, those regarding non-land-dwelling social groups made up of individuals of species that have developed over millions of years in an altogether different physical medium. Characterized by the largest brains on earth and brain–body size ratios comparable in some instances to that of humans, cetaceans provide a chance to study other social beings with mental organization of the world that may be of a kind altogether different from humans' mental complexities.

The Issue of Limited "Knowledge"

An assessment of the state of current information about these animals suggests that many humans who have claimed to "know" their "true natures" had a profoundly limited conception of these and other animals' lives. The continuum of beliefs includes a very negative pole near which one would find the negation of these animals' interests inherent in the Catholic Church's 1994 claim that all other animals are *by nature destined for human use.* At the opposite end of the continuum are several different kinds of views. The "animal rights" positions are diverse, and well-known proponents of this general view offer very different kinds of reasons for insisting that these animals have "interests" or "rights" that make any intentional *and* unnecessary infliction of suffering on them *immoral.*[14] Also at the more positive end of the continuum are the views of many indigenous cultures that are outside the sphere of major religious traditions. These have often exhibited a modus vivendi in which what was claimed as "knowledge" of other animals was different from what is counted "knowledge" today in industrialized societies.[15]

A review of the wide differences in opinions about nonhuman animals reveals that such views characteristically have a very specific, traceable history. Further, this history often shows that crucial factors in such beliefs are *not* discernible features of the lives of the animals evaluated, but other factors such as traditions of discourse or exclusivist, even ideological, claims to the effect that only human lives are morally considerable. A bias for the "human" has arguably been as true of "scientific" views as it has been of religious and other traditional views.[16]

Sometimes the limitations that appear in the views of other animals have obvious causes, such as the fact that those who make claims about them do not live with or anywhere near the animals in question. Sometimes there are far more subtle reasons, such as occurs when the framers of opinions are both dramatically ignorant of other animals and *not* predisposed to notice or take them seriously. In the midst of this ignorance, as McGrew notes (1992, 11–12), the mere absence of evidence is sometimes construed as conclusive evidence of absence. Clark (1977, 97) argues similarly that a common pattern is the transmutation of ignorance into knowledge of the negative of a proposition.

"Ignorance" regarding the key animals is, then, a many-sided phenomenon, ranging from lack of good information about real lives to reasoning poorly while knowing almost nothing about the emergent or supervenient qualities of individuals that arise as a result of complex individuals interacting in socially complex situations.

Why a Limited Number of Animals Are Examined

Choosing a limited number of species also allows two other sets of issues to be framed. First, there are important distinctions between (1) the issues raised by the exclusion of the more complicated nonhuman animals from fundamental moral protections and (2) the somewhat overlapping but distinguishable set of issues raised by the exclusion of *other animals generally*. Second, environmental concerns that have become very prominent in secular and religious traditions in the latter half of the twentieth century can be distinguished from the very specific issues that arise when a moral agent impacts a specific individual nonhuman animal that has the complexities described in this chapter.

As to the first of these two sets of issues, an important response to the exclusion of *all* nonhuman animals from certain morality-inspired protections has been the approach of creation theologies that base the moral considerability of nonhuman animals on their status as creatures of God.[17] Such approaches sometimes claim to be "theocentric" as a way of repudiating what is perceived to be the arrogance of purely anthropocentric accounts regarding which animals "really matter."[18] "Theocentrism," however, is a difficult concept to work with, especially for those moral agents who do not find theologically inspired traditions of discourse to be helpful. Particularly significant is that "theocentrism" provides no easily discernible basis for distinguishing one form of nonhuman creaturehood (say, viruses) from other, arguably more complicated forms (say, sentient mammals). Further, focusing on "creation" calls to mind the classic but recently questioned distinction between "history and creation." This distinction rested on the view that the biblical authors treated God acting in human history as distinctive while the rest of "nature" or "creation" was a theologically less significant realm idolatrously worshiped by Israel's neighbors and therefore properly subordinated to human history. This interpretive framework has dominated Christian theology's view of the distinctiveness of the Hebrew religious awareness since the nineteenth century. Classic statements of this distinction can be found in the writings of von Rad and Wright.[19] Although this view has been described as one of the dominant orthodoxies of twentieth-century Christian theology (Barr 1963, 193–94), the position has recently been challenged as problematically originating in nineteenth-century anthropological and philosophical models (in particular, Hegelianism) and as inadequate for understanding the biblical attitudes toward nonhuman phenomena.[20]

The second distinction (namely, that between so-called environmental issues and more individual-oriented "animal rights" issues) is also very complicated. Environmental analyses draw on many different conceptual schemes to assess ethical traditions' awareness of these problems and possible tradition-based solutions or guidelines.[21] While the matters discussed under notions of "the environment" (or, sometimes, "ecology") are of great importance and obvious relevance,[22] the range of concerns considered under this rubric is clearly *not* identical to the range of concerns for the status of nonhuman animals. The former is, generally, far broader, especially since "animal rights" or "animal liberation" advocates have notoriously been focused on individuals rather than species and their niches in ecosystems.

Focusing on only the key animals narrows the inquiry to a specific, manageable set of problems that is not related to the status of nonhuman animals collectively, creation as a whole, or the environment generally. Instead, focus is directly on the possibility of morally considerable aspects occurring in the lives of specific, identifiable nonhuman biological individuals. In particular, the moral agent can identify these individual animals easily and assess impacts directly and quite definitely. Under the far more general concerns that attach to discussions of the status of "all animals," "creation," or "the environment" (or even specifiable ecosystems), moral agents often struggle because the specific issues and a realistic praxis are often far harder for the individual moral agent to identify and assess.

Of equal importance and of particular relevance to the moral agent assessing the consequences of intentional actions is the fact that observation-based information, including certain scientific information, on the key animals is often some of the best information available, even if at times it is still fundamentally incomplete. Such a narrow focus on *only* the key animals, as opposed to other animals or the broad issues raised by the more generalized concerns, however, is *not* meant to suggest that the animals or communities in ecosystems not included could not be morally considerable or otherwise morally significant. The narrow focus merely permits certain very real problems to be seen clearly.

Epistemological Challenges and Sociology of Knowledge

There is a complex set of problems raised by a question that has consistently been asked, Is it *possible* to know the mental realities of other animals *without* the benefit of a common language? The debate on this issue has been wide-ranging, as evidenced by the arguments made by the Stoics and Augustine that are mentioned in part IV. Granting the common assumption that other animals do *not* have *human* language, relevant issues still remain. These include, among others, questions such as, Is what other animals do when communicating with one another similar, analogous, or functionally equivalent to some of the things humans do with their biologically based languages? or the more general question, Are the lives of some other animals rich enough on their own terms to merit the consideration of moral agents?

It is assumed here that empirical inquiries are relevant to answering such questions. The following sections review some of the empirical evidence regarding the conceptual abilities of the key animals. The conclusion is drawn that there exist individuals *outside* the human species that have conceptual and symbolic capabilities, as well as self-awareness, "intentionality" (defined later), and the ability to recognize others as "others." Further, it will be suggested that human learning about other species, and indeed even limited cross-species sharing of feelings, is *possible* because the common neurological bases of life produce functionally comparable, and presumably similar, experiences in humans and some nonhumans. Clark notes, "We can reason our way to understand the world and its denizens, if indeed we can, because the ways of the world are embedded in our very being" (1993, 32). We can learn and use phrases like "I have pain" because facial grimaces, body language, and other physical clues provide some common ground among humans, and this same extension can in some instances be applied to some extent to *some* other animals. Savage-Rumbaugh, on the basis of long experience with other great apes, notes that humans and chimpanzees inhabit a common perceptual world, "a sort of joint awareness that leads to joint perception and joint knowing" such that "what gains my attention is often the same as what gains theirs."[23] The *physical* similarities have long been known. As important, fully acknowledging them has at times been controversial, as evidenced by Linnaeus's comments in 1747:

> I demand of you, and of the whole world, that you show me a generic character . . . by which to distinguish between Man and Ape. I myself most assuredly know of none. I wish somebody would indicate one to me. But, if I had called man an ape, or vice versa, I would have fallen under the ban of all ecclesiastics. It may be that as a naturalist I ought to have done so.[24]

Beyond these purely physical similarities, *psychological* similarities have repeatedly been asserted in modern times, as when experiments that inflict harm on other primates are carried out for the sole purpose of understanding *human* psychopathology.[25]

Clark comments broadly about the significance of sharing certain cognitive abilities and features:

> And it is these non-verbal recognitions, abilities and judgements which we share most certainly with the non-human animals, and particularly with our mammalian next of kin [cite omitted]. We [list of animals] share quite enough of a common perception of the world, common curiosities, common disinclinations to betray or injure travelling or working companions, common affections for the small and defenceless. . . . for a sense of community to be entirely possible. (1977, 25–26)

It is possible, then, that even though humans and other animals do not share human language, the interested observer can still use natural abilities to seek fundamental features of the mental realities of other animals (by, for example, intuiting anger or fear in another animal that is unable to communicate the feeling verbally). The issue is not whether we can know exactly what it is like to be a member of another species. The issue is, rather, whether we can know that there is either some general similarity or a high degree of mental complexity, whether similar or not to the riches of human experience. In terms of the "interests" cited in chapter 2, humans as moral agents may not know precisely, or perhaps at all, what having interests is like for other, nonhuman biological individuals. That limitation is, however, logically distinct from whether one can realistically assert, perhaps even *know*, that other animals have interests *at all*.

Sociology of Knowledge Problems

Another complex of problems is related to the manner in which humans in a community of discourse make claims and hold information about subjects generally. For example, information held about other animals is often held "socially," that is, the principal component of an individual's claim such as "I know about elephants" is not personal experience with elephants. Rather, it is what the humans in that cultural system say and think generally about elephants. What is said and thought can, in turn, be understood best by reference to the background against which the realities of elephants are understood (such as the possibilities of elephant existence, the relation of elephants to humans, and the relation of elephants to other animals). A *general* understanding of elephants, then, is rarely based solely on experience with elephants; also relevant are generalized images of elephants and background views and values that one learns as a member of one's linguistic community.

In the next chapter and in parts III and IV generally, it is argued that this phenomenon of socially held knowledge plays a determinative role in views of other animals. This exemplifies the point that any person's assertion of *inherited* views of other animals occurs amid a complicated set of problems attaching to any socially held and transmitted "knowledge." This cultural conditioning is especially evident in the range of vocabulary that any speaker inherits. The arguments in chapter 5 and in parts III and IV about the words and traditions of discourse inherited by, respectively, contemporary English speakers, Buddhists, and Christians focus heavily on "generic" words used for other animals, that is, on words that convey broad generalizations such as "all other animals." To be sure, references to specific types of animals, and even occasionally to individuals of other species, exist in the vocabularies considered. It will be argued that these more specific references were, however, subordinated to the far more significant vocabulary of generic terms that dominated the writings of each tradition.

It will *not* be argued that such generic words themselves were *solely* responsible for the habits of reference that can be found in each tradition, as if by some magical quality related to the dominance of "language" the mere existence of certain words controlled the speakers. In fact, the prevalence of the generic words considered here reflects a habit of mind, the origin of which is difficult to identify. The pattern of occurrence in the early Buddhist and Christian traditions does reflect, however, that adherents in these traditions who learned the standard terms for expressing the possibilities of other animals were subjected to traditions of description and understanding that had at least the following features. First, the traditions of descriptions and understanding had profoundly exclusivist tendencies. Second, they were often as demonstrably ignorance-based as they were confidently used, given that the prevailing theories regarding other animals' lives were systematically underdetermined by the facts of those animals' realities.

The Role of Factual Realities

Answers to the question, Are there living beings which are morally considerable? are, whether affirmative or negative, logically reliant on a *claim to know at least some relevant aspects of the realities* of the living beings with regard to which one answers. More specifically, explicitly or implicitly comparative claims that have the general form "A is better than B," "A is more than B," or "A has traits or features which B does not" require, as a logical matter, knowledge in the relevant domain regarding not only A *but B as well*. Thus, claims that other animals lack those very features that make the interests of humans morally considerable are logically reliant on a claim to know relevant features of the lives of other animals as they "really" are. Exploring what might be called generally, though somewhat vaguely, "factual realities" is, then, pertinent to any view of other animals. The attempt to engage the "factual realities" of other animals provides a means of assessing whether the many human claims about the relative standing of humans and other animals meet logically mandated criteria regarding the conclusions being drawn.

Further, any ethical system that includes the provision that moral agents are responsible for the consequences of their intentional acts implies that the agents should seek to know the consequences of their acts. Knowledge of the impacts of one's acts on other beings can only be determined with reference to *those beings' interests*. This implies that one must know something of the being that is impacted rather than simply assuming the problem away on the basis of uninformed preconceptions. Thus, no ethical system can systematically ignore the natural world's factual realities, or the processes by which consensus about relevant factual realities is achieved, because ethics purports to be about the relations of natural world entities as they are. This is not to say that the specific consequences of any act are or should be the principal concern of ethical systems, though such a claim is made in consequentialist theories. It is to say, however, that consequences are to some extent relevant under *any* ethical theory which accepts that essential features of moral agency are awareness of, choices about, and responsibility for the results of one's own intentional actions.

Some Factual Realities: Other Great Apes

Although apes or monkeys of some kind were, as noted in parts III and IV, frequently depicted in Buddhist and Christian materials, the portrayals can be characterized as inaccurate, even caricatures, since they are poor descriptions of the day-to-day factual realities of the other great apes. The standard by which such apparently harsh judgments of "inaccurate" and "caricature" can be made is a picture of the lives of other great apes that has only begun to emerge since the early 1960s, and that today remains fundamentally incomplete.[26]

The Individual Kanzi

In 1994, researchers published the story of Kanzi, a language-trained bonobo (Savage-Rumbaugh and Lewin 1994). By a serendipitous turn of events, that is, without the benefit of experimental design for this particular purpose, researchers discovered that this young bonobo had learned to use a system of abstract symbols, which his adopted mother had not been able to learn. The dramatic differences between Kanzi's success and his mother's failures can be accounted for by the fact that Kanzi had been exposed to the abstract symbols at a time when he was peculiarly ripe for learning. Bonobos happen to have a window for learning that is very much like a well-known feature in humans. This is the ability of human children to learn *any* human language if they are exposed early enough in their development. This flexibility is typically lost in early adolescence.[27] Savage-Rumbaugh describes the window somewhat poetically:

> The first two years of an ape's life are something of a magical time. During this period, if exposed to brightly colored geometric symbols, apes learn to tell them apart as easily as if they were looking at different kinds of foods. If exposed to human speech, they

become responsive to the phonemes and the morphemes so that spoken language no longer sounds like a string of noises. (Savage-Rumbaugh and Lewin 1994, xii)

In summary, the researchers concluded that Kanzi's use of language is "evidence that bonobos can learn a simple grammar, but more interesting and more important, they can invent new protogrammatical rules—that is, simple grammatical rules never demonstrated by any human or animal in the chimpanzee social environment."[28]

Savage-Rumbaugh's work is based on a distinction between language production and language comprehension, and she has consistently pointed out that an important precursor of language competence is the comprehension of nonspoken referential symbols. The work with Kanzi built on her earlier work with Sherman and Austin, two chimpanzees that "had developed a capacity of fundamental importance to language—the ability to use arbitrary symbols representationally."[29] Her success with Sherman and Austin suggests that Kanzi's abilities with human language are neither unique nor freakish, and the continuing study confirms this, as other individuals of the bonobo species have shown similar abilities (Savage-Rumbaugh and Lewin 1994, 177).

Kanzi and "Language"

There has been a great deal of work on language with other apes, and far too much to summarize here.[30] Much of it has been generated not by an interest in what other great apes do in their own lives but by the search for evolutionary origins of *human* language. Greenfield and Savage-Rumbaugh point out that

> the search for grammatical competence among apes has been very anthropocentric. Not only have ape researchers looked for human grammar in a general sense, but they have also assumed that the grammatical development of apes, if it occurs, will resemble that of young human children (especially American children) down to the very details. It may be that apes can develop grammatical rules, but that, at least in part, the nature and developmental order of their grammar derive from their species-specific and individual way of life. If that is the case, we would expect *details*, if not the overall structure pattern, of chimpanzee grammatical development to diverge in some respects from that observed in human children.[31]

This makes it clear that using humans as a paradigm can be misleading, for the search then is a search for human dimensions in other animals, rather than the realities of other animals which, even if analogous, are missed because of the unrelenting anthropocentrism implicit in the unstated model. Kanzi's researchers noted regarding a rule created by Kanzi, "It was a rule that clearly manifested the interests and life-style of a pygmy chimpanzee, rather than a human."[32] Given the other complexities of the life of bonobos (some of which are described later), this will be surprising *only if* one assumes a paradigm like that governing Descartes's reasoning about other animals' failure to speak:

> [W]e may also determine the difference that exists between men and brutes. . . . [T]here are [no humans] so depraved and stupid, without even excepting idiots, that they cannot arrange different words together [to make public their "thots"]; while, on the other hand, there is no other animal, however perfect and fortunately circumstanced it may

be, which can do the same. . . . And this does not merely show that the brutes have less reason than men, but that they have none at all, since it is clear that very little is required in order to be able to talk. (Descartes 1952/*Discourse on Method*, V, paragraph 10)

It will be suggested in parts III and IV that the Buddhist and Christian traditions have often been dominated by this kind of a paradigm, assuming that the failure of other animals to do human "things" is decisively telling about their complexity.

Language Ability and Moral Considerability

Great emphasis has been given to the possession of language abilities as an indicator of intelligence in other animals, reflecting the centrality of emphases on "language" in the classical arguments for the distinctive place of humans relative to other animals. For example, the Stoics[33] and Augustine[34] were Descartes's intellectual predecessors in advancing the thesis that membership in humans' language community is the critical factor for moral considerability. Rollin (1992, 72) observes that the possession of language has often been given a paramount position in arguments about human uniqueness because it is the means by which we learn of others' mental realities and interests. He hypothesizes that it is this link between language and counting as an object of moral concern, rather than the Kantian argument that linguistic ability is constitutive of rationality, that makes the possession of language seem a touchstone of moral considerability.

Seeking to confirm language abilities in other animals is, of course, an attempt to refute the influential positions that only humans have language and thus are morally considerable. Yet, by framing the challenge as one of direct refutation of, for example, Descartes on *his* terms, there is the risk of embracing a traditional set of assumptions about what it is that makes an individual morally considerable. Presumably, what is at issue is the complexity or richness of the communication, especially as that bears directly on features of the individual attempting to communicate and that individual's relation to the targets of the communication. Whether or not the complexity is in a precisely human form is not, then, the issue. Rather, the issue is the existence of qualities of life that moral systems seek to protect, such as occurs in humans by virtue of the constellation of awareness of self and others, attachment, sentience, intelligence, intention, and individuality.

Other Bases for Moral Considerability

Apart from the mental complexity suggested by the capacity to comprehend some features of human language, there are several general features of the "in-context" lives of nonhuman great apes on which one might premise moral considerability. These are:

1. The occurrence of complex individuals who possess distinct, identifiable interests.
2. The occurrence in social groups of (a) attachment between and among family and other community members, and (b) interactions characterized by communication, social norms and expectations, and individual choices regarding compliance with such norms.
3. Sentience and the capacity to suffer mentally and physically.

Complex Individuals and Unique Interests

While there remains considerable controversy over how to express the insight that there are biological bases of *human* intelligence, values, and social interactions, and there is currently no single vocabulary or tradition of discourse in which the insight is expressed, it is clear that intellectual development in humans is a constructed event. Humans must learn at an early age, in a sequence of stages, in a particular type of protected, nurturing environment. If they do not, their learning is so impaired that we no longer recognize the end result as normal human intelligence (Gibson 1990, 114). This phenomenon has been shown as well in other great apes. As Gibson says, "[P]rimate and human *intellectual* developments exhibit striking parallels" (114; cites omitted). In all great apes, humans included, a long and natural development advanced by the nurture of others creates the fundamental features of, as well as constraints on, the form that fully grown structures will have (Antinucci 1990, 157). Because each individual great ape's cognitive abilities and intelligence are developed in a unique complex of circumstances that include familial and social elements, the result is considerable variation in the complexities exhibited by each biological individual.[35] Further, if an individual that can, because of its genetic potential, go through these stages is pulled out of the normal familial and social contexts (as happens when, for example, young members of the key species are captured), the individual so removed is deprived of vitally important developmental inputs and will very likely be significantly damaged.

Social Realities

The upshot of the occurrence of individuals with distinct personalities and interests is that social dimensions of life become much more complex.[36] In fact, social reality and the features of individuality in bonobos, chimpanzees, gorillas, and orangutans cannot be separated from one another, any more than they can for humans. For analytical purposes, however, several distinctive features of the social reality can be examined apart from issues pertaining to individuality. Recent discoveries include recognition in the 1980s and 1990s, particularly through the work of de Waal, of the role of reconciliation, political intrigue, social compacts, and rules and expectations regulating social behavior of other primates.[37] This empirical work suggests that reciprocity and obligation, the building blocks of morality, are recognizable in some nonhuman primates.

Yet even the best of contemporary ability to perceive the realities of the other great apes is, in large part, merely an ability to see macro-aspects of their social lives. These include family interaction, social structure, friendship connections, political alignments, cultural transmission, learning processes, and behavior-regulating features related to social realities amid which individuals live. For example, bonobos remain the "least studied of all the great apes," with "a social organization that is only beginning to be understood."[38] It has been determined, however, that the social and sexual patterns of bonobos are more like those of humans than are such patterns of any other animal (Savage-Rumbaugh and Wilkerson 1978, 341). The fact that a bonobo (Kanzi) can learn from *human* teaching suggests considerable flexibility in bonobos' ability to learn, a trait that is undoubtedly used in the natural setting. The reasoning used to suggest that bonobos in the wild are doing "something" with their obvious capacities for intelligence and interaction is the accepted scientific view that "the high metabolic costs of large cortices" will have corresponding benefits that exceed the high costs.[39] Bonobos' abilities could easily be developed more fully by parents and other bonobos in a natural setting than by human researchers in laboratories, and almost certainly in completely different ways. It would be naïve to assume that those important bonobo abilities that have been identified "out of context" (that is, in the laboratory) are exhaustive, or even representative, of more natural lives of bonobos. Such an assumption runs counter to the insight that there is a formative relationship between the development of intelligence and the context of development.[40] It is reasonable to assume, then, that the complex mental realities demonstrated in the laboratory are manifested in different, though analogous, ways in the wild.

Communication

As to the content of the great apes' communication, there have been many studies in captivity that confirm the abilities of other great apes to use signs in complex ways that are conceptual.[41] The most prominent example of work with an orangutan is the study of Miles with Chantek.[42] The most publicized work with a gorilla is that of Patterson with Koko.[43] Work with chimpanzees has a longer history and is arguably even more detailed, including that with Sherman and Austin described by Savage-Rumbaugh in her book on Kanzi, and the Foutses' work with Washoe and other common chimpanzees.[44] Savage-Rumbaugh also observes that the *nonverbal* language of bonobos is "far more humanlike than that of the common chimps" (Savage-Rumbaugh and Lewin 1994, 107) and that bonobos' hand gestures, when videotaped, can be shown to be "a truly abstract communication system" (113).The issue of the *content* of these communications remains elusive and difficult to discuss, for the issue of content in the wild is subject to a level of ignorance suggested by McGrew's comment that "[t]he relative lack of study of natural communication by apes means that even basic processes remain unknown" (1992, 222–23).

Mental Organization of the World

Thomas comments, "That there are some footsteps of reason, some strictures and emissions of ratiocination in the actions of some brutes, is too vulgarly known and too commonly granted to be doubted" (1983, 124 n. 18). In the second decade of the twentieth century, after extensive study of captive chimpanzees as they solved problems, Köhler suggested that certain "insight" processes (*Einsicht*, which can also be translated "intelligence") *"occur in chimpanzees, exactly as in man."*[45] In contemporary life sciences dealing with the mental activities of other animals, it is now accepted broadly that general terms such as "mental organization," "consciousness," and "awareness" are viable tools when attempting to describe the mental realities of individual nonhuman great apes, for as Terrace notes, "for the first time, ample evidence is available of the existence of animal thought."[46]

Byrne, using the language of the cognitive sciences, says that

> intelligence must involve an individual animal's ability to: (1) gain knowledge from interactions with the environment and other individuals (and specify whether there are constraints on the type of knowledge it can represent, and the circumstances from which it can extract knowledge); (2) use its knowledge to organize effective behaviour, in familiar and novel contexts; and (3) deal with problems, using (if it is able) "thinking," "reasoning," or "planning"—in fact, any ability to put together separate pieces of knowledge to create novel action. (1995, 39–40)

This observation and others[47] make it clear that "intelligence" can be many things, with no one manifestation of it exhausting all the possibilities. While the modern vocabulary for what has been colloquially called "intelligence" can be similarly quite complicated, it often reflects the traditional assumption that human mental organization has a paradigmatic quality. When Augustine claimed that "when man was created he received in addition a rational soul not produced from water and earth like the souls of other animals" (*City of God* 13.24), he assumed that humans had the highest level of earthly intelligence. This view implicitly invokes a linear scale or hierarchy of what it means to be intelligent. Such linear or hierarchical thinking is the background to the argument that humans, as possessors of the "highest" or "most" intelligence, can (1) comprehend what and how any other animal can think and (2) think differently *and* better than other animals.

The terms "mental organization" and "information processing" are now used commonly of some other animals. Employment of these terms by the science establishment is a by-product of the "cognitive revolution" that has gradually (and only in part) replaced behaviorist thinking in psychology since the 1960s.[48] Such terms convey more neutrally than does the term "intelligence" what is at stake in evaluating those mechanisms of any animal, human or otherwise, that are involved in modification of behavior during growth and after experience. In addition, the terms allow one to focus more accurately on the complex relationships among cognition, learning and development, information processing, representation, imitation, and problem solving generally. Cognitive theorists are committed to the view that many animals' minds are representational systems and that manifestations of cognitive abilities are *context-specific* realizations of any animal's abilities developed according to genetic constraints. Minds manifesting intelligence, then, might be very different, even if each is self-aware, conceptually able, intelligent by any measure, social, caring, and possessed by an individual who can be distinguished by moral agents who care enough to notice and take such realities seriously.

This is not to suggest that there is no overlap between the abilities of members of different species, or that closely related species cannot be ranked with regard to some of their overlapping abilities. Average humans, for example, can be counted as "more intelligent" than those average members of the other great apes species in important and morally significant ways. This does not mean, however, that the other great apes' mental lives have no moral implications, for such a denial requires one to argue, as noted earlier, that partridges cannot be said to fly because hawks fly higher. The extraordinary nature and complexity of humans' mental organization surely creates special levels of moral significance, but this alone does not imply that the existence of humans' special qualities automatically eclipses the significance of realities of other animals that live on the basis of different genetic endowments.

Intentionality, Tool Making, Large Brains, and Self-Awareness

"Intentionality" has an important history as a measure of consciousness and intelligence. Dennett's terminology regarding multiple levels of intentionality is often cited as a valuable way of framing the issue.[49] That of a simple machine is "zero-order intentionality." Simple animals which intend that a result be achieved through their actions display "first-order intentionality." "Second-order intentionality" is conveyed by the sentence "I want him to think xyz."[50] This involves representing another's mental state and is relevant to actions such as teaching and deception. The Cartesian tradition of interpreting animal behavior relies heavily on zero-order intentionality, as do behaviorist theories.[51]

Second-order intentionality is important because the attribution of mental states to others suggests high levels of complex mental activities in the intentional individual. The ability of nonhuman great apes to deceive others intentionally has received attention because it has been widely suggested that planned deception requires certain concepts and intention.[52] Second-order intentionality has, according to Byrne (1995, 124–44), been found in the wild among other great apes in several forms such as tactical deception and counterdeception, deception during play, and teaching. There appears to be a sharp discontinuity between great apes and all other nonhuman primates on this issue (Byrne 1995, 220–25).

As to tool making, *before* other great apes were known to make tools, it was argued that making tools for future use "implies a marked capacity for conceptual thought."[53] Goodall (1971, 50–53) was the first in the Western science establishment to confirm tool making in other animals. It has since been learned that "chimpanzees in all settings use tools regularly" (McGrew 1992, 44). Indeed, some have been shown to have a tool kit (that is, a set of tools, some of which are for several different uses), which they make themselves and use in situations other than those in which they have been made (in other words, they plan ahead; Savage-Rumbaugh and Lewin 1994, 201 ff.). Bonobos and orangutans have also been shown to make tools while in captivity (McGrew 1992, 49; Lethmate 1982).

Other circumstantial evidence that the other great apes have significant mental abilities comes in the form of the size of their brains.[54] While large brains and intelligence can be linked, the precise relationship is not known; the relationship surely is not "the bigger the brain, the more intelligent the being." Jerison has reasoned that the significant relationship is "the increase in *relative* brain size" (he refers to this as the "encephalization quotient," or "EQ"; 1985, 21). The highest EQs are shared by humans and bottlenose dolphins, with the other great apes and cetaceans all ranking very high. In fact, the ratio of brain size to body size is now widely held to be an easily identifiable physical correlate of where mental organization occurs.

Correlating large brains *and* language skills is not, however, a simple process. It is commonly argued that humans have had language for 40,000 years but brain sizes comparable to modern human brain sizes for approximately 130,000 years.[55] Thus, large brains can exist without language. If it is posited that humans prior to the development of language were morally considerable, it then must be posited that moral considerability can flow to those without language, and, of course, this is potentially relevant to members of all large-brained species.

Although the structure of brains has also been shown to be crucial (since the increased size of the neocortical association area provides the condition for more complex cognition), it must be noted for purposes of the argument being made here that the human brain has no unique structures (Gibson 1990, 112). Because the human brain is larger than that of its immediate evolutionary cousins, the other great apes, it is not unreasonable to conclude that the human brain is the culmination of the *primate* trend toward enlarged neocortical association areas. Those who draw this conclusion, however, must be wary of two very important qualifications. First, the brains of other primates are so like the human brain (in terms of structure and microscopic details) that any argument that the human brain is the basis of complexity would suggest that levels of complexities *might* be found in other great apes. Second, concluding that the human brain is the culmination of the primate trend does not justify the conclusion that the human brain is the culmination of all brains. As noted later, cetacean brains are also very large and, while similar in macroscopic features, somewhat different in their microscopic features.[56]

Additional circumstantial evidence that the other great apes have significant mental complexities comes from experimental evidence regarding their awareness of themselves as distinct selves. "Self-awareness," a highly prized feature suggesting individuality, complex mental capacities, and the possibility of moral considerability, is, in certain sciences, now recognized as occurring outside the human species.[57] Griffin notes, "The question of self-awareness is one of the very few areas of cognitive ethology where we have some concrete experimental evidence."[58] The experimental method was developed in the early 1970s by the work of Gallup on chimpanzees' recognition of themselves in mirrors (abbreviated MSR, for mirror self-recognition).[59] Generally, the evidence is that the other great apes, as well as a few other animals (such as bottlenose dolphins), are capable of MSR.[60]

Arguably, there is great significance in the mirror test as a measure of a special level of cognitive ability, but MSR itself is not necessarily indicative of "self-awareness" as this term is used generally. As Byrne notes, "[Other] great apes do not carry out the full range of behaviours that a human would do in front of a mirror, so their idea of 'self' probably differs from a human one" (1995, 117). Further, there is much variation in MSR tests, even in chimpanzees that regularly pass (Byrne 1995, 114–15). As Griffin notes, an individual may fail "for some other reason to correlate the appearance and movements of the mirror image with those of their own bodies" (1992, 250). Self-awareness need not be "all or nothing," as using the MSR test as *the* criterion might be taken to suggest. Since it is known that the acquisition of a sense of self in humans is greatly affected by the social nature and conditions of each individual human,[61] it stands to reason that the senses of self among the other great apes might be similarly affected. One implication of this is that, while the MSR test may suggest the existence of a concept of self, the full range of any sense of self in eminently social beings must be understood in context. In the end, however, it is clear that MSR is, as McGrew noted, "a most elegant index of intellectual capacity."[62]

Ignorance Considerations

Glover has noted, "The philosophical literature about our knowledge of other minds is strikingly silent and unhelpful about the animal boundaries of consciousness" (1990, 48). More specifically, as has already been suggested by the many references to what is *not* known, human ignorance of the lives of other great apes, and the accompanying errors in assessment, tend to go in the same direction, namely, underestimation. Despite the prevailing ignorance, opinions about the other great apes have been among the most strongly held of all beliefs about other animals, and tinged with very negative features. Apostolos-Cappadona summarizes the portrayal of nonhuman apes in the Western Christian iconographic tradition:

> Signifying the baser forms of human and animal existence such as lust, envy, cunning, and malice, apes represented the Devil in western Christian art. An ape eating an apple denoted the Fall of Adam and Eve. Depictions of enchained apes in scenes of the Adoration of the Magi were personifications of sin conquered by Christ. Mirroring human failure such as lust and sloth, apes were associated with orgiastic sexuality. In particular, female apes were believed to have lascivious natures, and thereby exposed their buttocks to male apes. As such, apes symbolized prostitutes or lustful women. (1996, 21)

Recognition and then appreciation of the significance of the impoverished state of such caricatures, as well as the development of accurate, "scientific" knowledge, have been retarded by the dominance of exclusivist ideas. Commenting on Goodall's commitment to become familiar with the factual realities of individuals, Gould notes that Goodall has challenged "the clinical view" and "taught us how the primary features of chimp society at any time are not direct consequences of first principles or measure of simple quantities (size, number of aggressive encounters), but irreducible and unique features of individual personalities and their complex interactions" (1995, 23–24).

Subsequent work on the same model has resulted in much greater awareness of the common features between human and nonhuman great ape lives, such that Gibson has commented, "All of the human-ape dichotomies so cherished by the anthropologists and psychologists of the early 1960s have fallen" (1990, 97, citing Ettlinger 1984). Importantly, the claim is not that mere *differences* have been eliminated, for those obviously exist. It is the claim "*fundamental divisions or dichotomies exist*" that has fallen. Thus, the claim of fundamental distance and separation that undergirds exclusivist attitudes has been openly challenged.

Elephants

Elephants provide the chance to consider animals that are radically different than great apes, human or otherwise. A description of the lives of elephants begins with the role of the matriarchs in elephant groups, for the matriarchs direct much of the communication, all of the decision making and defense of the stable groups, the opportunities for play, and the sharing and passage of knowledge among the members, both male and female. While this social envelope is the context for the development of individuals, communication, learning, and the individual-to-individual activities portrayed so vividly in many accounts,[63] the Western scientific tradition identified the centrality of matriarchal social grouping in the lives of elephants only in the late 1960s (Douglas-Hamilton and Douglas-Hamilton 1975, 59; and Chadwick 1994, 47). And, as argued in part III, even the patient observers in traditional India misgauged the crucial role of matriarchy in elephants' lives.

The varied series of noises by which elephants interact has been known, in part, for thousands of years, as have the emotional greeting displays so characteristic of group reunions. That elephants communicate formed a part of the claims about elephants made by ancient humans who, across the millennia, drew various conclusions about the nature of elephants, but many specifics obviously were not known. Discoveries in the mid-1980s revealed that elephants also communicate with sounds that are *subsonic* for humans.[64] Various observations of elephants' behavior corroborated this discovery, made possible by the availability of sophisticated sound recording equipment. It had often been noticed that elephants at a distance frequently act in concert, moving and changing direction simultaneously despite physical separation that would prevent visual contact. The subsonic nature of these communications had prevented our ancestors from experiencing this "hidden" feature of elephant social and mental lives. Payne, noting that only one-third of the elephant "calls" recorded were in the audible range, suggests that the "network [of communication] has something to do with the ability of elephants to maintain an elaborate hierarchical society" and that the constant communication "reinforce[s] the social bonds that are key to the elephants' survival" (1989, 266).

Apart from the different forms of elephants' communications, there are other dimensions of elephants, such as their individualities and intelligence, that must be included in any informed description. Before addressing these other dimensions, a description of the life of an individual will serve to convey some fundamentals.

Pra Barom Nakkot

The daily life of Pra Barom Nakkot is described by Chadwick:

> And he rocked, constantly, tugging on chains that bound his legs to the slightly raised platform on which he stood. . . . [T]his bull was never let out of the pavilion. . . . So for decades now, he had been here on his raised dais, rocking, straining, surging back and forth with unfathomable power. . . . Surging, swaying, pulling this way and that, forever and a day—the heaven-sent king of elephants, born of clouds and rain, colored like the sacred lotus, a captured god but now an obsolete one, something out of a distant time and kingdom, his purpose all but forgotten. . . . [A]lone in his dark, golden-spired pavilion. Forever alone. Colossal. And very likely insane. That was the message in those eyes: madness. (1994, 352–53)

A striking irony in this obviously attenuated life is that this is an honored elephant, singled out because he has, from the human vantage point, a distinctive appearance, for he is a *white* elephant.[65] The geography of Pra Barom Nakkot's birth put him "[a]mong the predominantly Buddhist kingdoms of Southeast Asia, [where] white elephants are seen as descendants of the original winged elephants that roamed the cloudscapes above Earth and as avatars of the Buddha."[66]

As a direct consequence of his status with humans, Pra Barom Nakkot is deprived of any chance whatsoever to pursue the development of his interests (or, perhaps more accurately, his potential for developed interests), including the possibility of interacting in the complex social network that characterizes all young elephants' lives. More precisely, captivity deprives him of the ability to develop interests that he can have by virtue of being born of a mother who possessed a large brain, was a member of complex social systems, had the ability to communicate, and lived amid experienced individuals (her own matriarchs). But rather than growing up amid the normal social network through which he would have learned to deal with the natural world and communicate with other individual elephants, after his capture Pra Barom Nakkot had limited training by humans as a youngster, but none thereafter (Chadwick 1994, 352).

Pra Barom Nakkot's many human-bestowed names include titles such as "he who will progress much among the elephants," and he is thought to "outrank" most humans; indeed, he is considered "like the highest of princes."[67] But Pra Barom Nakkot is used as a kind of instrument or symbol, since the reality is that he is a prisoner of a traditional belief that his presence augments the power and prospects of the Thai royal family. He is a contemporary example of a long-standing reality in Buddhist-influenced cultures, namely, a complete acceptance of the morality of overriding the interests of creatures like Pra Barom Nakkot in favor of human interests.[68] It has, however, been known since time immemorial that human ownership of an elephant makes it unsocial and a psychological misfit (Chadwick 1994, 311). In summary, human intervention has distorted Pra Barom Nakkot's reality, and his relatively impoverished life contrasts markedly with the full social envelope that is a central feature of noncaptive elephants' lives. The significant issues in the circumstances of Pra Barom Nakkot's life, in contrast with that of wild elephants, can be broken down into the categories of social realities for elephants, individuality, communication, and mental organization of the world.

Social Realities

Elephant social realities, although still not well understood, clearly play a constitutive role.[69] Wilson notes that this "largest land mammal is also distinguished by one of the most advanced social organizations" in which "[t]he degree of cooperation and altruism displayed with the family group is extraordinary" (1980, 240–41). The groups are *always* led by matriarchs (Sukamar 1994, 90). A leading expert notes, "An elephant's place in the social system is determined by its sex. Once adults, male and female elephants lead completely different lives. Females experience intensely social lives, surrounded by close relatives and always in the company of other elephants, sometimes in herds over 500. Males lead more or less solitary lives" (Moss 1992, 110).

The levels of society include the immediate matriarch-led family that is the primary level, and a larger grouping called various things.[70] In this "complex and sensitive system of social interaction" (Sukamar 1994, 93), young elephants learn the skills that are essential for survival and social interaction. "The family setting is thus indispensable for the normal growth and development of the young elephants. . . . Within the family, the calves are protected, nourished, nurtured, and taught the rules of living" (Sukamar 1994, 102). Juvenile males and females stay with the matriarchal group through youth.[71] The maturing males leave and wander in a fashion that is not now known to be socially structured (Sukamar 1994, 92). However, mature males constantly visit a wide range of the core matriarchal groups, and so have some society with many elephants. They do not provide group leadership, quite contrary to the patriarchy-inspired visions of many cultures such as that of the Buddhist animal tales discussed in part III.

The social dimensions also provide the matrix within which the "large and varied repertoire" of tactile, chemical, visual, and acoustic communication occurs.[72] The range of communication in the wild is only now being explored, but it has long been apparent that several kinds of communication, including tactile, postural, hearing-related, and visual, function as a linchpin in the life of wild elephants.

Because the social circumstance of elephants is their crucible of learning, it bears directly on the nature of elephant knowledge and intelligence. Humans and elephants are both at the extreme end of the scale of time in taking care of their young. Elephants are born with a brain weight of approximately 35 percent of their adult brain weight, very much like humans, who are born with 23 percent (Douglas-Hamilton and Douglas-Hamilton 1975, 93; Chadwick 1994, 77–78). This is contrary to the once-dominant thinking among humans that human brain size and development are distinctive. Chadwick makes an explicit comparison with humans: "Like humans, elephants are designed to learn most of what they need to know. The extended period of nurturing is part of that process, and they continue to learn throughout their long lives" (1994, 78). The individuals go through an extremely long adolescence, during which they are provided a protected environment of nurturing that is full of learning opportunities. This permits adolescents the opportunity to acquire important skills such as recognition of other individuals and their needs and interests. It is within and through interaction with knowledgeable elders that each elephant's intelligence is molded.

Additionally, the breadth of elephant social life requires special skills. Unlike many other large-brained, social animals (such as primates) which live in bands that constitute virtually their entire social reality, elephants constantly interact socially with a wide range of other individuals that are not part of their core group. Although they typically stay within a home range, elephants are not, as are primates, territorial in the sense of excluding others from that home range (Moss 1988, 125; Douglas-Hamilton and Douglas-Hamilton 1975, 222 ff.; and Chadwick 1994, 76). This results in them having broader social lives, which in turn requires special skills of recognition and sensitivity to the nuances of behavior in others.

Individuality and the Differing Interests of Individuals

It is in the development of individuals *within a social context* that the emergence of interests can best be seen. While there are group interests, there are also individual interests that are not identical to either the group interests or other individuals' interests. Sukamar notes, "Each elephant is different from every other elephant, not only by virtue of its distinctive genes, but also because it has undergone unique experiences in life" (1994, 106). Thus, apart from the fact that each elephant is an individual in the logical sense, each has a distinctive history in a social context populated by others with distinct histories.

Communication

Buddhist tales (discussed in part III) abound with references to elephant communication, and indigenous peoples who lived around elephants described their communication more specifically and in some instances much more accurately.[73] However, contemporary scientists repeatedly suggest that not much is known about elephant communication. Poole, a leading researcher, notes that "we're just beginning to scratch the surface of the language—all their body language communication" (Chadwick 1994, 68). The 1984 determination that elephants produced infrasound (a notion that is very human centered, "infra" being measured by the range of human hearing) has stimulated additional research. Indeed, Chadwick reports that Poole has identified a minimum of thirty-four distinct elephant vocalizations; importantly, however, as Poole admits, "translations of known elephant vocalizations are still rudimentary at best and . . . many more calls and variations on them may yet be uncovered."[74]

As with humans, there are also *other* kinds of communication that do not rely on audible (for elephants) sounds. An analogue to the great expressiveness of the primate face is to be found in the trunk, and this appendage is the subject of much early learning in elephants.[75] Douglas-Hamilton and Douglas-Hamilton comment, "Although their faces were relatively immobile, the infinite variety of trunk postures and movements lent to elephants all the expressiveness of a primate's visage" (1975, 35). When body language is added to this list, the result is a wide repertoire.

Intelligence in Context

Both Aristotle and Pliny designated elephants as the animals closest to humans in intelligence. Pliny claimed further that elephants recognize the language of their homeland, obey orders, remember what they learn, and possess "virtues rare even in man, honesty, wisdom, justice, also respect for the stars and reverence for the sun and moon."[76] The frequency of observations that elephants are, in terms of intelligence, remarkable is not surprising given that elephants possess one of the very largest brains (about four times the average human size).[77] Sikes says, "A close examination of the elephant brain . . . combined with actual experience of living elephants in the wild and captivity, yields abundant evidence that the elephant both possesses the mechanism and demonstrates the capacity for intelligence" (1971, 97). While the relationship between brain size and intelligence is not a matter of consensus, every contemporary thinker on the subject recognizes that there is some relationship between larger average brain size and greater intelligence-like activity.[78]

Generally, then, one cannot, if looking closely and sympathetically, fail to notice that elephants' lives involve a kind of complex mental construction. One developmental psychologist refers to elephants' creation of "seemingly complex cognitive maps" to meet the need to identify and map the environment for the purpose of locating widely dispersed foods (Gibson 1990, 112). Elephants also show other features often associated with intelligence, such as (1) noticeably different mental states or moods; (2) complex cognitive skills, including the ability to use mirrors to locate hidden objects (Gergely 1994, 55); (3) play;[79] (4) boredom;[80] (5) deception;[81] (6) tool use;[82] (7) knowledge of medicinal plants;[83] and (8) the possibility of self-awareness.[84]

Ignorance Considerations

In the past, human claims about elephants have often been extremely inaccurate, and the underlying ignorance has by no means been characteristic of religious traditions only. The fact and pace of discoveries suggest the need for humility, for as Chadwick notes, "What we are learning is that a great many of the limitations we ascribe to such animals may have mainly to do with limitations in our viewpoint" (1994, 14).

Whales and Dolphins

A recent experiment with captive bottlenose dolphins provides an introduction to the nature and state of contemporary scientific knowledge of cetaceans. The experiment involves two dolphins working together while each follows commands based on two concepts learned previously.[85] Bottlenose dolphins can be taught a command by which they understand that they are then to perform some behavior in tandem. It is also possible to teach bottlenose dolphins certain concepts such as "left versus right" and "before versus after."[86] A particularly interesting example of the conceptual ability of bottlenose dolphins is their ability to learn the concept of "novelty."[87]

The experiment reported in 1995 concerns these dolphins' response to humans combining the concept "novelty" with the command to do simultaneous behavior. The following is a description of the experiment:

> When two dolphins are asked to create a behavior not yet performed, and to do it in tandem, both dolphins will respond to the command, and emerge from the water in astonishing synchrony to perform identical behaviors. How do they do it? That's a puzzle we have yet to solve.[88]

The significance of this is that the dolphins must decide together, after each such command, what they are going to do as the novel behavior. One cannot simply follow the other, for the ability to do movements together requires anticipation and cooperation that are not always possible by simple mimicry.

Bottlenose Dolphin Abilities

The bottlenose dolphins used in this experiment are, according to one highly respected measure, extraordinary creatures, for they are members of a species that, along with the human species, has the highest ratio of brain size to body size. The abilities being studied in Herman's tandem behavior experiments are comprehension and conceptualization, both important aspects of the cognitive abilities that have been discussed in previous sections. The experiments require not only conceptual abilities but also flexibility on the part of the bottlenose dolphins in order to learn in the attenuated captive environment. They must survive being removed from their native societies, learn to interact with humans, and display an ability to learn human-designed concepts. These particular abilities are not bottlenose dolphins' only or most characteristic abilities. Other abilities include social and familial skills, sensory apparatus capable of exploring their native ocean environment with an array of sensibilities quite foreign to terrestrial creatures, large brains with cognitive abilities very different from those of humans, and arguably even awareness of themselves as individual beings (this is discussed further later). In fact, a wide range of diverse, often fundamentally alien, abilities is the full context in which the isolatable intelligence features focused on by the experiment are actually found.

It might be argued that the tandem novel behavior experiment, especially when seen against a background of having performed well in the language experiments, reveals that "dolphins are intelligent." But in very important ways this answer is too simple, for it assumes that "intelligence" can be identified by isolating a few cognitive features in an experiment designed by humans. As noted previously, understanding intelligence out of context is certainly not a simple task, and may not be possible at all. Thus, one might say that a kind of intelligence is hinted at by these bottlenose dolphins' responses, but its complexities and uses in native environments are left open by the experimental approach. What is shown by this experiment with *these* bottlenose dolphins is the tip of the iceberg in at least two senses. First, the experiment does reflect that some bottlenose dolphins do combine concepts in the limited circumstances of their captive life, but this does not necessarily represent what other cetaceans are doing. The seventy-five-plus cetacean species are internally quite diverse, even if they are characterized generally by large brains, complex social interactions, rich communication patterns, and long developmental periods that can create unique individuals. Second, the abilities to learn and act in tandem that are the precondition of the experiment are, in the wild, used for *other* purposes. The individual dolphins through which these abilities were glimpsed had previously developed their individuality in a particular social context involving connections to family and fellow group members. These connections were irrevocably cut off by an experimental design driven by the paradigms of idealized science.[89]

Cetacean Social Realities

The nature of the lives of these dolphins "in the wild" is difficult to consider. The ocean is a fundamentally different medium than terrestrial existence, not the least because sound and light travel differently. Further, the constraints of gravity compete with the counterbalancing effects of the buoyant medium (water), which supports bodies differently than does the atmosphere-land interface amid which terrestrials live. In water, the social dimension plays an all-important role, for the lack of barriers means that predators can be nearby anytime. Constant alertness beyond the ability of any one individual is required to survive for very long "in a world in which there is no lagging behind, not even for a minute" (Norris 1991, 182).

Some of the cetaceans have developed social systems that, when coupled with echolocation, provide a measure of security within these constantly changing circumstances. Norris describes how and why echolocation works in this world:

> The dolphin's echolocation shield is its own special defense. With it these mammals buy an advantage in the costs of predation over their silent antagonists. . . . Given that seemingly insignificant advantage, they can then afford to express all the complexity and individuality of their mammalian heritage. . . . [T]hey can let down the school's shield long enough to afford nurture, instruction, tradition, and even culture. (180)

It is not merely a case, then, of individuals seeking to use their isolated echolocation abilities for their own benefit. Rather, the school itself relies on constant communication to create the possibility of survival. The social dimensions of life of these marine mammals, then, are conditions of the possibility of a life lived among ever-present predators. Norris notes that schooling dolphins like the spinners are "utterly alone outside their schools" because they are born into and survive because of the cooperative nature of their "magical" social envelope. Individuals are bound together by the school's "sensory integration system" "because every animal in a school can send messages to all others through movements or sounds" (186).

These are features of schooling dolphins, and they do not apply to all cetaceans. Familiarity with them leads to the conclusion that social realities for large-brained individuals in other species can come in circumstances and styles altogether unfamiliar to humans. Indeed, studies have gradually shown that at least some cetaceans' social lives are complex and very unlike the paradigms offered by primate lives or any other terrestrial lives.[90] Norris comments, "It took my entire two decades with spinners to formulate a theory for how they worked" (1991, 178). Herzing, the author of a multi-year study of a community of spotted dolphins (*Stenella frontalis*) in the wild, comments that in "the 1990s our knowledge is broad enough to know that dolphins are long-lived social mammals, that they form long-term bonds, and that they learn and grow in their multi-generational societies and use many senses to communicate, especially sound" (1995a, 24).

But many fundamental features of cetaceans' lives are not known, even if there are glimpses of large brains working in complex ways that lead to complex actions by individuals. This, of course, bears on the ability of human theorists to comment on, but especially to deny, the existence of morally relevant characteristics such as intelligence, social regulation schemes, individuality, or emotional attachments. For example, Connor and Norris (1982, 363), noting well-developed altruistic tendencies in some cetaceans, argue that mere reciprocal altruism (that is, "altruistic" acts performed with expectation of reciprocity) alone is *not* sufficient to explain observed behavior of some dolphins. They postulate, instead, the existence of generalized altruistic tendencies in dolphins.[91]

Communication

For cetaceans, as for terrestrial mammals, there are several different media of communication between members of the same species. These include several kinds of sounds and various tactile and visual means of communication (through, for example, body rubbing and postures). Tactile communication is particularly important, as noted by Norris: "As much as 30 percent of a spinner dolphin's day may be spent in complicated caressing bouts that have a syntax all of their own" (1991, 40). Much of what follows focuses exclusively on the vocalization-like communications, as opposed to the other forms. This emphasis is a result of the immense importance we, as humans, have put on human language and the possibility of finding analogues in other animals. The historically dominant emphasis on language as critical seems to have been based on an assumption that, upon examination, may not bear up. This is the assumption that confirming the existence of a communication system which is like humans' conceptual and feelings exchanges via language is the best, and perhaps only, way to confirm the existence of features or traits that we deem morally considerable. But, as noted earlier, seeking in other animals analogues to human experiences is a risky and potentially unfair business. Richness of communication need not come in only human forms.

Complications abound when one tries to assess cetacean communications, for seeking cetacean communications' nature and role requires one to enter an unending circle. The communications are a manifestation of social realities in the lives of other animals, just as they are with humans. To understand these communications, one must know the *social* realities; but in order to know the social realities, one must be able to tap into the communications. Where to start in the circle is a difficult question, particularly for any creature that is not a part of the species being studied.

The best studied means of communication characterize many of the odontocetes (toothed whales) that school together, but some odontocetes and many of the mysticetes have different social structures and communication patterns that have been far harder to ascertain. The work of Norris and others (Norris 1991; Norris and others 1994) on the spinner dolphin communities off of Hawaii gives some data for one species. Herzing's studies provide material on one community of another species (spotted dolphins).[92] The dialects of orcas in the Northwest have been closely studied and carefully distinguished by Ford (1983, 1984). Sperm whales,[93] narwhals (Watkins and others 1971), and belugas[94] have also been given much attention. There remain, however, dozens of species of the odontocete branch of cetaceans that have never been studied.

The status of studies with the other major branch of cetaceans, the mysticetes, is much less developed.[95] Our ability to extrapolate findings is subject to question because the two groups are not closely linked evolutionarily (Watson 1981, 18). The vocalizations of humpback whales, apparently the most complex communication outside human language, have been studied since the Paynes' discovery in the late 1960s that these "songs" had intricate structure.[96] Blue whales have received some attention, but the logistics of studying such large, fast-moving animals have been overwhelming. Research in the 1990s, though considerably more sophisticated, remained rudimentary.[97] The studies which have been done show that "communications" between the members of any one species are diverse, and not necessarily like the communications of members of other cetacean species.

It is known that some cetaceans use precise and identifiable vocalizations. Norris describes "contact calls," which announce "the position and state of one animal to the others" (1991, 204). Distinctive vocalizations called "signature whistles" have also been identified,[98] and these work something like an identifier or name. These can be modified to carry further meaning, as in the case of a warbled whistle working as a distress call for a particular individual,[99] and can transmit a great deal of information between dolphins.[100] Norris found the Caldwells' discoveries to be "the first demonstration that dolphins do not have anything like a human language. Instead, they use a here-and-now system of signs, some of them metaphors for ongoing events, to get across their information and intent. Such a system is vastly more ponderous than language" (1991, 316).

Despite these efforts to identify the function of vocalizations, on the whole thinking about cetaceans' communications in the wild remains very general and speculative. Norris theorizes that spinner dolphins do *not* communicate with a system that stores abstract symbols, but rather communicate with each other by associating the state and timing of other dolphins' voices with events as they are happening. He says of these voices and events, "[T]hey are metaphors of each other, and thus the communication is precise. But unlike our human language, this communication is good only for the immediate present in which it occurs" (208). The "synchrony" of the group, that is, the timing of vocalizations in response to other vocalizations, is, according to Norris, a method particularly adapted to the marine world because while the ocean's physical features "distort sound in unpredictable ways, . . . [w]hat it does not distort nearly so severely is the timing with a series of sounds given close together" (208). Norris repudiates the notion that what the dolphins are doing is communicating symbolically: "That dolphins use such metaphor as a central element in their communication is an indication that they do not also use a sophisticated symbolic language like our own" (209).

Despite the difficulty of grappling with a suggestion of such alien forms of communication and despite Norris's vague language, one generalization can be confidently made, namely, *that the communication occurs* among large-brained creatures and precedes social movements. But just how such communication works for the individual members of the distinct groups within each species is still as mysterious as ever.

Cetaceans and Intelligence

All of the cetaceans have large brains, and the EQs are high as well,[101] but the structure of cetaceans' brains is in some respect unique among mammals. Deacon describes the similarities to other large mammalian brains:

> The highly advanced features of the dolphin brain are largely macroscopic morphological features, including large brain size, a high degree of encephalization, a highly convoluted cortex, a high ratio of neocortex to total cortex (and therefore a high ratio of neocortex to limbic cortex), and apparently (although this is difficult to assess accurately), a large percentage of association.[102]

The dissimilarities are highly technical "microscopic features," which Deacon hypothesizes are related to "their unusual and relatively complete adaptation to the aquatic habitat."[103]

It is generally thought, but not universally agreed, that large brains in cetaceans do mean high intelligence.[104] There is also abundant evidence for an imperfect but existent correlation between measures of intelligence and measures of relative brain size.[105] Herman's work with dolphins establishes that some cetaceans have some ability to handle concepts, make generalizations, possess beliefs about their world, follow inferences, and understand negation.[106] If this work is seen in conjunction with the widespread occurrence of legends about dolphins' abilities,[107] it is not unreasonable to inquire if some odontocetes might be complex in ways that inquiring moral agents can recognize. In addition, some cetaceans have passed self-awareness tests.[108] These observations suggest several possibilities: (1) some cetaceans may be mentally complex in rich ways comparable to the mental complexity in humans in *some* ways; and (2) some cetaceans may be mentally complex in *other* ways as well.

Ignorance Considerations

Knowledge of cetaceans is a good measure of certain features of human claims about the place and significance of humans on this earth. Although humans possess a more complex communication system than the other great apes, the conclusion that humans possess the only really complex communication systems is premature if based on that evidence alone. The argument assumes that the evolutionary grouping of primates is the relevant area of inquiry. Humans have not explored well the communication systems of other animals, for both the obvious reason of epistemological limitations *and* the less obvious reason of a failure to be prepared to notice or take seriously the possibility of complex individuals or richness of communication systems in other forms of life.[109] Numerous "discoveries" have been made about cetaceans in the last half century, and such discoveries suggest that a realistic view of at least some cetaceans will be far more complicated than standard views of "beasts" and "animals" that dominate many traditions of ethical thinking.

The Significance of Basic Facts about the Key Animals

Several features of the empirically verifiable realities of the key animals described here, and in particular the newness of the information and its radical disagreement with the demeaning, standard caricatures often found within various Buddhist and Christian materials, prompt the conclusion that the *nature* of claims purporting to be about *all* other animals, such as those found in the Christian and Buddhist traditions, must be looked at very carefully. It is, of course, possible as a logical matter to affirm the importance of human existence while at the same time acknowledging the value of at least some nonhuman individuals. In light of the conflict between the traditional caricatures and contrary information recently developed, claims to the effect that the constellation of abilities so characteristic of human individuals is the *only* constellation that produces morally considerable individuals can be questioned on several grounds. One of these grounds is increased awareness that the distribution of mental and other valued abilities across the taxonomy of life is more complicated than suggested by misleading and facile claims along the lines of "all humans are intelligent, no animals are." The dualistic thinking explicit in such claims, signaled by the conceptuality "humans versus other animals," can seriously mislead when it is used as an unassailable principle of exclusion. It has, in fact, been observed that the distribution of mental abilities "does not fit a simple grade-level model" (Parker 1990a, 47). In other words, if one explores the lives of nonhuman animals, it will be apparent that the distribution of increasingly complex cognitive abilities, self-awareness, and awareness of others does not occur in a linear fashion, as is suggested by the dominant image of a recognizable, simple hierarchy leading up to humans. It is conceivable, then, not only that there are some nonhuman individuals possessed of abilities that humans do not have, but even that some such nonhuman abilities, or constellations of abilities, might in and of themselves make some nonhuman individuals morally considerable for the inquiring moral agent.

Parts III and IV attempt to show that, in the past, comparisons between humans and other animals have been ideologically determined. Clark has noted that "we are always comparing our ignorant conception of animal being with an overdrawn picture of a very cultivated man" (1977, 25). A fairer comparison would be to compare *real individuals* of each species to be compared, rather than collective images held to be representative of the entire species. For example, to assess how "complex," "sophisticated," or "complicated" humans are relative to nonhumans, it would be fair to match a technologically unsophisticated human with a realistically described representative from one of the *most complex* nonhuman species.[110] Of course, it is not necessarily the case that high-EQ, intelligent, and otherwise mentally complex beings from one environment will be able to understand creatures with analogous features from another environment that is radically different. But it is essentially problematic to attempt to resolve these admittedly difficult issues by clumsy use of a standard that relies *solely* on humans' mental organization of the world as the paradigm.

Other Viewpoints: An Implication of Existing Ethical Systems

Our ethical traditions often presuppose that we can see from another's viewpoint. This is true in any system that limits self-interested acts. This occurs despite the fact that *we* do not know exactly, or even approximately, what it is like to be another complex *human* individual.

This principle of considering other points of view has, of course, been extended often to nonhuman individuals. It can be found in ancient Greece, as shown by Sorabji's scholarly analysis mentioned in chapter 8, and is implicit in many of Augustine's views, also discussed in chapter 8, such as the *De Musica* 1.4–6 passages regarding birds singing because they enjoy their own songs. The same principle is more explicit in (1) many of the indigenous traditions mentioned in this book, (2) late eighteenth-century secular utilitarianism, and (3) Buddhist concerns for the sacredness of nonhuman lives (discussed in part III). It can be argued that it is also a core part of traditional Christian concerns for cruelty to nonhuman animals (although, admittedly, some prominent explanations of prohibitions on cruelty focus *solely* on its effects on moral agents).

It is theoretically possible, then, for the moral agent to attempt to extend his or her calculations to nonhuman complex individuals' viewpoints and interests. One argument for doing this is the following three-part claim:

1. What makes humans morally considerable is *not* mere membership in the human species but, rather, human individuals' possession of a constellation of general characteristics leading to rich social relationships among complex individuals.
2. Some individuals of some other species may, on the basis of empirical evidence of the kinds listed earlier, be reasonably claimed to have the same or a similar constellation of characteristics, or even a different constellation that nonetheless leads to rich social relationships among complex individuals.
3. Such constellations produce in these large-brained individuals, as in humans, recognizable capacities for intelligent, individualized choices, family and social loyalties exhibited in favor of distinct individuals, intraspecific communications, and sentience of both physical and mental sorts.

A failure to explore the possibility of these features existing in complex individuals among *other* species risks the possibility of *missed opportunities* asked about in this chapter's title.

Descartes Was Wrong in Several Ways

The foregoing review of information about the key animals reveals that the assertion "dumb animals do not think" is not based on familiarity with a full range of other animals, nor is it based on a commitment to know other animals and the realities of their lives. Descartes, then, in part relying on the Christian Weltanschauung that supported the monolithic notion of "animals" in the sense of all nonhumans, simply erred about whether any other animals think, for, arguably, there is no informed way in which it can be claimed that *some* of them do not "think" or have significant mental realities. As van Hoof observes, "Clearly there are different cognitive realms that are spread in different ways over animal taxa. The ability to attach symbolic labels to conceptual categories is clearly not restricted to our nearest relatives" (1994, 278). Thus, in asserting his exclusivist prejudice so boldly, Descartes missed some animals as opportunities to understand better the realities of living beings.

Descartes was wrong for a second reason as well, namely, in asserting that there is no prejudice to which we are *more* accustomed. There is at least one prejudice to which we are certainly more accustomed. This is the common assumption that we can talk about all other animals easily and with simple generalizations such as those that underlie the use of the word "animals" to mean "all nonhuman living creatures that are not plants." This prejudicial way of speaking and thinking, to which we are far more accustomed than the notion that other animals think, is addressed in the next chapter.

5

What Is an Animal?

Men are indeed a tangle, whereas animals are a simple matter.
—Majjhima-Nikāya

The first four sections of this chapter attempt to answer the question, What do and can we mean when we talk about "animals"? The concluding section asks, What does it mean to talk about a species or an animal of a particular type?

The Basic Problem

There is a broad, conventional two-way classification of *all* organisms into "plants and animals" which is characteristic of human cultures. How this two-part classification is further broken down is described by Sebeok as "ultimately (although, of course, within limits) a personal matter (1994, 64). Whitaker broadens this classification into three fundamental "kingdoms" on the basis of modes of nutrition:

1. Plants, or producers, which derive their food from inorganic sources, by photosynthesis.
2. Animals, or ingestors, which derive their food—preformed organic compounds—from other organisms.
3. Fungi, or decomposers, which secrete digestive enzymes into their surroundings and thereby break down their food externally, then absorbing the resulting small molecules from solution.[1]

Within the "animals, or ingestors" group, however it is defined, astonishing internal differentiation is easily recognized. For example, Gotama says, "Brethren, I see not any single group so diverse as the creatures of the animal world"[2] The life-forms that fit into this broad category "animals" include not only the tiny organisms that form the "aeolian plankton" or "rain of planktonic bacteria, fungus spores, small seeds, insects, spiders, and other small creatures which falls continuously on most parts of the earth's land surface" (Wilson 1992, 20) but *also* the complex individuals discussed in chapter 4. This diversity is so great, in fact, that it is problematic to use a single term for purposes of description. The exclusions that are the subject of this book reflect recognition that at least one group of animals, namely, humans, are not well understood if approached solely as members of the diverse group defined as "ingestors, which derive their food—preformed organic compounds—from other organisms." Members of the human species clearly have features that are foundational for any adequate understanding of their interests, and thus it is understandable that humans have most characteristically been dealt with as members of a category distinct from the general and vague classification "animals." However, *all* other, nonhuman "ingestors" have remained grouped into one large class in the Buddhist and Christian traditions, and this is what here is called "the basic problem" because it is the foundation of so many comments that purport to be dispositive about other animals. Here are two examples:

1. Pope Pius IX is reported to have said to the English Catholic antivivisectionist Anna Kingsford, "Madame, humankind has no duties to the animals."[3]
2. Gotama is reported to have said, "Humankind is a tangle, but the animal is open enough."[4]

These comments rely on a conceptualization scheme collecting *all other animals* into one group. The problematic feature of the scheme stems not from the fact that it is a generalization, for generalizations are of course indispensable tools in thinking. As James notes, "The whole universe of concrete objects, as we know them, swims . . . in a wider and higher universe of abstract ideas, that lend it its significance" (1923, 56). The issue is, rather, the *quality and accuracy* of this particular generalization. In fact, use of this coarse generalization scheme as the *principal* means of understanding and describing other animals is problematic for a wide range of reasons that will be discussed in this chapter.

Augustine, Gadarene Swine, and Logical Leaps

Augustine's reasoning about the Gadarene swine incident (Matthew 8:28–34; Mark 5:1–20; Luke 8:26–39) provides an opportunity to look at an instance of the basic problem: "Christ himself shows that to refrain from the killing of animals . . . is the height of superstition for, judging that there are no common rights between us and the beasts . . . , he sent the devils into a herd of swine."[5]

There are several logical leaps in the argument, including the deduction of humans' right to *kill* other animals from Jesus' act of exorcism and the subsequent entry of the demons into the swine.[6] The logical leap that is directly related to "the basic problem" is the assumption that a few individuals of one type of nonhuman (here, some pigs living during Jesus' lifetime in the country of the Gadarenes) represent *all* other nonhuman animals. Augustine specifically reasons that if Jesus' act was directed to these individual members of one kind of nonhuman (the swine), then it is an act that has implications for all nonhuman animals at all times in relation to humans. Since Augustine was a master of rhetoric, there is little likelihood that he did not intend the obvious logical leap by which *all* other animals and not just swine in general or even all domestic animals were covered by the principle of evaluation that Augustine found in this Gospels-based story.

The generalization used by Augustine to refer to the diverse group of biological individuals outside the human species is represented by the term *animalium*, and it clearly means all other, nonhuman animals. This sort of broad grouping is also a feature of Gotama's statement that "animals are a simple matter." The following argument suggests that this kind of reference reflects a process of thinking which relies on a troubling overgeneralization. This mental habit is described more fully later as a complicated series of habits, the common element of which is that all other animals are thought of as belonging to one category that, of course, does *not* include humans. The overgeneralization permits a rigorous thinker like Augustine to make the conceptual leap to all other animals when an incident has symbolic overtones that could equally have been construed to bear on only a few animals' importance relative to humans. This has significant consequences because, as discussed in part IV, this coarse generalization is an organizing principle in Augustine's thinking.

Coarse Grouping as the Central Problem

Coarse grouping is arguably *the* dominant form of reference for most contemporary English speakers when we talk *and think* about other animals, especially when we compare nonhuman realities and interests to human realities and interests. To designate this mental habit, the word "lumping" will occasionally be used. There are, of course, non-"lumping" words in each language, but when it comes to general evaluations or comparisons, there is a culturally pervasive habit of bypassing the more specific words in favor of far more generic language even though it is often very inadequate for the task at hand.

The convention by which we use the word "animal" to mean "all animals other than members of the human species" is commonplace not only in ordinary discourse but also in scholarly works. Eliade observes that "the spiritual universe of the Paleolithics was dominated by the mystical relations between man and animals" (1978–85, 1:19). McDermott's essay (1989) on other animals in Buddhism is entitled "Animals and Humans in Early Buddhism." Linzey's (1994a) theological discussion of other animals utilizes the term "animal" to mean "all other animals," as is evident in his title *Animal Theology*. Such uses of the word "animal," which group all other animals together while implicitly placing humans into a separate group, are no less characteristic of discussions within other religious traditions. For example, the text of *The Declaration of the Parliament of the World Religions* uses "animals" in this sense (Küng and Kuschel 1993).

Such habits of reference are also a common feature of modern discussions regarding ethics, and it can be found regularly in the discourse of professional philosophers. Carruthers, who presses negative conclusions regarding the moral status of other animals, starts his book in this manner: "The task of this book is to consider whether animals have moral standing—that is whether they have rights that we may infringe by killing them or causing them suffering, or whether there is some other way in which we have direct moral duties towards them" (1992, 1). Frey's (1980) extended argument against "animal rights" is subtitled "The Case against Animals." Perhaps the most obvious example is the common locution "animal rights" where the word "animal" plainly means "animals other than humans."

In these examples, especially as they are typical of general use, collecting all other animals under a single term is a conceptual move that implicitly relies on the validity of the dualism "human animals and all other animals." This traditional way of dividing the universe of natural world animals can be quite unresponsive, especially when it is the *principal* means of understanding biological individuals outside the human species. Simply stated, it can be too coarse an instrument to guide moral agents in their discrimination of the world.

Is "Lumping" Descriptive or Evaluative?

Grouping all other animals together often operates as a description, especially since the prevalence of the habit clothes ordinary uses of "animals," in the sense of "other animals," with such an aura of factuality that the division seems uniquely realistic. It has already been suggested that, regarding the more complicated animals such as the key animals, this convention can seriously distort reality because this kind of coarse grouping is, in fact, very shy of description. Good description requires carefully crafted knowledge of the world, while the peculiar generalization of "lumping" thrives on nonobjective criteria and the peculiar kinds of refusals characterized in chapter 2 as ideological.

Use of this mental habit, then, rather than operating well as description, arguably involves contemporary speakers in a perpetuation of traditional, culturally constructed views of other animals. Thus, use of the term can operate as a predescriptive, evaluative move that, in its immunity from correction by reference to natural world phenomena, risks the serious drawbacks of any claim which is immune to counterfactual information. Consequences of the widespread practice of habitually referring to all other animals under a single, collective term can be broken into three distinct problems.

1. It minimizes the differences among other animals.
2. It implies that a sameness is shared by all other animals.
3. It causes humans as moral agents not to notice other animals.

First Problem: Minimizing the Differences among Other Animals

The facility with which one can refer to other animals is exceeded only by the vagueness of doing so. As Clark notes,

> [T]he orthodox perennially imagine that all creatures that are non-human are members of one, homogeneous class—just as the more naive of Greeks supposed that all non-Greeks were of a kind. In both cases this was arrogance: the conviction that the failure to be Greek, or human, is a property so important as to overshadow any differentiae between animal species. (1977, 89)

The sheer vagueness of the term allows some very indiscriminate thinking to go forward, for, as Midgley (1995, 206) notes, it is vacuous to talk of what distinguishes "man" from "the animals" without saying *which* animals. Despite this, the generalization "all other animals" is *central* in the history of ethical thinking. It operates as one of the two principal components (along with the notion of species membership for humans) in statements such as the following: "So far as animals are concerned, we have no direct duties. Animals are not self-conscious and are there merely as a means to an end. That end is man. . . . Our duties to animals are merely indirect duties to mankind" (Kant 1963, 239). Kant's claim appears to be premised on the specific factual assertion that no other animals possess the important trait of self-consciousness; but, more functionally, the statement is evaluative because it makes irrelevant the obvious differences that occur among animals outside the human species.

Using "animals" is this way, that is, as a reference to all nonhuman living things other than plants, will, in the analyses of parts III and IV, be referred to as a "second-level generalization." The term "first-level generalization" will be used to describe any term whose referent is all living beings (sometimes including plants but usually meaning "humans and all other animals").[7] The flatness of second-level generalizations is one of the principal themes of parts III and IV. The predominance of second-level generalizations also plays an important role in the arguments in parts III and IV that the Buddhist and Christian traditions failed to engage the diversity of nonhuman life even though they clearly recognized many of the obvious differences among other animals. Consider the attitude toward other living things in this Buddhist passage:

> They [nonhuman animals] knew neither mother nor father, neither brother nor sister, neither teacher nor teacher's pupil, neither friend nor kinsman. They devoured one another and drank one another's blood. They slew and strangled one another. From darkness they passed into darkness, from woe into woe, from evil plight into evil plight, from ruin into ruin. They suffered thousands of divers miseries, and in their brute state it was with difficulty that they survived. (Mv. I, 22, verse 27)

This kind of description is also characteristic of some Hebrew, Christian, and Hellenistic thinking, and it sometimes is found with the added dimension of other animals warring against humans. An example is Philo's distorting image of a *continuous* war with other animals "whose hatred is directed . . . towards . . . mankind as a whole and endures . . . without bound and limit of time" (*De Praemiis et Poenis*, 85). Such statements about other animals are extremely problematic in that, like Kant's formulation as to which biological entities should be direct beneficiaries of duties, profound differences are glossed over by the sheer flatness of the statements.

There is, of course, another use of the word "animal" to mean "all animals, including humans." This is the first-level generalization sense of the word we have when we read Aristotle's dictum that "man is by nature a political animal" (1984, *Politics* I, 2, 1253a, p. 1987). This inclusivist sense, however, is not the primary sense of the English word "animal" today, even though the OED lists first the logically prior, and more accurate, use of "animals" to mean "living thing[s]."[8]

Because use of "animals" in the sense "all other animals" (that is, the second-level generalization) is potentially problematic in the senses already discussed, it can be misleading. Descartes exemplifies well problems that occur when one carelessly uses the concept "all other animals." Using French and Latin cognates from which the English "brute" was derived, Descartes argued in *Discourse on Method* V, 11:

> For next to the error of those who deny God . . . there is none which is more effectual in leading feeble spirits from the straight path of virtue, than to imagine that the soul of the brute is of the same nature as our own, and that in consequence, after this life we have nothing to fear or to hope for, any more than the flies and ants.

Descartes's ability to use "flies and ants" as representatives of any nonhuman animals that might have souls or an afterlife is a by-product of the differences among "brutes" having been minimized. Such a rhetorical ploy reflects the same mental habit displayed by Augustine in his analysis of the meaning of the Gadarene swine incident.

The Logic of the Concept "All Nonhuman Animals"

There is, from the standpoint of the logic of the underlying concept, a peculiar problem with the word "animals" when employed to convey the second-level generalization "all nonhuman animals." In the underlying concept, the idea "nonhuman" may seem to be a definition or attribute, but as a predicate the description "nonhuman" is only trivially true of the animals that are not members of the human species. Living things outside the human species are, of course, "nonhuman," but what the moral agent really wants to know is if they have any features that make them distinctive such that they are important in an ethical sense.

The concept "nonhuman animal" is, like many negative definitions, a virtually useless piece of information, *unless* the hearer already values the negation implicit in the use. In a human-centered society, knowledge that a living thing is outside the species line is a valued piece of information, *but only because* an anthropocentric *and* exclusivist paradigm is already assumed. Absent that paradigm, the information that an animal is a nonhuman animal is not particularly helpful. That speakers of contemporary English regularly accept the word "animal" as a meaningful substantive employed in opposition to the substantive "human" signals the risk that an exclusivist paradigm is already at work.

Second Problem: The Implication That All Other Animals Are the Same

Diamond notes that the principal use of the word "animal" "implies that we consider centipedes, chimpanzees, and clams to share decisive features with each other but not with us, and to lack features restricted to us" (1992, 1). It is difficult to identify, however, any *verifiable* feature that *all* nonhuman animals share which humans also do not share, other than the trivially true features that are related to their status as "nonhumans."

The claim that sharing "nonhuman-ness" is more important than mutual differences leads to other animals being spoken of together by means of various generic terms such as "animals," "beasts," or "brutes." Under this mental habit, the differences between the many kinds of other animals are more than minimized; they are made irrelevant. The habit makes it easy to slip into the "one animal is just as good as any other" or "any animal represents all other animals" mentality exhibited by Augustine's Gadarene swine reasoning and Descartes's flies and ants comment. The obvious risk of such reasoning is the fallacious conclusion that if *some* nonhuman animals can be used instrumentally, then *any nonhuman animal* can be so used.

The tendency to extrapolate conclusions regarding one nonhuman animal to all other nonhuman animals is often further complicated by selection of a particularly *unrepresentative* animal to represent the class of nonhuman animals, as Descartes did in the flies and ants passage. The peculiar approach of using a relatively simple animal that is a social pest to represent the general possibilities of other nonhuman animals obviously biases the inquiry. But use of representatives with limited abilities not only trivializes; because it is inadequate, such a rhetorical ploy will also *mislead* to the extent the example fails to signal that there are *some* other animals whose realities would make a better comparison.

Third Problem: The Failure to Notice and Clark's Maxim

The dualism "humans and animals" can be misleading in another sense that is, arguably, particularly important for moral agents. Clark notes that "one's ethical, as well as one's ontological framework is determined by what entities one is prepared to notice or take seriously" (1977, 7). Moral calculations can be affected not merely by the fact that other animals' mutual differences have been minimized as irrelevant and even totally ignored. As important, other animals' peculiar realities often are not even *seen* because use of the dominant discourse deadens the ability to be alert to the sometimes subtle, sometimes obvious differences among nonhuman animals.

The Negative Side of the Dualism "Humans and Animals"

The generalization "all other animals" not only coexists with but also arguably *produces* a complex of interrelated consequences, including (1) a lack of awareness, (2) unfamiliarity, and (3) indifference, the ultimate effects of which are greatly diminished abilities to see other animals. It has been noted that "[w]hat knowledge will be sought in a society depends on the axiological system which reigns in that society" (Stark 1967, 477). What any one moral agent seeks to know, then, will in large part be governed by what the adults of a society train the youth of the society to value. It is in this area that the traditions of discourse discussed in parts III and IV play such a determinative role. If one is taught to speak in generalizations that rely on ignorance, the underlying exclusivist mentality becomes a self-perpetuating and thus self-validating enterprise.

It is not as if *merely* seeing or being told about the realities will make someone ethically sensitive to those realities. To claim this would be a form of the Enlightenment fallacy.[9] It is equally clear, however, that a failure to look for a reality can result in it being unfairly ignored. Recall Midgley's comment quoted in chapter 3 to the effect that ethological investigation has shown "Western urban thought" to have been "ill-informed" relative to "local superstition" because the allegedly sophisticated and cultured urbanites "had consistently attributed to animals a vastly *less* complex set of thoughts and feelings, and a much smaller range of power, than they actually possessed" (1984, 123).

Not unlike this phenomenon is the fact that in the Buddhist tradition, a dominant view is that "existence as an animal is a very unhappy one, much more painful than human existence" (Schmithausen 1991a, 16). Schmithausen notes that one of the reasons given for this is "that one animal kills or devours the other, especially the weaker one. This argument is also used to prove that animals are particularly malevolent and hence even morally inferior to man" (16, cites omitted).

A "lumping" mentality permits this kind of conclusion to apply broadly to *any* nonhuman animal. The risk, then, of such a deprecatory overgeneralization is that it misleads, for many animals are strictly vegetarian[10] and peaceful in their interactions with other animals. Such deprecation comes in many forms, ranging from mild depreciation to outright dismissal. It thrives especially when we compare an idealized, overdrawn, *and* culturally conditioned image of humans with a depreciated image of other animals based on caricatures of their worst features (such as are evident in Apostolos-Cappadona's summary of ape images in Western Christian art, quoted in chapter 4).

In cultures that have been part of the Christian tradition, reactions to nonhuman great apes provide many instances of how peculiar this deprecation really is. For example, the nineteenth-century Anglican bishop who succeeded Wilberforce, Charles Gore, commented that zoo chimpanzees made him "return an agnostic. I cannot comprehend how God can fit those curious beasts into his moral order. . . . When I contemplate you [the chimpanzee, which was roughly 99 percent identical to him genetically], you turn me into a complete atheist, because I cannot possibly believe that there is a Divine Being that could create anything so monstrous" (cited in Sagan and Druyan 1992, 272). This kind of gross overstatement, that is, a feigned atheism upon viewing another being obviously similar to humans, might be explained by Midgley's general assessment, "We distance ourselves from the beast without for fear of the beast within" (Clark 1977, 20, citing Midgley 1973).

There are, to be sure, various uses of the simplistic generalization "other animals" that are not harmful. Bauckham's and Linzey's Christological analyses (discussed in part IV), as well as the bodhisattva notion discussed in part III, rely on certain references to all other animals, and such generalizations are arguably benign. For example, Bauckham comments on the brief passage at Mark 1:13 regarding Jesus and other animals: "The animals are not said to fear him, submit to him, or serve him. The concept of human dominion over the animals as domination for human benefit is entirely absent. The animals are treated neither as subjects nor as domestic servants" (1994, 20). In that Jesus is described as having a "companionable presence with the wild animals" (20) and these animals are used as representatives for all other animals, Bauckham has used "lumping" to positive effect. Nonetheless, the risks of habitually glossing over the internal diversity previously discussed are very high because this habit offers no means of sorting out how individual animals are impacted by the actions of moral agents.

Other Aspects of Contemporary Discourse about Other Animals

Countless additional examples can be drawn from ordinary discourse that reflect the dominance of the view "humans alone really matter." In fact, many phrases that crassly and directly demean *all* other animals are regularly employed with no perceived loss of intellectual integrity. Use of the generalizations "brutes" and "beasts," together with their related negative adjectives, comes immediately to mind. Diamond points out that the English language is rich in animal names used as pejoratives

(1992, 269), and Dunayer lists many deprecatory words for other animals that target women in particular.[11]

Uses of the Word "Animal": The Modern Animal Rights Movement

The entrenched position of the habit of using "animal" or "animals" to refer to all nonhuman animals but not to human animals can be seen in the titles of leading books in various fields of the "animal movement":[12]

Animal Liberation (Singer 1976)

The Case for Animal Rights (Regan 1988)

Animals and Why They Matter (Midgley 1984)

The word "animal" in each instance is meant to designate only those animals outside the human species. In these works, however, the coarse grouping implicit in the titles coexists with strong repudiations of historically dominant views of other animals and, in some instances, traditional practices affecting some other animals. There is a peculiar tension in such uses, however.[13] The phrases "women and people" and "blacks and humans" grate on the contemporary English speaker's ears because the two components in each are not logically equivalent to one another. The problem is a simple one—the second component encompasses the first, while the separation in the phrase (at least as it is normally used) implies that the categories are exclusive of each other. The separation, of course, is made for the psychological purpose of implying a value-laden distinction. The terminology "humans and animals" has the same shortcoming but is backed by a powerful tradition of discourse that validates the use of "animals" as a second-level generalization.

Traditional Legal Conceptuality and Contemporary Legal Language

The same dualism and coarse grouping of other animals is a primary feature of traditional legal conceptuality. Consider the Roman law codes, "the most important and influential collection of secular legal materials that the world has ever known" because "[a]ll later Western systems borrowed extensively" from them. These codes feature the human–other animal distinction prominently and in a manner that dramatically biases the possibility of seeing other animals.[14] As Wise notes, "the legal thinghood of nonhuman animals was a Roman axiom" and so ingrained "that history reveals not a single instance of a Roman jurist questioning its legality or even its propriety" (1996, 492–93). To be sure, within Roman law there were distinctions made regarding different kinds of animals such as wild animals (*ferae bestiae*) and domestic animals (*pecus*) (Berger 1953, 469, 625). Yet, this is of minor importance, for Roman law has as its most fundamental division the distinction between a member of the human species (*persona*) and all other things (the category *res*). This latter category included all animals outside the species line.[15] This is confirmed by the fact that even human slaves, which were legally in the *res* category, were referred to as *persona*, while no other living things were placed outside the *res* category.[16] Similarly, while one meaning of the Latin word *animal* includes humans, the principal use in the codes is "all animals other than humans."[17] This basic division has been inherited by Western religious and secular legal systems.[18] For example, it is a feature of Catholic canon law,[19] and Wise documents how the common law traditions of England and the United States perpetuate the Roman conceptuality.[20] An additional feature of the conceptual background is that humans owe duties to no other animals; rather, duties relevant to how other animals could be treated were duties to the owners. Thus, legal relations provide a paradigmatic example of how exclusions based directly and solely on the species membership line between humans and other animals are perpetuated by the central secular institutions in Western culture.

What Is at Stake: The Possession of "Unique" Traits and Differentiated Value

Contemporary English discourse employs two distinct senses of the word "unique" that are relevant to the issues of moral standing. "Unique" can be used as an adjective to convey the idea that members of one species have a trait that no other animals have, and this sense will be referred to here as "unique-different." "Unique" can also be used to mean that the members of one species are more valuable than are members of another species. Consider, for example, the phrase "Humans are unique, but no other animals are." This second sense will be referred to as "unique-better." These two senses are not, of course, mutually exclusive, since the attribution "unique-better" is often based on claims about who possesses "unique-different" traits, but it is helpful to distinguish the two senses carefully.

"Unique-different" is the more purely descriptive term and can be further broken down into absolute and relative senses. Diamond (1992) lists many traits characteristic of humans that are unique in an absolute sense. Among these are many that are simply irrelevant to the issues of moral considerability,[21] but at least the following are potentially relevant to such issues: (1) hierarchical language; (2) capacity to learn from distant others and those in the distant past; (3) writing; and (4) the making of compound tools.[22] These are some of the grounds cited in traditional claims that humans are distinct from all other animals, although the status of these items as absolutely "unique-different" depends on how one understands certain animal precursors or analogues such as those described in chapter 4.

Another sense of "unique-different" addresses the existence of *relative* differences, that is, features characteristic of a species in something other than an absolute, exclusive sense. Such a list can also be drawn from Diamond's work (1992) and includes art, intelligence, tools, agriculture, genocide, language, speech, brain size, genitalia, female menstrual cycle, menopause, rapid cultural change, life cycle, food-gathering techniques, complexity of our society, and xenophobia. Chapter 4 might be viewed as an extended argument that some traits cherished as particularly human are merely relative differences, because analogues occur in complex individuals outside the human species.

It is true that many species are composed of individuals that are unique in both these senses, since some nonhuman animals display absolute and relative levels of abilities and social arrangements that no other animals, including humans, possess.

Clearly, some of these differences are *mere differences* from the standpoint of the inquiring moral agent. For example, members of a bird species that have uniquely colored feathers would exhibit a trait that is "unique-different" *but* without importance in the area of moral considerability.

"Unique-Better"

Some differences between the members of one species and the members of another species are, however, regularly held to be more than mere differences. For example, when humans prefer to kill bacteria because they are making a valued individual sick, the bacteria are killed because the life of the sick animal (whether human or not) is held to be more valuable than the lives of the bacteria. The life saved is thought of as "unique" and "better" in an evaluative sense that is integrally related to moral significance.

While the relative valuation of humans and bacteria is generally uncontroversial, it is more controversial to assert that (1) members of the human species are distinguished by differences (2) which justify extinguishing the interests of any nonhuman animals whenever such an act promotes the lives and welfare of individual humans. Such "unique-better" claims can be controversial for several reasons. For example, the claim that the relevant difference is absolute might be challenged. Alternatively, if the claim is based on relative differences, the weighting of those differences might be challenged. Third, the relevance of the difference to the extinction of interests might be challenged (this is one of the Rachels's strategies described in chapter 2).

Certain exclusivisms, such as racism, have relied heavily on "unique-better" claims. Such exclusivist claims have been broadly repudiated because the shared features of humans have been deemed more important than alleged differences between races. It is, of course, far more controversial to bring this kind of challenge on behalf of, for example, nonhuman complex individuals. One reason for the greater controversy is the fact that any claim that some other animals "share what humans have" (whether this is a particular trait or some constellation of traits) is not easily proved. This is especially true in an intellectual climate where nondomesticated, nonhuman animals are ab initio neither noticed nor taken seriously.

An interesting feature of claims that humans are "unique-better" is that they can be phrased in terms that appear to be quite specific, as when Augustine argues, along with the Stoics, that no other animals have reason.[23] But apparently specific claims of this kind can be quite vague.[24] Even apparently verifiable bases of "unique-better" claims can be difficult to work with. For example, Clark describes the reaction to recurring challenges to species-specific "unique-better" claims based on humans' exclusive possession of language:

> [W]e remain doubtful that animals could be said to have a language. In part, this doubt is a mere device of philosophy: it is not that we have *discovered* them to lack a language but rather that we define, and redefine, what Language is by discovering what beasts do not have. If they should turn out to have the very thing we have hitherto supposed language to be, we will simply conclude that language is something else again. (1977, 96)

This skeptical view of some apologists' tactics hints that ideology (in the narrow sense of chapter 2) may underlie the attempts of defenders of traditional exclusions to find ways of construing "unique-different" traits to be grounds for the conclusion that humans are "unique-better." In a general sense, insisting that all parties focus carefully on the realities of other animals is a strategy designed to level the playing field, so to speak.

Such a strategy has three effects. First, it foregrounds the fact that many traditional claims about nonhuman animals were not based on any meaningful inquiry into their realities. Second, it offers an acceptable information base that all parties can draw on. Finally, it offers the possibility of providing kinds of information that can be relevant to any challenge to the merits of a specific, traditional claim that all humans are "unique-better."

Challenging the vagueness and difficulty of working with some "unique-better" claims does not amount, however, to claiming that "unique-better" does not, or should not, work as a concept. There are many extremely important "unique-better" claims that are evident and important in everyday life (such as the human-bacteria example used earlier, or the common claim that membership in an animal species characterized by a central nervous system is more morally significant than membership in a plant species). Generally, the meaning of these simple examples of "unique-better" claims is more readily accessible than is the meaning of vague or controversial claims. In the next paragraphs, attention is turned to certain formal features of the important but complex nature of "unique-better" claims.

Principles of Differentiated Value

Attempts to divide the realities around us according to some principle by which the value of some things is differentiated from the value of other things are legion, and they repeatedly follow two basic principles. First, living things are typically valued more than nonliving things. Second, among living things, some are valued more than others are. Neither of these principles is per se controversial, for *every* value system reflects such divisions. The question is not whether to differentiate value, but where.[25] What is being challenged when traditional uses of the generalization "all animals other than humans" are questioned is the validity of doing so along the lines of the dualism "humans and animals," for this division begs many questions.

Claims that it is only humans who are "unique-better," and indeed the claims of any form of exclusivism, including blatant speciesism, are *formally* similar to more inclusivist animal rights positions and many other attempts to say what it is in the world that moral agents ought to value.[26] Each follows some principle by which the value of other beings or mere things is differentiated. In effect, all such claims share the formal features of asserting that some parts of the world are (1) more valuable than others and, thus, (2) especially relevant to the moral agent's decisions as to when and where the consequences of decisions and actions must be assessed.

To be sure, some principles of value differentiation are relatively more exclusivist, such as radical egotism, racism, and patriarchy. These can be contrasted with those principles that are relatively more inclusivist, such as the biocentrism of "deep ecology"[27] or the principles of the Jains by which life characterized by one faculty can be killed but those with more cannot.[28] Speciesism, when seen as an example of such a principle, might be understood as an intermediate form on the continuum of possibilities. That continuum runs between one pole where one finds the most radical exclusivism (for example, egotism) to another pole where one finds the most radical inclusivism (for example, deep ecology). Speciesism is, when seen in this context, broader than some principles that do not advocate the application of moral protections for all humans, and it is narrower than those principles that seek fundamental moral protections for some nonhuman animals. The notion of "complex individual" used in chapter 4 is another intermediate form on the continuum suggested here, for it does not include biological entities without the constellation of features listed in chapter 4.[29]

It is argued later (in the analysis entitled "The Relevance of Species Membership to Moral Issues") that, given the nature of the interaction between living things (particularly the biological inevitability of some ingesting others), it is necessary for the moral agent to make some division according to a principle of differentiated value. Historically, exhortations to expand existing principles of differentiation have been characteristic of various movements not usually associated with one another, such as political revolutions, agitation for religious toleration, social justice demands, environmental protection, and various trends often collected under terms like "the animal protection movement." In each of these, proponents of an expanded sensibility challenge the contemporary moral agent's rote acceptance or ignorance of harmful practices that imply *where* the dividing lines can legitimately, that is, morally, be drawn.

Species, Essences, and Natural Kinds

Attention is turned here to the notion of "species," since clarification of this concept is, of course, extremely important for an assessment of the validity of decisions based solely on species membership considerations. The idea of species membership has been central in the history of thought, but the notion is, despite an appeal that seems intuitive, far from simple.

Balme noted, "Since Porphyry, the traditional interpretation has tended to treat essence and species as synonyms referring to the first order of generality above particulars, and to regard this generality as an absolute form characterising all the species-members alike" (1980, 6). Indeed, the long-standing tradition of equating shared membership in a species with possession of identical "essences" has been, in Western circles at least, one of the most prominently used conceptual tools for understanding the realities of animal life. But essentialist interpretations of the concept "species" are not obviously true, even if they seem to many intuitively correct. Mayr notes, "There is probably no other concept in biology which has remained so consistently controversial as the species concept" (1982, 251). It is suggested here that the species notion has been not only a confused one but also in important ways an abused one, especially as it has so often been used to the advantage of human animals and to the disadvantage of nonhuman animals.

Two distinguishable concepts have functioned under the one notion "species" and must be isolated from one another to specify how any single instance of the word "species" is being used. Mayr uses two different terms to untangle the related, but very distinct concepts. The first is "species taxon," which is used to designate some of the most basic and easily discerned biological continuities and discontinuities that surround us. If we examine the animals or plants in a particular area, it will be readily apparent that they can be grouped into classes that differ from one another in numerous respects. Certain individuals have similar or complementary body structure and integrated lifestyles, and they interbreed to produce offspring. The term "species taxon" is used to describe each of these natural world populations that share spatiotemporal unity and historical continuity. The obvious existence of such populations is matched by equally noticeable gaps or discontinuities between different species taxa. The notion of a species taxon, then, is the common tool with which we distinguish the natural world populations from one another.

Membership in such groups is not at all the same as having a shared ancestor, since, importantly, a species taxon can *not* be defined solely with reference to common origin. Such an approach fails to take into account the separation of one population of animals from another, which, across time and due to genetic changes, results in the two populations no longer being able to interbreed. The two populations will then have become separate species taxa. Common origin is commonly addressed by the term "clade," which designates "a coherent evolutionary group" (Byrne 1995, 11). Thus, all of the great apes, including humans, constitute a clade because they have a common origin—that is, they share an ancestor—but are not, obviously, of the same species. All elephants also constitute a clade, as do all cetaceans.

Mayr explains that each of the species taxa, as readily distinguishable interrelated groups, is "a concrete zoological or botanical object" (1982, 253). It has been argued that each species taxon is, ontologically speaking, an *individual*, such that individual members as products of that gene pool are *parts* of the species *rather than members of a class*.[30] This view is not universally accepted,[31] but the thrust of the claim is clear enough. Because of spatiotemporal unity and historical continuity, individuals in a species taxon have a unique relation to each other. This relation is qualitatively distinct from relations to other biological individuals who are not part of the species taxon. But, and this is of the utmost importance, these closely related individuals are *by no means identical* to one another, as is explained later.

To be distinguished carefully from the notion of "species taxon" is another notion that has gone by the name "species"; this is the "species category" defined by Mayr as follows: "The species category is the class, the members of which are species taxa. The particular definition which an author adopts determines which taxa he must rank as species. The problem of species category is simply one of definition" (1982, 254).

Besides the species category and apart from the important category of individuality, other important categories or levels of noticeable, interrelated biological phenomena are (1) the immediate family (parents and immediate offspring), (2) a population, (3) a subspecies, (4) a genus, (5) a taxonomic family, (6) a phylum, and (7) a kingdom. Of these categories, however, the species category has some particularly important features, for it is "the lowest level of genuine discontinuity above the level of the individual" (Mayr 1982, 251). The species category, then, is of great significance in understanding the continuities and discontinuities that occur between and among the many biological individuals that populate the earth.[32]

For the ancients, there was no consistent terminology to describe what a species taxon was, although they recognized continuities among populations and discontinuities between species taxa, as reflected in their use of differing names. Despite the lack of a common vocabulary, there was, according to Mayr, a consistent *essentialist* interpretation of what a species taxon was, and "each species was thought to be characterized by its unchanging essence (*eidos*) and separated from all other species by a sharp discontinuity" (1982, 256). Mayr understands this "dogma of essentialism" to stem from Plato; whatever its source, subsequent authors have been dominated by an essentialist approach, and this appears in common discourse even today when people speak of an animal's "essence" or "nature."[33] Interestingly, this pronounced tendency to essentialism did not lead the ancients to recognize the integrity of each species, for authorities (such as Aristotle and Theophrastus) accepted that one kind of seed could produce another kind of plant, and that hybridization across species lines was a frequent occurrence.[34] It was not until the Reformation period of Christianity that an important change in the attitude toward the absolute fixity of species taxa occurred. Mayr argues, "The fixity and complete constancy of species now became a firm dogma . . . [because a] literal interpretation of Genesis required the belief in the individual creation of every species of plants and animals on the days prior to Adam's creation" (1982, 255).

In the following, consideration is given to some of the confusions that may explain why essentialist uses of species membership seem so intuitively appealing but are, upon examination, problematic from both a factual and an ethical standpoint.

Natural Kinds and Species

There are, of course, many other naturally occurring classes that are readily identifiable. These include various classes with fixed characteristics or traits, examples of which are designated by the names of the periodic chart (for example, oxygen, gold, or silver) or of mineralogy (for example, quartz or granite). These consistent realities are fully defined in terms of a set of properties essential for membership in the class. Each of the elements of the periodic table, for example, is defined by a unique atomic weight, and all members of the class by definition have this "essential" trait. The species concept in chemistry and mineralogy, however, is *fundamentally* different from the species concept employed in contemporary biology (Mayr 1982, 251). The species taxa as "concrete zoological or botanical objects" are quite different from the kinds of natural objects dealt with in chemistry or mineralogy, for as noted later, members of a species taxon differ from one another in very important ways.

The traditional way of dividing up the physical world according to different kinds of things is found in the notion "natural kind." The classic theories are those of Aristotle and Locke.[35] For Aristotle, natural kinds are ontological entities of an unchanging kind, a claim that has particular bearing upon the validity of the notion as applied to animal species. Locke gave a different answer, described by Ruse: "[W]hereas for Aristotle natural kinds are ontological entities, for Locke they are at best epistemological concepts" (1987, 229). Locke, although he assumed that reality lies in the underlying particles that go to make up substances, doubted we could know these. Locke, then, thought natural kinds were made, not found.[36]

Species taxa traditionally were treated as natural kinds of the same type as non-biological natural kinds. It is, however, a category mistake to equate species taxa, as natural objects, with the natural objects of chemistry and mineralogy,[37] since species taxa are fundamentally different from paradigmatic, nonbiological natural kinds in very relevant ways. Species taxa are living objects composed of a population of nonidentical members who, through sexual or asexual unions and division, produce new members that are unique relative to the parents. Thus, members of a species taxon, and indeed the whole species profile, can change in unpredictable ways. This is in great contrast to the natural kinds of chemistry and mineralogy, each of which is meaningfully thought of as fixed and thus characterized by an unchanging essence. Simply said, species taxa have a radically different character. There is, then, a misplaced essentialism if species taxa are understood on the basis of paradigmatic natural kinds that can be defined in terms of a set of properties essential for membership in the class.

Essentialism and Notions of Other Animals

The foundation on which the dominant ways of talking and thinking about other animals were developed is the pre-Darwinian notion that species taxa are characterized by an identifiable, unvarying essence. Essentialist understandings of species taxa and the species category are, however, no longer dominant in biological thinking because recognition of the history and phenomena of biological evolution has undermined the belief in the fixity of species.[38] Biologists proceed now on the assumption that the primary unit of significance in ecology is not the species but, rather, populations of individuals. "Populationist," as opposed to essentialist, thinking in biology stresses the uniqueness of everything in the organic world. Individuals form populations, and while populations (groups of individuals) can be analyzed for an arithmetic mean or statistical variation, it is *only* the individuals that have reality, not the statistical mean.[39]

To argue that populationist thinking is "accurate" and essentialist thinking in biology "inaccurate" is not to claim that species are not "real" in crucially important senses, for the existence of species taxa is one of the most striking realities when one examines the world of living things. It does not follow from the existence of species taxa as an indisputable biological datum, however, that one can draw the conclusion that identification of an "essence" must be a central feature of either the species category or species taxa. Careful study of the animals grouped into different classes will reveal that the distinguishing characteristics are by no means constant within the classes. If we extend our investigation of any group of animals, including humans, in both space and time, the limitations of both the similarities inside a particular species and the differences between separate species become increasingly apparent.[40]

Varying Traits and the Moral Status of Individuals within the Population

An implication of the view that *populations* are the reality, rather than an identifiable essence shared by each member of the class, is that the real point of measurement must be the *individual*. Because traits possessed by different members of a species taxon will vary from one individual to the next (this being a consequence of the mechanisms of biological inheritance), an inquiry that seeks only the alleged traits of the species is pursuing a fiction. Traits occur in individuals, who are not identical to each other. A mean or an average may be a telling figure, but it will not be exhaustive of the traits possessed by the members of the species taxon. Mere membership in one group as opposed to another, then, is not necessarily a good criterion of the relative status of two individuals from different species. Membership in one species versus another *may* in some situations be controlling. This would be the case if the relationship of the genetic endowments of the two species is such that there is no chance of respective interests being similar, as is arguably the case in the complex individual versus the bacterium examples already used. But, as a general matter, when the interests of two individuals are in conflict, the relevant inquiry will be each individual's possession of traits that bear on decisions as to whose interests the moral agent might favor.

The wide range of variations within the human species is the starting point of the "marginal cases argument" discussed in chapter 2. In fact, the range of traits exhibited by members of the class "biological humans" is so vast that some other animals' abilities in the areas of cognition, communication, intelligence, and emotion easily overlap with those of some humans. Further, as argued in chapter 4, it is not merely that other animals match or exceed the abilities of the so-called marginal humans. Some nonhuman animals, such as members of the key species, have abilities that are unlike those of any human but still possibly relevant to the issue of moral considerability.

The implications of such arguments are not always clear. Consider how the philosopher Rachels argues the case:

> If Darwin is correct, there are no absolute differences between humans and the members of all other species—in fact, there are no absolute differences between the members of *any* species and all others. Rather than sharp breaks between species, we find instead a profusion of similarities and differences between particular animals, with the characteristics typical of one shading over into the characteristics typical of another. As Darwin puts it, there are only differences of degree—a complex pattern of similarities and differences that reflect common ancestry, as well as chance variations among individuals with a single species. Therefore, the fundamental reality is best represented by saying that the earth is populated by individuals who resemble one another, and who differ from one another, in myriad ways, rather than by saying that the earth is populated by different *kinds* of beings. (1991, 174)

Rachels appears to be suggesting that the human-bacterium division is *not* a basis for the moral agent *automatically* favoring the human. It will be suggested later that this is taking the argument too far. That humans overlap in features with the members of some other animals would not justify the claim that they overlap in features with *all* other animals.

There are some potential benefits that might accrue from use of Rachels's guidelines. It can be argued cogently that such a "moral individualism" (Rachels's own description is quoted in chapter 2), *if and when* it can be done as a practical matter (a critical qualification that is addressed later), produces a consistent application of the principle of equality. In such situations, species-neutral rules of morality then govern the moral agent's treatment of all creatures. Under such a guideline, individuals are treated in the same way unless there is a relevant difference. For the inquiring moral agent, this is of significance, since in the everyday world there are often conflicts in which species membership itself is not a difference relevant to resolution of the conflict.[41]

Such an approach based on inquiries at the level of the individuals' realities and traits requires the moral agent to know the impact of his or her avoidable actions, especially since no one difference in traits will have moral relevance to all differences in treatment. As Rachels argues it, the general principle is "Whether a difference between individuals justifies a difference in treatment depends on the kind of treatment that is in question. A difference that justifies one kind of difference in treatment need not justify another" (1991, 178). "This has an important corollary: "[T]here is no *one* big difference between individuals that is relevant to *all* differences in treatment" (178). The moral agent's conclusion as to how to act will depend on what kind of treatment is involved *and* what kinds of traits are involved. This, in turn, requires knowledge, including some awareness of the complex pattern of similarity and differences between those individuals, *whether human or not*, who are impacted by intentional or avoidable actions.

The Alternative Claim That There Are Traits "Proper" to a Species

A prominent alternative to the claim that the relevant inquiry is consideration of the specific features that individuals exhibit is the argument that what really matters is the species-level phenomenon of traits "proper" to the species taxon. "Proper" is a word that has extremely varied meanings, but in this context its meaning is confined to the particular, even if vague, sense conveyed by these OED meanings: "(1) belonging to oneself . . . [a] property of the thing itself, intrinsic, inherent. . . . (2) belonging or relating to the person or thing in question distinctively (more than to any other), or exclusively (not to any other)." The OED uses these synonyms: "special, particular, distinctive, characteristic, peculiar, restricted, private, individual, of its own."

The thrust of the word, then, is twofold. First, features, traits, properties, or characteristics[42] that are proper (in this sense) belong to the individual as a consequence of what might be called "its basic nature." Second, at times a claim is made that "proper" features belong "distinctively" or "exclusively" to their possessors.[43]

The claim that some features are "a property of the thing itself, intrinsic, inherent," is not the clearest of notions but is, rather, somewhat elusive. Some clarity comes from the common assertion that the features "proper" to a *species*, as opposed to an individual, are those exhibited by healthy individuals and not those exhibited by unhealthy, marginal cases within each species. It is not immediately apparent, however, that the healthy members are fully representative of what it means to be a species member, for healthy humans are not in fact more human, in a biological sense, than are marginal cases. This is, nonetheless, how the term "proper to a species" is used. Note also that the OED definitions of "proper" are directed primarily at features characteristic of *individuals*, not necessarily species. Expanding these senses of the word "proper" to the *species* level suggests that the "proper to the species" argument relies heavily on the notion that species taxa are classes, the members of which share basic features by virtue of that membership. Arguably, then, even though the two concepts "proper to the species" and "species essence" are in important respects distinguishable, they have similarities that cause them to be used in conjunction with one another. At times, they are even used interchangeably or conflated into one operative concept. Both rely on the assumption that membership in a species taxon is membership in a class of individuals who, by virtue of that class membership, participate in, or are otherwise importantly linked to, some foundational paradigm. Thereby, individuals are said to have the "essence" of their class, or to get credit for traits "proper" to their "kind."

One possible objection to any claim reliant on such notions of "class" has already been stated. The underlying notion of class membership is applicable to paradigmatic natural kinds (for example, elements in the periodic table) but only questionably, even if traditionally, to *biological* kinds.

Another possible set of objections deals with the issue of "potentiality" for traits. The "proper to the species" analysis often functions as an integral part of an attempt to rebut arguments claiming that it is the *actual* possession of features that confers moral considerability. One can argue quite forcefully that the potential to possess traits must be considered, for it cannot be only those traits actualized in a particular moment that matter. This would render irrelevant dormant traits (for example, when someone is sleeping) or unrealized potential that will, if unimpeded, be realized. This is an important objection that can be dealt with by a richer sense of "actual" than the narrow notion "being actualized right now." If we decide to use the notion "actual possession of features" to mean (1) "actualized in some way now," (2) "capable of being actualized now," *or* (3) "an individual's potential to actualize at some time in the future" (such that an embryo or young member of a species can be credited with traits it will develop if unimpeded), we can deal with the most obvious objections to the narrower sense of what is meant by an individual "actually possessing" a feature.[44]

There remain problems, however. Arguments that use the notion "proper to the species" go further than considering whether an *individual* has the potential to have a trait. For example, suppose a human child has a debilitating disease that precludes it as an individual from having the potential for some feature characteristic of human life (say, self-awareness). The "proper to the species" argument has been used, as in the Catholic arguments regarding fetuses already cited in chapter 2, to argue that this individual is a member of a species for which the missing feature is "proper," and therefore this individual should, on the issue of basic moral protections, be accorded protections equivalent to the protections accorded those who do in fact have (or have the potential for) self-awareness. This is also the kind of argument made to protect marginal cases even if their relevant abilities do not match those of certain nonhuman individuals.

In an important sense, this argument is using species membership as an indicator of a certain kind of potential, although this is obviously a different sense of potential than is used when one speaks of an *individual* having potential for a feature. The "proper to the species" analysis, then, is for some a means used to grant marginal cases moral considerability because marginal cases are members of a species to which certain features are "proper" and thus in a sense, albeit a special sense, have "potential" for crucial features. Whether this approach involves an equivocation in the meaning of "potential" is discussed further later.

But it is not immediately clear why nonpossessors of the allegedly "proper" trait get the same moral protections as the actual possessors. If it is only because they are members of the species, we have, through use of the "proper to the species" concept as a means of including candidates within the moral circle, assumed that mere species membership is morally relevant, by virtue of what species membership usually, but not always, entails. But this is precisely what is at issue. The "proper to the species" argument has at least this anomaly, then: some members of the class are without features that are "proper" to the class. This arguably is accounted for by the fact that there are two senses of class operating. The first class is composed of those with the genetic endowment that, by definition, means membership in the species. The second class is the group of healthy individuals, which has potential in the ordinary sense. This kind of reasoning, to the extent it relies on changing senses of the notions "potential" and "class membership," risks the fallacies that equivocation in definitions all too easily permits.

The "proper to the species" notion, then, can be strangely at odds with the approaches and empirical evidence that have led to populationist theories and the demise of essentialist thinking about species taxa. Arguably, any moral agent's operative notion of species should be an empirical matter, or at least subject to adjustment in light of what is the case in the natural world. If the operative definition of what species membership entails derives all its strength from culturally conditioned prejudgments about the significance of species membership, traditional prejudices will control. Further, if the "authority" called upon by contemporary moral agents to justify their analysis of a situation is *solely* (or even primarily) the range of concepts and words that are now operative in an existing tradition of discourse about humans and other animals, rather than openness to the empirical realities of the individuals whose interests are at issue, then the moral agent risks failing to take responsibility for the consequences of his or her actions.

Of course, as discussed in the next section, the practical demands of everyday life in *some* situations (to be specified later) require prima facie presumptions as to the significance of species membership. But our need in everyday life for such assumptions should not be confused with the propriety and accuracy of essentialist thinking about species membership. It is a mistake to make the practical necessity of using rebuttable assumptions an excuse for essentialist conclusions (or their functional equivalents) regarding which *individuals* should benefit from characterizations of features as "proper to the *species*."

The Relevance of Species Membership to Moral Issues

It is commonly said that species membership is not a valid criterion for moral decisions.[45] The obvious point being made in such claims is easily seen when considering certain natural world situations. For example, it makes no sense to favor chimpanzees over orangutans simply because chimpanzees have membership in one species while orangutans have membership in another. Ward's comment that "[c]onsiderations of group membership cannot override considerations of justice" (1986, 57) suggests that there are other, non-species-membership criteria that, by consensus, govern moral decisions.

While this general point about the irrelevance of species membership works well within a certain range of natural world circumstances, much talk about "species membership" being a "morally irrelevant characteristic" seems wrong. There are two reasons for this. First, historically, much of the talk about species membership being morally irrelevant has been an attempt to make the point that membership in *one* species alone (the human species) cannot be the only criterion of moral considerability. This point, valid in a limited sense, does not carry over well to all situations.

A second reason that general statements about "species membership" being a "morally irrelevant characteristic" seem counterintuitive and confusing is that the point appears not to be valid when applied to *all* conflicts between different forms of life. Many common practices and approaches seem to go forward on the assumption that mere species membership is morally relevant. Thus, in some conflicts membership in a species is not just an important consideration but sometimes the overriding one. In fact, group membership considerations are, on an everyday basis, used to determine who the candidates for protection are. Some simple examples show this. Even highly sensitive moral agents do not have the same kind of qualms when cutting up lettuce as they do when cutting up any mammal.[46] Similarly, we generally are not troubled by washing our hands in order to kill the "germs" that accompany all forms of macroscopic life. In important ways, then, criteria that seem to be those of species or other group membership, or at least very much like these membership concerns, are, *in some instances*, used if we are asked to decide whether terminating one form of life for the benefit of another is going to raise a moral issue.

In reply, it can be argued that in the lettuce-mammal and "kill the germs" examples, where we justify our action in terms of species or higher taxonomic group membership, such expressions are really only shorthand for a different judgment. In essence, the argument goes, this is the product of experience which has shown us that any individuals of species A are *always* more valuable (in some relevant sense) than any member of species B (this is, again, the bacteria-mammal example as worked out in real life). So the phrases we use which invoke species membership simply reflect our previous determination that there are necessarily great differences between the qualities of the lives of the so-called higher animals we prefer and the qualities of those we kill without too much compunction.

Interestingly, the practice of using genetic endowment (which is, in effect, the equivalent to using mere species membership) as a morally relevant criterion is common in the animal liberation movement as a shorthand method for determining which animals are to receive attention. Practices inflicting death are typically questioned by animal rights activists *only* in those cases where the organisms are roughly comparable to humans on the phylogenetic scale (thus, for mammals and birds, less often for fish, but almost never for yeast, viruses, and plants). In such cases, descriptions relying on group membership criteria are used to say something about whether the impacted living things have the potential to possess characteristics that we might protect. Of course, in those special cases where the impacted individuals are (1) recognizable individuals, (2) complex in some important sense, or (3) generally comparable to the benefited organism, reliance on species or group membership alone becomes more problematic. It has already been suggested that whenever the impacted individuals are at all complicated, comparisons of natural world individuals rather than of species membership considerations give the moral agent a better understanding of what is at stake in the conflict.

Common practices and approaches, then, make questionable the assertion that *species membership is always morally irrelevant.* Such an assertion is an enthymeme, that is, an instance of syllogistic reasoning in which an important premise is suppressed (usually because it is not noticed). The missing premise in this case is something like "The different taxonomic groups (whether species, genus, family, order, class, phylum, or kingdom) to which the competing biological entities belong are not obviously greatly different in terms of biological features."

When the pattern of species membership questions as "sometimes relevant/sometimes irrelevant" is seen clearly, a more subtle and responsive, and thus more important, question can be asked: Does use of species membership result in unfair results relative to individual-based comparisons?

In the end, how one resolves the relevance of species membership depends on how one construes the meaning of species membership. If one is willing to equate genetic endowment with species membership, and arguably that is what species membership literally means, species membership is a fact of life that is relevant to resolution of many of the inevitable conflicts that arise in a biological world where living beings *must* consume other living things. In such a world, the moral agent who continues to live must constantly make decisions that favor one organism over another. If our moral agent adds the view that species membership is *not* always automatically dispositive, because traits vary within and across species such that various species can have overlapping abilities (whether identical, analogous, or functionally equivalent), then species membership considerations will often not be conclusive as to which individuals matter.

No matter how one understands species membership, however, there appear to be interesting cases in which we do use "species membership" or its functional equivalent as a morally relevant criterion. It may only be shorthand for another assessment, that is, that membership entails certain genetic endowment, which is pertinent to potential and actual abilities. Even if this is true, it is clearly the case that group membership considerations are regularly spoken about and used as conflict resolution criteria. Simply stated, we may not be complex enough creatures to do without this kind of shorthand. We *are* complex enough, however, to do so with some other living things (and, in particular, the higher mammals), as is clear from the fact that many already do this. But *no one* can do the calculations necessary to extend moral individualism to all living things.

This approach of using species membership in some cases differs from speciesism in dramatic ways. To have elevated mere membership in *one* particular species into a morally crucial characteristic is the problem being addressed by the anti-speciesism critique. This is different than using the concept "species membership" to assess the likelihood of qualifying for the moral circle. Once moral agents have determined that *some* members of a particular species have features that make them candidates for moral protections, then it is common to go forward on the rebuttable presumption that other members of that species are candidates as well. In this way, use of mere species membership as a relevant criterion *in some circumstances* can be a valid exercise.

Recapitulation

The concepts and words commonly used to describe other animals suggest both (1) a general failure to consider realities of nonhuman complex individuals and (2) an excessive reliance on certain serious inadequacies in our dominant traditions of discourse. In effect, mere membership in the human species overdetermines the qualities of any individual human, while membership in the vague, undifferentiated group "other animals" underdetermines the features of many of the diverse biological individuals in that group, such that species membership of other animals often becomes irrelevant. This asymmetry is accepted because the status of human qua member of the human species taxon has been a favored status, whereas the status of any other biological individual qua nonhuman or member of its species taxon has been a disfavored status.

PART III

IS THERE SPECIESISM
IN BUDDHISM?

Consideration is turned to specific questions that follow from the general inquiry of whether the concept of speciesism helps one understand attitudes about other animals that are common in the Buddhist tradition. To raise these questions, the following two chapters provide a review of the Pali canon's passages involving other animals (chapter 6) and the claim that the Buddhist tradition is ethically sensitive to other animals (chapter 7).

6

Other Animals in the Pali Canon

*I [the Buddha] . . . comprehend animal birth [tiracchānayoni] and the way
leading to animal birth and the course leading to animal birth, and that according to how one is faring along one uprises, at the breaking up of the body after
dying, in animal birth.*

—Majjhima-Nikāya

It is a challenge to assess how the first Buddhists saw other animals. The opening
section of this chapter presents some general features of the vocabulary, including
tiracchānayoni,[1] available to, and used by, the early Buddhists in their scriptures when
they mentioned other animals generally. The next section describes the extent to
which Buddhists lived near or around the key animals. The concluding eight sections
analyze the references to the key and other animals that occur in various sections of
the Pali canon.

Early Buddhist Generalizations about Living Things and Other Animals

References to other animals in early Buddhist materials reveal that several different
levels of generalization dominated the views of other animals. These are examined
in detail in order to assess whether their use involves some or all of the problems
with coarse overgeneralizations that were described in chapter 5.

In the Pali canon, the broadest generalizations can be seen in the nouns (and their
inflected variations) *satto, jīvo, bhūto,* and *pā.no*. Consideration of how these generic
terms are used, as well as how they are translated, shows that these words (1) are not
used in strictly defined ways but are used rather loosely and (2) do not represent or
present distinctly defined concepts but, rather, overlap in many ways.

Satto

The noun *satto*[2] is found often, and occurs regularly as the lead noun in various strings
of generic terms that are clearly intended to include all types of beings.[3] It is the first
in a list of four descriptive nouns found in the *Dīgha* and *Majjhima*:[4] *sabbe* [all] *sattā;
sabbe pā.nā, sabbe bhūtā, sabbe jīvā*.[5] Translations of this string are:

Horner: "all creatures [*sattā*], all breathing things [*pā.nā*], all beings [*bhūtā*], all living
things [*jīvā*]" (M. II, 406–7)

113

Rhys Davids: "all animals, all creatures (with one, two or more senses), all beings (produced from eggs or in a womb), all souls (in plants)"[6]

Walshe: "all beings, all living things, all creatures, all that lives" (DW 95)

The list can be seen as an attempt to encompass all living things rather than as a true breakdown of the classes of living things. Rhys Davids, citing Buddhaghosa's attempt to explain these terms, notes, "The explanation is very confused, and makes the terms by no means mutually exclusive" (D. I, 71 n. 1) Schmithausen adds, "It is much more probable that originally in these phrases the terms are used as quasi synonyms, with a tendency towards coextensiveness, or at least no stress on specific delimitations" (1991c, 59).

Like all of the generic terms, *satto* is translated variously, sometimes within the space of a few lines.[7] The *Pali-English Dictionary* gives "a living being, creature, a sentient & rational being, person" (VIII, 132). Hare uses "living beings" in his translation of the passage where Gotama mentions that "trade in living beings [*sattā*]" is one of the "five trades [which] ought not to be plied by a lay disciple" (A. III, 153). Schmithausen uses "sentient being" (1991c, 1 n. 7), while Norman,[8] Chalmers,[9] and ~Nā.namoli[10] translate *sattā* as "creatures." *Sattā* can also mean just human beings,[11] but generally the sense is much more generic.

Bhūto

A common noun form related to one of the fundamental forms of the verb "to be" (*bhu*) is *bhūto*, literally "what has become." It appears in the string of generic terms described earlier, where it is variously translated as "beings" (Horner), "beings (produced from eggs or in a womb)" (Rhys Davids), and "creatures" (Walshe). Mrs. Rhys Davids translated the word as both "creatures"[12] and "beings,"[13] while Schmithausen restricts himself to "beings" (1991c, 1 n. 7). T. W. Rhys Davids makes it clear how generic *bhūto* is when he comments that it includes "man, animal, god, ghost, fairy, or what not" ([1881] 1969, 117).

The overlap with *satto* can be seen in Horner's comment that Buddhaghosa explains *bhūtā* by reference to *sattā* (M. I, 8 n. 1), and in Schmithausen's comment that "the use of *bhūtā* as more or less equivalent to *pā.na* and/or *satta* does not seem to be problematic for the Buddhist point of view" (1991c, 2 n. 7). The term, then, is used plastically.[14]

Jīvita.m and Jīvo

Jīvita.m (plural, *jīvitāni*) and *jīvo* (plural, *jīvā*) are other generic terms that appear less often than *sattā* and *bhūtā*. *Jīvita.m* and *jīvo* are related to the verb "to live" and are usually translated, respectively, "life" and "soul or life principle."[15] In the string of generic terms referred to earlier, the translations are:

Horner: "all living things"

Walshe: "all that lives"

Rhys Davids: "all souls (in plants)"

~Nā.namoli and Bodhi: "all souls"[16]

Pā.no

Pā.no in the string referred to earlier is translated:

Horner: "breathing things"

Rhys Davids: "creatures (with one, two or more senses)"

Walshe and ~Nā.namoli and Bodhi: "living things"

Etymologically it is related to the word for "breath" or "breathing," and since it can itself mean "breath" (Warder 1991, 403), it is sometimes translated as "breathers."[17] The generic qualities of the term are evident in the PED definition: "living being, life, creature" (V, 73). It is a central term in the Pali canon in the sense that it occurs often and in extremely important passages, such as the Vinaya passage dealing with the obligations of monks to other living beings: "Whatever monk should intentionally deprive a living thing [*pā.na.m*] of life [*jīvitā*], there is an offence of expiation."[18] The scope is narrowed in the succeeding lines: "*Living thing* [*pā.no*] means: it is called a living thing that is an animal [*tiracchānagatapā.no*]."[19] Although it can clearly function as a first-level generalization (encompassing all living beings, human and otherwise), it also often designates, as here, "other animals only"[20] or merely humans alone.[21] In these uses, its signification is something like "mobile breathers" and does not include plants.[22] Sometimes, however, *pā.nā* even includes plants, as in the *Suttanipāta*.[23]

The plural form *pā.nā* occurs as part of the standard formulation of the common injunctions against the taking of life (known generally as the "First Precept" and discussed generally in chapter 7). The pivotal concept of this precept is *pā.natipātā*, which translates as "destruction of life, murder" (PED IV, 74); "onslaught on creatures" (M. I, 53, 375); "kill living beings" (MNB 125); and simply "kill" (MSBB 31).

Pā.nā also occurs frequently outside the First Precept statements[24] and is commonly translated simply as "living creatures"[25] "life," or "living things."[26] The word occurs as part of the compounds *pā.nabhūtā* and *pā.nabhūtāni*,[27] which mix two generic terms, acting, as do all of these generic terms, as a reference to a broad and diverse group of living things.

Second-Level Generalizations: All Nonhuman Animals

There are other generic terms that are not as broad as the four just considered but that still are so broad as to be the kind of generalizations about other animals which risk the problems discussed in chapter 5. The most common of these is *tiracchāno* and related compounds. The Vinaya passage quoted previously using *tiracchānagatapā.no* makes it clear that *tiracchāno* is a very broad notion, encompassing the great diversity of nonhuman life of which the early Buddhists were keenly aware. Gotama, for example, says, "Brethren, I see not any single group so diverse as the creatures of the animal world."[28]

The term *tiracchāno* is a classic second-level generalization. The *gata* portion of the compound *tiracchānagata* is a past participle form that literally means "gone away, arrived at"; in applied meaning, its sense is "gone in a certain way, i.e., . . . fared, fated, being in or having come into a state or condition" (PED III, 71). *Tiracchānagata* thus means something like "the realm of animals." Importantly, humans are *not* part of this realm but rather part of their own realm. In this compound, then, *tiracchāna* means "all animals other than humans" and is the equivalent to the most common use of "animal" in contemporary English. This can be seen in the translations of inflected forms of *tiracchānagata* as "animal kingdom" by ~Nā.namoli (KhpA. V 171, VI 138, 96, VII 30); "brute creatures" by Mrs. Rhys Davids[29] and Woodward;[30] and "animal world" by Woodward.[31]

In one passage, Gotama breaks down this second-level generalization into third-level generalizations, and in doing so reflects several things, including the classifications of folk taxonomy, the Buddhist penchant for subdivision and classification, and recognition of some of the natural history of different animals:

> There are, monks, animals [*tiracchānagatā*], breathing creatures [*pā.nā*] that are grass eaters. These eat moist and dry grasses, chewing them with their teeth. . . . Horses, cattle, asses, sheep, deer, and whatever other. . . . There are [also] . . . creatures that are dung-eaters. . . . Cocks, swine, dogs, jackals, and whatever other. . . . [There are also creatures that] grow old in the dark and die in the dark [such as] [b]eetles, maggots, earth-worms and whatever other. . . . There are [also] . . . creatures that are born in water, grow old in water, die in water. . . . Fish, turtles, crocodiles, and whatever other. . . . There are [also] . . . creatures that are born in filth, grow old in filth, and die in filth. [The following sentence describes animals living in rotting fish, carcasses and rice, and pools near villages.][32]

The *second*-level generalization aspects of the *tiracchāno* notion can be seen in the fact that, even in the face of this kind of recognition of internal differentiation among other animals, the dominant conceptualization of all other animals was as members of one realm *distinct* from the human realm. *Tiracchāno* literally means "horizontal goer" (PED IV, 137), in the sense of walking parallel to the earth, and this description operates as the generic term designating all nonhuman animals, even if some are not "horizontal goers" (for example, birds or climbing animals). Another example of the second-level generalization use of *tiracchāno* appears in the assertion attributed to Gotama at the beginning of this chapter.

It will be argued later that *tiracchāno* as a generalization is reliant on a derogatory view of all other animals. This feature is evident in certain English translations of compounds that connect the exclusion of members of the human species from this realm *and* a related negative view of the realm. For example, the compound *tiracchānakathā* means, literally, "animal talk."[33] Rhys Davids translates this as "low conversation,"[34] while Walshe translates it as "unedifying conversation" (DW 70). Buddhaghosa's commentary on the *Dīgha* explains the reasoning behind this description, noting that as other animals walk parallel to the earth ("horizontal goer"), so this kind of talk does not lead upward.[35]

There are other words that are sometimes translated as "animal" and are meant to work as second-level generalizations. For example, *pasu*, which usually means "cattle," appears as a generic term in its plural form (*pasavo*) in the passage quoted earlier: "Humankind is a tangle, but the animal is open enough." Generally, however, none of these alternative second-level generalizations is nearly as common as is *tiracchāno* when the referent is all nonhuman animals.

Third-Level Generalizations: Large Groups of Other Animals

At a narrower but still very general level, there are many different words that describe large groups of animals. These are sometimes translated loosely as "animals," but these generalizations are not nearly as encompassing as the first two levels of generalization. An example of this third level of generalization is the word *migo*, which is, in the plural form, sometimes translated as "beasts of the forest."[36] It can signify a very broad reference to other animals, as in *migarājā*, an epithet for the lion that means "king of beasts."[37] But it also means "a deer, antelope, gazelle,"[38] and in a compound form (*sākhāmiga*; literally, "branch beast") is a word for a nonhuman primate.[39] It also occurs in compounds such as *migapakkhīsu*, meaning "beast(s) and birds."[40] This compound designates less than all living things but clearly is "generic" to some extent in that it covers a very broad range of other animals.

Other groupings of animals are "water-dwellers" (*dakāsaya*), "forest-dwellers" (*vanāsayā*), and "those that dwell in holes" (*bilāsayā*).[41] The "footedness" of creatures provides another set of lower-level generalizations: footless (*apadā*), bipeds (*dipadā*), quadrupeds (*catuppadā*), or those of many feet (*bahupadā*).[42] There are also fairly narrow generalizations, clearly not encompassing many animals, but nonetheless generic in at least some sense. Examples include some biologically distinct groups such as "birds" (*pakkhin*; PED V, 4) but also groups that are composed of members not biologically related and actually quite diverse. An example of the latter is *siri.msapā*, "creeping things."[43] This lower-level generic category can be translated more generically as "creeping things," or more specifically, but still somewhat generically, as "reptile" (PED VIII, 170) or as "insects."[44]

These examples do not exhaust the Pali canon's more generic references to other animals, but they do show that many levels of generalization are used to describe the existence and realities of other animals. Since it is clear that there are several levels of generalization and certainly other words in Pali for other animals,[45] that very variety suggests that the tendency to coarse generalizations referred to in chapter 5 as "lumping" was not the only approach used in describing other animals.[46] It will be argued later, however, that at the most fundamental *evaluative* level, Buddhists did not differentiate among other animals.

The Overlap of Buddhism and the Key Animals

Buddhists surely encountered the key animals, but the overlap between Buddhists, on the one hand, and each group of the key animals, on the other hand, differs in significant ways. An extensive overlap occurred between Buddhism and elephants early on because *Elephus maximus* is as native to that area as are humans. Elephants were, then, a feature of life in the Indian subcontinent and Southeast Asia, and a significant part of Indian iconography and lore.[47] The lands into which Buddhism moved in its early stages, Sri Lanka, central Asia, and Southeast Asia, are also home to related subspecies (Haynes 1993, 8). In fact, the natural range of the three subspecies of *Elephus maximus* is almost coextensive with the areas into which Buddhism spread.[48]

The overlap with great apes is much less extensive, though the overlap with gibbons, remotely related "lesser" apes, is very great.[49] Thus, while early Buddhist literature and iconography reflect frequent exposure to many cousins of the great apes, including gibbons and the many species of small, so-called Old World monkeys common in that part of the world, it is difficult to confirm exposure to any of the much larger brained species that constitute the nonhuman great apes.[50]

The overlap of Buddhists with cetaceans has a very different pattern. It can be reconstructed on the principle that the distribution of cetaceans during the development of Buddhism, which began in the fifth century B.C.E.,[51] was most likely to have been somewhat like it was only several hundred years ago, before human intervention disrupted many populations and social groupings of cetaceans. The cetaceans to which Buddhists were exposed would likely have ranged from large whales (coastal humpback whales in the south and occasional sperm whales stranded on their shore) to a dozen or so varieties of much smaller coastal dolphin families and social groupings. In addition, India and China were home to unique species of river dolphins.

The Key Animals in the Jātakas

Elephants are the nonhuman animals most commonly referred to in the *Jātakas*, with references to them in at least 83 of the 547 stories.[52] There are stories in which the Buddha in a former life exists as an elephant,[53] and these, with two exceptions (humans and other primates), outnumber instances in which the Buddha is any other animal. The overwhelming majority of the references to elephants, however, presents them as instruments for human use. In fact, the stories are always told against a background acceptance of captivity and instrumental uses of elephants. Accordingly, they most frequently appear as tools of war,[54] vehicles for transportation,[55] work machines or possessions of ordinary humans,[56] or royal possessions.[57]

These stories suggest that the early Buddhists recognized many aspects of elephants' lives. These include elephants' social nature, natural haunts,[58] trumpeting,[59] antipredator behavior,[60] curiosity,[61] play,[62] fear,[63] and musth (a Hindi word referring to a physiological and psychological state that males come into periodically) and oozing glands.[64] Though there are arguably factual inaccuracies in the pictures given (discussed in chapter 7), a high degree of familiarity with these animals' natural history is undeniable.

In terms of the concepts argued for in chapter 4 (that is, the features of elephants' lives are such as to produce complex individuals with cognizable interests specific to individuals), the *Jātakas* reveal the early Buddhists' recognition that (1) elephants are possessed of interests and can be subjected to harms short of death, (2) elephants prefer freedom to captivity by humans, and (3) elephants suffer when in captivity. Consider, for example, the description of an elephant that has broken away from its trainers (of relevance here is the fact that chapter 7 contains two graphic descriptions of high levels of physical violence involved in the initial domestication of elephants and their subsequent use as domesticated animals):

> And they tied the elephant up fast to a post, and with goads in their hands set about
> training the animal. Unable to bear the pain whilst he was made to do their bidding,
> the elephant broke the post down, put the trainers to flight, and made off to the

Himalayas. . . . [T]he elephant lived in the Himalayas in constant fear of death. A breath of wind sufficed to fill him with fear and to start him off at full speed, shaking his trunk to and fro. And it was with him as though he was still tied to the post to be trained. All happiness of mind and body was gone, he wandered up and down in constant dread. (J. 105/246)

In addition, other negative consequences of captivity were recognized.[65] Some passages in the *Jātakas*, then, reflect the early Buddhists' recognition that the interests of individual elephants were overridden, even eclipsed, in captive situations.

The *Jātakas* also reflect that naming of individual elephants is common in Buddhist texts, as evidenced by the references to *Bhādavatikā*, *Somadatta*, *Nālāgiri*, and *Māta"nga*.[66] *Chaddanta* is also the name of an elephant (J. 514/20), but this is a generic name in the sense that *Chaddanta* is the name of one of the types or clans of elephants specified by the Buddhists.[67]

Apes in the Jātakas

At least thirty-four stories mention primates, although these are surely monkeys more often than great apes, as is evident from the descriptions.[68] While in a significant number of stories the Buddha in a former life is reincarnated as a monkey,[69] and in some even acts valiantly,[70] cleverly,[71] or loyally,[72] the overall view of these animals is quite negative. For example, though the Bodhisattva (capitalized here because it is a reference to the historical Buddha) has intelligence when he is incarnate as a primate,[73] rarely is any other primate that is *not* the Bodhisattva pictured as an individual with any significant abilities. In essence, it is the Bodhisattva who is honored in the stories, usually as the king of many kinds of animals.[74] Since there are many stories of wise kings of different animal kinds, the stories that accord an individual primate the status of king who, as the Buddha in a previous life, acts in intelligent ways arguably do not constitute recognition of the peculiar complexities of primates.

The early Buddhists did recognize the similarity of humans and other primates, as is evident when Gotama as a bird says to a monkey:

> Monkey, in feet and hands and face
> So like the human form,
> Why buildest thou no dwelling-place,
> To hide thee from the storm?

The reply is:

> In feet and hands and face, O bird,
> Though close to man allied,
> Wisdom [pa~n~na], chief boon on him conferred,
> To me has been denied.[75]

This story reflects the important claim that humans have a crucially important ability (*pa~n~na*). *Pa~n~na* is often translated as "wisdom" but it is more akin to what in the West is referred to as propositional knowledge; Griffiths notes that in Pali the word means that which can be put into a statement (contained within a *ti* clause; 1981, 611). Keown argues that it is misunderstood if translated "wisdom," and is, instead, "essentially knowledge of facts," "essentially cognitive" (1992, 80).

The attitude that nonhuman primates (and, in fact, all other nonhuman animals) lack this crucial ability is consistent with the *Jātakas'* generally negative view of nonhuman primates as simple. In fact, one might assert that more than a mere belittling of these evolutionary cousins occurs; what arguably takes place is a dismissal of their possibilities and realities, for they are considered stupid[76] and malicious.[77] In one story, the Bodhisattva says, "You don't know the ways of a mischievous monkey, or you would not praise one who little deserves praise" (J. 175). The Bodhisattva then makes several other comments about the ways of monkeys and their witless nature. The view that other primates have a nature that precludes them from making anything constructive appears when it is asserted that "the proper way of monkeys" (J. 280/266) is to destroy but not to make things. Indeed, capricious men are compared to monkeys.[78]

Dolphins and Whales in the Jātakas

There are many fewer possible references to cetaceans in the *Jatakas*. Stories 537 and 545 appear to have references to cetaceans, and perhaps stories 32 and 270 do as well, since in the latter two stories a fish named Ānanda is chosen as king of fishes (*machā*). The word *machākinnari* is listed in Pali dictionaries as the word for "dolphin."[79] But the argument that there are *any* references to cetaceans relies on indirect evidence, for there are language and vocabulary problems associated with confirming that any text refers to real cetaceans. The circumstance which suggests that *machā*, or at least *mahāmacchā* (great fishes), is possibly at times a cetacean reference is the association of that word with other words that are more likely "cetacean referring" words. An example occurs in the following passage: "Once upon a time there were six monster fishes [*mahāmacchā*] in the ocean. Amongst them were Ananda, Timanda, Ajjhohāra—these three were five hundred leagues in extent—Tītimīti, Mi"ngala, Timirapi"ngala—these were a thousand leagues long—and all of them fed upon the rock-sevala weed."[80]

Timi is "a large fish, a leviathan; a fabulous fish of enormous size" (PED IV, 137). In the Pali canon, this word always occurs in the formula *timi timingala timitimingala*;[81] according to PED, the latter words are variations meaning "greedy or monstrous fisheater, a fabulous fish of enormous size, the largest fish in existence."[82] The plant on which the *Jātaka* text says these creatures feed is seaweed,[83] but this makes it questionable whether the creatures are cetaceans because, while some cetaceans frequent kelp beds, they do not feed on them. It is clear, however, that these are large marine creatures, and some of the cetaceans that early Buddhists would very likely have seen, or perhaps only heard about, are the largest marine creatures. There are, of course, also very large fish in the ocean, such as the whale shark, which are much larger than many of the smaller cetaceans.[84]

One translation mentions "crocodiles are here and porpoises and tortoises," but "porpoises" is a translation of the Pali word *su.msumāra*;[85] this is more properly, or at least far more frequently, translated as "crocodile."[86] Similarly, while the term *makare* can be translated as "monsters of the deep"[87] or even "leviathan" (a term discussed fully in chapter 8), it can be any large marine creature and even a mythical being, for one of the translations is "a mythical fish or sea monster" (PED VI, 135). This is the translation used when a marine creature, maddened by musical sounds, destroys a ship (J. 360/124).

While cetaceans *may* occasionally be referred to in these stories, there is no story that focuses on them. The paucity of references is not too surprising for at least two reasons. First, given that humans typically have a terrestrial bias, cetaceans are not likely to receive too much attention. For example, the animals whose flesh was forbidden to monks were solely terrestrials: humans, elephants, horses, dogs, snakes, lions, tigers, leopards, bears, hyenas (Vin. IV, 350). Flesh of marine creatures, under the generic term *macchama.msa* ("flesh of fish"), was allowed in some circumstances.[88] Second, it is not unusual for terrestrials not to notice marine animals, especially fast-moving and intelligent species that learn to avoid predators.

Other Legend Collections

The *Dhammapada*, which is a short text of 423 verses purporting to be the utterances of Gotama, has been described as "the basic text of Buddhism."[89] Amid the references to various domestic and wild living creatures that occur in thirty different verses, two of the key animals are mentioned. The brief reference in verse 334 to a primate, *vānaro*, is negative; a human who is wanton or thoughtless, going from one thing to another, is described "as ape in forest seeking fruit" (Dpda. 1931, 111). Not all of the references to other animals are as negative as the primate image (for example, the bird images of verses 91–93 are neutral). Indeed, the elephant images discussed in the following have some interesting, though complicated, positive aspects.

Chapter XXIII is entitled *Nāgavaggo*, "The Elephant Chapter," and in this section Gotama uses the elephant as an image of restraint.[90] The first image (v. 320) is that of an elephant enduring the arrows and injuries of human wars, and Gotama uses this as a means of conveying his own endurance of abuse by others. In verse 321, instrumental use of elephants in war is again mentioned, as is the use of elephants as royal transportation. Verse 322 contains a reference that at first appears positive but is, upon reflection, rather negative about elephants on their own. *Wild* elephants (*ku~njarā*, a term used regularly in the Pali canon for elephants) are unfavorably compared to *trained* elephants, in that the latter alone are *varam* ("elect," "noble," "splendid," or "best"; PED VII, 61).

Verse 326 reflects awareness of the realities of the control of captive elephants. Gotama says, "Now I can rule my mind as the mahout controls the elephant with his hooked staff."[91] Arguably, statements attributed to Gotama also reflect recognition of captivity's inevitable abrogation of several different interests of individual elephants. Noteworthy among these is the loss of society and its consequences (v. 324): "[R]oyal elephant in rut-eruption [musth] hard to check, captive he would no morsel eat, mindful he . . . of the wood where (roamed) his peers" (Dpda. 1931, 109). A striking contrast, perhaps unintentional, with this captivity image can be found in Gotama's very positive image of a free individual elephant living in conditions it has chosen for itself: "So one should live alone, do no evil, and be carefree like the elephant Māta"nga roaming alone in the forest" (Dpda. 1990, 115, v. 330).

In The *Buddhava.msa,* or "The Lineage of the Buddha,"[92] both the key animals and other animals generally have receded into the virtually featureless background of being "lumped" together, found only as abstract images designed to convey the importance of special human qualities.[93] Other animals are mentioned more prominently in the *Cariyā-Pi.taka,* or "The Collection of Ways of Conduct" (Law 1938). This work is also relevant in that it is the only work in the Pali canon that deals systematically with the ten perfections, or *pāramitās,* which are the ideals of conduct (*cariyā* means "conduct" or "daily duties"; Law 1949, 13). It is instructive to consider how the working out of these ethical ideals is applied to other animals, which are mentioned in seventeen of the thirty-five stories.

Elephants feature very prominently in three of the stories.[94] Two are part of the chapter dealing with the goal or perfection of giving (*dāna*). In one story, Gotama is, in a previous life, the king Dhana~njaya.[95] Brahmins from another kingdom beg for a special elephant as a remedy for drought and famine. The king reasons that, because of his vow to reach the perfection of giving, he should give a royal elephant to them. When he does so, the ministers of his own country complain that the best elephant has been given away, and they specifically refer to the military benefits Dhana~njaya's kingdom received from this elephant.

This recurring story[96] displays the background assumption that elephants are human property. There is an implicit assumption that an individual elephant can be given as an object for human benefit, *and* that this is ethical and *even* required, though another instrumental use favoring the giver (namely, war benefits) is eliminated. The background and propriety of instrumental use are simply assumed.

The first story of the second chapter is "the story of the pious elephant-king."[97] In the opening verses, Gotama indicates that he is a male elephant supporting his mother in the forest. This is an interesting complex of good and bad natural history, since social cooperation in feeding is common. Importantly, however, the sexes are reversed relative to what occurs in real elephants' lives. The story concludes with the Bodhisattva allowing himself to be captured because this is one way of fulfilling the perfection of morals. As in the previous stories, acceptance of the propriety of instrumental uses involved in captivity lies "behind" this story.[98]

These stories (especially those regarding elephants) are good examples of the Buddhist belief that one should give generously to "others," and that one should not violate moral principles even if it is extremely disadvantageous to do so. But the stories also reveal that it is humans, rather than other animals, who are the beneficiaries of this kind of thinking. It can be asked, why shouldn't the elephant individuals who were given away to other humans benefit from the same principle that the moral agent should not be selfish? One apparent answer for the early Buddhists is that elephants are deemed to be in a different category than are humans.

The Vinaya *Pi.taka*: Connection amid Disconnection

The Vinaya *Pi.taka* is the ancient section of the Pali canon that addresses the life of Buddhist monks. As such, it is the central text for the core group of the tradition.[99] It exemplifies an important tendency or discriminating sense that at times dominates the Pali canon; this tendency is reflected in the fact that definitions and distinctions of kind abound. Particularly relevant to this study are the prescriptions and proscriptions touching on daily life and interaction with other living things, amid which many positive details about various kinds of other animals and many distinctions between kinds of living things are presented.

A simple example occurs in the following attempt to describe various classes of animals using the criterion of "footedness":

> Creature [*pā.no*] means: what is called a human creature [*manussapā.no*]. . . . "Footless" [*apada.m*] means: snakes and fish. . . . "Two footed" [*dvipada.m*] means: men and birds. . . . "Four-footed" [*catuppada.m*] means: elephants, horses, camels, bullocks, assess, cattle. . . . "Many-footed" [*bahupada.m*] means: scorpions, centipedes, live maw-worms.[100]

Such references to variety in living things are complemented by rules providing that actions terminating the life of even the simplest living things should be avoided, a concern found in the disciplinary rule already quoted.[101]

In characteristic Buddhist fashion, the importance of *intention* in determining the level of moral culpability if a life is taken is repeatedly emphasized, and intention includes even culpable negligence: "If he [the monk] is in doubt as to whether [water] contains living things (and) makes use of it, there is an offence of wrong-doing" (Vin. III, 3). Here, a certain "benefit of the doubt" is given to the protection of living things, such that the monk, as the paradigmatic human actor and moral agent, must not casually ignore the fact that his actions affect other forms of life. Life is sacred, and doubt is to be resolved against those who take life.[102]

This general concern for other life is a significant, indeed a radical, message, for in Buddhist lands there were significant dangers to humans from *some* other animals who occupied the same areas as did human beings. This is not to say, of course, that *all* animals, or even any animals at *all* times, posed the kind of threat that called for self-defense. Generally, other animals did not pose lethal threats, and those humans who voluntarily killed other animals as a regular matter—such as butchers, fowlers, hunters, fletchers (arrow makers), and animal tamers (*sārathi*)—are described in the Vinaya as suffering horrible deaths because of these intentional deeds. Horner notes that the Vinaya "posits one of two bourns and uprising for those who make onslaught on creatures . . . either downright woe in hell, or rebirth in the womb of an animal."[103] It is noteworthy that this concern for the sacredness of life was not the exclusive province of the Buddhists, for the Jains and various Brahmin ascetics had similar rules proscribing intentional taking of life.[104]

Distinguishing Humans from Other Life

In the midst of the recurring concerns for other animals and even plants,[105] the Vinaya includes numerous passages that distinguish humans from *all* other animals. It might have been the case that the discontinuity asserted was no more than the obvious discontinuities between biological kinds, which arguably underlie strict prohibitions on sexual intercourse with other animals.[106] But the separation of humans from all other animals, and the suggestion of a decisive discontinuity, is much more radical than mere enshrinement in a taboo or moral rule that limits sexual activity to contact between members of the same species. The assertion of a radical discontinuity is based, instead, on the assumption that *all* creatures outside the human species are *decisively* lower than *all* members of the human species in the universe's fundamental moral order. Even though it is clearly assumed that all life has value, it is *also* assumed that human life is of a qualitatively *better* kind than is the life of any other animal. The lives of other animals, therefore, are lacking in the greater, qualitatively more important significance which humans have by virtue of their mere participation in humanity. Other animals are, thus, all alike in being less than human and can be meaningfully grouped, in relation to humanity, as a single group. This "out group" is the realm of *tiracchānagata*, which is considered one of the "states of woe" (along with the hells and the realm of ghosts).

The Vinaya reflects this discontinuity and the underlying simplification and depreciation of other animals in a number of ways. The penalties provided by the Vinaya reflect the division "humans on one side, all other living things on the other side." Because Buddhists conceived of killing a human as a fundamentally different kind of offense than killing any other animal, the penalties for a monk who intentionally killed a human were the most severe possible (Vin. I, 125–26), while the penalty for an intentional killing of *any* other animal was far less drastic. There are many of these lesser offenses, referred to as *pācittiya*, such as

1. destroying vegetable growth (Vin. II, 227)
2. digging the soil and thereby killing "living beings" (*jīvā*) that "are in the ground"[107]
3. sprinkling water containing living things (*pā.nā*)[108]
4. killing a crow and, more generally, depriving an "animal" (*tiracchānagatapā.no*) of life (*jīvitā*)[109]
5. walking during the raining season and "injuring life [a form of *jīvo*] that is one-facultied and bringing many small creatures [a plural form of *pā.no*] to destruction"[110]

The critically important discontinuity appears in the fact that *intentionally* killing an elephant merits no more punishment than does intentionally killing vegetable growth or earthworms or negligently causing the destruction of life by sprinkling water containing "living things." The penalty for these offenses is the same. Further, in the passage discussing levels of intention when acting so as to deprive a living thing (*pā.na.m*) of life (*jīvita.m*), the difference in penalties again reflects that all other animals are treated as (1) the same and (2) less than humans. For example, if a pit is dug and a human falls in and dies, the offense is of the highest type (a *pārājika*, or defeat) and requires expulsion from the order. If an imaginary *yakkha* or *peta* being is killed, or an "animal in human form" [*tiracchāna-gatamanussaviggaho*], the offense is of a lesser type known as a *thullaccaya* (grave) offense. Yet, if any natural world animal (*tiracchānagato*, that is, an animal other than a human) falls in and is killed, the offense is an even lower level offense requiring only expiation.[111]

The second *pārājika*, or offense requiring expulsion, prohibits "taking" from others what is not given, but only humans are included in the category of "others" who are recognized as rightful owners of things. Gotama declares, "Monks, there is no offense in taking what belongs to animals."[112] Apparently, Gotama believed that only human individuals have that peculiar kind of interest which can be abridged or harmed by a taking, or which the Buddhist moral sense should recognize as important or capable of being overridden or cancelled.[113]

All other animals are seen as lacking a certain crucial level of intention and thus incapable of reaching the level of intention that creates the critical level of responsibility which humans have. For example, no offense is committed if the human actor is in any of various unintentional states, including being "in the animal world."[114]

The Vinaya provides that it is an offense to use "low modes of address," which are defined as calling some other human by the name of an animal, or the general allegation "animal" [*tiracchānagata*].[115]

Discontinuity is also reflected in other proscriptions. The Vinaya provides that *pātimokkha* (monastic rules of personal conduct) should not be recited before a *tiracchāno*, among many other beings, and other animals are listed among those who cannot constitute the Order; indeed, one of the questions to be asked of an entrant to the Order is "Are you a human being?"[116]

Elephants in the Vinaya

Elephants are the first of the "four-footed creatures" mentioned (Vin. I, 87), eating their flesh is banned, and rugs made of their hides are prohibited (Vin. IV, 257). As elsewhere throughout the Pali canon, some instrumental use of elephants, though not as food, is simply assumed to be normal. For example, Gotama says to a woman who has refused to give him a robe, "It is as if, sister, a man giving an elephant should caparison its girth" (Vin. II, 38). The Vinaya also reflects the realities of elephants in Indian society at the time, noting that elephants are an integral part of the army (Vin. II, 375, 379) and handled by a tradition of elephant trainers (Vin. IV, 494).

Some passages in the Vinaya reflect positive attitudes toward elephants, for some individuals are mentioned by name, such as the female Bhaddavatika (Vin. IV, 392) and the bull Nālāgiri.[117] There is some accurate natural history about elephants, including their fondness for water, their eating habits and diet, the process of learning from elders,[118] and their habit of dusting themselves (Vin. V, 273–74). A positive attitude also appears when the Buddha compares his mind with that of the bull elephant that has sought solitude.[119]

Other Great Apes in the Vinaya

Humans are the only great apes who make any clear appearance in the Vinaya, although there are prominent references to some other primates (most likely lesser apes or monkeys). Most of these appear in the sections prohibiting intercourse with nonhuman animals.[120] There are derogatory references to monkeys, including the rules of the *pātimokkha*, which enjoin monks not to climb trees "like monkeys" (Vin. V, 193). Monkeys are more positively treated in the story of the monkey, elephant, and partridge who argue over seniority and memories of the banyan tree. Each undertakes the basic moral precepts and then goes on to be reborn "in a happy bourn, a heaven world."[121]

Cetaceans in the Vinaya

One passage includes a series of images of the ocean, and certain large animals (possibly cetaceans) are called one of the eight strange and wonderful things about the ocean: "the great ocean is the abode of great beings . . . : the *timis*, the *timingalas*, the *timitimingalas*, *asuras*, *nāgas*, *gandhabbas*."[122] This passage occurs in a series of metaphors about the ocean, which is compared to *dhamma*. These beings are said to be the "eighth wonder" of the ocean, and their image is used in describing the four categories of human believers (the stream attainer, the once-returner, the non-returner, and the *arahat*).

The Abhidhamma *Pi.taka* and Mapping Animal Existence

The Abhidhamma *Pi.taka* reflects a preoccupation with a "level of truth" which is different than the "level of truth" that preoccupies many other parts of the Pali canon. The Buddhist tradition has asserted that there are two levels of truth, the first or more conventional level being *sammuti* or *vohāra-sacca*, which is the level of people, other animals, and things existing just as they appear to naïve understanding. The second level, or *paramattha-sacca*—"ultimate truth"—deals with existence as a mere process of physical and mental phenomena within which, or beyond which, no real ego entity nor any abiding substance can ever be found.[123] Since the realities of any individual animal, human or otherwise, and indeed the whole doctrine of karma and rebirth, have their validity only in the realm of conventional truth, it might be expected that references to other animals in general, whether key animals or not, would disappear from this kind of treatise. Yet, while it is true that for vast stretches of the Abhidhamma other animals and even humans are invisible (as occurs, for example, in the sections known as the *Dhatu-Kathā* and the *Pa.t.thāna*), a few sections mention other animals regularly. For example, the short book or portion known as *Designation of Human Types* (*Puggala-Pa~n~natti*) mentions at least seventeen species.[124] The animals mentioned are those integral to life on the Indian subcontinent, and a preponderance of them are domesticated. However, since an atomistic or reductionist approach dominates in the Abhidhamma, references pertaining to nonhuman living things, when they occur, are most characteristically generic.[125]

The Buddha's Mapping of Animal Existence

Buddhist teachings about any animal, whether human or not, generally are premised on at least two assumptions: (1) that Gotama correctly assessed his own existential situation and the corresponding need for cessation of *dukkha* and (2) that Gotama's evaluation applies to all other animals (and, indeed, to all other beings).[126] The second assumption is worth examining, since it is not self-evidently valid.

Dukkha is commonly translated as "suffering," but it is a commonplace that the underlying notion is not adequately conveyed by any single English word. The gist of the notion may more adequately be represented by a string of English words like "unsatisfactoriness, suffering, impermanence." The term is universally considered in the Buddhist tradition to apply not only to all other humans but also to *all* other animals and beings. This assumption that Gotama's mapping of his own existential terrain is not only relevant but, more radically, *conclusive* as to the realities of other, nonhuman animals is related to the pan-Indian assumption of an equivalence between microcosm and macrocosm. Gombrich describes the peculiarly Buddhist version of this assumption:

> [T]he historian can see in the Buddha's teaching an important trace of the brahminical equivalence between microcosm and macrocosm. Where the Brahmin had to discern the true identity between his own soul and the world soul, for the Buddha the emptiness in the centre of man—his "no soul," *nairātmya*—corresponded on the macrocosmic level to the lack of any supreme omniscient god and indeed to the absence of any religious significance in the world as such. (Gombrich 1991a, 12)

The notion that a human who knows himself or herself well knows the possibility for all others, whether human or another animal, shows the peculiar and very anthropocentric aspects of such a belief. That the predicament of one human might be a model by which we can understand the existential situation of *all* other *humans* is one issue, requiring assumptions about the similarity of each human to all others (which are often made by virtue of some kind of essentialism or its equivalent). But assuming that *human* experience provides insights into all other animals' existence is an altogether different kind of claim. If one asks, "Why make *any* assumption about other animals at all?" the answer seems to lie in the Buddhist tradition's acceptance of the pan-Indian notion of the special, paradigmatic status of humans relative to all other animals.

The *Dīgha-Nikāya* and *Majjhima-Nikāya*

The *Dīgha Nikāya*'s thirty-four *suttas* provide many examples of the dominance of generic terms in discussions about other animals, but specific animals are also mentioned often. This is particularly evident in the historically important antisacrifice diatribes that mention the specific victims of the proposed sacrifices such as oxen, goats, fowl, and pigs.[127] There are also good examples of the power of imagery based on certain realities of other animals, as in the discussion of the thirty-two marks of the *Mahā-purisa*, or "Great Man." This being has legs "like an antelope"; the "front half of his body is like a lion's"; "his jaw is as a lion's"; he has a "divine voice like the *karavīka* bird's" (Indian cuckoo); and he has "the eyelashes of a cow."[128]

The only key animals prominently mentioned in the *Dīgha* are elephants. They are mentioned regularly as one of the seven "treasures" or gems (along with the wheel, horse, gem, woman, treasurer, and adviser) that, according to an ancient, pre-Buddhist legend, appeared at the time of a universal emperor.[129] This is a recurring positive reference,[130] although admittedly it is heavily invested with non-elephant reality, in that the "elephant treasure" (*hatthi-ratana*) is "all white . . . flying through the sky" (D. II, 204), decorated with ornaments, and "a fine elephant of noble blood long since well trained."[131] While the image can be said to reflect a kind of respect for natural world elephants, it is only slightly related to elephants in the wild.

Another positive image of elephants is created by a description of Gotama who gazes with "an elephant look."[132] Similarly, Buddhaghosa notes that some of the descriptions of the *Mahā-purisa*, such as the tongue touching the ears, nostrils, and forehead, are related to elephant traits.[133] Somewhat positive as well are the references to elephants in the series of three identical sections known as the *Sīla Vagga*, or "Section Containing the Sīlas" (virtues), which appear in each of the first thirteen *suttas*.[134] This series is a listing of moral duties or virtues and includes explication of what those duties entail. The first duty listed is "putting away the killing of living things" (*pā.nā*; Rhys Davids/Carpenter, I, 4); the explication specifically mentions elephants, though they are not prominently featured but rather included in a long list of domesticated animals that cannot be possessed by monks.[135]

Counterbalancing these positive references are the common incidental references that, though condemning the worst abuses and uses of elephants, nonetheless involve a general acceptance of some instrumental uses of elephants.[136] Additionally, although ownership of elephants by monks is condemned in the recurring morality passages, this is not a condemnation of *lay* ownership of elephants. The similes involving elephants are also mixed.

(1) E'en as an elephant with heat oppressed,
    Hies him to some still pool . . .

(2) E'en as an elephant fretted by hook, dashes unheeding curb and goad aside. . . .
    (D. II, 301, 303)

The first is good natural history, for elephants do suffer from heat and must be kept cool (DW 686 n. 587); the second mentions a goad used in controlling domesticated elephants, which is like the instrument of harm described in chapter 7.

The Majjhima Nikāya

The frequency of this text's consideration of other animals can be seen in the sheer volume of references to the Buddhist concern for "the onslaught on creatures" (Horner's translation), which number in the dozens.[137] These reflect well the Buddhist conviction that treatment of other living beings has ramifications in the moral order. Elephants in particular are the subject of frequent and major references.[138] There are two discourses on "the Simile of the Elephant's Footprint,"[139] but only the first mentions elephants, using the image of "a skilled elephant-tracker" who enters "the elephant forest." Upon seeing a large footprint, the tracker refrains from concluding that it is evidence of a great elephant until further information is obtained; in the end, the process is compared to seeing the Buddha's "four foot-prints."[140] The story contains good natural history, focusing on differences in sizes and differences between males and females, as well as on feeding and traveling habits. It also reflects a developed vocabulary for elephants:

1. Both *nāga* and *hatthi* are used to mean "elephant."
2. *Nāgavaniko* means elephant tracker.
3. The elephant's footprint (*hatthipada.m*) is "long and broad."
4. Elephant forest is *nāgavana.m*.
5. The great bull elephant is *mahā nāgo*.
6. Stunted she-elephants are *vāmanikā*.
7. Normal she-elephants who have tushes (short tusks) are *uccāka.lārikā*.
8. Other she-elephants with stumpy tusks are *uccāka.nerukā*.[141]

The second important parable featuring elephants clearly reflects the background of instrumental use. Gotama tells a story of the use of a royal elephant to capture a wild forest elephant; after tying the wild elephant to the king's elephant, "The king's elephant brings him out into the open. . . . But . . . the forest elephant has this longing, that is to say for the elephant forest." The king tells the elephant tamer, "[T]ame the forest elephant by subduing his forest ways, by subduing his forest memories and aspirations and by subduing his distress, his fretting and fever for the forest, by making him pleased with the villages and by accustoming him to human ways" (M. III, 178).

In response to this royal order to override the elephant's interests, the elephant tamer drives a great post into the ground and ties the elephant to it "by his neck" (M. III, 182). He addresses the elephant with "words as are gentle, pleasing to the ear, affectionate, going to the heart. . . . [T]he forest elephant, on being addressed . . . listens, lends ear and bends his mind to learning" (M. III, 178–79). The tamer makes "the king's elephant" (for this is now the captive forest elephant's designation) do many tasks, some of which are very complicated. One involves a shield tied to the trunk and men with lances, and is obviously military in nature.

The subduing of the forest elephant is compared to the "four applications of mindfulness" (M. III, 182–83). It should be noted that there is at least one limited aspect to this analogy, which is that the process of *self*-discipline is chosen for one's *own* self, and does not involve coercion of another individual against its will. That the text could use this limited analogy *without* mentioning this material difference suggests acceptance of the inferior status of elephants' interests relative to the human interests that are advanced by its captivity. The story concludes with the suggestion, clearly for purpose of analogy to humans, that a king's elephant which dies in old age untrained "is reckoned as one that has died untamed," and similarly with middle-aged and young elephants; the implication is that training of elephants is not harmful to them.[142]

The Term Nāga

Although this term is used regularly for elephants in the Pali Canon, its principal meaning is as a reference to imaginary creatures that are described as physically quite different than elephants: "water lizards with big heads and tails like needles" (J. 304/10). Vogel notes, "It has never been satisfactorily explained in what manner the word [Nāga] came to be applied to an elephant, an animal which bears little resemblance to a snake."[143] Gombrich notes that *nāgas* are cobras, and that the Sanskrit word for cobra is *nāga* (1971, 167). Mrs. Rhys Davids notes in her translation of the *Theragāthā*'s chapter about a monk named *Mahā-nāga*, "The name = great-wondrous being or spirit, applied equally to a serpent, an elephant, a thera [monk], and to a class of fairies" (Tag. 210 n. 1). The beings referred to by the term include, then, humans, cobras, snakes in general, and, mostly, mythological creatures.

The Sa.myutta-Nikāya and A"nguttara-Nikāya

Primates (of a kind other than humans) are mentioned in the Sa.myutta more frequently than in the other sermon collections mentioned thus far, although they are not mentioned often.[144] Generally, the references are in similes or metaphors intended to convey negative messages. One passage compares the normal, untrained, natural mind of humans to "a monkey [makka.to] gambolling in a forest and leaping from branch to branch."[145] A more complex image of primates reminds that the flesh of nonhuman primates was not on the list of proscribed meats, "Now those monkeys who are free from folly and greed, on seeing [the trap] keep far away from it," while those who are "greedy, foolish" get caught and eaten (Sam. V, 127).

Elephants are mentioned an astonishing number of times in this collection, including the normal range of references to instrumental use.[146] There are also many incidental references to elephants, such as the recurring image of the elephant's footprint being large enough to encompass any other footprint (a simile regarding understanding and insight).[147] Knowledge of elephants' natural history also comes through in some references, such as the lack of experience and indiscretion in immature elephants[148] and their natural fear of lions.[149]

Specific Animals Mentioned

In the Sa.myutta, the usual domestic animals are mentioned, but also wild animals such as tortoises, tigresses, mules, myna birds or rice birds or thrushes, dung beetles, vultures, crows, falcons, swans, herons, peacocks, "eke the dappled deer," and flamingos.[150] There are also very positive aspects to the use of some specific animals as images, including Gotama as the "bull of men" and in the traditional image of a lion's posture (sīha-seyya.m).[151]

Awareness of the diversity of life is further evidenced by the number of references to specific kinds of animals throughout the Pali canon. As noted previously, the Puggala-Pa~n~natti mentions at least seventeen different species. In the Suttanipāta, counting conservatively, at least twenty-eight species are mentioned.[152] The variety in the specific kinds of animals mentioned in the Majjhima is also startling. Apart from instrumental use and indirect references such as the lion's roar,[153] references occur as parts of similes to the water snake (which, if wrongly grasped, bites, as does the dhamma if grasped wrongly; M. I, 172), and the crab which young boys smash (as does Gotama his opponent in a debate; M. I, 287). Some rarely mentioned animals, such as crocodiles and fierce fishes or sharks, appear in the Majjhima.[154] In the A"nguttara, the many references to specific kinds of living things range from the largest animals on the earth (the largest cetaceans) to some of the smallest that are visible to our unaided eyes. Bears, hyenas, leopards, lions, tigers, centipedes, scorpions, and snakes are listed as sources of death (A. III, 81), and there is a recurring list of what "creeping things" had to be endured by a monk: flies and mosquitoes (A. II, 122), gadflies and gnats (A. III, 123, 276), and centipedes, scorpions, and snakes (A. III, 219). The names of specific animals are also featured in many place-names appearing in the *Sa.myutta*, such as Elephant Town and Deer Park (where Gotama preached the first sermon after his enlightenment).[155]

The frequency of these references is, arguably, another aspect of Buddhists' important sense of community with all living things. There does not appear to be any one reason for this, although one basis surely is the fundamental assumption that life has an intrinsic value. Keown lists valuing of "karmic life" (that is, life-forms that are traveling through the *karma/sa.msāra* "system") as one of the three basic or foundational goods of Buddhist ethics (along with friendship and knowledge).[156] The second basic good listed by Keown ("friendship," which could well be translated "community") also suggests that a fundamental feature of the Buddhist tradition is a concern for other life-forms. One reason given for this concern is related to the belief in rebirth and the very long periods over which beings cycle through *sa.msāra*; this belief appears in recurring statements that all other beings have at one time been one's own father or mother.[157] There are, accordingly, many powerful injunctions against killing, perhaps the most specific of which is Gotama's view that those humans who carry out such acts will suffer a severe downfall.[158]

The A"nguttara Nikāya

Elephants again are mentioned an astonishing number of times, while primates are not a factor and the brief reference to cetaceans (A. IV, 136) is essentially the same as that which occurs in Vinaya. There are the standard dozens of references to elephants as (1) property, (2) human transportation, (3) part of the battles of an army, (4) a royal possession, and (5) "better if trained for human purposes."[159] More relevant to the early Buddhists' knowledge of elephants' lives are statements attributed to Gotama that accurately portray elephant panic behavior (A. II, 37) and playing in water (A. V, 140–41). Especially relevant are extended similes in which Gotama's words are used to convey the claim that some traits in an elephant are not to be desired, while other traits are.[160]

> Monks, possessed of five things a rajah's elephant is not worthy of a rajah. . . . Take the case, monks, of a rajah's elephant going forth to fight, when he sees a force of elephants, horses, chariots or foot soldiers, he loses heart, falters, stiffens not and cannot go down to battle. . . . And . . . when he smells the smell of the dung and urine of those finely bred rajah's elephants, whose home is the battle ground, and loses heart. . . . [Or] . . . when, pierced by the piercing of arrows, he loses heart. (A. III, 120)

This is merely an image for the listeners, the ultimate point being the possession by monks of traits such that the monk is worthy of offerings. But the background (instrumental use of elephants by humans) is not only present; it is actually promoted by the characterization of what is worthy in an elephant:

> [H]e is a hearer, destroyer, a warder, an endurer and a goer. . . . And how is he a destroyer? . . . the rajah's elephant gone forth to fight, destroys an elephant, destroys the

rider . . . chariot . . . horse . . . foot soldier. . . . And how is he an endurer? . . . He endures the blow of the spear . . . sword . . . arrow . . . axe. (A. III, 121–22)

Such passages and many others make it clear that elephants were deemed important. They were honored with the name *nāgas*, understood to be presences or at least images to which a Buddha could be compared, and held to be able to possess qualities that would make them fit possessions of a human king. But, arguably, elephants were valued not for their individual selves but as tools and property, a peculiar form of apparent "valuing" seen to be without ethical problems. *Beyond* this, however, is the belief that the right to the benefits of instrumental use of elephants is a *reward* for acts in conformity with the moral norm which the Buddhist tradition held to be the key to reality and moral living. This belief is evident in the story of what Gotama says when he sees fishermen who have caught fish and are selling them. He asks the monks if "as a result of such deeds, of that way of living [that is, killing the fish]," the fishermen have then been seen "going about on an elephant or on horseback . . . or living in the abundance of great wealth" (A. III, 216–17). He clearly is condemning the killing of living things and pointing out that there are negative karmic consequences to such acts (the results of karma are known as *vipāka*). The comparison, though, reveals that there were not negative consequences to riding around on a captive elephant. Rather, that is seen as a reward for good acts: "Indeed, monks, he who gloats evilly on creatures being slaughtered . . . shall not go about on elephants." (A. III, 217). The acceptance of a background assumption of the propriety of instrumental use of elephants could not be clearer.

The Interrelation of Instrumental Use, Human Separation, and Deprecation of Other Animals

The *A"nguttara* contains classic expressions of the Buddhist view of the predicament of other animals. They are already in a low state, and they have limited abilities. The missing abilities include the critical *pa~n~na*, "and hence [they] cannot attain liberating insight as long as they are animals."[161] Recall that nonhuman animals, represented by a monkey, were said to be without *pa~n~na* (J. 321), which, as previously suggested, should be carefully translated with reference to its propositional and cognitive nuances. Schmithausen cites a passage from the *Milindapa~nha* in which Nāgasena attributes *manasikāra*, translated by Horner as "attentive consideration" (Miln. I, 43 n. 5), to *some* animals but denies them *pa~n~na*. Note how this is done: "[C]onsideration (*manasikāra*) is one thing, wisdom another. Of these (two) . . . goats, sheep, cows, buffaloes, camels and donkeys have consideration, but they have not wisdom (*pa~n~na*)" (Mil. I, 43). The assumption appears to be that if *these* particular animals don't have *pa~n~na*, then *no other animals* do. This broad conclusion is, arguably, a product of the conceptualization of all other animals as a class sharing fundamental characteristics. Most certainly, however, this is not a conclusion drawn after exhaustive inquiry; it is an assumption used to interpret reality. Animals that are more complex than these domesticated animals (by definition subservient to humans) are disadvantaged by the assumption that these domestic animals' complexities suffice to represent the complexities of the many other kinds of animals.

Further, it is not merely that other animals lack *pa~n~na*. What in fact other animals lack, according to the Buddhist view, is the *ability* to have such insight or level of world awareness, for many humans are without *pa~n~na* but can achieve it through effort. In summary, for the Buddhists generally, the place of other animals is, as Vetter notes, a "vicious circle of evil deeds and bad results," citing the *Majjhima* story analogizing a fool's chance of regaining human status to those of a blind turtle that surfaces once a century, putting its neck through a yoke cast onto the vast ocean.[162] Consider Gotama's description of those lucky enough to return to human status:

> Monks, if some time or other once in a very long while, that fool came to human status (again), he would be born into those families that are low: [There is a description of many low-status jobs]. Moreover, he would be ill-favoured, ugly, dwarfish, sickly, blind or deformed or lame or paralysed, he would be unable to get food or drink, clothes.[163]

Even these human positions which the Buddhists considered the *worst* of human life were thought to be better than the *best* of any other animal's life. The human pauper or outcaste is better off than the elephant king. The moral law somehow, then, sanctioned the preeminence of mere membership in the human species, while membership in any other earthly species, that is, being born in an "animal womb," was a place of punishment.

The *Suttanipāta* and *Udāna* of the *Khuddaka-Nikāya*

Widely understood to be one of the oldest portions of the Pali canon,[164] the *Suttanipāta* contains (1) an abundance of references to other animals (already listed), (2) references that suggest a "background acceptance" of instrumental uses of some other animals,[165] and *also* (3) recurring injunctions not to harm animals.[166] The historically important *Metta Sutta* (vv. 143–52) provides some remarkable, nonspeciesist passages, such as: "Just as a mother would protect with her life her own son, her only son, so one should cultivate an unbounded mind towards all beings, and loving kindness towards all the world" (Sn. 149–50). But even the caring attitude of these passages is laid atop, and thus relies on, the notion that all other animals are fundamentally different from and inferior to all humans.

The Ultimate Separation

Many of the references to specific kinds of living creatures occur in a remarkable passage citing the "divisions in the kinds [*jāti*] of living things."[167] Gotama explains that there is diversity in the many kinds of living things, each of which has a birth that is its distinctive mark. After listing diverse kinds other than humans, Gotama says, "Each after his kind bears / His mark" (M. II, 382). Humans are then differentiated from any other animal in this way:

> [I]n man there is not manifold ["I.e. no variety of marks."[168]]
> Not in the hair or head . . . [long list of physical attributes]
> . . . or thighs, colour or voice,

Is mark that forms his kind as in all else [that is, all other animals].
Nothing unique in men's bodies is found:
The difference in men is nominal.

~Nā.namoli translates the last line, "Distinction among human beings is purely verbal designation" (MNB 801). The commentary explains (per ~Nā.namoli's paraphrase):

> [A]mong [other] animals the diversity in the shape of their bodily parts is determined by their species (*yoni*), but that (species differentiation) is not found in the individual bodies of brahmins and other classes of humans. Such being the case, the distinctions between brahmins, *khattiyas*, etc., is purely a verbal designation; it is spoken of as mere conventional designation. (MNB 1298 n. 902)

The passage is complex, in that it appears to say that humans are not, as are all other animal kinds, characterized by a physical trait (the "mark") that distinguishes the species. But the passage actually asserts the unity of the human species through its argument that "the alleged differences among members of the human species are merely nominal." Humans thus are different from all other animals, but like each other. The common factor is that, though they may not act correctly, they are nonetheless like each other and distinct from all other animals by virtue of having the potential to understand the universe *and* to act correctly, that is, in harmony with the normative in the universe.

It is an implication of the fact that other animals can eventually move out of the *tiracchāno* category that they, too, can, and must, act in conformity with some norm. Indeed, this must be the moral norm of the universe identified by Gotama, for there is no other in Buddhist thinking. But other animals' conformity apparently is only conformity of lower abilities with lower possibilities, the result of which is a move "up" in the hierarchy. What it means for humans to conform to the normative in the universe is much more complicated, requiring an engagement with morality, mindfulness, and *pa~n~na* in ways that are, to the Buddhist mind, totally foreign to any other biologically identifiable being. Thus, here again, the Buddhist sense of continuity is counterbalanced by a much stronger tendency to separate humans from other animals through elevating humans while deprecating other animals. This human–other animal distinction also occurs in the Buddhist scriptures in some very subtle ways, one of which is the favoring of civilization over what might be called "wild nature." As Schmithausen has noted, there is in the Buddhist tradition an attitude "clearly in favor of civilization," and the ideal is areas heavily populated with humans.[169]

The Udāna

This short collection of cryptic verse and prose reflects many different kinds of contact with other animals; in addition, the key animals are mentioned prominently. Cetaceans are referred to in the standard passage about wonders of the ocean,[170] and there is the briefest of allusions to a "mutilated monkey" as a simile for comparative ugliness. Elephants again are the most frequently mentioned key animals, and of note is the story about a senior male elephant (*hatthināga*) that seeks solitude because his grass stalks are eaten by others:

Then that elephant-nāga stepped aside from the herd and approached the root of the auspicious sāla-tree in the Rakkhita jungle thicket at Pārileyyaka, approached the Lord and, having approached, there at whatever spot the Lord stayed, such spot that elephant-nāga rid of grass, and with its trunk provided for the Lord water for drinking and water for washing. (U. 71)

Gotama thinks about how he has been crowded by others, and then the elephant has the same thought. Gotama comments, "This heart of the elephant, of the one with tusks like poles, coincides with the nāga, with the heart of the nāga, in that it delights alone in the grove."[171]

The Psalms of the Early Buddhists

The *Theragāthā* and the *Therīgāthā* of the *Khuddaka-Nikāya*[172] are poems in which the frequent references to other animals, including the key animals specifically, betray a tension between (1) an emphasis on other animals in their natural places and the beauty of that, and (2) a profound acceptance of the background of captivity. The emphasis on "natural surroundings" can be found in many lines, of which the following are examples relevant to the key animals:

> Those upland glades . . .
> Where sound the trumpet-calls of elephants:
> Those are the braes wherein my souls delights.[173]

> I'll to that jungle that I love, the haunt
> Of wanton elephants, the source and means
> Of thrilling zest to each ascetic soul.[174]

> [A] rocky world,
> Haunted by black-faced apes and timid deer . . .
> Those are the highlands of my heart's delight.[175]

Coupled with the common first precept passages protecting life, these suggest a strong appreciation of other life in its natural environment. Such images, however, as common as they are, are dominated by both acceptance of instrumental uses and negative images of other animals. The acceptance of instrumental uses of other animals, and elephants in particular, is reflected in the many militaristic images, of which Mrs. Rhys Davids said, "Metaphors from warfare are less frequent in Buddhist than in Christian literature, and the few contained in this work almost exhaust them."[176] Nonmilitary instrumental use also is heavily reflected, such as the references to the goad or hook used to control elephants.[177]

There are eight passages that refer to nonhuman primates, an unusual number given the few references to apes or monkeys outside the *Jātakas*. Some of these are potentially positive images, such as the passage about natural environments quoted earlier.[178] The others are not positive, however. Some convey the image of nonhuman primates as restless:

> Within the little five-doored hut an ape
> Doth prowl, and round and round from door to door
> He hies, rattling with blows again and again.[179]

Since the other images of primates in the *Theragāthā* are of a heedless animal[180] or a deceptive one,[181] and the final one suggests another instrumental use of other animals as food or material,[182] the view of these animals is, overall, very negative. In the *Theragāthā* (162, v. 436), primates are also briefly mentioned in a belittling manner when Isidasi recalls her past lives, one of which was as an ape. This inferior state was clearly the result of past bad acts, and in her life as an ape she lives only seven days, for "such was the fruit of my lasciviousness" (Tīg. 162, v. 437).

Summary

The many references in the Pali canon to other animals feature both positive aspects, especially the prominent injunctions not to kill, and negative ones, epitomized by a recurring derogatory tone. Chapter 7 attempts to explain the tension between these features by summarizing the tradition's view of other animals.

7

The Buddhist Understanding of Other Animals

Buddhism takes into full account the animal's latent capacity for affection, heroism and self-sacrifice. There is in Buddhism more sense of kinship with the animal world, a more intimate feeling of community with all that lives, than is found in Western religious thought. . . . So in Buddhist texts animals are always treated with great sympathy and understanding.

—Story, *The Place of Animals in Buddhism*

Variations on these themes can be found in the claims of both adherents and scholars. Two practicing Buddhists claim, "The healthy rapport between plants, animals and humans, underlined by boundless compassion, was the basis of Buddhist life." (Ariyaratne and Macy 1992, 80). Similarly, a Buddhist nun says, "Buddhists . . . have never believed humanity superior to the rest of the natural world" (Batchelor 1992, 12). Very much in this vein, the literature of the Royal Society for the Prevention of Cruelty to Animals (RSPCA) states that in Buddhism, "nature is sacred and humans are not more significant than any other living being. . . . Buddhism contrast[s] markedly with Judaism, Islam and Christianity, which are human-centred religions" (RSPCA 1994, 6). Finally, Singer describes the Buddhist tradition as "kinder to animals than our own."[1] Such claims, either that "Buddhism is better" or that "Buddhism is good to animals," are examined in this chapter.

The opening section of this chapter outlines a prima facie case for the claim "the Buddhist tradition is ethically sensitive to other animals." The next four sections address the components of that argument, and the sixth section then states in detail the conclusion that there are extremely significant weaknesses in the prima facie case. The seventh section provides a general characterization of the Buddhist view of other animals, and the final section addresses what it means to characterize this tradition as speciesist.

A Prima Facie Case: Buddhism Is Ethically Sensitive to Other Animals

Before stating the prima facie case, attention is turned to a simple, logical point that underlies the criticism which this chapter will bring to bear on such claims: the Buddhist tradition could be "better" in this area than are other traditions without necessarily being "good for animals." With this caveat in mind, consider the following argument.

There are prominent features of the Buddhist tradition which reveal that Buddhism has an altogether healthier view of other animals than do the Semitic traditions. These features are not merely peripheral points in the tradition but, rather, belong to the core of the tradition and are the foundation of Buddhist morality (*sīla*). Four features that in concert produce an ethically sensitive attitude to other life are (1) Buddhist recognition of the continuity between humans and other animals; (2) the prominence accorded the virtue of compassion as the primary ethical value; (3) the existence of the moral guideline known as the First Precept; and (4) the high profile of other animals in the tradition.

The first point in the prima facie case is Buddhism's keen, recurring sense of the continuity of humans with all other living things. This is expressed in countless ways and is arguably central to the core Buddhist notions of reincarnation, karma, *skandhas*, and *anātman*.[2] This basic continuity is expressed in the reasoning used to support arguments as to why people should be kind to other animals:

> Since all male creatures have at one time been our father, they should be regarded as our father. And since all female creatures have at one time been our mother, they should be regarded as our mother. . . . all living things throughout the six realms can be considered as our father and mother. So to catch and eat any living creatures is surely equivalent to killing our own parents and eating our own body?[3]

A sense of this continuity also appears in the Buddhist view that all living creatures, human and nonhuman alike, are subject to karma, and all must act according to certain standards in order to progress. Humans and nonhumans are, then, subject to the same laws and conditions in this world. Similarly, any individual animal, whether human or nonhuman, is composed of strands or *skandhas*, with no strand in itself or in concert with others constituting an abiding, essential self. Thus, in these several ways, central beliefs in the tradition suggest strongly that Buddhists are fully committed to the view that humans and other animals are in continuity.

The second element in the prima facie case is the prominence given to the virtue of compassion. Indeed, Buddhists see this orientation to the suffering of others as a sine qua non of ethical life. The notion of compassion is given an especially prominent place in the *Mahāyāna* branch of the Buddhist tradition by virtue of its association with the central ideal of a bodhisattva, although concern for living things is conceptually no less central in the *Theravādin* branch.[4] The bodhisattva is known, and even defined, by his or her commitment to the salvation of other beings, and this, it can be argued, entails that the status of other animals has a place of importance in Buddhist morality.

The existence of the First Precept is the third element of the prima facie case, since the Buddhist tradition has from its very beginnings identified a commitment to abstain from the destruction of life as the core of ethical life. Finally, the high profile of stories about animals suggests that they are an important ethical concern in the tradition, and "illustrate the position that animals occupy side by side with men in the Buddhist world-view" (Story 1964, 11).

In summary, this prima facie case is built on core features of the Buddhist tradition and accounts for "Eastern beliefs [being] said to stress harmony of man with nature in contrast to the Western concept of dominance and exploitation."[5]

Problematizing the Basic Continuity Claim

Although the Buddhist tradition does assert a fundamental continuity between humans and other animals, there is an even stronger tendency to assert a basic *discontinuity*. Thus, one can quite properly accept claims that there is an important sense of continuity, expressed by Schmithausen's observation that the tradition displays "a broader sense of a community comprising all living or sentient beings" (1991a, 40) while *at the same time* holding that the tradition also asserts an overriding discontinuity. Consider how continuity and the important accompanying sense of discontinuity are reflected in the notions of reincarnation and karma.

Reincarnation

The belief that the current life of an individual is not his or her only life is characteristic of beliefs from the Indian subcontinent.[6] A representative Buddhist belief is the notion that all sentient creatures are subject to rebirth and redeath, and ancient parts of the Buddhist canon reflect that rebirth was clearly taken as a literal reality.[7] This fact suggests that continuity with other animals was taken as literally true. The many passages suggesting that all other creatures have at some time in the past been one's parents convey the Buddhist sense that rebirth must occur many times before the possibility of release can be achieved. The *Jātaka* stories also exemplify the central place of reincarnation in the Buddhist view of reality, for those stories relate the history of the single most successful individual going through the process of reality, and he is reborn thousands of times.

There is, however, a competing sense of an even *more radical discontinuity* that is an aspect of Buddhist thinking on this subject. Humans are, simply said, the pinnacle of the rebirth-redeath system.[8] This can be shown by reference to several features of the tradition.

First, as noted throughout chapter 6, the status of humans is very special and thus, while connected to "animal status," also very different. Conze notes that the Buddhist approach of exhorting humans to liberation by "de-identifying" with the conditioned world "requires, of course, that we should take a very exalted view of ourselves" (1975, 111). A story from the *Mahāvagga* illustrates what this means for other animals. A serpent wanted to be a priest and was told by the Buddha, "You . . . are a serpent and not capable of growth in this doctrine and Discipline; go you, remain in your state as a serpent, and keep fast-day . . . ; thus shall you gain release from your state as a serpent, and quickly become a human being" (Vin. IV, 110–11). It is true that a few passages suggest that other animals can attain enlightenment without first being reborn into human form,[9] but the overwhelmingly dominant view is that humans alone can gain enlightenment and other animals must come through human status to reach the more exalted planes of existence, let alone attain enlightenment. Indeed, it is the dominant view that men alone can gain enlightenment, although Gross (1993, 34) argues that this is a later developing view, which was not the view of the historical Buddha. Conze (1975, 155) notes further that neither women nor animals were thought to populate many of the idealized heavens—the so-called Pure Lands—of some of the *Mahāyāna* subtraditions.

Second, the belief that humans cannot "regress" to the status of "animal" once humans have reached a relatively low level of spiritual achievement is an ancient assertion in the tradition, and another feature that confirms the powerful sense of discontinuity. One need reach only the first of the four levels of spiritual achievement (in Pali, *sotāpanna*, or "stream-entrant") to assure oneself that one will never again be reborn as a "lower animal."[10]

Finally, the belief that regression to status of being born as a nonhuman animal was the worst of circumstances, especially when contrasted with the elevated sense of what it is to be *any* member of the human species, confirms the belief that there is a radical difference between humans and other animals.

These claims suggest that a belief in a fundamental difference between humans and other animals is at least as central a part of the tradition as is the competing sense of continuity. To be sure, one can argue, as do many scholars such as McDermott, that there is "no permanent or ultimate distinction between beings in these two (human and animal) courses of existence" (1989, 270). Kapleau, an American Zen master, states with regard to the possession of the fundamental Buddha nature, "There is no demarcation between human and animal nature" (1981, 6). Such arguments slightly mislead if not placed alongside observations about the discontinuity that is also a central feature of the tradition's claims. There may not be a "permanent or ultimate" distinction as to "fundamental" nature, but there is a crucially important distinction for the Buddhist mind between current existence as a member of the human species and membership in any other species. As Keown notes,

> A creature's physical nature is, according to Buddhism, a manifestation of its moral status. . . . We might say that human nature is itself the product of moral evolution. No animal, therefore, can be more valuable than a human being, however intelligent the animal or however handicapped the human being. (1995, 48)

The important claims regarding continuity thus should not be allowed to obscure the fundamental discontinuity that is a very pronounced feature of the Buddhist view of nonhuman animals relative to members of the human species.

Karma

In the *Milindapa~nha*, the continuity of all beings, humans and other animals alike, is described in this way: "All beings . . . are heirs of their karma; they are sprung from their karma; their karma is their kinsman; their karma is their refuge; karma allots beings to meanness or greatness."[11] This central notion of karma, described by Gombrich as "Be done by as you did" (1971, 68), was inherited by the Buddhist tradition from its general cultural milieu. Von Glasenapp characterizes karma as a "central dogma," describing it as "the assumption of a moral world order manifesting itself through the cosmos. Its expression is the automatic law of cause and effect implicit in all activities, and thus the conditioning factor for reincarnation" (1970, 48).

This general view can be seen as having positive implications for other animals. Since humans and nonhumans both are completely subject to the same process, continuities among all karmic forms of life are implied (further, such continuities are often explicitly asserted, as in the Abhidamma). Another implication of the karma notion is that other animals, like humans, must live up to a standard of some kind, for each individual must act consistently with the moral order of the universe in order to advance from lower to higher states. Other animals might thereby be seen as "responsible," since, as Bowker points out regarding the karma notion, any individual's position is the result of "an exact moral balance of the universe" (1970, 201). Because this "balance" is both moral and exact, other animals, responsible for their own fate after death, logically must have a chance to act one way versus another. This has positive, even if not thoroughly worked out, implications for the abilities of other animals.

The karma doctrine, however, has the negative implications about other animals already pointed out in chapter 6. Since each being is currently reaping the results of actions in past lives, the fact that a being is now a nonhuman animal, as opposed to its now being a human, suggests that it is at a lower level *by virtue of its own decisions and ways of living in the past*. The karma notion, then, implies that any creature lower in the hierarchy of beings has not acted as well as any being higher in the hierarchy. This reasoning is sometimes taken beyond an explanation of current status to an explanation of current *treatment* by others. For example, "Śāntideva argued, "Since sorrow comes from my own offense, why should I be angry elsewhere? . . . Those who injure me have been prompted by the impulse of my Karma."[12]

In a sense, the karma notion is scaffolding built on the logically prior notion of a hierarchy. As such, it has a built-in prejudice in favor of those creatures that have reached the levels considered "privileged." It can thus operate as a justification for a negative view, and perhaps even harsh treatment, of those who are in a "lower" realm (such as a member of the *tiracchāno* realm). The karma notion, then, at times in subtle ways reinforces the belief that humans are the pinnacle and an altogether *separate* realm in the reincarnation system, at least relative to any other living beings that one can go out and meet in the natural world. The continuity implied by the karma notion is, then, again accompanied by a very pronounced emphasis on the privileged, separate status of membership in the human species.

In summary, since in the tradition humans and other animals are deemed to share the same world and, except for the mental and moral features crucial to enlightenment, the same conditions of existence, it is not surprising that the central notions of the tradition reflect a sense of continuity between humans and other animals. The notions of composite existence and no-self clearly reflect this.[13] What is equally important, however, is that both the reincarnation and karma notions also reflect the important sense of discontinuity between humans and other animals that sustains the tradition's constant, dominant emphasis on the kind of achievement which *mere* membership in the human species is believed to be.

Compassion as the Primary Ethical Value

The virtue of compassion has a primary place in the Buddhist tradition and is expressed in many forms, ranging from the ancient statements of the *Theravādin* canon to the classic *Mahāyāna* vows of the bodhisattva. In the *Theravādin* canon, where Gotama is often described as "kindly, compassionate towards all creatures,"[14] there is no single word or concept of compassion. *Metta* (often translated "love") is described as having the power of counteracting anger and hatred,[15] while *karu.nā* (compassion) and *muditā* (sympathetic joy) counteract, respectively, harmfulness and displeasure (Keown 1992, 75).

The bodhisattva ideal and its elaboration are invariably mentioned when *Mahāyāna* is contrasted with *Theravāda*.[16] Williams (1994, 198) has noted that while there are no ontological absolutes in *Mahāyāna*, compassion is "an ethical absolute" for *Mahāyāna*. Thus, in the *Mahāyāna* texts, statements about compassion abound; one of the most frequently quoted is from the Diamond Sutra: "As many beings as there are in the universe of beings . . . all these must I lead to Nirvana" (cited at Williams 1994, 50).

While such a commitment is only one of many different vows which a bodhisattva is described as taking, it clearly includes all other animals, the ideal thus having great *potential* for ethical sensitivity. It should be added, however, that other animals fare no better in *Mahāyāna* scriptures than they do in *Theravāda* scriptures. Each of the subtraditions regularly demeaned other animals as other animals; the *Mahāyāna*'s views on this subject, then, seem not to have been ameliorated by the extraordinary emphasis on compassion. This very likely stems from the heavy commitment to the characteristic Buddhist assumption about the inferior status of "nonhuman" animals *and* the related negative view of the very existence of other animals *as other animals*. Yet, on the whole, because the bodhisattva ideal need *not* be advanced in ways that cancel interests of other animals (for example, the bodhisattva could simply help other animals be what they most truly are), it, along with *Theravādin* versions of compassion, offers support for the prima facie case.

The First Precept: Equivocations and Nonlethal Harms

The substance of the First Precept is a proscription on, at least, killing. This provision is regularly listed as the first of the five principal moral commitments or "undertakings, expressed in the first person" (Gombrich 1988, 65) known generally as the "Five Precepts." It is often the first part of the Buddhist message announced, as in the story of a victorious warlord who, proclaiming the message of the Buddha to the vanquished kings, begins, "Ye shall slay no living thing" (D. III, 63). Adherence to this precept, along with the other four precepts, was used as a sign of who was, and who was not, a Buddhist. Consider the advice given by monks to the Sri Lankan king Duttagamani in response to his remorse over a great wartime slaughter:

> That deed presents no obstacle on your path to heaven. You caused the deaths of just one and a half people, O king. One had taken the Refuges, the other the Five Precepts as well. The rest were wicked men of wrong views who died like (or: are considered as) beasts.[17]

That the individual who had taken only the Three Refuges (that is, in the Buddha, the *dhamma*, and the *sa.mgha*) *and* not the Five Precepts was counted as only "a half people" shows that the Five Precepts were considered a defining aspect of adherence to the tradition (other features of this passage are discussed later). The centrality of these precepts in Buddhism is also reflected by their status as a critical part of the path to a good rebirth. Indeed, along with generosity and cultivating the mind, they are considered to "summarize the Buddhist path to a good rebirth and ultimately from all rebirth" (Gombrich 1988, 65).

The first four of the Five Precepts also occur repeatedly in one of the oldest parts of the Buddhist scriptures, the opening group of thirteen discourses in the *Dīgha* known as the *Sīlakkhandhavagga*, or *Collection on Moral Practices*.[18] In addition, one of the principal reasons A"soka is such a prominent figure in the tradition is because he famously attempted to integrate the First Precept into his rule. The texts of the edicts that he had posted around his large realm testify again and again to a respect for the lives of other animals.[19]

A proscription on killing for living beings, then, is central to the Buddhist tradition. Indeed, it is in fact one of the few common features across the vast Buddhist tradition and its many sects, strands, and branches.

What Does the First Precept Cover?

It is very difficult to specify all that the First Precept covers, for at least two reasons. First, there are several versions of the First Precept. Whatever the reason for the variation, it makes for some confusion, for, as will be shown later, there are two different thrusts in the First Precept formulations. One thrust surely concerns the *killing* or *murder* of living things, while another seems concerned with *injuries* or *harms* that fall short of murder but, nonetheless, are very serious harms that might be the subject of ethical concern.

Second, because the Five Precepts are negative, there is no guide to what is positively required. Gombrich has noted that since they only "tell one what not to do," "as advice for positive action they are—necessarily—vague" (1988, 88). The existence of such a rule *could* be taken to suggest that the life so respected is important, but it can also be taken to suggest that the act of killing is of a such a nature that the moral agent should avoid it for his or her own good. The latter interpretation does not *require* that the living things protected by the prohibition be considered important in and of themselves.

If the operative insight behind a commitment not to kill other animals is that their lives are valuable, then such a broader concern should manifest itself elsewhere in the tradition. For example, the existence of attitudes suggesting respect for the integrity and freedom of living things might also be deduced from the manner in which nonhuman animals were viewed generally *and* treated in everyday life. If there is Buddhist sanction or even authority for handling and treating nonhuman animals in ways that involve important harms or obvious suffering, the mere occurrence of a prohibition on killing in the Buddhist scriptures will not be conclusive as to the substance of the Buddhist attitude toward other living things.

Some Scriptural Passages and Commentary

Buddhaghosa comments extensively on this undertaking regarding other life. In doing so, he makes it clear that, in his opinion, intentional killing is what is at issue:

In order to make the matter clear we must understand what is meant by the terms *a living being, killing a living being, one who kills a living being,* and *the means of killing a living being.* In everyday language *a living being* means "a creature" (*satta*), but in terms of Buddhist philosophy we mean the "life faculty." What is being said is that in attacking the life faculty the living being is attacked. *Killing a living being* refers to the intent which sets up some means for destroying the life faculty: it is that intention to kill which is *killing a living being,* and *one who kills a living being* as a person who has such an intention.[20]

This seems to make it clear that, at the very least, the First Precept prohibits intentional killing. Yet the First Precept has not been taken as a categorical prohibition, as already noted with reference to the advice given by monks to Duttagāmani. Schmithausen (1991b, 46–47) notes an interpretation by the Korean monk Chajang, who justified much killing of nonhuman animals when it suited human needs.

A Possible Equivocation: Narrowing the Protected Class

The vagueness of this negative undertaking has made it possible to construe rather narrowly who or what the beneficiaries of the First Precept are. In such narrowness lies the *possibility* of many different kinds of exclusivist thinking, including exclusion from basic moral protections solely on the grounds of species membership. Consider the narrowing of protection that is an obvious feature of the monk's advice to Duttagāmani (quoted earlier). That advice was premised on the view that the killing of non-Buddhists presented no obstacle because, of all the creatures slaughtered in the war, only "one and a half people" were really important. The relevant part of the advice is that only some humans mattered because "[t]he rest were wicked men of wrong views" who were considered the equivalent of nonhuman animals.

Such a narrowing of the First Precept cannot itself be considered speciesist, for it excludes many humans, and therefore the exclusion is not drawn along species lines. The monks' advice involves a narrower exclusivism, namely, one based on expression of the "right views." The relevance of the passage to the *possibility* of speciesist thinking is its comparison of humans holding "wrong views" to the generic category "beasts." The passage can be taken to suggest that the death of nonhumans need not merit the king's attention. He is told that he need not heed the death of those who hold the wrong views, for they are (quoting Gombrich's English rendition of the passage) "like (or: are considered as) beasts." This suggests that only a human could matter, and even though some humans do not, because they hold "wrong views," the species membership issue is part of the conceptuality implicit in the comparison of humans holding wrong views to nonmembers of the species ("beasts"). So, although exclusivism based on the human species line is not part of the advice, the underlying conceptuality is present.

Beyond the hint of species-based exclusivist thinking, the monks' advice suggests two other things:

1. The First Precept's general prohibition on killing can be rationalized away by narrowing the class to which it applies; in this case, the advice given makes a mockery of the protection that the First Precept offers to humans.

2. The givers of this advice disrespected nonhumans as a class so fundamentally that it was considered a sufficient explanation of the removal of protection for those humans holding "wrong views" to equate them with "beasts" who, presumably, were understood not to be covered by the prohibition on killing.

Generally, however, the monks' advice is not representative of the Buddhists' understanding of the First Precept, and indeed is a serious abrogation of it. Yet the exclusivist overtones in the advice, particularly in the negative image of all other animals, are *not* uncommon in the Buddhist tradition.

A Possible Objection: What about Injuries Short of Death?

There are other major injuries that, arguably, are *as important as the extinction of life*, for the mere continuation of life cannot be a value in isolation. It is possible to keep some creatures alive but in pain or impoverished conditions, such that the common phrase "they would be better off dead" applies.

Quality of life is consistently a central theme in moral theories, although to be sure this issue is most typically worked out in terms of *human* goods. Nonetheless, moral theorists have very often argued that (1) goods other than continued life and (2) evils short of death can be morally considerable.[21] Thus, human value systems have as a matter of course held many acts to be immoral even if the injury they inflict falls short of destruction of life. In the definition of "moral circle" used in chapter 2, the second and third elements (freedom from captivity and intentional infliction of unnecessary harm) reflect that essential concerns are not tied solely to the issue of continued life. Injuries and harms that impact quality of life, then, can be a basis for fundamental moral concern.

Nonlethal Harms: The Case of Elephants in Captivity

A specific example conveys how significant injuries and harms other than death would have been known in many early and later Buddhist communities. Consider Chadwick's description of contemporary Thais breaking a young wild elephant:

> After tying it to a tree, men would poke and prod and beat it with sticks for days on end . . . until the youngster quit lashing out at its tormentors and stood dazed and exhausted and wholly subdued. Once the animal stopped reacting, the men would start touching it with their hands rather than sticks, and, rather quickly, the animal accepted their dominion and became receptive to their demands. If it did not, it might have wounds inflicted in its neck and salt rubbed into them, then a rattan collar with embedded thorns placed around the neck to make the animal more responsive. (1994, 378)

As noted in chapters 4 and 6, domestication of elephants is a very old tradition in India, and it has always required this kind of domination. The pain and torment do not stop once dominion has been established, for as Chadwick's account shows so graphically, the dominion is maintained by ongoing, intentional infliction of pain:

> Some of the traditional methods of handling elephants in India are extremely harsh. To restrain a newly captured, willful, or musth animal, its leg may be clamped in an

iron hoop with inward-pointing spikes. The harder the animal strains against the device, the deeper the points bite. A long pole, called a *valia kole*, is used to prod the giant in the sensitive ankle and wrist joint while the handler keeps out of reach of the trunk and tusks. Some of these goads have blunt ends and are thrust so as to bruise the small bones that protrude near the surface of the lower foot. Others are actual spears but have a hilt on the blade to limit penetration.

Mahouts usually carry a *cherya kole*, a short rod with a blunt metal end, also used for walloping joints or, when mounted, the top of the skull. Close to the Nepal border, I rode on several occasions behind mahouts who whacked the top of the elephant's head with the dull edge of the large, curved *kukri* daggers men carry in that country. Crueler yet is the technique I saw of incising a wound atop the elephant's head and worrying it with a knife blade to get the animal to respond. One Nepali mahout carried a hammer for pounding on his elephant's head. Whether the weapon was a hammer, knife, or *cherya kole*, the giants would stagger with a loud groan when struck. (1994, 297)

Apart from this intentional infliction of pain and suffering on captive elephants, it is easy enough to recognize that the interests of a large, trainable, intelligent captive are abridged by captivity in that it entails elimination of the native social reality of the captive individual.

Does the First Precept address such obvious harms to elephants? In answering this, the differing statements of the First Precept come into play.

Various Formulations of the First Precept

While most of the statements of the First Precept focus on the extinction of life, some formulations mention harms or injury other than death. Some of these begin by focusing on the destruction of life and only then go on to include a reference to other harms. Consider the second sentence in the following passage: "Putting away the killing of living things, Gotama the recluse holds aloof from the destruction of life. He has laid the cudgel and sword aside, and ashamed of roughness, and full of mercy, he dwells compassionate and kind to all creatures that have life."[22] These sentences are followed by many proscriptions, one of which is "He abstains from accepting elephants, cattle, horses, and mares."[23]

Apart from passages such as this, which begin with a focus on destruction of life as the harm to be avoided and then turn to other harms, there are passages in which "killing" is replaced by "injuring." An example can be found in the A"*nguttara Nikaya*, although the following translation is somewhat awkward.

> Seeing hell's fearfulness, shun wickedness;
> Wise men shun that, firm set in Ariyan Dhamma.
> Not harming aught that breathes where progress is. (A. III, 156)

The portion translated "not harming aught" is *na hi.mse pā.nabhūtāni. Pā.nabhūtāni* is one of the generic terms discussed in chapter 6, and *na* is simply a negative meaning "not." *Hi.mse* (from the verb *hi.msati*, which means "to harm")[24] is related to the classic Indian term *ahi.msa.*[25] This language expresses clearly a concern for harming that is short of the taking of life. Schmithausen points out that in the commentarial literature, *hi.msā* and other words regarding harm "are taken to include, among other things, 1. killing . . . 2. fettering or confining . . . 3. injuring by means of the hands, lumps of earth, sticks, weapons, etc. . . . 4. torturing . . . and even 5. lack of compassion" (1991a, 42 n. 233).

Since (1) tools of oppression are laid aside, (2) harsh treatment is condemned, and (3) possession of some domestic animals, including elephants, is proscribed, such passages suggest that injuries short of death were viewed as harms that have moral dimensions. That the Buddha is described as avoiding these activities is of the utmost significance, since the Buddha's conduct is the ideal of moral behavior. Keown shows that, because the major preceptual codes are "based upon the conduct of Gotama the *Sama.na*" (1992, 31), "the conduct of the ideal *sama.na*[26] . . . becomes the foundation for Buddhist ethics" (29); this leads Keown to comment generally, "To observe the precepts, therefore, is to model one's behaviour on that of the Buddha" (31).

Can one argue, then, that the First Precept amounts to an indictment of the intentional infliction of such harms? Several scholars describe it thus. Chapple says, "The treatment of animals is included in the first Buddhist precept—not to harm or injure living things. . . . In some instances the qualifier 'needlessly' is added to this precept" (1986, 221). He cites wide-ranging sources, several of which are *Mahāyāna* sources, for this proposition. Evaluation of these sources shows that his argument is not strong. First, Chapple argues:

> In the *Bodhisattva-bhumi* discussion of *dana* ("giving," which is the first of the six perfections), there is a proscription on giving anything that "may be used to inflict injury on other living beings," nor is he allowed to give "poisons . . . and nets for the capture of animals."[27]

Arguably, this is an example of a Buddhist recognition of two distinct facts: first, that there are injuries other than death, and, second, that capture and captivity for other animals can involve either pain or deprivations which are harmful and thus injuries. The argument is relevant to the recognition of such injuries, but it does not grapple with either (a) the dominant wording of the First Precept, namely, the focus on killing and not on other harms or (b) the fact that in an overwhelming number of places the Buddhists, including Gotama himself, clearly accepted some instrumental uses of elephants as part of a moral universe. The next three sources that Chapple cites for the proposition that the First Precept is more than an injunction against killing, however, are even less relevant.

Second, the passage Chapple cites from the *Da'sabhūmika Sutra*[28] states merely that one "must not hate any being and cannot kill a living creature even in thought." This does not address the issue of harms short of death.

Third, the *Mahavagga* passage (from the Pali canon) cited by Chapple enjoins monks not to destroy intentionally "the life of any living being down to a worm or an ant"[29] and thus focuses only on the destruction of life.

The fourth example Chapple cites is a *Jātaka* story dealing with an indictment of animal sacrifice.[30] While this story has all of the human-animal continuity elements that come with the Buddhist notions of karma, rebirth, respect for life, and compassion, it does not expressly recognize that injury occurs short of death.

In summary, at least one of Chapple's citations (that from the *Bodhisattva-bhumi*) does directly support the position that nonlethal harms are to be avoided if one wants to follow the First Precept. The general argument, however, that the First Precept can be described as an injunction "not to harm or injure living things," while arguably consistent with the *spirit* of other core insights of the Buddhist tradition (such as compassion and the belief that all life is interconnected and similarly situated in *sa.msāra*), is nonetheless not well supported. Further, the argument does not address many other statements in the Buddhist scriptures that are inconsistent with this claim.

Schmithausen also addresses this issue of killing versus other harms:

> Actually, killing animals is the grossest form of violating their interests, just as in the case of men. Besides, at least in urban and agricultural societies it can in fact be avoided to a considerable extent. The same would hold good for *other kinds of injuring* like hurting or torturing, which, though not explicitly prohibited by the wording of the standard form of the Precept (*pā.nātipātā pa.tivirato hoti*), can hardly be taken to be, on that account, allowed.[31]

This sets out well the tensions in arguing that the First Precept addresses harms other than death. The standard formulations simply are not explicit in condemning nonlethal harms. Schmithausen's concluding comment hints obliquely that the Buddhist tradition has an insight, embodied in the First Precept, that goes beyond a prohibition on killing. In other places, Schmithausen is much more direct in stating the claim that nonlethal injury is covered: "the old Buddhist teaching" was "that animals, as sentient beings, should not be killed *or injured*" (1991a, 11, emphasis added). He notes, "For at least in traditional ('Hinayana') Buddhism, the prohibition to kill *or injure* living beings is categorical" (35, emphasis added). His basis for this claim is, among other things, the "occasional" passages in which the First Precept is framed in terms of injury rather than killing.[32]

It has been suggested earlier that one way to address this issue of whether the First Precept addresses harms short of death is to look at other elements of the Buddhist tradition. If the same insight occurs elsewhere, the generalization of Chapple and Schmithausen (that the First Precept addresses injury short of death) is plausible. If the insight does not occur elsewhere, or there are Buddhist practices or views that are contrary to this interpretation, then Chapple's and Schmithausen's characterizations of the First Precept must be qualified.

It was argued in chapter 6 that the early Buddhists recognized that injuries short of death also constitute harms to, for example, elephants, and that, despite this, there were both acceptance and, at times, promotion of some instrumental uses. Thus, one could argue that the insight regarding harms other than death was not an insight *consistently* played out in the early Buddhist tradition. The coexistence of such contradictory signals calls into question the broad characterizations of the First Precept as "categorically" covering harms short of death. I do not wish to be understood to say that there was no concern for other harms because, as has already been shown, there are, to be sure, instances where that insight is clearly stated. Rather, I am arguing that, if one considers other practices and features of the Buddhist tradition, the better conclusion is that the early Buddhists were extremely inconsistent on this point. In effect, the goods and interests of other animals were so insufficiently recognized that the subsequent tradition failed to follow up the insight that captivity-created harms short of death in *another animal* could be a moral issue on the order of killing that animal. Thus, though the earliest strands of the Buddhist tradition clearly recognized captivity as a harm, the tradition generally fails to resolve the tension between (1) recognition of such harms, evidenced both by various observations about the activity of animals in captivity and by "occasional" expressions of the First Precept which proscribed harms short of killing, and (2) promotion of human interests to the exclusion of the interests of other animals.

Bluntly stated, Buddhists simply coexisted with daily, obvious harms to nonhumans. Therefore, while the First Precept may legitimately be read as a prohibition of *some* intentional harms short of murder, the tradition must *also* be read as allowing *other harms* to exist. At times, some statements even seem to suggest that it is *moral* to allow such harms to exist (for example, the harms that inevitably occur from acceptance of the captivity that allows humans to ride and even own elephants as a reward for compliance with the moral order). In the end, then, some elements of the early Buddhist tradition do not promote noninjury generally. Rather, some nonlethal injuries were accepted, perhaps because they were only inconsistently recognized, or perhaps because *human* interests were so prized that the early Buddhists accepted the exclusion of the interests of other animals because such exclusions were consistent with the elevated view of humans.

The factors that permitted this odd circumstance—clear recognition of the immorality of killing, attended by a failure to address many recognized harms short of death—are (1) the vagueness of the First Precept as a negative injunction, (2) the standard language of the First Precept which focused on *killing*, and (3) an inadequate understanding of other animals occasioned by the preoccupation of Buddhists with humans. This resulted in the First Precept often being interpreted as *merely* a prohibition of killing and thus, as suggested by both explicit and tacit approval of the treatment of captive elephants, narrowly construed and practiced.

The High Profile of Other Animals in the Tradition

Other animals are mentioned frequently enough in the Pali canon to justify a claim that they have a high profile in the Buddhist tradition. This is also true of extracanonical writings in the *Theravādin* tradition (such as the commentaries) and of the *Mahāyāna* texts generally. Ishigami notes more broadly, "Throughout the writings, sculptures and paintings of Buddhism, instances in which references are made to animals are truly innumerable" (1965, 667). Schmithausen argues that the stories of the previous incarnations of the historical Buddha (described in chapter 6 and referred to here as the "animal stories") are characterized by a view of other animals that is more positive than the pro-civilization and "one-sidedly depreciative view of animals and wild nature" that dominates other, more central Buddhist texts.

> [I]n most of these stories animals . . . are accorded value in their own right, and not depreciated wholesale as miserable and ill-mannered or evil creatures, and in view of the popularity of texts like the Jatakas this has probably exercised considerable influ-

ence on people's attitude towards animals in at least some Buddhist countries. (Schmithausen 1991a, 20–21)

The position taken here is that, while the animal stories do provide a basis for positive views of other animals and *some* information about the lives of those animals, ultimately they provide almost no really valuable and accurate information about the actual complexity and subtleties of the lives of the different kinds of animals mentioned in them. Of course, to assert the limited value of the animal stories *in this regard* is not to question their great significance in other respects. As von Glasenapp notes, "[The *Jātakas*] serve a dual purpose: they have to demonstrate the presence of a moral order in the world, and they specially stress that even the greatest of all living beings did not possess his venerable position inherently, but like every man worked himself to it in the course of aeons" (1970, 69). Since the stories are, in essence, human tales about human foibles to be heard by human listeners,[33] the references to other animals are secondary and even incidental, a feature that results in them having shortcomings as tools for conveying accurate information. They are limited, then, as a source of insights into (1) the realities of other animals' lives, (2) the possible ethical significance of those realities, or (3) any non-human-centered understanding of other animals.

What the Animal Stories Do Tell Us

Although providing limited information about the animals themselves, the animal stories do provide information about the Buddhist view of nonhumans. As a collection, they confirm the following:

1. Some nonhuman animals clearly were noticed and were considered an integral part of the same world as humans.
2. The early Buddhists evaluated the status and abilities of any nonhuman as always fundamentally inferior to that of any human.

That mere membership in the human species was so valued is evident not only by virtue of the direct statements in this regard presented in chapter 6 but perhaps even more significantly in the recurring acceptance of captivity and other instrumental uses. Arguably, the intentionally inflicted harms of captivity are, when identified, not consistent with core Buddhist values such as the importance of intention and the connectedness and importance of all karmic life forms. One can easily distinguish the instances and kinds of suffering that captivity creates from the suffering that the lives of all other animals would, in the Buddhist view, necessarily entail, since the suffering of captivity is intentionally imposed on other animals by humans for human purposes. This is a qualitatively different aspect of suffering in the world, since it need not exist and only human choice makes it exist. The moral agent's choice to inflict it, then, has a special moral dimension that is not associated with the more general kind of suffering that is not a matter of choice. To use Schmithausen's uncompromising language, "[A]nimals are enslaved by man: used as vehicles, beaten and exploited" (1991a, 15). The absence of a challenge to this additional, intentionally created suffering, especially as manifested in the obvious and inevitably harsh realities of captivity, suggests how dominant the attitude that all nonhumans are inferior to humans is in the tradition.

3. Nonhuman animals were not noticed very accurately.

The animal stories are not a good source of accurate factual information about the animals mentioned. The stories, of course, do not make this claim, but the arguments noted earlier (namely, that the stories opened listeners up to the animals) must be qualified by the observation that the portrayal of the animals is not accurate. This problem goes well beyond the trivial examples of inadequate natural history. The most significant example is both a surprising and revealing error. What is arguably the most important aspect of elephants' existence, namely, the most characteristic feature of family and social grouping, is completely misrepresented, and perhaps even misunderstood altogether. In summary, the Buddhist storytellers simply got the realities of elephant social structure wrong. The misrepresented fact is the dominance of males in the elephant groups, for, as noted in chapter 4, elephants are *eminently* matriarchal in their social groupings. This obvious reality of elephants is missing from the Buddhist tales, and while this is perhaps the product of patriarchal values,[34] it is so wrong as to positively mislead because the feature is as central to the lives of elephants as any. That the early Buddhists always portray the elephant groups as being led by a male, usually a king, is especially strange, since not only are the group leaders always female but Indian female elephants are easier to differentiate from Indian males than are African females from African males because Indian females typically have no tusks. In other words, matriarchy is an especially obvious phenomenon among Indian elephants.

One reasonable conclusion is that, because references in the animal tales to elephants are not very helpful in understanding natural world elephants, they *cannot* teach listeners well about them.

Inaccurate Information and Anthropomorphization

Because the extreme anthropomorphization so characteristic of the animal stories makes it only too obvious that the traits of the animals portrayed are not those of the natural world counterparts, the inaccuracies are generally rather harmless. Further, even though the stories are religious texts that were not written to convey facts about elephants, or at least that was not their primary purpose, they do convey some facts in the occasionally accurate portrayals of some of elephant natural history. Additionally, as Ishigami mentions, reference to other animals made for "easy comprehension of the meaning of the teachings" (1965, 668–69), and this suggests indirectly that use of other animals as storytelling devices reflects how ingrained the notion of a connection to other animals was.

But the appearance of animals in the *Jātakas* and other legend collections in the Buddhist scriptures hardly demonstrates conclusively that the Buddhist tradition is "very open" to other animals. Such openness may or may not be the case, but the animal stories as a group provide a questionable basis for that conclusion.

Summary of Problems with the Prima Facie Case

There are shortcomings in some of the principal points supporting the prima facie case. This is so not only because the early Buddhists did not know some animals well but more significantly because their acceptance of some harmful instrumental uses contradicts the claims (1) that other animals are, or were, "always treated with great sympathy and understanding" or (2) that "Buddhists . . . have never believed humanity superior to the rest of the natural world." Simply stated, what is said in the texts, what is done in Buddhist societies, and the general tenor of the Buddhist depreciation of all nonhuman animals are inconsistent with these claims.

Thus, there are complications with bald assertions such as "the Buddhist tradition is ethically sensitive to other animals." This claim is true in some important senses, particularly in light of the central concern about not killing living beings intentionally. This alone justifies some of the "Buddhism is better" comments, such as those by Keown regarding the tradition's "wider moral horizon," Passmore's claim that the tradition has resources not found in the "West" for an extension of ethics, and Singer's claim that this tradition is "kinder to animals than our own." As Keown notes, "[Buddhism] treats [life-forms] as moral beings simply by virtue of what they are, namely, living creatures. The evidence from Buddhist sources suggests that living beings are worthy of respect simply by virtue of the inherent dignity which is inalienably theirs as living beings. In other words, for Buddhism, life has intrinsic worth" (1995, 36–37).

This is a profound emphasis, but it is *not* conclusive on the issue of the nature of the exclusivist attitudes that arise when interests conflict and the interests of other animals are subordinated to those of humans as a species. Recognition that other animals have some moral significance can coexist with exclusivism, in that (1) *some* level of concern can be accorded to other animals when their interests are not in conflict with the interests of humans, or (2) as in early Buddhism, lethal harms can be prohibited even as some nonlethal harms are tolerated and even subtly promoted. For example, Ruegg (1980, 234) argues that vegetarianism is a logical corollary of *ahi.msā*, but that vegetarianism is not practiced or much discussed in the Buddhist tradition. Since, as Ruegg notes, "*non-harming* is universally acclaimed as a principle of primary importance for Buddhist thought and practice" (234), the lack of emphasis on the "logical corollaries" of this practice (in Ruegg's analysis, vegetarianism, and, in this study's analysis, nonacceptance of instrumental uses that entail the intentional infliction of suffering) is revealing. It suggests that the claim that the Buddhist tradition is *fully* ethically sensitive to other animals' interests is unjustifiable because it obscures some central aspects of the Buddhist conception and treatment of other animals.

It can be argued, then, that while some features of the tradition, such as the insights into continuity and the primacy of the ethical, do moderate the overtly exclusivist and anthropocentric features of the tradition, the end product is nonetheless a dismissal of other animals in some very important senses.

The Buddhist Tradition's General Understanding of Other Animals

If the prima facie case is not correct, what is the place in the Buddhist tradition of the individuals from other species that exist in the world at this present moment? In particular, what is the place of other complex individuals, such as elephants and nonhuman great apes in Africa and Southeast Asia, as well as in zoos and experimental labs, or of the cetaceans off any coast away from terrestrial humans? Clearly, the tradition expresses concern for the key animals as fellow voyagers in *sa.msāra*. It can be said, then, that they have a place of some importance. This is, however, the *same* status that all other animals have in the tradition and is, of course, subject to the conclusion of this analysis that overall the tradition is negative on nonhuman animals' existence, moral standing, and abilities relative to those of members of the human species.

To be sure, any attempt to say something general about the Buddhist tradition is complicated by the extraordinary internal diversity of the tradition. As Gombrich has noted, "About *all* Buddhists few valid generalizations are possible" (1988, 2, emphasis in the original). On the complex and difficult issue of "other animals," however, it can be forcefully argued that there is unanimity of a kind on the significance that real, live individuals of other species have in the minds of Buddhists.

The Deprecation of Other Animals

It has been suggested that the texts considered feature a constant disparagement or belittling of any biological being outside the humans species, and that this deprecation is closely allied with the coarse grouping of all other animals in the *tiracchāno* category. In summary, these nonhuman animals are conceived of as follows:

1. There is a negative view of the very fact of birth as any kind of animal other than a human animal.
2. The product of bad conduct is existence as an(other) animal. Importantly, it is not only nonhumans who are deprecated but also those humans who are non-"standard," that is, impoverished, ugly, or handicapped in some way. Here the rebirth system assumed to exist is arguably *not* speciesist, although there is that overtone given the great divide between humans and all other animals and the implication that even the ugly, deformed human is better than the best of other animals.
3. There is, then, in the Buddhist view a kind of culpability in (other) animality.
4. All other animals are simple and easily understood by humans. Such "lumping" potentially limits adherents' ability to notice the realities of the more complex nonhuman animals.
5. Other animals are pests or not rightfully in competition with elevated humans. The images here range from the view of other competing living things as pests—such as "flies, mosquitoes . . . and creeping things" to be endured by a monk[35]—to the view that what other animals do is "anti-human," "inhuman," and low by human standards, such as the recurring image of dead human bodies being eaten by crows, ravens, vultures, dogs, jackals, and other "vermin."[36]

All of these factors lead to descriptions of other animals that are fundamentally negative. This brings us back to the Buddhist view that, in a most fundamental way, (other) animals' existence must be unhappy, for the "bourn" or realm composed of all nonhuman animals is one of the places of woe to the Buddhist mind. Humans are the paradigm, or, better said, membership in the human species is one paradigm, and once a being has attained membership in the human species, there is an additional paradigm set out by Gotama's teachings. The status of members of other species is set out by Gotama's evaluation—"so many are the anguishes of animal birth" (M. III, 213)—which was considered by the early Buddhists, and indeed the whole tradition, to be a definitive description of other animals' realities.

In summary, then, the tradition separates humans from all other animals as a result of claims about the paradigmatic nature of human existence relative to that of other animals. The underlying claims draw great strength from the Buddhist tradition's heavy investment in hierarchical thinking. Because of the dominant understanding of the relative value of existence as a human versus existence as any other kind of animality, the tradition has never emphasized seeing other animals in terms of *their* realities. Rather, the dominant claims about other animals tend to the ideological, in that there is a prejudgment about possibilities and an underdetermination of views by factual realities. Further, the negative view of other animals *as other animals* results in systematic depreciation, and at times dismissal, of the diverse realities of the many different kinds of other animals. These views were adopted as a whole and applied to all nonhuman animals. They have been maintained *regardless of the course of events* and without regard for careful investigations of the day-to-day lives of the more complicated of other animals such as members of the key species. In an important sense, then, the Buddhist tradition has not enhanced its adherents' abilities to understand animals beyond the species line.

The Argument That the Buddhist Tradition Is Speciesist

Chapter 2 proposed this definition of speciesism: "Speciesism is the inclusion of all human animals within, and the exclusion of all other animals from, the moral circle." Any argument that the Buddhist tradition has excluded other animals from what has been narrowly defined as the moral circle must rely primarily on the tradition's acceptance of harmful instrumental uses of other animals. These are relevant because they involve intentional deprivations and the infliction of pain, psychological as well as physical, in order to create and maintain subservience. In particular, the general circumstances of instrumental use of elephants, especially the necessary denial of their social realities and the eclipse of important and formative associations between family members and their matriarchs, result in individual elephants' essential concerns being overridden, thus denying them fundamental moral protections. Note that it is the second and third essential concerns (freedom from captivity and intentional infliction of unnecessary pain) that are eclipsed, not the first essential concern (the right to life).

If the argument made here regarding the Buddhist tradition's views of instrumental uses of elephants is correct, this is *suggestive* of, but not conclusive as to, the existence of the pervasive species-based exclusions challenged by the anti-speciesism critique. The definition requires exclusion of *all* other animals from the moral circle, not just elephants. The existence of a "no unnecessary lethal harms" rule (that is, the First Precept construed as certainly covering intentional but unnecessary kill-ing) goes a long way toward minimizing the eclipse of many other animals' essential concerns, for many other animals cannot be held captive (the second essential con-cern) or are not sufficiently near humans to be otherwise harmed (the third essen-tial concern).

It is arguably the case, however, that the early Buddhists accepted humans' domi-nance of other animals when humans could, for their own benefit, effect such. This, in combination with the emphasis on the significance of membership in the human species, makes the description "inclusion of all human animals within, and the exclu-sion of all other animals from, the moral circle" a potentially valuable tool in the following ways. First, it can help in identifying features of the early Buddhists' im-plicit and sometimes explicit sanctioning of the harmful treatment of nonhuman animals. Second, it can be particularly helpful in ferreting out principal features of the dominant Buddhist view of the relation of humans to the rest of the animal king-dom, including the most complicated of the biological individuals outside the humans species.

PART IV

IS THERE SPECIESISM
IN CHRISTIANITY?

The early Christian tradition paid some attention to other animals, but it will be argued here that the focus and concern of what now might be called "the mainline tradition" were confined primarily to very broad generalizations employed most characteristically for the purpose of contrasting an idealized version of human life with a caricature of any biological life outside the human species. The biological realities that were obviously shared with other animals were thoroughly subordinated to those features of human mental and social life believed to be qualitatively, even ontologically, unlike any features of the lives of any other animals. The operative principle of differentiation thus became the "humans–nonhuman animals" division discussed in part II. It will be argued here that the early Christian views, like those of the early Buddhists, exemplify the fact that how one construes the moral significance of other animals has a great deal to do with the story one accepts of their relationship to oneself. Chapter 8 assesses references to the key and other animals that played a part in the formative stages of the tradition. Chapter 9 concludes with general discussions of dominion, sacrifice, and whether the Christian tradition narrowed the attitudes toward other animals that it inherited generally from the Hebrew tradition.

8

Other Animals in the Christian Tradition

And God created the great whales . . . and God saw that it was good.

—Genesis 1:21

The opening section of this chapter provides information on the "overlap" of the Christian tradition with the key animals. The next section engages Old Testament views of nonhuman animals, for without an understanding of this foundation it is not possible to comprehend the Christian tradition's assessment of the key and other animals generally. The third section addresses what can be said of the New Testament views of other animals, while the fourth section assesses pre-Augustine views. The pivotal views of Augustine are the subject of the concluding section.

The Overlap

The first creation account in Genesis mentions that on the fifth day "living creatures" were created (Genesis 1:20–21 RSV). The two Hebrew words rendered by RSV as "living creatures" are *nephesh .hayyâ*.[1] A literal translation of these might be "swarmers having a soul of life" (Green 1976, 1) or "swarming things, living creatures" (IB I, 478). This combination of words is clearly a reference to animal life.[2] Immediately following the generic reference to "living creatures" are more specific references, first birds (*'ûph*) and then *hattannîmim* (Green 1976, 1), a combination of definite article and plural noun translated in KJV as "the whales"; literally its meaning is closer to something like "the sea-monsters" or "sea animals."[3] When this passage was translated into Greek, the translators of LXX chose the word *kētē*,[4] while Jerome in the Vulgate used *cete* (Vul I, 5). The Greek and Latin words are the roots of the modern English term "cetacean," which appeared in English usage in the mid–nineteenth century.[5]

While it is not clear that *tannîmim* is in this passage a reference to natural world cetaceans (this is discussed in the next section), it is clear that natural world cetaceans did exist near the areas where the compilers of the Genesis accounts lived. There is limited information in Aristotle's treatises about different kinds of cetaceans, and the contemporary distribution of cetaceans in the area indicates that perhaps as many as sixteen or more species of cetaceans could have been known.[6] There were, then, many kinds of cetaceans along the coasts, in the rivers, and in the deeper waters off the land masses occupied by those who put together the Genesis accounts and other materials constituting the Hebrew Bible. Similarly, the earliest

Christians lived in a world thoroughly familiar with the existence of cetaceans. For example, the coins of Carthage, Syracuse, and imperial Rome displayed dolphins, and a dolphin figure often appears as a Christian symbol of the fish (Hall 1996, 19).

Overlap with Other Great Apes

The overlap of Christians with the other key animals is of a different quality altogether. The native ranges of the nonhuman great apes are far removed from (1) the Mediterranean basin and the Middle Eastern cradle of the tradition and (2) the dominant trade routes among the peoples of the first millennium B.C.E. Thus, even though adherents of the Christian tradition at many later times and places overlapped with the other great apes, the overlap was, both geographically and historically, delayed and very irregular. As for other, smaller-brained primates, McDermott (1938) and Janson (1952) provide many examples of the frequent references in art, literature, and lore from eastern and western Mediterranean areas. Aristotle in particular mentions other primates prominently, aware of the difference between apes and monkeys.[7] His reference to baboons as bigger than apes (1984, 502a19–20) mildly suggests that he was not familiar with the nonhuman great apes, since each of them is, on the average, noticeably larger than baboons. Generally, however, it is not possible to determine if the apes Aristotle mentioned were nonhuman great apes or members of the lesser apes.

Overlap with Elephants

Direct references to elephants in the tradition's scriptures are confined to the twenty or so occurrences in the Maccabees books. These were written about the mid–second century B.C.E. and reflect the military realities of the post-Alexander world. LXX and the Vulgate use cognates for "elephant," as these animals were well known, valuable commodities even before Alexander's wide-ranging conquests, although they probably no longer occurred naturally in the Greek world at the time of the early extant references.[8]

As Christianity expanded, it often spread into areas where humans had extinguished local elephant populations (such as Asia Minor and more recently North Africa, where elephants disappeared in the second century C.E.; Chadwick 1994, 32). Thus, the elephants that existed in or near Christian societies were, at least until expansion outside the Mediterranean basin, imported captives rather than naturally occurring inhabitants in normal social groupings. Elephants have, nonetheless, had a high profile in the tradition, as is evidenced by their appearance in seminal texts like the *Physiologus* (discussed later) and the subsequent iconographic tradition.[9]

The Starting Point: Old Testament Views of Other Animals

One source suggests that a cetacean is referred to in one of the Old Testament passages: "In Psalm 104:26 Leviathan's character is different: he is . . . probably the dolphin" (*New World Dictionary-Concordance* 1970, 369). A similar comment was made by B. D. Erdmans in 1939 regarding a reference to "Leviathan" in Job 41:1.[10] Although it will be suggested in this section that there appear to be no references in the Hebrew Bible providing any helpful details of what was known about the more complex animals outside the humans species, it remains the case that Old Testament translations, beginning with LXX and later the Vulgate, and concluding with the influential English versions cited in the following, do include words that, on their face, are often taken by ordinary readers as references to the key animals. Thus, even the references referred to here as mythological are not irrelevant to the development of Christians' views of the key animals. Day notes that the circumstances of description suggest that the authors did think the creatures actually existed,[11] hints that no doubt reinforced later interpretations that the referents were natural world creatures.

Given these circumstances and complications, it will be helpful to keep in mind these distinguishable issues: (1) whether the author(s) believed the referent was real (in which case we might be able to glean information about attitudes toward other animals from the original textual references); (2) whether the referent was in fact a natural world animal; and (3) whether later adherents, relying on subsequent translations, thought the references had purchase on the natural world.

Attention is first focused on passages containing words that *could* be references to the key animals in the Old Testament. This will provide some context for assessing the kinds of problems that arise when trying to identify what might have been thought about the more complex animals outside the human species. Attention is then turned to the generalizations that reflect Hebrew Bible/Old Testament attitudes toward nonhuman animals.

Possible Cetacean References

The historically important Genesis 1 account of Creation, which became for Christians "a primary means for revealing and defending basic attitudes and values" (Pagels 1988, xix), reads in the influential KJV as if cetaceans were the first animals created: "And God created the great whales, and every living creature that moveth . . . and God saw that *it was good*" (IB I, 480, emphasis in the original). In 1611, when the KJV was published, the word "whale" was used to refer to the largest of the cetaceans. The word had already been in common use for hundreds of years as a means of specifying the large cetacea, which were hunted, feared, and poorly known.[12] There is some plausibility in the KJV's translation of *tannînim* as "whales," for, as noted earlier, the LXX and Vulgate translations of the Hebrew use cognates for the late developing English word "cetacean." But the Hebrew reference is not specific, and since it, together with the plural form of the adjective *gādhôl*, literally means "the great sea-monsters" (Green 1976, 1), *tannînim* could be taken to refer to other creatures in the sea (some of which, unlike cetaceans, prey upon humans and are fearsome in the extreme).

Day, in his thorough analysis of the biblical imagery of "God's conflict with the dragon and the sea,"[13] concludes that, generally, such references are mythological (his argument is, in part, stated in the following).[14] It is not, however, universally agreed that *tannînim* in Genesis 1:21 is a mythological reference. S. Parker argues that while some uses of the word may involve mythological allusion (he gives Ezekiel 32:2 as an example), "there is certainly [no mythological reference] when the words *tannin* and *leviathan* are used to refer to the monsters of the deep created by God (Gen 1:21 . . .), summoned to praise God, and beyond human capture."[15]

The context in which *tannînim* occurs in Genesis 1 supports the claim that the reference is a mythological use of language, for cosmic themes abound in the passage. Murray, on the other hand, notes that the passage avoids the "faintest trace of personification" (1992, 1), a feature of many of the other references to be discussed later. Day agrees that this particular passage is different than other references, noting that there was an "anti-mythological tendency which led to the substitution of 'great sea monsters' in Genesis 1:21 for the more mythological term Leviathan of the parallel passage in Psalm 104:26" (1985, 74; see also 55). Generally, however, the style of discourse in this passage of the Old Testament suggests that, even if some specific animal types (birds, for example) are mentioned, these opening passages are meant to speak poetically rather than specifically and referentially. Translators of this passage into English have generally honored the nonspecific quality of *tannînim* as a referent, as RSV, NRSV, JB, and NEB use some variant of "sea monster."

Forms of the word *tannînim* occur elsewhere in the Hebrew Bible. For example, the singular form (*tannîn*) occurs in Job 7:12 in the first cycle of Job's dialogues with friends (Green 1976, 446). The verse in the RSV is "Am I the sea, or a sea monster, that thou settest a guard over me?" The word itself, and whatever its reference, is not a major feature of the story. The LXX translators did not, when translating *tannîn* here, use the same Greek word which they used when translating Genesis 1 (*kētē*); instead, they used *drakōn*, reflecting the common references to dragons in ancient Near East mythology and iconography.[16] Jerome, on the other hand, uses the same word that he used in his translation of Genesis 1:21, *cetus* (Vul I, 738).

The English translations of the Job 7:12 passage reflect variety. KJV again uses the word "whale." The RSV and JB use the more literal "sea monster," while the NEB uses the similar "sea-serpent." The NRSV uses the English cognate "dragon" for LXX's *drakōn*, a translation that suggests mythological overtones rather than a reference to living creatures. This is plausible, given that in the cosmogonies of Israel's neighboring peoples, large, obviously mythological sea creatures are involved in the birth of the gods and then subsequently subdued. Examples are the Babylonian story of Tiamat, the Hattic myth of the dragon Illuyankas, and the Ugaritic myths from Ras-Shamra, which refer to various monsters defeated by the storm god Baal or his sister Anath.[17] Day (1985, 4–7, 61) concludes that the source of the references is Canaanite. Also in accord is Murray's view that *tannîn* in this passage is "a fully mythical monster" (1992, 2). As such it can trade on the existence of culturally held views of large marine creatures but is, in the end, irrelevant to providing information about them.

Three other occurrences of *tannîn* are equally inconclusive. First, in Psalm 148:7,[18] a plural form of *tannîn* occurs in a cosmic hymn of praise. Both the LXX and the Vulgate use dragon cognates.[19] Interestingly, the KJV does not use "whale" again; rather, it uses "dragons." Similarly, more recent translations generally use non-cetacean words. RSV, NRSV, and JB all use variants of "sea-monsters."

Second, in Ezekiel 32:2, the word occurs in a proposed address to Pharaoh of Egypt.[20] While KJV uses "whale" in its translation of this passage ("thou *art* as a whale in the seas"), the terms of this extended image suggest that the passage is, at best, an inconsistent reference to cetaceans. Further, *if* it is a reference to a natural animal at all, the other words in the passage suggest that it is more likely a reference calling to mind another kind of animal altogether. Day (1985, 94 and 139) argues forcefully that it is *not* a reference to natural world animals but rather to the mythological chaos monster. While the LXX (II, 826) and Vulgate[21] again use dragon cognates, and are followed in this by RSV and NRSV and to some extent by NEB ("like a monster"), JB translates with the altogether different word "crocodile."[22] Given that the animal's *feet* are referred to, translation of *tannîn* with an animal image other than that of a cetacean seems reasonable, and KJV's "whale" is misleading.[23]

Third, in Psalm 74:13 the plural *tannînîm* appears (Green 1976, 487). The RSV verse reads: "Thou didst divide the sea by thy might; thou didst break the heads of the dragons on the waters." In the Septuagint, where the Psalm is number 73, the translators stayed with the plural *drakontōn*, and Jerome in the Vulgate used the Latin cognate *draconum*.[24] The KJV translators used "dragons" here when they used "whale" for the same term in Genesis 1, Job 7, and Ezekiel 32, all of which suggests that the translators had a choice and thus intentionally chose the word "whale" in the first three passages.[25]

In summary, these occurrences of *tannîn* do not suggest strongly that natural world cetaceans were the referents.[26] The term occurs elsewhere in the Hebrew Bible as a reference to "jackals," "serpent," and "dragons,"[27] and thus its general value as a reference to cetaceans in any specific context is difficult to affirm. What is particularly significant in the Christian tradition, though, is that the translations of the word as "whale" (or non-English equivalents) have often been taken as references to natural world animals. This anomaly (namely, the Hebrew word being without an obvious natural world referent, while later translations use words that make the passage seem to have natural world relevance) has affected interpretations of just how referential the passages involving *tannîn* might be. Thus, even if one concludes that the original use of the term had nothing to do with cetaceans, it clearly has been taken as such at later times and thus has seemed to adherents to provide a referent or image regarding the place of cetaceans in the scheme of things envisioned in the tradition's sacred writings. This, as noted later, has been a recurring pattern.

"Leviathan"

Psalm 74 (which is Psalm 73 in LXX and the Vulgate), at verse 14, uses *livyāthān*,[28] which at times has been construed as a cetacean reference. For example, Feliks (1972, 16), in listing the natural world animals mentioned in the Hebrew Bible, indicates that *livyāthān* is a reference to "whale." In LXX (II, 78), *livyāthān* in verse 14 is translated as *drakontos*, which is the same word used by the LXX translators for *tannîn* in verse 13. The Vulgate (I, 861), on the other hand, simply uses the cognate in verse 14. Preserving the term has become something of a tradition in the English translations, as in KJV, RSV, NRSV, JB, and NEB. That the referent (Leviathan) has multiple heads suggests mythological associations that are well attested in the scholarly sources.[29]

Livyāthān is also found elsewhere in the Hebrew Bible, and these other occurrences make it clear how predominantly mythological, rather than exclusively natural world referential, the references to *livyāthān* are.[30] In Job 41, the opening lines of the extended passage are "Can you draw out Leviathan with a fishhook . . . ?" (RSV 41:1). While the LXX translators used *drakonta* (the same term used by the translators for *tannîn*), the Vulgate uses *Leviathan*.[31] Most English translations, such as RSV, NRSV, and KJV, also use the cognate. The footnote to the word "Leviathan" in RSV 41:1 is "or a crocodile"; this is echoed by NRSV and JB, the latter noting, "The name, in its strict sense, indicates a monster of primeval Chaos, believed still to be living in the ocean. Here it is used of the crocodile, though the description still bears traces of the primeval monster which Yahweh subdued" (JB 40:25, n. "j").

Suggestions that this passage is a reference to natural world animals have included not only the crocodile but also the hippopotamus and the tunny fish (Day 1985, 65–67). Using a combination of philology and deductions from clues in the physical descriptions of the text, Day (1985, 68, 72, 74) concludes that the passage is not a reference to *any* natural animal, including cetaceans.

NEB uses "whale" for this passage,[32] a translation that has precedents in the scholarship addressing this verse. Driver originally suggested that the passage referred to a whale and then later suggested that it referred to a dolphin.[33] Day notes that the text's physical descriptions do not fit these interpretations. Driver had based his conclusion on the familial nature of whales, interpreting the root of leviathan as "to accompany." But this etymology will not hold, since the root clearly is "to twist."[34] As to Driver's later suggestion that the Job 41 reference is to a dolphin, Day argues that the claim is "a series of nonsequiturs." Driver had based his suggestion on an anecdote about a group of dolphins pleading for a companion, which parallels the Job 41:3 text's references to pleading. Day notes that "all of this is very learned but splendidly irrelevant" (1985, 67), since in Job 40:25 and following Leviathan will *not* plead for mercy. Day concludes, "We may rest assured, therefore, that Leviathan is not the dolphin!" (67).

The occurrence of *livyāthān* at Psalm 104:26 has aspects which suggest that it, unlike some of the references considered previously, could be a reference to natural world animals. The RSV translation of verses 25 and 26 is "Yonder is the sea, great and wide, which teems with things innumerable, living things both small and great. / There go the ships, and Leviathan which thou didst form to sport in it." The passage goes on to say that these "living things" (*hayyôth*; Green 1976, 497) are dismayed when God's face is hidden (verse 29), suggesting in verse 30 the common Hebrew Bible theme that humans and nonhumans share the same fate when God takes away their "breath" (*rû.hām*) and they return to "dust" (*'phārām*; Green 1976, 497).

Livyāthān in this passage is again translated in LXX as *drakōn*, and in the Vulgate and the English translations simply as *Leviathan*.[35] The IB commentary, which consistently emphasizes the mythological aspects of other references, suggests that leviathan here "seems" to refer to "an enormous marine animal" (IB, IV, 556). Since Psalm 104 is full of references to other natural world animals (such as wild asses, birds, cattle, storks, wild goats, badgers, and young lions), and since verse 25 refers to "the sea . . . which teems with . . . living things both small and great," there is some plausibility in a suggestion that "leviathan" in this passage trades on knowledge of the existence of the large, dimly understood cetaceans that populated the seas bordering the Near East.

The text itself is not clear and has elicited other interpretations that this is indeed a reference to natural world cetaceans.[36] The Hebrew is capable grammatically of bearing two different meanings: either "leviathan whom you formed to play with" or "leviathan whom you formed to play in it" (Day 1985, 72–73). Day opts for the interpretation of this as a reference to a "chaos monster" that "has undergone a process of depotentization" (74).

In summary, the occurrences of *livyāthān* provide little, if any, information regarding cetaceans, and there often is little basis other than tradition for translating the passages with words that suggest references to natural world cetaceans.[37] Nonetheless, translations using cetacean-referring words have at times given adherents the impression that these passage have some purchase on what the authors of the tradition's sacred literature thought about cetaceans.

Jonah and the "Whale"

Another Hebrew Bible reference, which occurs in the story of Jonah.[38] has been taken as a reference to cetaceans. The Hebrew for the creature that swallowed Jonah is *dāgh gādhôl*, which is literally "a great fish."[39] The word chosen by the LXX translators (II, 527 Jonah 2:1) was an inflected form of *kētē*. The Vulgate (II, 1398; Jonah 2:1) uses *piscem grandem* and then merely *piscis*. Principal English translations, such as RSV, NRSV, JB, KJV, and NEB, use the word "fish" and thus suggest no cetacean associations.[40] The dominance of the version of the story in which a *whale*, as opposed to a fish or some other large marine creature, swallows Jonah might come from influential English translations of the passage at Matthew 12:40 referring to the Jonah story:

KJV: For as Jonah was three days and three nights in the *whale's* belly

RSV: in the belly of the *whale*[41]

Some other modern translations of the Matthew passage use "great fish" or "huge fish" (for example, the *New International Version, The Living Bible,* and *Today's English Version*); others use the term "sea monster" (NRSV, JB, NEB). The IB comments suggest that the whale association derives directly from the New Testament itself: "Matthew has rewritten the verse; he is like many other Christians who, when they think of Jonah, can remember only the whale" (IB VII, 403). That KJV uses "whale" for the New Testament passage is peculiar, since Matthew's word is the same Greek word (*kētē*) that appears in the LXX version of Jonah, which KJV at Jonah 2:1 translates as "great fish."

This provides another example of subsequent understanding or translations which create the impression that passages in the foundational scriptures of the tradition address in some specific way the natural world animals known generally as "whales."

Other Key Animals

There are only minor references to the other key animals in the Old Testament. The most obvious are the twenty-three references to elephants in the series of Maccabees books written in the second century B.C.E.[42] The Hebrew text cannot be analyzed because there are no extant Hebrew versions of these books.[43] The Greek and Latin versions use cognates of the English "elephant" for these references, which are mostly martial in nature. There are no references that suggest the Hebrews had contact with the elephants other than as parts of the invading armies fighting against them. Consequently, these references are of very little use in assessing what was known or thought of elephants.

It was a common view until well into the seventeenth century that the Job 40:15–24 passage mentioning "Behemoth" was a reference to elephants. In 1663 Bochart rejected this view, and it appears no modern scholars advance this idea.[44] This is not to say, however, that the existence of the earlier tradition of interpretation did not affect adherents' views of natural world elephants.

Minor references to key animals appear in virtually identical passages at 1 Kings 10:22 and 2 Chronicles 9:21. The RSV translation of 1 Kings 10:22 is "Once every three years the fleet of ships of Tarshish used to come bringing gold, silver, ivory, apes, and peacocks." The Hebrew *shenhabîm* suggests the possible connection to elephants, for it translates "ivory,"[45] but the references are incidental. Part of the products or curiosities brought back to Solomon include simians, for which the Hebrew is *qōphîm* (*pithekon* in LXX, and *simias* in the Vulgate). Thayer opines that this is probably a word of foreign origin.[46] Each of the English translations being considered here uses "ape." HBD comments, "The apes mentioned in 1 Kings 10:22 and 2 Chronicles 9:21 are probably monkeys, possibly *Papio hamadryas*, a baboon once common in Egypt and Somalia" (35).

In summary, these minor, incidental, and vague references make it obvious that the complex individuals discussed in part II do *not* have a high profile in the Old Testament. What is relevant to this study, however, is that in spite of limited information about these and other animals, their lives, though conceived of as in some ways connected to the phenomenon of life in members of the human species, were generally thought of as not only different but also far less important than human lives.

It is argued below and in chapter 9 that the general vocabulary of the Hebrew Bible reflects tensions between competing senses of connection and separation. This tension appears in the different attitudes toward wilderness.[47] Nash, pointing out that this notion occurs 245 times in the RSV Old Testament, contrasts the hostile, rain-parched desert (the "wilderness"), which dominated the geography of the ancient Near East, with the fertile strips of land that benefited from four or more inches of rain annually; he argues, "The Old Testament reveals that the ancient Hebrews regarded the wilderness as a cursed land and that they associated its forbidding character with a lack of water."[48] However, the Hebrews, recalling their experiences following the Exodus, also regarded the wilderness as a sanctuary from sinful society and a place to draw near to God (an overtone of the Mark 1:13 passage mentioned previously). Thus, the bald claim that all nonhuman spaces were only negatively conceived in the Hebrew scriptures is overstated.[49] Nash (1973, 16) contends, however, that there was no real fondness for the wilderness itself. Since this nonhuman space was the domain of "wild animals," passages frequently use such animals as metaphors for human enemies,[50] and thus they exemplify the negative associations that often carried over to the nonhuman inhabitants of areas not dominated by humans.

Generic Features of the Hebrew Bible's Vocabulary for Other Animals

The conceptualization regarding other animals that dominates the many different views expressed in the Hebrew Bible is reflected in features of the word choice and vocabulary of various texts. In general, these provide an example of one of the problems described in chapter 5, namely, the relation between (1) heavy reliance on generic terms and concepts as foundational tools for comprehending and describing the realities of the many different kinds of other animals, and (2) an inability, or perhaps an intentional failure, to notice or take seriously those realities.

Although there are no words that clearly designate any of the key animals other than the now lost Hebrew references to elephants in the Maccabees series, many other animals are mentioned in the Hebrew Bible. Feliks (1972, 10–16), for example, lists 113 kinds, including (1) domestic animals, (2) a limited number of familiar wild animals that were nonthreatening (including birds), (3) threatening terrestrial mammals, (4) marine animals generally, and (5) other mammalian and nonmammalian forms such as rats and insects, which were considered pests. Despite the variety of life mentioned in many contexts, attempts to understand the realities and possibilities of animals beyond the human species line were dominated by high-level generalizations that can be broken down into several categories.

First-Level Generalizations

As in the Pali canon, consideration of when and how the Hebrew Bible's generic terms for life beyond the human species are used, as well as how they were translated in the Old Testament and used in the New Testament, is illuminating. As with the Buddhist terms, they are not used in strictly defined ways, nor do they present, relative to one another, distinctly defined concepts.[51] They are reliant on a highly generalized conceptuality through which the vaguely known realities of other animals were presented. As with the English term "animal," sometimes the same term is used differently, such that at one point it is a generalization of the highest or broadest level that includes all animals whether human or not, while at another point the same word functions as a generalization of a lower, that is, narrower, level.

Two words together that *can* work as a paradigmatic example of a first-level generalization are *nephesh* and *.hayyâ*, which occur in Genesis 1:20–21. *Nephesh* is a feminine noun that can cover a wide range of living things. Weingreen gives the English terms "soul, life, person" as definitions.[52] The second word (*.hayyâ*) is a modifier meaning "living."[53] In Genesis 1:21, these two terms are further modified by an adjective meaning "all" or "every" (*kol*), and the threesome is often translated by the phrases "every living creature" (for example, KJV, RSV, NRSV), "all living creatures" (NEB), and "every kind of living creature" (JB). It is clear, however, that the group designated does not include *all* living creatures, for humans are not created until the sixth day. These words together in Genesis 1:21, then, work as a generic term, but as a *second*-level generalization, since some living beings (humans) are not included. Thus, in this passage the two words operate together to signify something like the term "animals" in its primary signification for modern speakers of English.

Nephesh appears in many other important passages such as the Yahwist's description in Genesis 2:7 of God's creation of man: "[T]hen the LORD God formed man of dust from the ground, and breathed into his nostrils the breath of life; and man became a living being [*nephesh*]."[54] Here, *nephesh* works as a first-level generalization. *Nephesh* can be found in many contexts, such as Genesis 35:18, where it is the soul of Rachel leaving as she dies, or Genesis 17:14, where it refers to a male human whose "soul" (RSV) will be cut off from his people if he is not circumcised. It is used regularly of other animals, as in Genesis 1:24 and 30 (again with the adjective *.hayyâ*), Ezekiel 47:9, and Proverbs 12:10. Importantly, the range and meaning of *nephesh* change depending on context and the use of adjectives. Without the adjective *.hayyâ* with which it so often occurs, the term can mean "a living being whose life resides in the blood."[55] It can also be used solely for humans, as in Jeremiah 37:9 (RSV, "do not deceive yourselves") and Numbers 31:35, 40, and 46 (where, modified by *'ādām*, it refers to various numbers of humans).

Adjectives and Nouns Related to .hayâ

There is a complex of words deriving from the verb form *.hayâ* ("to live" or "have life"; Brown, Driver, Briggs 1976, 310–313) which have very generic qualities. As with *nephesh*, the connotation and import of the *.hayâ*-related adjectives and nouns vary significantly. At times the noun *.hayyâ* operates as a first-level generalization as in Genesis 8:21, when God says to Noah, "[N]either will I ever again destroy every living creature as I have done."[56]

Often, however, occurrences of words in the *.hayâ*-related series signal second- or third-level generalizations. Examples of *.hayyâ* doing work as a second-level generalization include the Priestly tradition's use in Genesis 9:9–10, "[M]y covenant with you and your descendants after you, and with every living creature that is with you," and in Genesis 9:12, "[T]he covenant which I make between you and every living creature that is with you." The standard translation of the Yahwist's comments in Genesis 2:19 ("whatever the man called every living creature, that was its name") reads as if the reference was meant to be a *second*-level generalization (that is, all nonhuman animals). Hiebert's analysis (1996, 60) of verse 19 in relation to the verse 18 reference to Adam's need for a "helper" suggests that the principal focus of this minor story of the creation and naming of "helpers" is *domestic* species that play a major role in Mediterranean agriculture. Thus, although the discourse is general, the referent may not have been *all* nonhuman animals. The Hebrew used as a generalized reference in all these passages is the *nephesh/.hayyâ* combination.

Third-level generalization uses of *.hayyâ* are very common because the Hebrews habitually spoke of several broad categories of animals such as "beasts" and "birds."[57] An example is Genesis 2:19, "So out of the ground the LORD God formed every beast [*.hayyâ*] of the field and every bird of the air." A similar example occurs in

Genesis 9:2, "The fear of you . . . shall be upon every beast [*.hayyâ*] of the earth, and every bird of the air." Other passages reflect the many different kinds of third-level generalizations which *.hayâ* is used to convey. In Leviticus 26:6 ("I will remove evil beasts [*.hayyâ*] from the land"), negative overtones regarding *some* other animals are suggested, but the group of animals is very limited, for the many beneficial animals, as well as the birds and marine creatures, are arguably not the referent.

In Hosea 2:18 the prospective covenant is with "the beasts [*.hayyâ*] of the field, the birds of the air, and creeping things of the ground." It is a reasonable interpretation that this combination was meant to be a very broad, second-level generalization (that is, a reference to all animals other than humans), since the tenor of this passage is the harmonizing of all creation, and thus the intent was likely to encompass all life on earth. In this passage, the word *.hayyâ*, of course, is not itself a second-level generalization, even if the multiple-part phrase itself was intended to function this broadly.

These many uses of *.hayyâ* suggest that its coverage varies rather dramatically, occasionally rising to first- and second-level generalizations, but primarily acting as a generic term that groups terrestrial animals into a complex aggregation that is a third-level generalization.

Additional Second-Level Generalizations in the Hebrew Bible

Unlike the Pali canon's regular uses of the word *tiracchāno*, the Hebrew Bible has no specific word that operates exclusively to group all animals other than humans together. It has been noted previously that some words, such as *.hayyâ* and the combination of *nephesh*/*.hayyâ*, do work in this way at times, and as such their use may involve coarse generalizations of the type described in chapter 5. Usually, however, second-level generalizations are produced in the Hebrew Bible by stringing together third-level generalizations, sometimes with the names of specific animals. The Hosea passage discussed earlier is an example of such a "string"; another occurs in Genesis 1:21, "So God created the great sea monsters and every living creature that moves, with which the waters swarm, according to their kinds, and every winged bird according to its kind." These strings abound, occurring particularly often early in Genesis[58] and regularly elsewhere. Clark (1968) lists several recurring formulas or sequences in the Hebrew Bible; these are two-, three-, and four-part series, and some are for mammals only, while others encompass all other living things. Clark, noting that these occur in both the Priestly and the Yahwist traditions (also indicated earlier by Hiebert's revealing comments about the difference between these two traditions in the *order* of the strings), suggests that the two different traditions drew on a common source, namely, the "domain of priestly ritual instruction" (1968, 446–49). Clark's analysis suggests that even though no *one* word acts as a second-level generalization, in the Hebrew tradition humans were distinguished from all other animals by use of these strings in a manner that is the functional equivalent of the human-*tiracchāno* division found in the Pali canon.

This suggests that it is the underlying conceptuality and habits of discourse that dictate the ways other animals are thought about. The existence of a specialized word, such as the Pali word *tiracchāno*, dedicated to the concept underlying second-level generalizations is one method; the Hebrew Bible's use of strings is another, providing the functional equivalent of the second-level generalization *tiracchāno* and the English word "animal" in its principal use.

The Special Place of Human Animals, and the Complex Views of Other Animals

Members of the human species are seen in the Hebrew Bible as a single, distinct group of animals that has been specially created and given dominion in Genesis 1:26 over all other animals described by a string of third-level generalizations at ("the fish of the sea . . . the birds of the air . . . the cattle . . . every creeping thing"). Since all humans were conceived of as descended from the same two ancestors, Adam and Eve, each of them had a special status from which even human slaves were not excepted.[59] Even the special election of the Hebrews (for example, Deuteronomy 7:6) does not produce divisions among humans that in any way pertain to the moral status of humans *relative* to that of other animals.[60] There was, then, a sense that all humans constituted a single group in a most important sense, *especially* in relation to all other animals.

Thus, even though other animals were thought of as creaturely, sharing with humans the biological realities reflected in the broad senses of *nephesh* and the *.hayâ*-related series (as well as *dām*, *bāśār*, and *rûa.h*), each and every one of them was nonetheless also conceived of as qualitatively different from members of the human species. It is possible to counter this argument by replying that, from another vantage point, the Hebrew Bible offers a "rich" range of possibilities for viewing other animals in themselves and in relation to humans, for there are extremely complex aspects and tensions in the Hebrew evaluation of animals beyond the species line.[61] When considering this complex picture, there is, as already noted with regard to the possible references to the key animals, a need to distinguish metaphorical from other kinds of language about nonhuman animals. As to the relative status of those animals within and those beyond the human species line, Murray summarizes as follows:

> The Bible contains, in fact, two models for thinking about humans and animals: one paradisal, the other this-worldly and realistic. The first way uses the picture of peace with and between wild animals as a metaphor for cosmic and social peace; the second way sees peace from them as a practical aspect of desired *šalom*. (1992, 34)

Of these two pictures, the second dominates in the sense that it is human interests, far more than the interests of any nonhuman animals, that are deemed critically important. This slant is evident in the notion "peace from evil animals," which can be found in Leviticus 26:5–6, 9, 12 and Ezekiel 34:25. Bauckham speaks of the "ancient tendency, at least in the Jewish tradition, to consider wild animals primarily as threats to human life" (1994, 8). This tendency to a negative view of the animals not under humans' control is represented well by Philo's image of a *continuous* war with *thēria*. There is, however, a certain irony in the dominant view of wild animals as evil, given that it is a common biblical theme that the disorder in nature comes from human actions. Murray notes, "[T]he biblical tradition presents us with pictures of a cosmic order established, broken and re-established, but still under threat and in need of reaffirmation. . . . [I]n the biblical world [the disorder] was regarded as essentially caused by persons" (1992, 44). This stems from both the responsibility of "archetypal human ancestors" and the unfaithfulness of Israel railed against by the prophets (Murray 1992, 123).

Murray summarizes the contrary but less dominant view: "But in the Hebrew Bible, even if wild animals are called 'evil' (Lev 26:6, Ezek 34:25), they follow their natures under God, who feeds them (Ps 104:21 etc) and proudly describes them to Job (Job 38:39 ff.). Animals appear not as examples of disorder but rather as examples of right order, to the discredit of humans" (1992, 60). This less dominant view can be seen as reflecting the important notion that God as the source of creation has conferred a goodness on it generally. Importantly, however, this less dominant view does not automatically translate into the distinguishable view argued in chapter 4 that the features intrinsic to the lives of some nonhuman animals result in those individuals having lives that moral agents might hold morally considerable. To be sure, as to a special place for other animals as opposed to humans, it must also be observed that the law codes (Exodus 22–23 and 34, Leviticus 22 and 25, and Deuteronomy between 14 and 26) contain many provisions that recognize, at least to some extent, the welfare of other animals.[62] Such "recognition" is, however, limited in an important respect, for the subject matter is primarily (1) the welfare of domestic animals, that is, those that work or produce benefits for humans, and (2) restrictions on the killing of the few animals that could be sacrificed.[63] It is difficult to argue convincingly from the existence of these limited provisions to the conclusion that other animals were valued in and of themselves (a topic discussed more fully in chapter 9).

Covenants and Nonhuman Animals

Other animals are mentioned in *some* of the covenants found in the Hebrew Bible. Most prominent is the first covenant (if one is reading from the beginning of Genesis), namely, the Noachic covenant of Genesis 9:9–16. Linzey makes a great deal of this in his works,[64] but Murray has observed that the preceding set of verses (Genesis 9:1–7) "has things to say about the relationship between humankind and animals which radically qualify the situation of God's animal covenant-partners in 9:8–17" (1992, 34). Thus, although the covenant is called an "eternal covenant" and has as partners God "and all that lives," other animals are "in the subordinate relationship to humankind which has already been set forth in Genesis" (Murray 1992, 33). The entire passage, that is, Genesis 9:1–7 and the covenant passage of verses 8–17, reflects the characteristic insistence on the preeminence of humans that dominates the Genesis Creation passages. Consistent with this conclusion is the fact that later covenants in the Pentateuch (though *not* all of the extra-Pentateuch covenants) ignore other animals entirely, and Murray argues that in the passage at Zephaniah 1:2–3, "what is pictured is nothing less than a cancellation of the covenant with humankind and animals in Genesis 9."[65]

There may well be other, more animal-friendly covenants that are important in, even integral to, the Hebrew Bible. Murray attempts to identify remnants of a broader, "cosmic covenant" in which "the heavenly and earthly spheres correspond and together are bound to one great 'right order' which, if it is duly observed by all its subjects, will be expressed in the harmony of the heavenly bodies, of the seasons and harvests, and of society and proper cult on earth" (1992, 70). He attempts to piece it together from ritual remnants, various modes of expression, and symbolic accounts of reality cast in a narrative form. The vision in Hosea 2, which does include other animals in a covenant of peace, is the most explicit statement of the cosmic covenant, and according to Murray (1992, 36), it shares a common origin in ritual with the inclusive covenant of Genesis 9:8–17. However, the dominance of the animal-exclusive Abrahamic, Mosaic, and Davidic covenants leads Murray to note, "But though we can find expressions of admiration or sympathy, a view of animals as our own covenant partners is scarcely to be found in the Hebrew Bible."[66] With these other covenants, the vision of harmony is less inclusive of other animals, being instead focused on the human community.

Background Beliefs and Generalizations Inherited by the Christian Community

The dominance of the generalizations described here and the more exclusivist versions of covenants with the divine reflect background beliefs about, and the centrality of commitments to, the importance of members of the human species relative to all other animals. These background beliefs can be found throughout the Hebrew Bible. They are particularly evident in the Genesis accounts of (1) the order of Creation, the naming of animals, the charge of dominion, and the image of God, and (2) the Flood story by way of its emphasis on stewardship, the focus on terrestrials, and the permission to eat other animals. The commitment to humans as a group to be distinguished from all other animals is an emphasis that the early Christians inherited, though it was changed in some significant ways (this is discussed later in this chapter and in chapter 9).

Thus, humans were conceived of as separate from the rest of life in critically important ways even though the breadth of generalizations about living beings, the number of specific animals mentioned, and observations about the variety of life confirm that the Hebrews noticed and appreciated, at least in some ways, the extraordinary diversity and interconnectedness of human and nonhuman beings mentioned in part II. To note that this sense of separation was important, however, is *not* to say that a universalism among the class of humans operated at all times, for it clearly did not. It is to say, however, that the Hebrews operated on the assumption that no other animal could possibly have the special gifts given to humans, and that other animals could therefore be generalized about in many of the ways discussed in chapter 5. This explicit belief that humans were, in the language of chapter 5, not merely "unique-different" but "unique-better" is the starting point which the Christian tradition inherited from the Hebrew Bible.

Earliest Views: The New Testament and the Mixed Cultural Background

Wallace-Hadrill asked, "The Christian stood at his door and looked out at a universe of earth, air, water, plants, animals, insects, and birds; skies and stars and sun and moon; . . . and amidst these, man. How much of it interested him? What in all this did he find important?" (1968, 2). In attempting an answer, it will be helpful to distinguish between (1) finding the whole system, whether called "creation" or "nature," interesting, good, or significant, and (2) attributing to component parts such as nonhuman animals, collectively or individually, such value. The first could, but does not necessarily, imply the second.

One major component of any answer will be the Old Testament set of views already considered, for the New Testament reflects fully the Old Testament's view of other animals, especially their place relative to members of the human species. Thus, even though Frear can argue that "the New Testament [is] bereft of any direct provisions for human care of animals" (1993, 7), there are passages that clearly reflect the early tradition's adherence to the animal-sensitive views described in the previous section. Since many of the issues, concerns, and concepts relating to other animals were taken as having already been fully stated and resolved in the inherited texts, the fact that they are not readdressed in the New Testament cannot be taken as an indication that they were unimportant.

The early Christians inherited the views of the Hebrew tradition in both Hebrew and Greek forms, for the LXX featured prominently in the lives of early Christians. Since the generic terms of both languages mediated possibilities for talking about other animals, the use in the LXX of the generalizations of Hellenistic Greek (discussed later) was extremely important in how the Christian tradition came to speak about other animals. Würthwein, noting that Augustine demanded that Jerome use the LXX texts, rather than Hebrew originals, as the bases for the Vulgate, adds,

> [T]he influence of the Old Testament upon the Christian world through the centuries, almost up to the present day, has been mediated linguistically and conceptually by the hellenistic forms it received in the Septuagint. We must acknowledge . . . that the Septuagint is a book of such critical significance that apart from it both Christendom and the western culture would be inconceivable. (1979, 49)

References to Other Animals Generally in the New Testament

The New Testament references to other animals are of several kinds. Some of the passages have no more to do with natural world animals than the phrase "love of money is the root of all evils" (1 Timothy 6:10) has to do with botany. Thus, although the use of animal images is common, Muddiman cautions, "We should remember that illustrations drawn from nature do not imply that one is talking about nature" (1995, 12).

There are many references, however, that can be used to explore New Testament views of other animals more specifically and directly. These consist mostly of references to domestic animals and generic references. The specific "wild" mammals mentioned, other than the "whale" of Matthew 12:40, include about five kinds of animals (fox/jackal, wolf, bear, leopard, and lion),[67] while the number of domestic mammals mentioned is more than double that and, not surprisingly, reflects a far richer vocabulary.[68] Even if the domestic animals are combined with nondomestic animals, the universe of mammals mentioned is quite narrow, the focus being on humans as the distinctive creatures of concern to God. Other living things, such as birds,[69] reptiles,[70] and insects (Louw and Nida 1988, 45 ff.), are also mentioned, and words that can be associated with marine animals are also common, but only because the word for fish (*ichthus*) occurs twenty times (Scott and others 1995, 27).

Key Animals in the New Testament

It has already been noted in the preceding section that some translations of Matthew employ the term "whale" even though the Greek word used by Matthew[71] can also be translated with generic terms such as "large fish" or "sea monster."[72] Nonetheless, the theme of "Jonah and the *whale*" has become a prominent image in the tradition, with the notion that it was a whale, rather than an unspecified marine creature, now found widely in stories and art.[73]

Other than this, there are no direct references in the New Testament to the key animals. This is not surprising, since, for the reasons already noted, there is no reason to expect great specificity of the New Testament as to particular kinds of animals. Rather, the vocabulary of the New Testament reflects general adherence to the Hebrew and Hellenistic views of other animals, especially as those otherwise very different worldviews are in agreement on some general features such as the superiority of humans. Of course, the explanations for this superiority given in the Hebrew tradition, on the one hand, and those found in Hellenistic cultures, on the other, were quite distinct from one another.[74]

Generic Greek Words for Other Animals

First-level generalizations were ready to hand in Hellenistic Greek. One could speak of all living beings with *zōon*, a late-developing word in Greek that means "living being."[75] This is the word Aristotle uses in his *Politics* when speaking of humans as "by nature a political animal" (*politikon zōon*; 1977, 8–9, 1253a3). It is related to *zōē*, a generic term meaning "life, existence" or "natural life."[76] One could also speak of living things generally with the idiom *psuchē zoēs*, which translates as "living soul" (Louw and Nida 1988, 37) or, in its components, as "the vital principle in creatures"[77] and "living."

Second-level generalizations were also quite common, as Hellenistic Greek had, quite unlike biblical Hebrew, single words that operated as descriptions of all other animals. *Zōon* could work in this manner,[78] but the most prominent of the words used as second-level generalizations is *thērion*. Lampe defines this with the English "beast," while Louw and Nida use "any living creature, not including man."[79] This is the word Aristotle uses in *Politics* when he says a man who cannot enter into a partnership "must be either a lower animal or a god" (1977, pages 12–13, 1253b29). *Thērion* is also used in LXX as part of many second-level generalizations, such as Genesis 8:1 and Genesis 9:2 (where the Hebrew is .*hayyâ*).

In Hellenistic Greek, third-level generalizations abounded, especially words for domestic animals. *Thērion* in a narrower, less generic sense could act as a reference to all wild animals (an example is Mark 1:13) or, as does the descriptive *tetrapoun*, to any four-footed creature. The smaller grouping of "domesticated four-footed animals, primarily livestock" was *thremma*, and there is a separate word (*chtēnos*) for the still smaller group "beasts of burden, riding animal, cattle." This word appears in 1 Corinthians 15:39, which is translated as the more generic-sounding "animals" in the RSV: "For not all flesh is alike, but there is one kind for men, another for animals [*chtēnōn*], another for birds, and another for fish."[80] There are, of course, third-level generalizations for nondomestic animals, examples of which are Paul's use of *ichthoōn* for fish in the passage just quoted and *enalios*, which occurs but once in a plural form in the New Testament (James 3:7, "sea creature" [RSV]). Second-level generalizations also occur in the style of the "strings" of third-level generalizations that dominate the Old Testament. An example is James 3:7, "man can tame any wild animal [*thērion* in the narrower sense], bird, reptile, or creature of the sea." Here, as in the Old Testament, the string of groups is meant to be all-inclusive with regard to other animals.

Generic References in the New Testament

Uses of generic references in the New Testament that reflect typical views of other animals include 2 Peter 2:12, Titus 1:12, and James 3:7. In 2 Peter 2:12, there is, as part of a discussion of false prophets, a comparison of unrighteous humans to other animals:

> RSV: like irrational animals, creatures of instinct, born to be caught and killed

> KJV: as natural brute beasts made to be taken and destroyed

The Greek word translated as "animals" or "beasts" is *zōa*. When coupled with the adjective *aloga*, *zōa* is part of a very common second-level generalization that occurs in classical Greek thinkers.[81] The description of other animals as irrational (*aloga*) relies on the view that all other animals lacked the feature(s) of human thinking traditionally called reason and/or rationality. This view calls to mind the influence of Hellenistic (and specifically Greek) notions in thinking about other animals, rather than characteristically Hebrew conceptuality.

The comparison to other animals in the passage, whether it is a reference to all or only some other animals, is meant to convey a negative message. The phrasing is built on several unstated assumptions, such as (1) human animals are essentially unlike other animals, and (2) other animals can be considered as a group without doing any real injustice to the differences that occur in that very diverse group. It is the reliance on these background assumptions that makes this passage representative of the New Testament's generic references to other animals. Similarly, in Titus 1:12–13, the writer assents to the adequacy of the following image, "Cretans are always liars, evil beasts, lazy gluttons." The Greek term for "beasts" here is *thēria*, and this is generally thought to be a quote from the sixth century B.C.E. figure Epimenides. While the adjective "evil" (*kaka*) is no doubt a factor in the negative image, the comparison again trades on the generally negative view of other animals relative to humans, such that a comparison was an insult or at best a pejorative term for human beings.[82]

James 3:7, "For every kind of beast and bird, of reptile and sea creature can be tamed and has been tamed by human kind," also contains attitudes toward other animals that are characteristic of the generalizations in the New Testament. The word translated "beast" is again *thērion*. "Kind" is a translation of *phusis*, which, though used for many purposes, here is a reference to the notion of the natural form, constitution, or "nature" of a thing.[83] This passage features the notion of human dominance over other animals, a theme that has both Greek and Hebrew precedents. It should be noted that the claim itself, however, ran against common experience, for it was clear that many wild animals could *not* be tamed. For example, the largest whales could not be caught (they were simply too fast and were not hunted successfully until the nineteenth century after the invention of steam-powered vessels), and many other kinds of wild terrestrial animals could not then, and cannot now, be domesticated or tamed. This was the precise reason for many of the concerns of the Hebrew Bible about security in the wilderness, as well as Aristotle's admission in *Politics* (I, 8, 1256b15–22) to the effect that some animals are not for humans' use.

These three examples provide a profile of the dominant generalized images of other animals in the New Testament. Of course, there are other New Testament images (such as Paul's much discussed comment about oxen, which is addressed in the next chapter) that are also significant factors in the early tradition's views of other animals. Importantly, some other images are not so negative. Mark's brief reference (at 1:13) to Jesus and wild animals uses *thērion*, with no adjective. This is a good example of *thērion*'s third-level generalization sense of "wild animals in the wilderness." Mark's reference is not derogatory in tone, though there have been negative interpretations. Bauckham (1994, 4–6) explores previous interpretations and notes that those suggesting demonic associations offer no textual basis for their analysis and misconstrue the Jewish view to be that wild animals were allies of Satan. Bauckham notes, "References to nature in the NT, especially the Gospels, have been persistently understood from the perspective of modern urban people, themselves wholly alienated from nature, for whom literary references to nature can only be symbols or picturesque illustrations of a human world unrelated to nature" (3–4). Bauckham adds that the prevailing view among modern exegetes is that the image suggests Jesus at peace in a paradisal state, and he argues for the passage as a Christological image for contemporary ecological concerns.

Some Aspects of the Cultural and Intellectual Background

Grant (1953, xv) makes the commonsense point that the study and interpretation of the New Testament, "which is, from first to last, a Greek book," must address both the emphases of the Aramaic-speaking early Christian communities in Palestine and the very different world of ideas and views that prevailed outside the original cradle of Christianity in northern Palestine. The first of these two elements can be seen in early Christians' use of so many of the categories, emphases, and stories of the Hebrew Bible. The second element addresses the fact that the surrounding Hellenistic cultures were sources of various views that are relevant to the manner in which the Christian tradition developed its claims about humans and their status relative to other animals. Stressing how varied Hellenistic religions were, Grant (1953, xv) opines that the early Christians saw little of the moral richness of this complex cultural mix. A wide range of options for seeing and talking about nonhuman animals generally was available in the environment of the tradition's first centuries. These options reflect diverse sources and factors, and include at least the following categories.

1. Views found in the Hebrew Bible. Though often filtered through the Greek of LXX, these included the opposing views discussed earlier, which were in tension with each other. Of relevance also were (a) the traditional dietary laws and attitudes toward sacrifice and cultically slaughtered animals (which, it will be argued in the next chapter, are only marginally relevant to views of the key animals and *wild* animals in general), and (b) the role of humans as the stewards of creation (also discussed in the next chapter).

2. The pluralism of the Hellenistic world. Diversity was especially pronounced in the area of religious claims and views of other animals.[84]

3. The greater Greek familiarity with the more complex animals outside the human species. There was greater familiarity with cetaceans and elephants, though probably not with nonhuman great apes.

4. The wide range of intellectual argument in the Greek world. This was particularly true regarding other animals' abilities and nature.[85] Of great importance also was the common heritage of the Greek language in which this debate took place.

5. The fundamental differences in views of the source of morality. Hatch, noting the many points of both difference and contact between the Hebrew and Greek traditions, says, "The main point of difference was that Christianity rested morality on a divine command" (1914, 158). He then notes that although the Stoics had a sense that moral laws are divine in nature, "they are so in another than either the Jewish or Christian sense: they are laws of God, not as being expressions of His personal will, but as being laws of nature, part of the whole constitution of the world" (158). Thus, the Hebrew and Greek traditions manifest different emphases in concluding alike that humans are "unique-better."

The diversity and syncretism of the Hellenistic environment resulted in many options being available to see the possibilities of other animals. Some of the more positive views have been alluded to earlier. Lecky argued that Plutarch was "probably the first writer who advocated strongly humanity to animals on the broad ground of universal benevolence."[86] The culture also offered numerous lifestyles and options, such as vegetarian living, that avoided unnecessary harms to other animals.[87] Clark, commenting on Matthew Fox's simplistic criticism of Plato's views, notes that "it was the Platonists who long maintained an attention to the welfare of our nonhuman kind" (1993, 69). Further, in the mix were many human-centered options that were extremely unfriendly to other animals, thus allowing less harsh but still anthropocentric views to seem reasonable and compassionate in comparison.

Still, amid these many options, claims about the paradigmatic qualities of humans' lives, whether backed by belief in a divine command or by confidence in the capabilities of human knowing, dominated and provided a meeting point for the Hebrew and Greek traditions. To be sure, *outside* Hebrew and early Christian circles the view that humans are and should be preeminent was so entrenched that it seemed axiomatic. Clark notes this was, indeed, "Aristotelian common-sense: that human beings display the basic form of life most clearly (very much as women were maimed males!), that it is in human life that the point of the universe is unveiled" (1993, 99).

The Early Centuries

In the early centuries of the tradition, views of other animals were not prominent topics of discussion, for several reasons. First, the formation of new Christian communities in the pluralistic, syncretistic culture caused the focus to be inward rather than outward. Meeks (1993, 37) argues that to understand the distinctive Christian morality that developed, its relation to other claims in the competitive urban environments must be seen. In such urban settings, early Christians developed morality that was very distinctive in some ways, even as the tradition was itself internally diverse on the kinds of things emphasized. Importantly, however, early Christian morality also shared important features with the general cultural milieu, especially its view of other animals. The continuity between the early Christians and their competitors (the non-Christians) on the issue of other animals can be accounted for by Meeks's observation that "[t]he language of virtue that Christians spoke was adapted from older traditions of moral discourse, rather than being invented from scratch" (2). Discourse about other animals, then, was one of the features of the existing discourse that did *not* change in its broadest features. This provided some continuity with the culture against which the tradition in so many other ways defined itself. Thus, even though the early Christians altered morality and even occasionally developed new vocabulary, the new features of Christians' morality did not pertain to the status of other animals.[88] Christian morality was, in this regard, another version of why it is that humans are special relative to the rest of the animal kingdom. That the behavior with which the community was concerned was *intra-species* behavior was simply a cultural datum, and thus often an invisible background assumption over which other debates about *which humans* mattered, and why, took place. In both Christian and non-Christian communities, the general method of describing other animals was reliance on traditional generic discourse in expressing a dismissive attitude.

The Physiologus

Before turning to influential postbiblical thinkers, some attention is given to the text that, outside the Bible, had the most influence on views of other animals generally and, in particular, on views of the key animals. Barber notes, "The *Physiologus* was enormously popular; if we include the bestiary as being a version of it, perhaps no book, except the Bible, has ever been so widely diffused among so many people and for so many centuries as the *Physiologus* " (1993, 9). Janson calls it "the basic compendium of 'Christian zoology' [which] wielded extraordinary influence in both the Catholic and the Orthodox world" (1952, 17). The original version, composed "in the second century, in Egypt or in Palestine, [by] a Christian monk,"[89] relied on Hellenistic vocabulary and concepts to articulate views of specific other animals. Although the principal sources were, according to Barber (1993, 9), Aristotle, Pliny, Lucan (39–65 C.E.), and Solinus (third century C.E.), the text had a different purpose than did these secular sources. As Barber notes regarding the bestiaries generally (including the later medieval tradition), the purpose of the bestiaries was

not to document the natural world and to analyse it in order to understand its work-
ings. The writers of bestiaries knew the laws of nature before they began their work,
and were concerned only to expound them. They knew that everything in creation
had a purpose . . . and they knew, too, what that purpose was: the edification and instruction of sinful man. The Creator had made animals, birds and fishes, and had given
them their natures or habits, so that the sinner could see the world of mankind reflected in the kingdom of nature, and learn the way to redemption by the examples of
different creatures. Each creature is therefore a kind of moral entity, bearing a message
for the human reader. (7)

As mainstays of Christian understanding of other animals, the *Physiologus* and
bestiaries were a source of information about the key animals (all of which are
described to some extent in these texts), often to negative effect. Janson notes generally in his study of the portrayal of other primates in the Christian iconographic
traditions:

[T]he reputation of *simia* [apes] had taken a decisive turn for the worse with the ad-
vent of Christianity. Patristic writers, familiar with the pejorative meaning of the
epithet "ape" in classical literature, applied the term to all enemies of Christ, whether
pagan, apostate, heretic or infidel. Even more damaging is the interpretation of the
animal in the *Physiologus*, which brackets the ape with the wild ass (onager) and asserts that both represent the devil.[90]

Although elephants and cetaceans are less negatively portrayed, the descriptions are
so brief as to be caricatures *if* relied upon by a moral agent for information or perspectives regarding these complicated animals. Thus, the consequences of intentional
actions affecting such animals could hardly be well understood if based upon such
descriptions. In general, as Barber's analysis of these collections shows, the views
and explanations of other animals found in these works were eminently anthropocentric and ideological in the narrow sense of chapter 2. In summary, the consequence of these texts being important tools by which viewpoints were transmitted
was the perpetuation of caricatures of the key and other animals.

Significant Postbiblical Theologians

The concerns and vocabulary of the early postbiblical theological tradition echo both
the view affirming the value of mere membership in the human species found in the
Old and New Testaments, and the dismissive attitude toward biological individuals
not a part of the human species. Generally, the vocabulary of the extant writings
regarding other animals from this period has the generic features already discussed
and only rarely reflects close engagement with other animals' realities.

Justin Martyr

According to the individual "generally regarded as the most significant apologist of
the second century," (Hinson 1987b, 220), "We have been taught that God did not
make the world aimlessly, but for the sake of the human race (*anthrōpeion genos*)."[91]
Similar views of the centrality of humans *as a group* can be found in 2 *Apology* 5.2,
where, to use Barnard's summary, Justin "states that all earthly things were made

subject to man while the heavenly elements and the seasons were ordained for man's advantage" (1967, 113). Such a stark, human-centered claim reflects an influential way of evaluating other animals that combines features of the Hebrew and Greek cultures. Justin was well educated in Greek ways of thinking.[92] Osborn argues that Justin's anthropocentric views have a Stoic, rather than an explicitly Platonic, origin, commenting that for the Stoics "plants and animals live for their use by man" (1973, 51). Indeed, Justin uses the characteristically Stoic word *oikoumenē*,[93] which Sorabji (1993, esp. chap. 10) points out is the central feature of the later Stoics' exclusivist and anthropocentric vision of justice and ethics.

While general references to humans collectively are characteristic of Justin's extant writings, there is an absence of specific, direct references to other animals. This can, to some extent at least, be accounted for by the fact that the primary purpose of these writings was apologetic. There are, to be sure, incidental references.[94] In the *Dialogue with Trypho* 4, the nonhuman animals used as examples in the passage are all domestic (horses, asses, goats, and sheep; Dods and others 1868, 91–92), the implication being that they are good representatives of all other animals. Justin seems to reason that the features of the nonhuman animals he knew, or had heard of, exhaust the relevant abilities of all other animals.

In 1 *Apology* 55 and 1 *Apology* 24 (1), the familiar *alogōn zōōn* appears as a second-level generic term (Pautigny 1904, 116 and 48). The context in 1 *Apology* 55 is this argument:

> The human figure differs from the irrational animals [*alogōn zōōn*] precisely in this, that man stands erect and can stretch out his hands, and has on his face, stretched down from the forehead, what is called the nose, through which goes breath for the living creature [*zōō*]—and this exhibits precisely the figure of the cross.

The underlying principle of differentiation is the traditional Greek notion that humans are distinguished by, and other animals lack, *logos*, which appears here as a "background" or culturally given perspective that Justin employs to describe and organize the world of living organisms.[95] Justin's use of *tetrapoda* as a second-level generalization at 1 *Apology* 43.8 is similar: "But God did not make man like other [beings], such as trees and animals [*tetrapoda*], which have no power of choice."[96] The dominant second-level generalization in Justin's work, however, is *thērion*, which occurs about a dozen times (Goodspeed 1912, 134). It is also used as a third-level generalization, as in 1 *Apology* 15.14, where it appears along with the word for birds in a stringlike phrase reminiscent of the Hebrew tradition (Pautigny 1904, 30). Such references to other animals are almost never to specific kinds of animals; instead, they are generic, totally reliant on existing views he inherited, and generally derogatory.

The underlying conceptual scheme relies on the view that all humans share essential features by virtue of species membership. But, in one sense, the species category *itself* is not important, for membership in other, nonhuman species is not judged of much consequence, at least from the standpoint of moral considerability. Rather, other animals are grouped together regardless of their species because it is their *non-membership* in the human species that matters. In summary, Justin's frequent and diverse emphases on *all* members of the human species can be contrasted with the few indirect and generic references to other animals. Although his anthropology diverges from that of the New Testament in some significant ways,[97] and his anthropocentrism is expressed in some concepts new to the Christian tradition (the Stoics' idea of the universal occurrence of the *spermatikos logos* being the most obvious example),[98] his views of other animals are in no way inconsistent with the New Testament view of other animals.

Irenaeus of Lyons

When Irenaeus argued "[F]or man was not made for its sake, but creation for the sake of man,"[99] he emphasized the Hebrew views which he inherited while, unlike Justin, offering few compliments for nonbiblical writers. His long treatise *Against Heresies* was written in Greek but remains only in a Latin translation, which Roberts and Rambaut described as "of the most barbarous character."[100] In this poor condition, it was "circulated widely and exerted a widespread influence on Christian theology in subsequent centuries, particularly in the West" (Hinson 1987a, 281), a fact that contributed to Robinson's assessment of Irenaeus as "the greatest theologian of the second century" (1920, 1).

Against Heresies is apologetic in nature, and the paucity of references to non-human animals is again explained, at least in part, by its detailed polemical refutation of Gnostic claims. Yet, in the details of his opposition, Irenaeus left numerous clues regarding his understanding of other animals. The Gnostic theories that are Irenaeus's targets can, in significant ways, be seen as radically anthropocentric, since these views generally ignored the existence of more positive perspectives, observations, speculations, and information about other animals that could be found in widely known texts in the second-century cultural mix. There are clues that Irenaeus knew at least some of these views (see, for example, *Against Heresies* 2.14.2 regarding Anaxagoras's opinions), but it is also clear from his opposition to the Gnostics that, to Irenaeus's mind, what was at issue was the proper form of anthropocentrism. Accordingly, his references to other animals are minor, generic, and incidental.

Irenaeus's Form of Anthropocentrism

In the idiom of the Western Christian theological tradition, Irenaeus's explanation of the relative place and purposes of all living and nonliving reality is told by means of a theology of Creation history. In such explanations, the created world can be understood by virtue of Christian revelation, which tells a discernible story, and a characteristic feature of Irenaeus's explanation is the recurring emphasis on humans as one group (particularly good examples can be found in *Against Heresies* 3). In fact, Irenaeus argued that humans as a group had been appointed by God to a place higher than that of the angels.[101] Just how central Irenaeus made humans in the broader creation has been disputed.[102] Wingren notes that claims of extreme anthropocentrism have "a certain justification . . . since the changing events of nature are quite definitely centred on that which befalls man."[103] Santmire refers to Irenaeus's views as "a qualified anthropocentrism" (1985, 41) because

Irenaeus's nuance is not that the world was created by God for the *sole* purpose of blessing humanity and offering humanity redemption, but rather that *when* it was created it was *arranged* or shaped so as to offer humanity blessings and to communicate salvation to humanity. (42)

This emphasis on the special place of humans does *not*, however, cause Irenaeus to repudiate the obvious continuities with other animals. Rather, Irenaeus, in great contrast to his Gnostic opponents, plainly acknowledges the "animal" dimensions of human existence as part of God's good creation.[104]

Yet, in the ways being addressed in this study, Irenaeus's version of which animals matter is not less anthropocentric than the views of the Gnostics he challenged, especially if the measure is the purpose of biological humans in the broader universe. In very significant ways, Irenaeus did not accept *other* animals' biological realities at all, since, from the vantage point of appreciating other animals for traits not held by humans, Irenaeus saw humans as absolutely more important than any biological competitors. For example, in *Against Heresies* 4.37.7, Irenaeus argued that all things in this world were arranged for "the bringing of man to perfection, for his edification, and for the revelations of His dispensations" (Roberts and Rambaut 1868–69, 2:41). Santmire thus admits that "Irenaeus's view of human life in nature is self-consciously anthropocentric. . . . But this is an administrative anthropocentrism, as it were, not an ontological anthropocentrism [like that of Origen]."[105]

Relative to beings in *this* world, however, the distinction between these two forms of human-centeredness makes no difference. From the standpoint of humans who opposed any form of radical anthropocentrism or from the standpoint of other animals' interests, the alleged distinction arguably amounts to a dispute over which form of exclusivist, anthropocentric thinking will prevail.[106]

Irenaeus on Other Animals

Irenaeus's references characteristically rely on the generic vocabulary and concepts that he inherited. For example, in the claims found in the extant original Greek of Irenaeus (that is, in the only portions of his works reliable enough to assess *Irenaeus's* choice of words, since the Latin is so "barbarous"), Irenaeus uses the standard generic terms found inside and outside early Christianity. In *Against Heresies* 1.5.4, Irenaeus, when recapitulating Valentinian claims about different kinds of matter, uses words that suggest how he divided up the universe of living organisms. In one sentence he uses the word *anthrōpon* (translated in the Latin as "hominem"), which he contrasts with the familiar second-level generalization *alogōn zōōn* and the third-level generalization *thērion*.[107]

Of other animals Irenaeus says generally that God has promised that they will "become peaceful and harmonious among each other, and be in perfect subjection to man."[108] In describing how this world has been ordered by God for members of the human species, Irenaeus argues that God "conferred on spiritual things a spiritual and invisible nature, . . . on angels an angelical, on animals an animal, on beings that swim a nature suited to the water, and those that live on land one fitted for land."[109] These passages, no longer available in the original Greek, express divisions that reflect the standard separation of humans from all other animals which characterized both the cultural traditions that dominated Irenaeus's training and beliefs. The passage that contains the most references to different kinds of animals (calves, lambs, kids, wolves, lions, leopards, vipers)[110] is dominated by the standard domestic-wild division, which is found in Isaiah (discussed in chapter 9). It also portrays other animals as "by nature mutually hostile and inimical" and compares humans who harm others as "brutal and beast-like because of selfish pride."

In summary, Irenaeus, admittedly with some special nuances relative to the main-line tradition,[111] legitimated the negative views of other animals that he inherited.

Clement of Alexandria

Clement of Alexandria took a more positive attitude toward Greek philosophy than that implicit or explicit in the criticisms of the dominant culture found in the works of Justin, Irenaeus, and Tatian.[112] Even scholars who have concluded that Clement's use of Greek philosophy was only instrumental (and thus did not substantially alter his Christian views) make it clear that Clement's work is steeped in the idiom of Greek ideas, whether they be directly from Plato, the Stoics, and Aristotle, or mediated by the "cultural synthesis as it appears in Philo, in Middle Platonism, and in Neoplatonism."[113] Whatever the answer to this debate, it is clear that Clement used the cultural forms of Hellenism, which were, as Dewart notes, "the cultural form of the *ecumenical* world" (1966, 133).

Clement took the negative side in the ongoing debate about the importance of the abilities and interests that occur in biological individuals outside the human species. His opinions provide a meeting point where certain Greek ideas about other animals are meshed explicitly with and indistinguishably from those views tending to subordinate, and at times dismiss, other animals which the Christian tradition inherited from the Hebrew tradition. His many and diverse references to other living things are characterized by confident assertions and wide-ranging claims. Murphy (1941) systematically lists the "nature" references in Clement's works, citing more than twenty-four species or groups of animals referred to in the *Protrepticus*. The more than one hundred references to other animals in the *Paedagogus* alone cover more than fifty species or groups of nonhuman animals, while the *Stromata* mentions more than thirty-five species or groups. Of the key animals, apes (or at least primates of some kind) and elephants are mentioned, while it appears that there are no references to dolphins or whales.

Clement's references, however, were framed within the narrow universe of discourse and concerns that had been developing in the Christian tradition exemplified by Justin, Irenaeus, and Tatian. In his extant works, the traditional Greek generic terms for other animals dominate the specific references. In *Stromata* 5.13, for example, Clement collects all other animals under the generic term *alogon zōon* when mentioning the views of Pythagoras, Heraclitus, Democritus, Plato, Aristotle, and Xenocrates regarding animals outside the human species (Migne PG 9, 127–28). As a participant in the debate described by Sorabji (1993), Clement argued, after the manner of the Stoics, that humans, but *no other animals*, are able to discriminate appearances; all other animals, described generally as *aloga zōa*, are, instead, "carried away by them."[114] This kind of confident assertion about other animals is also found throughout the *Protrepticus*, as in 10.80, where Clement makes the standard argument that humans are not merely set apart but, indeed, above all other animals (Butterworth 1953, 216–17).

The term used in discussing living beings is *zōōn*, which appears regularly in the *Protrepticus*. At times it stands unmodified as a first-level generalization, as at *Protrepticus* 3.37 (Butterworth 1953, 94–95), where it is a reference to "all living creatures."[115] At other times, it stands unmodified as a second-level generic term, as in *Protrepticus* 10.80 (quoted earlier), where it is used in the plural as a reference to all nonhuman animals.[116] The changing meaning of this single word is modulated by the basic, background understanding that while humans are animals, they are completely different than any other animals, such that the remaining animals need not be distinguished from one another when the human–other animal distinction is used.

The many references to other animals collectively and by their individual species names are characterized by a recurring instrumental or negative attitude *despite* the fact that Clement, in a general sense, upholds the "goodness" of creation against the Gnostics of his time.[117] Clement also exhibits the standard view of Greek and Hebrew cultures that other, *wild* animals are savage.[118] Clement's comments, then, are generally not sympathetic. They are also not particularly "informed" in any sense other than following traditional views. His assumption that all animals outside the human species can be meaningfully grouped together can be seen in a number of ways, including the lack of references to the more complicated animals described in part II. He does include an incidental reference to an unidentified nonhuman primate when discussing the views of Basilides,[119] but his extant works do not include any reference to the notorious claims of Celsus and others about elephants. In general, the more complicated nonhuman animals do not seem to have made any impression on him.

In summary, Clement's species-based thinking took the form of advocating the then new universalism within the species taxon that was being emphasized by both Christians and the Stoics.[120] All humans were deemed by Clement to have within them (this spatial image is used loosely) "the image of God" simply by virtue of being a species member, and it was this ontological feature that "forever recalled them to a more godlike life."[121]

Origen

In *Against Celsus*, Origen claimed, "The Creator . . . has made everything to serve the rational being and his natural intelligence."[122] Origen's position on which animals are rational beings is, of course, related to membership in the human species. Thus, his human-centered claims are commonly found intertwined with negative positions regarding other animals, an example of which is the colloquial *Against Celsus* 4.85, "He who looks from heaven upon the irrational animals [*alogois*], even though their bodies may be large, will not see any origin for their impulses other than irrationality, so to speak" (Chadwick 1953, 251; Migne PG 11, 1160). The latter is a particularly good example of how confidently Origen made his assertions about all other animals despite relatively little exposure to the natural world beyond his eastern

Mediterranean milieu. It appears that nothing could shake Origen's conviction that all of nonhuman sensible reality was, to use Santmire's words, "made not for the sake of the whole, and each creature for its own sake as part of the whole, but ... for the edification of the human creature" (1985, 50).

Origen's views on other animals are, then, in a decisive way dominated by what Williams referred to as "[t]he most extraordinary and explicit formulation of the anthropocentric view of nature."[123] Other animals are "not bearers of the fallen spirits, as humans are; the animals exist solely as agents of purgation for the moral education of humanity."[124]

These views have been of some consequence in the tradition because Origen has been variously described by scholars as the "greatest of ante-Nicene fathers" (de Lubac 1966, vii) and "towering above the Greek fathers as Augustine towers above the Latins" (Butterworth 1966, xxvii). Jerome at one point pronounced him "the greatest teacher of the Church after the apostles" (Butterworth 1966, xxiii), although he later gave less ardent opinions. Because some of Origen's views were later attacked, his works were destroyed; there remain some fragments of Greek originals, but most of what remains of "a massive body of writings numbering close to a thousand titles" (de Lubac 1966, vii–viii) are Latin translations, which have often been questioned. Butterworth commented when reviewing the state of these translations, "we can never be quite sure that we have Origen's thought as he himself expressed it" (1966, xlvii). Fortunately, some of the central passages in *On First Principles* dealing with other animals occur in the extant Greek and allow one to see how it is that Origen himself talked about other animals. These show that, on the issues being discussed here, Origen is in the same tradition of discourse as Clement.[125] He uses Greek idioms and ideas to explicate a fundamental commitment to the authority of Old and New Testament scriptures as they were then understood. In doing so, his comments about other animals are, though interesting and of great importance, simply not as novel or profound as many of the theological formulations and philosophical arguments that produced his fame and eventually his censure. Instead, Origen passed along the views of other animals that he received, offering interesting rationalizations along the way.

At the very end of the first book of *On First Principles*, Origen argues:

> When the soul falls away from the good and inclines towards evil . . . unless it turns back, it is rendered brutish by its folly and bestial by its wickedness . . . and it is carried towards the conditions of unreason and, so to speak, of the watery life. Then, as befits the degree of its fall into evil, it is clothed with the body of this or that irrational animal [*zōou alogou*].[126]

The passage is related to Origen's belief that the entire cosmic process is a mistake, due, as Butterworth says, "to the misuse of free-will" (1966, lviii). This is, of course, alien to the "goodness of creation" emphasis that is characteristic of the Hebrew tradition and sounds more like the declining universe that one finds portrayed in the *Timaeus* (of which there is an echo in the derogatory reference to "the watery life"; Plato/Jowett I, 68, paragraph 92).

Origen's emphasis on the importance of "reason" as the distinguishing mark of valuable beings is also not new. It is, rather, another example of a kind of perfectionism characteristic of Platonism and its intellectual offspring, which are bound up with the elevation of certain mental processes of humans and a characterization of the realities of animal/biological life as "imperfect" because they are subject to change. Further, the lack of other animals' participation in the community of human speech (the external *logos*[127]) and their apparent lack of ability to reason like humans (that is, mentally organize the world by use of internal *logos*) resulted in the dismissal of other animals' mental abilities. This dismissal is epitomized by the dominance of the recurring negative description *aloga*, which is perhaps best translated as "without the mental and speaking feature(s) deemed to be characteristic of humans and any truly intelligent life."[128] Arguably, however, the notion *a-logos* is not conclusively helpful on its own, that is, without a corollary assumption that there are not *other* kinds of intelligence; in other words, use of *a-logos* as a valid description and point of comparison requires the assumption that human intelligence is paradigmatic. This second, often unstated assumption was a cultural given in the intellectual environment of the times, evidenced by the common claim that humans share rationality with God, the angels, and celestial bodies, but no other creatures.

The Debate with Celsus

Origen's "debate" with Celsus, an educated Greek who attacked Christianity on many grounds about fifty years before Origen's detailed reply in *Against Celsus*, is a telling event regarding the manner in which the early Christian tradition handled the status of other animals. Celsus's challenge to the claims of Christians was a wide-ranging critique, and the portions dealing with other animals, contained primarily in Book 4, are only one part of the dispute, although given some prominence. Chadwick notes:

> For the pagan Platonist the refutation of the Christian thesis requires an extended argument to prove that animals are not less rational than human beings. The argument was a well-worn theme in the debates between Academic and Stoic philosophers of the hellenistic age. . . . Origen decisively identifies himself with the Stoic side of the argument (1966, 106).

In participating in this debate, Origen, who categorically refused to accept the possibility of centering concern on any group of animals other than an exclusively human group, relied on both Christian and Stoic arguments to sustain the propriety of an exclusivist anthropocentrism. In essence, Origen argued that Celsus's attempt to put humans at the same level as other animals, that is, on the level of "irrational" creatures, is destructive of the dignity of humans who are created in the image of God. Celsus had argued for a leveling of human interests with those of other animals in several ways. As part of his argument, Celsus ridiculed what seemed to him the preposterousness of the Christian version of anthropocentrism.[129] In effect, Celsus argued that the claim makes no sense to the individual who lives his or her life in the natural world, which seems *not* to be anthropocentric. Celsus supported his argument by referring to claims that other animals exhibited a measure of rationality in sometimes being able to, using Amundsen's summary, "cure themselves when ill by having recourse to substances of which they would not otherwise avail themselves."[130] In reply, Origen assumed that this must occur "by nature" rather than through the use of reason or any other important, discriminating mental faculty. His general approach, then, is to assume that the claim cannot be true (the burden being placed on the claimant). Using this method, he concludes that it is "obvious" that other animals do not possess "wisdom or reason" (*Against Celsus* 4.87).

Celsus also argued that it was obvious, when one observed other animals, that it was as likely that the features of the world had been set up for their sake as for the sake of humans. For example, rain exists as much for the sake of other animals as for the sake of humans. In reply, Origen asserted unequivocally that there is a clear hierarchy within nature. This is an interesting argument, because it does ring true that some animals are more "complex" (many words would fit here) than others. But the argument, if acceptable, pertains to more than just humans, because some *other* animals (for example, members of the key species) are also obviously more complex than some other biological individuals or parts of nature. Origen's counterargument completely missed, or perhaps simply glossed over, this point. Instead, for Origen, all things are primarily for humans, secondarily for other animals, and only then for the plants that supply the needs of other animals (*Against Celsus* 4.74–75). As Wallace-Hadrill argues, Origen's "principle is that the lower order can only be understood in relation to its end. To understand the plant one must look to the animal; to understand the animal one must look to man" (1968, 114). The analogy (as all plants are for all animals, all animals are for all humans) was widely known in the ancient world, appearing in the writings of Aristotle and Cicero.[131] The analogy involves a category mistake or equivocation, since the category "plant" excludes any animals, while the category "animals" does not exclude humans. Relying on the second claim "all animals are for all humans" on the basis of the validity of the prior claim "all plants are for all animals" is a questionable move, then, because the comparisons are not logically equivalent. In short, the second claim relies on an artificial removal of humans from their natural category.

Another example of the negative attitude and degradation of other animals implied by the coarse grouping so characteristic of Origen's thinking can be seen in *Against Celsus* 4.74:

> [The Stoics] quite rightly put man and the rational nature in general above all irrational beings, and say that providence has made everything primarily for the sake of the rational nature. Rational beings which are the primary things have the value of children who are born; whereas irrational [*aloga*] and inanimate things have that of the afterbirth which is created with the child.[132]

This argument has several salient features other than the degradation and generic grouping of all other animals. Origen cites authority from within the Greek tradition, an effective rhetorical ploy that attempts to refute Celsus on his own terms. The appeal to the image of human children as the standard of value is also interesting; it suggests that the biological species was the standard, since children are not developed members whose "rationality" is fully in place. Sorabji comments, "Origen's position is an extreme one. He does not accept, as Basil was later to do, that animals exist also for their own sakes. On the contrary, he identifies himself with the Stoics who maintain, he says, that irrational animals are made primarily for rational beings"

(1993, 200). As Santmire summarizes, "Below humans in the hierarchy Origen depicts a world that resembles a pernicious wilderness, much more than a life sustaining home" (1985, 50).

Origen's claims at *Against Celsus* 4.81–89 regarding the instructional purpose (for humans) of the existence of other animals go far beyond the allegorical value suggested by many stories. At *Against Celsus* 4.78, Origen argues that, like the domesticated dogs and oxen who lived in community with humans, other animals also had purposes *to benefit humans*: "Similarly the species of lions and bears, leopards and boars, and animals of this sort, are said to have been given to us in order to exercise the seeds of courage in us" (Chadwick 1953, 246). This kind of reasoning opens up Origen's insistence that *all* other animals benefited humans to the charge of ideology, since he appears committed to superficial rationalizations that gloss over well-known realities that were radically inconsistent with such a claim.

Concerning nonhuman animals, then, Origen was positively conservative. His use and perpetuation of inherited assumptions about the realities of biological individuals outside his own species remained unquestioning and to the disadvantage of all other animals.[133]

Attention is now turned to the Western Christian tradition as a prelude to dealing with Augustine's influential views of other animals.

The Latin Generics

The broad generalizations for describing living things available in Latin at the beginning of the common era included *animalia*, *animantia*, *beluae*, *bestiae*, *ferae*, *iumentae*, *pecora*, *quadrupedia*, and *viventia*. Of these, several could operate as first- or second-level generic terms depending on context. For example, *animal* (in plural form, *animalia*) could operate as a first-level generalization meaning "a living being" (in the plural, "all living beings"). Lewis and Short's definition of *animal* includes "in the widest sense, ζῷον" (1962, 122), a reference to the dominant Greek generic term for living beings discussed previously. They give several examples from classical authors that show the generic features of the term. *Animal*, however, had a second, more common use, usually doing work as a second-level generalization.[134] Similarly, inflected forms of *animans* could be used broadly to include humans, other animals, and plants, although Lewis and Short note that the plural form *animantium*, like *animalia*, usually stood for all other animals "in opposition to men."[135]

There were other words that could operate as second-level generalizations, such as *bestiae*. *Bestiae* was most often employed much as "beasts" has been employed in English, that is, not only to indicate the status of nonhuman animal *but also* to add the judgment that the referents were without the critical human mental faculty often called "reason" (Lewis/Freund 1993, 234; and Glare 1982, 231). *Bestiae* could also be used as a third-level generalization.[136] *Brutus*, an adjective meaning variously "heavy," "dull," "stupid," "insensitive," or "unreasonable" (Lewis and Short 1962, 253; Glare 1982, 243), at times worked in the manner of a second-level generalization in early Latin, and is of course related to the English terms "brute" and "brutal." As an adjective, when it was used for other animals, it conveyed the evaluative sense of "irrational" or "very animal-like" (in a negative sense). Lewis and Short (1962, 253) note, however, that it was only in later Latin that *bruta* came to be used as a substantive that operated as a second-level generalization.

Another word in pre-Christian Latin that operated as a broad third-level generalization (that is, for large groups, but not all, of nonhuman biological life) was *ferae*, a term used much as *thēria* in its narrower sense was used, that is, for wild animals beyond humans' control (Lewis/Freund 1993, 741). It also could be used to mean wild animals other than fish and birds (Glare 1982, 685). Narrower third-level generics included (1) *pecus* (usually reserved for domesticated animals; (Glare 1982, 1317); (2) *quadrupes* and variants (Glare 1982, 1532); and (3) *iumenta*, generally used like the English phrase "beasts of burden" (Glare 1982, 981).

Latin Translations of the Old and New Testaments

Even though classical Latin did not become the dominant language in Rome in matters of religion and philosophy until the third century,[137] there were influential Latin translations of the writings deemed important by early Christians that no doubt contributed to ways in which early Latin-speaking Christians spoke about other animals. Augustine wrote, "In the early days of faith, everyone who happened to get possession of a Greek manuscript and who thought that he had any facility in both languages, however slight it may be, ventured to translate it."[138] The dominant early translations, generally known now as "the Latin Versions,"[139] had come to prominence as early as the late second century.[140]

The Vulgate was a late development in the Western church, in that by the time it was commissioned in 382 and completed in 405 (Würthwein 1979, 91–92), specific and generic words for other animals were already well established. These, of course, reflected the cultural consensus as to the relative standing of humans versus all other animals. Jerome's choice of words for the passages describing other animals was also heavily influenced by the fact that his commission was to translate existing texts that were already being read as saying something narrow about other animals. Thus, the very nature of the project was not likely to produce revolutionary views of other animals. Rather, as might be expected, the Vulgate's language perpetuated the established tradition of viewing all other animals as a group distinct from members of the human species. The Latin words that appear in Jerome's translation of Genesis 1, then, reflect the same habits of reference to other animals that have been discussed with reference to Justin, Irenaeus, Clement, and Origen.

For example, in Genesis 1 the phrase *anima vivens*, in inflected forms, appears repeatedly (vv. 20, 21, 24). *Anima* has many meanings in Latin, most of which are directly related to a basic sense expressed by the English phrase "the air breathed by a living creature." In this sense, it has obvious first-level generalization qualities. Glare (1982, 132) lists four definitions having such broad application, and only in the fifth definition is there a hint of the other, *nonmaterial* senses that have been historically important as well (such as "soul" or some vital principle abstractly considered). Jerome's coupling of *anima* with *vivens* (from the verb "to live") emphasizes the great breadth of the reference.

In Genesis 1:20 and 21, the same two-word combination works in the manner of a third-level generalization, since the referent is marine creatures alone, and some other animals are still to be created (including humans). In verse 24, *animam viventem* also works as a third-level generic term because the referents are terrestrial (as opposed to marine) animals. It is followed by a string of narrower third-level generalizations (*iumenta* [domestic cattle], *et reptilia, et bestias terrae*), which, as noted earlier, is typical of the Hebrew scriptures.[141] The work done by these third-level generalizations in combination is that of a second-level generalization. Verse 28 in the Vulgate includes a word that in Latin can function as a true second-level generalization, the inflected participle *animans* used in nounlike fashion. The RSV translation is "and have dominion over the fish of the seas and over the birds of the air and over every living thing [*animantibus*] that moves upon the earth." The Hebrew is again a string of third-level generalizations (marine, air, and land creatures).

Jerome's translation of Genesis 8 and 9 also contains standard generic terms used to convey the broad generalizations that occur in the original Hebrew passages (exemplary is Genesis 9:10, "I establish my covenant with . . . every living creature [*omnem animam viventem*] that is with you, and the birds [*volucribus*], the cattle [*iumentis et pecudibus terrae*], and every beast of the earth [*universis bestiis terrae*] with you").

The New Testament portions of the Vulgate reflect a similar pattern. In the 2 Peter 2:12 passage regarding "irrational animals" (discussed earlier), Jerome's term for the Greek *aloga zōa* is *irrationabilia*. In Titus 1:12, where Cretans are said to be "always liars, evil beasts," Jerome uses *bestiae* for the LXX *thēria*. Interestingly, the oft-cited passage at Romans 8:19–21 about creation groaning in travail does *not* use words that were especially associated with nonhuman animals. Instead, the Latin *creatura* is used, which, as with the Greek *ktisis*, has a sense that can include both other animals and inanimate objects as part of the created order.

Additional Comments in Early Christianity about Other Animals

There were, of course, many other figures in early Christianity who commented on other animals. Of particular interest are the comments of Augustine's mentor, Ambrose of Milan. Characteristic of the hexaemeral tradition as it had been decisively influenced by Basil,[142] Ambrose mentions many other animals.[143] In many of his references, a positive sense and even exuberance are conveyed.[144] His information is, however, largely derivative, in that he relies on Basil (who first introduced the hexaemeral tradition to anecdotal information about other animals and plants). Importantly, Basil had also relied on sources who drew from the writings of Aristotle, Aelian, and the *Physiologus* tradition.[145] Ambrose's accounts of other animals were, then, more often than not a matter of passing along inherited views that had their root in (1) the language and concerns of the Genesis passages being explicated, and (2) certain highly anthropocentric presuppositions of the *Timaeus*, which was foundational for the whole hexaemeral tradition. It should be noted as well that, although at times the rich and interesting hexaemeral tradition provided the best information available on some other animals, this information was entirely secondary to the focus on the Creation and humans' special place.

Augustine and Other Animals

On the central issue of the moral dimensions of a member of the human species killing any nonhuman animal, Augustine in *City of God* (1.20) interpreted the commandment "Thou shall not kill" as follows:

> [S]ome try to extend this commandment even to wild and domestic animals [*bestias ac pecora*] and maintain that it is wrong to kill any of them. Why not then extend it to plants. . . . Hence, putting aside these ravings, if when we read, "Thou shalt not kill," we do not understand this phrase to apply to bushes, because they have no sensation, nor to the unreasoning animals [*inrationalibus animantibus*] that fly, walk or crawl, because they are not partners with us in the faculty of reason.

This explanation invokes the traditional *sorites*, or "slide," argument, "if you spare animals, you will have, absurdly, to spare vegetables."[146] Elsewhere, Augustine adds reasons such as humanity's similarity to angels but not to any nonhuman animals.[147] As with the argument regarding the Gadarene swine incident analyzed in chapter 5, there is little likelihood that Augustine as a master of rhetoric was unaware of the many logical leaps that such arguments require.[148] The argument is more likely appealing because it justifies existing practices and a way of life, rather than because it is logically compelling.[149]

That this argument has been influential is not surprising,[150] given that Augustine is, by consensus, a leading figure in the Christian tradition. As on so many subjects, he has had great influence on how later Christians would talk about and see other animals. Robbins notes, for example, that Augustine was "the second greatest innovator of the Hexaemeral tradition and the chief authority of the mediaeval Latin writers on creation" (1912, 64). His innovations in the hexaemeral tradition were of a particular sort, for Augustine "does not, like Basil and Ambrose, introduce a mass of detail concerning the life of birds and beasts, illustrative of God's providence in their creation" (Robbins 1912, 70). Rather, his status in the hexaemeral tradition came from the influence of his views on Genesis generally (dealt with later).

More broadly, his great and admittedly complex influence on the subject of how other animals are to be understood was generally of a negative and exclusivist nature. Sorabji states unequivocally, "[T]he Stoic view of animals, with its stress on their irrationality, became embedded in Western, Latin-speaking Christianity above all through Augustine. Western Christianity concentrated on one-half, the anti-animal half, of the much more evenly balanced ancient debate" (1993, 2).

By arguing later that Augustine had a negative impact in reinforcing exclusivist reasoning and views of other animals, I do *not* mean to suggest that he did not refer to other animals often, for his works contain a wide range of references to many other kinds of animals. Holman lists approximately fifty kinds of animals (species, or small groups of species, as opposed to larger, third-level generalizations) that are in some way mentioned by Augustine.[151] She concludes, "[H]is knowledge of nature was wide and varied, and presupposes a close personal observation and study. His treatment of nature is serious and earnest" (1931, 120). Holman adds an important qualification to this evaluation when she notes that "the nature-imagery in St. Augustine is always subordinate to the thought or doctrine he wishes to develop" (147). It will be suggested later that features of Augustine's *style of reference*, with all its implications for seeing other animals' realities, justify the characterization of Augustine's overall view of other animals, as well as his impact on subsequent views, as "negative" and "exclusivist." These features are evident in the five separate works where Augustine addresses the opening chapter of Genesis.[152] Augustine's recurring fascination with this first and more cosmically oriented Creation account reflects the fact that the inherited Old Testament text addressing the origin and organization of the world and its biological beings became *the* template and justification for later views of other animals.[153] This tradition of interpreting the Genesis 1 story as paradigmatic has made Christian attempts to understand other animals resistant to counterfactual information and hence potentially ideological in the sense defined in chapter 2.

Augustine's five studies of the opening chapter of Genesis are:

1. *De Genesi contra Manichaeos libri duo* (*A Commentary on Genesis: Two Books against the Manichees*)[154]
2. Books 12 and 13 of the *Confessions*[155]
3. *De Genesi ad litteram inperfectus liber* (*The Literal Meaning of Genesis: An Unfinished Book*)[156]
4. *De Genesi ad litteram duodecim* (*The Literal Meaning of Genesis: A Commentary in Twelve Books*)[157]
5. Book 11 of *City of God*[158]

Augustine's attempts to interpret this text reveal that a foundational assumption for him was that the Genesis 1 passages offered definitive descriptions of humans and all other animals.

Augustine's First Attempt at Explicating Genesis 1

In *De Genesi contra Manichaeos libri duo* 1.15–16, (Teske 1991, 71–74), Augustine addressed the very negative view of other animals that the Manichees advanced. He rebuts Manichean objections to the account of Genesis 1:20–23 regarding the origin of certain animals using the words *animalia* and *multa animalia* by referring to unnamed "learned men who carefully investigate these matters."[159] This approach of appealing to "investigation" suggests (1) that Augustine viewed the Genesis 1 passages as realist claims (that is, as referent-based and referent-accurate claims) that were informative about the existing realities of the biological world and (2) that Augustine believed empirical investigation supported the Genesis 1 descriptions. Although Augustine thus implicitly acknowledged that an empirical approach is a valid one, he did not go further and suggest that such empirical investigation is either necessary or important. Rather, Augustine's comments about other animals remain conservative, in the sense that they are couched in traditional categories that were generally underdetermined by facts and overdetermined by theories which, on the whole, were driven by factors other than the realities of the animals being described.

Augustine often stated the important theme (discussed in more detail later) that "all things are beautiful to their creator" *even if* humans remain unaware of their uses

(1.16.25). Regarding seemingly insignificant or noxious animals, he states candidly, "I admit that I do not know why mice and frogs were created, or flies and worms. Yet I see that all things are beautiful in their kind, though on account of our sins many things seem to us disadvantageous" (1.16.26). He uses the second-level generalization "all living things" when arguing in the same passage that not every being need be useful to *humans*: "Surely all living things [*omnia animalia*, Migne PL 34, 185] are either useful for us, or harmful, or superfluous." Such observations, though mildly suggestive that other animals might have purposes or possibilities distinct from the purpose and possibilities of humans, did *not* lead Augustine to nonanthropocentric formulations of rules for interacting with other animals. Instead, he generally reaffirmed the existing anthropocentric and exclusivist tendencies. For example, in 1.18.29 and 1.20.31 (Teske 1991, 76–79), Augustine reiterates the claim that humans are designedly dominant over the "beasts" (*bestias*; Migne PL 34, 187), even though "men are killed by many wild animals [*multis feris*]" (1.18.29). As noted in the discussion of Origen's similar claim, this is simply not an obvious feature of life on earth, and the claim begs some explaining. Augustine's explanation resorts to his characteristic position that sin has removed humans from their rightful position. He adds, apparently as evidence of humans' high place despite their sin, "But even man's state of condemnation involves such power that he rules many animals [*multis pecoribus*]" (1.18.29).

The Second Attempt: The Confessions

In the *Confessions* passages of Book 13 where Augustine again deals with the import of the Genesis 1 claims, he reemphasizes the importance of allegorical interpretation (that is, he goes beyond the literal meaning). Importantly, he does not use this interpretive tool to move away from the views he inherited regarding the ontological differences between humans and all other animals. Those views were not, in his opinion, mere allegories that assert the importance of humans. Rather, the "human animals/nonhuman animals" contrast is ontologically real and always remains a principal feature of his interpretation, as at 13.23 (pages 434–35), where he contrasts "Man" (*homo*) in his intellectual dimension (*per mentis intellectum*) with "unreasonable beasts" (*iumentis insensatis*).[160]

Generally, the portions of the *Confessions* dealing with other animals in the Creation story (book 13, chaps. 20–32) are extremely formulaic, in that they constantly rely on the "string" categories for descriptions of other animals (the groupings of flying, swimming, crawling animals are constantly the units of reference).[161] Thus, the vocabulary is the standard series of third-level generalizations, as in 13.23, which reiterates that humans by God's design have dominion "over all the fish of the sea [*piscium maris*], and over the fowls of the air [*volatilium caeli*], and over all cattle and wild beasts [*omnium pecorum*], and over all the earth, and over every creeping thing that creepeth upon the earth."

In 13.32, Augustine summarizes by using *animal* as a first-level generalization and then, employing centrally important theological language, by contrasting the significance of humans with all other animals described by a second-level generalization (*inrationabilibus animantibus*):

> We behold the face of the earth decked with earthly creatures [*terrenis animalibus*], and Man created after thine own image and likeness, even through that very Image and likeness (that is the power of reason and understanding) made superior to all unreasonable creatures [*cunctis inrationabilibus animantibus*].

In general, then, the *Confessions* reflects well the fundamental feature of Augustine's understanding of biological lives, that is, on one side, all human animals, and on the other side, all other animals, defined negatively by virtue of their not having the paradigmatic mental qualities that all humans have.

The Third Attempt

In *De Genesi ad litteram inperfectus liber*, even though Augustine worked very hard to find literal interpretations of the Genesis 1 claims,[162] he goes beyond literal interpretation to implement the "humans–other animals" contrast. At 16.54, he argues regarding Genesis 1:25, "Here the name 'cattle' [*pecorum*], I believe, signified all the quadrupeds [*quadrupedia*] that live under man's care" (Teske 1991, 182–3; Migne PL 34, 241).

In the next passage (16.55), after citing the Genesis 1:26 passage about humans being made in the image and likeness of God, Augustine oscillates between different broad, vague generalizations by using language that on its face reads easily enough but is, upon further examination, undergirded by a complex taxonomy of life. The relevant portion of the passage reads:

> Here we should note how all of the animals [*animantium*] are grouped together and yet kept separate. Scripture says that man was made on the same day as the beasts [*bestias*]; for they are all alike earthly animals [*terrena animalia*]. Yet on account of the excellence of reason, according to which man is made to the image and likeness of God, it speaks of him separately, after it had finished speaking of the other earthly animals [*caeteris terrenis animantibus*].

Augustine begins with a reference to *animantium*, which in this context is ambiguous. It could be construed as a reference to all living beings, including humans, but, more likely and as the context of the passage suggests, it is a second-level generalization grouping all *other* animals under one term. Augustine goes on to mention *bestias*, which in this context is clearly a third-level generalization exclusive of humans and some other animals such as marine creatures and insects. He then refers to the group *terrena animalia*, which is a narrow group of terrestrial animals that here includes humans. He ends the passage with the phrase "other earthly animals" (*caeteris terrenis animantibus*), which under the logic of *caeteris* (other) here excludes humans but which otherwise would have included them (since they are terrestrial living beings). Context again suggests that his referent is all other animals, since the contrast is with humans generally.

This complex oscillation is easy for the reader to miss and even intentionally ignore, since the passage is prefaced with the claim that humans are in the image of God and *unlike* any other living beings. Thus, an underlying feature of the text, as with all of Augustine's writing, is that the biological beings that really matter are members of the human species, while the other groupings are secondary. The words chosen by Augustine, then, do not always *on their face* "lump" all other animals into just one group that is constantly contrasted to a second group composed of all humans. Rather, Augustine often uses the vague generic terms rather loosely. But the underlying message cannot be mistaken.

De Genesi ad litteram duodecim

A fourth treatment of the Genesis 1 creation account is the longest. It had an important impact on how the later Christians viewed other animals, for, as Robbins observes, this work "exercised the most influence on the Hexaemera" (1912, 64 n. 1) of Augustine's accounts of Genesis 1. In *De Genesi ad litteram duodecim*, other animals are principally addressed in book 3, chaps. 8–18. Here Augustine reveals his familiarity with the views of unnamed others regarding some other animals. In 3.8.12, where his argument aims to uphold the Genesis account in its specifics, he refers to "authors who have recorded many astounding phenomena observed in fish ponds"[163] in order to rebut unnamed others who "have failed to observe the facts of experience." Although this is another appeal to the value of empirical observation, these empirically based arguments are tactical replies in the service of Augustine's passionate commitment to rebut challenges to the scriptural tradition and other inherited, cherished values. In many other contexts, Augustine repudiated the general validity of empirically based arguments, for, as Pagels notes, "Augustine . . . argued for a view of nature utterly antithetical to scientific naturalism" (1988, 130).

Augustine's commitment to the Christian views he inherited is evident in his creative attempts to justify the specifics of the Genesis 1 passages. At 3.11.16, he takes great pains to explain what the individual words of Genesis 1:24–25 mean:

> There is, of course, no doubt about the kinds of animals [*animalium genera*] that the earth produced at God's word. But because the terms "herds" [*pecorum*] and "beasts" [*bestiarum*] are often used to indicate all irrational animals [*animalia omnia rationis expertia*], there is reason to ask which animals are meant here. . . . [L]ions, panthers, tigers, wolves, foxes, and even dogs and apes [*simiis*], and the other creatures of this kind are normally called beasts. But the term "herds" is more appropriately restricted to domestic animals, which help man with his labors. (Taylor 1982, 89–90; Migne PL 34, 288–89)

Augustine goes on to discuss the referent of terms such as *quadrupedia, omnia reptilia terrae*, and *ferae*, making it clear that he takes the language of Genesis 1 to be a "realist" inventory of living beings. He also assumes that the surface features of the Genesis account (that is, the fact that specific claims purport to cover only some animals but not others) must, and can, be accounted for. For example, he states an argument at 3.13.21 (Taylor 1982, 89), explaining why the command "increase and multiply" was addressed to only some categories of other animals and not others.

Augustine's attempts to provide literal meaning for specific passages in Genesis 1 are characterized by explanations which presume that all other animals can be (1) seen together as (2) lacking important features which (3) make humans alone morally considerable. At 3.12.20, Augustine explains, "[A]fter his fall, [man] has been joined with senseless beasts [*pecoribus insensatis*] and has become like them" (Migne

PL 34, 287). This use of the plural of *pecus* as part of a second-level generic is unusual, in that the term is usually reserved for the narrower group "domestic animals" (as in 3.11.16, discussed earlier). Its employment as a description of *all* nonhuman animals is one of the subtle ways in which all other animals are rendered faceless and subordinate to humans.

Augustine's project of using the Genesis 1 passages as a literal guide to understanding other animals leads him to ask questions that arise from even minimal familiarity with the biological world as it surrounds us. He tries, for example, to account for the innumerable small forms of life that appear not to be included in the list of "macro" life-forms which dominate the descriptions of Genesis 1. At 3.14.22–23 (Taylor 1982, 89–90; Migne PL 34, 288–89), Augustine addresses "certain very small forms of animal life" (*minutissimis animalibus*), which everyone assumed had their origin in decaying creatures. After arguing that these commonly derided life-forms have "a special beauty proper to [their] nature," Augustine attempts to account for the origin of these life-forms that seem not to be mentioned in the Genesis account. To explain their occurrence while at the same time preserving the status of Genesis 1 as an all-encompassing account, Augustine suggests that those animals mentioned explicitly in the Genesis 1 account carried "seminal principles of animals [*animalium*] later to appear."

Here, as in each of these studies,[164] Augustine displays great confidence in the descriptive value of Genesis 1, operating as if its ordering of the biological world, together with its descriptions of other animals, is not only adequate but also *definitive*.

Positive Features of Augustine's Views of Other Animals

Before detailing how these habits of reference are also characteristic of *City of God*, the argument that there are certain *beneficial* implications for other animals in some of Augustine's views needs to be addressed.[165] First, Augustine's views of other animals are clearly far more positive than many other views found in the Hellenistic-Roman environment. For example, the creation account of Mani from the third century C.E., the details of which Augustine surely knew, is, relative to Augustine's, very negative. In Mani's Zoroastrian-inspired dualistic account, "the animal world . . . springs from abortions of the daughters of Darkness at the sight of the Messenger and similarly keeps Light-substance imprisoned" (Jonas 1963, 225). Augustine's move away from Manichaeism can be seen, then, as a move from an extraordinarily negative view of other animals to possibilities for a far more positive view.

Second, Augustine enhanced these possibilities in some significant ways, the most commonly cited of which is his repeated emphasis on the goodness of creation. As already noted, he argued that other animals that do not benefit humans (such as reptiles and vipers) are, nonetheless, good. Apart from the "creation is good, so other animals must be good" passages discussed previously, there are many places in his works where some interest, and even fascination, is clear. In *De Musica* (1.4–6), for example, Augustine inquires why birds sing, answering that they enjoy their own songs. He notes in these same sections that elephants and bears respond to their human trainers and enjoy music.[166] Further, Augustine made interesting arguments about the experience of nonhuman animals at *De Trinitate* 8.6.9: "[S]ince brute animals [*bestiae*] also perceive that not only themselves live, but also other brute animals interchangeably, and the one the other, and that we ourselves do so."[167] Augustine in this passage goes on to make an argument from analogy, that is, extrapolating from one's own experience of mind to the existence of mind in another: "[W]e both know the mind of any one from our own, and believe also from our own of him who we do not know."[168] It is *not* clear from the passage that Augustine necessarily attributed this process to other animals, although the context suggests that he may have been claiming that something similar occurs. Of other animals, he stated only vaguely that they see "the movements or the body, and that immediately and most easily by some natural agreement." At the very least, these arguments suggest that Augustine was at times concerned to explain the behavior of other animals.

But it is *not* clear how foundational such positive views of nonhuman creation are in Augustine's thought in general. For example, Pagels, when discussing her thesis that Augustine marks a radical departure from the earlier tradition, argues that he repudiated "the twin foundations of the Christian faith: the goodness of God's creation; and the freedom of the human will" (1988, 131). Her argument is not that Augustine failed to say that Creation was good, for he regularly stated that assertion when arguing against views that Creation was a mistake or otherwise not to be respected. Rather, the thrust of Pagels's argument is that there are *other* elements in Augustine's views that are in extreme tension with the recurring claim that Creation was basically good.

An examination of Augustine's specific comments about other animals suggests that, despite the prominent passages where he emphasizes that other animals need not be pleasant to or useful for humans, Augustine's overall view of other animals remains decidedly negative. In fact, a recurring disdain for other animals is in constant tension with, and arguably finally overcomes, the potential, but not actualized, benefits of the argument that "creation is good because it is the product of a good Creator."

In addition to the tension between "good creation" and prominent negative features of Augustine's view of other animals, there is arguably another tension created by his subscription to the grades-of-being notion that came out of the Greek tradition.[169] Belief in this notion appears not to have generated a positive evaluation of those animals that were near humans at the top of the scale. Nor does this view seem to have implied to Augustine that other animals were near to humans in the sense of physical relatedness, consanguinity, similarity of ability or possibility, or competing importance. The other animals that were next to humans in the scale seem have been thought of as completely different in the qualities that matter most, despite a claim that fine gradations and continuity existed. Simply said, subscription to this view did not affect the more important belief that all other animals were ontologically separate from, and to be subordinated to, humans.

The Related Elevation and Criticism of Human Nature

The Christian tradition had inherited a skeptical vein in the Hebrew views of humans generally; especially prominent examples are Adam's sin, the Noah story, the prophets' appreciation of sin, and the psalmists' awareness of the fragility of human enter-prises (as in Psalm 39). The New Testament also contains many passages that ex-plicitly challenge humans, particularly in its expression of the need for salvation of the unspiritual man (such as 1 Corinthians 2:14). Additionally, for much of the early Christian tradition, human sexuality was, as Brown points out, "an unmodi-fied outcrop of the alien, 'animal' world into which the serpent had first led Adam and Eve" (1988, 95). Pagels argues controversially that Augustine effected an im-portant shift in the tradition's view of central features of human existence (espe-cially free will):

> [F]or nearly the first four hundred years of our era, Christians regarded *freedom* as the primary message of Genesis 1–3—freedom in its many forms, including free will, freedom from demonic powers, freedom from social and sexual obligations, freedom from tyrannical government and from fate; and self-mastery as the source of such freedom. . . . [But Augustine had a different reading of the Adam and Eve story.] What they had read for centuries as a story of human freedom became, in his hands, a story of human bondage. . . . Adam's sin not only caused our mortality but cost us our moral freedom, irreversibly corrupted our experience of sexuality (which Augus-tine tended to identify with original sin), and made us incapable of genuine politi-cal freedom. Furthermore, Augustine read back into Paul's letters his own teaching of the moral impotence of the human will, along with his sexualized interpretation of sin. (1988, xxv–xxvi)

Brown also notes that Augustine, "deeply preoccupied by the idea of the basic unity of the human race," held that "nothing is more rent by discord than this human race, in its flawed state."[170]

Thus, the Christian tradition and in particular Augustine, even as they are anthro-pocentric and exclusivist, are also very humble at times about humans' current reali-ties. The skepticism, however, does not necessarily demean humans. Humans may be a problem, but they, as a collective, are the centerpiece and raison d'être of the creation. This elevation is reflected in the central claims that (1) members of the human species alone are in the image of God, (2) the species collectively has been given dominion over all other animals and the earth, and (3) Jesus is the God-human who, as the "new Adam," rectifies the imbalance in all members of the species brought on by an act of the first man and woman.

In the tradition's mainline story about which biological individuals matter, then, other animals, however innocent they may be of any wrongdoing or membership in a species whose progenitors were guilty of some wrongdoing, are not, from the very beginning, capable of being as important as the progeny of Adam. It is their lack of membership in the human species that is the problem, for they cannot, under the inherited paradigm of who is "in the image of God," be a member of the class that really matters. The notion of "image of God" is, of course, a difficult standard to apply, and arguably has not been a static concept over time. Murray (1992, 98), for ex-ample, argues that the original use arose out of the ancient ideology of kingship, and that it is a postbiblical tradition to relate the claim to spiritual or intellectual quali-ties of humans. Whatever the interpretation of the specific meaning of the "image of God," the notion has been widely held applicable to all human beings but to no other animals. Continued heavy reliance on this notion suggests how the Christian tradition is heir to Hebrew presuppositions about the cosmic significance of member-ship in the human species.

References to Other Animals in City of God

McCracken comments that *City of God* "is the flower of the mature thought of Augustine . . . [and] [i]ts influence upon the men of its own day was doubtless great, but far less than that upon succeeding generations" (1966, liv, lvi). It is full of refer-ences to particular kinds of animals, including some of the key animals. As with the interpretations of Genesis 1 discussed earlier, in *City of God* Augustine wants to account for biological diversity greater than that mentioned in this foundational section of the tradition's scriptures. He thus addresses which animals were in Noah's ark (15.27) in order to respond to the obvious problem occasioned by interpreta-tions of Genesis 1 as an exhaustive description of what animals exist. To address the shortfall between the animals listed in Genesis 1 and the far greater biological diversity in the surrounding world, Augustine argued that the animals in the water were not included in the ones to be preserved in the ark.

His wide-ranging references include incidental comments regarding elephants (for example, 5.7 and 8.15), as well as words that normally would have been taken as references to whales. For example, at 22.24 he refers to the "huge bodies of whales" (*ballaenarum*) when arguing that animals (*animantium*) are of so many sizes, suggest-ing that humans admire the smallest most, since we marvel even more at the work of ants and bees than at the size of whales' bodies.[171] Dolphins are also mentioned incidentally in 1.14, which passes along the recurring story of a human saved by riding on the back of a dolphin (*delphini dorso*), as a justification for believing the Jonah story.

Primates are also mentioned, but as a way of pointing out the unity of human-kind. At 16.8 there is a discussion of "monstrous races of men":[172]

> Yet whoever is born anywhere as a human being [*homo*], that is, as a rational mortal creature [*animal rationale mortale*], however strange he may appear to our senses in bodily form or colour or motion or utterance, or in any faculty, part or quality of his nature whatsoever, let no true believer have any doubt that such an individual is descended from the one man who was first created.

He immediately follows this reference with the caveat that, since humans do not know why God created many things, humans should not censure abnormalities:

> For if we did not know that apes [*simias*] and long-tailed monkeys [*cercopithecos*] and chimpanzees [*sphinges*] are not human beings but beasts [*bestias*], those same natural historians who take pride in curious lore might with unscathed vanity foist them upon us as divers distinct tribes of men.

In this passage, two important things collide. The similarity of some other primates to humans (such that some may try to pass them off as humans) collides with Augustine's (and the tradition's) great emphasis on species membership as the critical factor. Similarity will not suffice; biological descent is the critical factor, for indi-viduals that are to be within the moral circle must be descendants of Adam and not merely humanlike. A corollary of the exclusive concern for only descendants of

Adam, but *not* for other animals even when they are somewhat similar to humans, is the emphasis on the universality of the human community:

> The society of moral men, therefore, spread everywhere throughout all countries and, no matter how great the variation of environment, yet retained in a way some bond of fellowship, as being of one and the same origin, though each group pursued advantages and satisfactions peculiar to itself.[173]

This heavy emphasis on humans, but not any other animals, leads to recurring emphasis on the traditional human-nonhuman contrast, as in 12.22:

> God's propagation of the human race [*genus humanum*] from the single man who he first created, was much better than if he had begun it with several. For in the case of other animals [*animantes*] he created some to be solitary and, so to say, lone-ranging, that is, animals who are more attracted to separate living, like eagles, kites, lions, wolves and so on, while others he created to be gregarious, animals preferring to live together in groups, like doves, starlings, deer, little fallow-deer and so on. Yet when he created these animals, he did not propagate both kinds from single specimens but ordered more than one to take up existence at the same time.

Although Augustine here emphasizes some internal variation in the group "other animals" and clearly here and elsewhere appreciates the diversity of animal life beyond the human species line, the principal thrust of his observations is not to discuss biological diversity.[174] Rather, Augustine's point is to emphasize humans as distinct from all other animals, as is evident in the succeeding lines:

> In the case of man [*hominem vero*], however, he proceeded differently. For he created man's nature to be midway, so to speak, between angels and beasts [*angelos bestiasque*] in such a way that, if he should remain in subjection to his true lord and with dutiful obedience keep his commandment, he was to pass into the company of angels, obtaining with no intervening death a blissful immortality that has no limit; but if he should make proud and disobedient use of his free will and go counter to the Lord his God, he was to live like a beast [*bestialiter*], at the mercy of death, enthralled by lust and doomed to eternal punishment after death.

The human–other animals contrast at the heart of Augustine's thinking could not be any better stated. The passage also displays well the constant juxtaposition in Augustine's thought of (1) the belief that humans are valuable and (2) a dismissal of the broad category "other animals" conveyed by means of derogatory uses of second-level generalizations such as *animalia, animantia, bestiae,* and *pecora.*

Augustine's Legacy

The subsequent tradition in the Latin-speaking parts of Christendom had many significant theological and doctrinal developments following Augustine, but *with regard to the status of other animals* the subsequent tradition has been, with few exceptions, a footnote to his views and those of the postbiblical theologians reviewed earlier. In essence, Augustine's views of other animals have provided the subsequent tradition with a template of the view that, for the moral agent, it is members of the human species *alone* who matter among the earth's animals. This template is part of the inherently conservative feature of Christianity as it is bound to its scriptural inheritance and its preoccupation with tradition. The result is that the early refusal to take *any* other animals seriously has become a central, even honored, feature of the tradition.

This is not to say that there have not been variations on the general theme of exclusivist anthropocentrism, or even occasional dissenters. In the main, however, even the dissenting factions of the tradition have held views that place humans in the center. Thus, in general, the tradition has been locked into the negative evaluation of possibilities and realities of nonhuman animals that Augustine inherited and then restated so forcefully.

9

The Christian Understanding of Other Animals

For many Christians, animals are a non-issue.
   —Linzey, *Christianity and the Rights of Animals*

Cosimo de Medici shut a giraffe in a pen with lions, bloodhounds and fighting bulls to see which species was the most savage. As Pope Pius looked on, the lions and dogs napped, the bulls quietly chewed their cuds, and the giraffe huddled against the fence, shaking with fear.
   —Dagg and Foster, *The Giraffe: Its Biology, Behavior and Ecology*

In the opening section of this chapter, various views of what it means to talk "about" other animals are discussed as a prelude to examination of several Christian notions of dominion. The next section provides a characterization of Christian views of other animals "in and of themselves," and the third section addresses the relevance of sacrifice to the general issue of the status of the key animals and other animals generally. The fourth section presents an argument that the Christian tradition narrowed the concerns about other animals that it inherited. The fifth section summarizes the dominant view of other animals in the tradition, and the concluding section presents the argument that speciesism as a concept illuminates features of the tradition's dominant view of other animals.

Christian Talk "about" Other Animals: Dominion and the Basic Division

An essential feature of the dominant manner in which the mainline Christian tradition has spoken "about" other animals appears in the paragraph 2415 provision of the 1994 Catholic Catechism already quoted: "Animals, like plants and inanimate things, are by nature destined for the common good of past, present and future humanity." This sentence is but one part of an integrated series of claims and explanations that also include other sentences in paragraph 2415 and the entire text of paragraphs 2416–18, summarized at paragraph 2457. This series represents an official Catholic Church position on the place of nonhuman animals relative to members of the human species and will be referred to here as "the 1994 Catholic claims."

   The language used in the 1994 Catholic claims refers to nonhuman animals in such a way that one can say that it is "about other animals," albeit in a distinct sense.

The balance of paragraph 2415 (which begins with a reference to the commandment "You shall not steal") adds:

> Use of the mineral, vegetable and animal resources of the universe cannot be divorced from respect for moral imperatives. Man's dominion over inanimate and other living beings granted by the Creator is not absolute; it is limited by concern for the quality of life of his neighbour, including generations to come; it requires a religious respect for the integrity of creation.

Instrumental use of other animals is, then, constrained by considerations that have a moral dimension. Admittedly, the first constraints (neighbors and future generations) are concerned only with other members of the human species, but the constraints are not related only to human interests.[1] The required "religious respect for the integrity of creation" is further explained in paragraph 2416: "*Animals* are God's creatures. He surrounds them with his providential care. By their mere existence they bless him and give him glory. Thus men owe them kindness. We recall the gentleness with which saints like St Francis of Assisi or St Philip of Neri treated animals."

This direct duty of kindness is limited in several important ways. In paragraph 2417, the notion of human dominion over the rest of creation, referred to in the Catechism as "stewardship," is used to speak about the propriety of harmful uses:

> God entrusted animals to the stewardship of those whom he created in his own image. Hence it is legitimate to use animals for food and clothing. They may be domesticated to help man in his work and leisure. Medical and scientific experimentation on animals, if it remains within reasonable limits, is a morally acceptable practice since it contributes to caring for or saving human lives.

This favoring of human interests (that is, humans' need for food, clothing, labor, leisure, and medical benefits) follows from claims about the special ontological status of membership in the human species. It is explicitly tied to the claim that humans, but not other animals, are created in the divine image, and this understanding is what gives members of the human species alone the status described in chapter 5 as "unique-better."

The reasoning in the passage is interesting, if only because the "hence" clause works in an unusual way. Ordinarily, use of "hence" signals that the substance of the phrase following "hence" has been deduced in some way from the preceding phrase(s). But this is arguably not the case with the phrases in paragraph 2417, for it does not necessarily follow from the claim "God entrusted animals to the stewardship of those whom he created in his own image" that "it is legitimate to use animals for food and clothing." Under many common senses of stewardship, though not all, the claim is a non sequitur, since it simply does not follow *automatically* that all of the property or living things over which one is a steward can be used instrumentally.[2] Here the "hence" implicitly relies upon the traditional claims for the special standing of humans discussed in chapter 8.

Another feature of the reasoning found in the 1994 Catholic claims is that membership in the *human* species is a pivotal notion. This is evident in the last sentence of paragraph 2417, since the lives to be saved are measured by such membership considerations, subject, of course, to the vague constraint of "remaining within reasonable limits." Another salient feature is that the 1994 Catholic claims intend to refer to *all* natural world animals outside the human species, and to do so regardless of their intelligence level, social realities, or individual complexities or personalities. In one sense, then, the 1994 Catholic claims are "about" (in that they purport to pertain directly to) Kanzi, Pra Barom Nakkot, and Herman's bottlenose dolphins. The core sentence of paragraph 2415 can then be understood to claim very specifically that these nonhuman individuals, as well as *all* others, "are by nature destined for the common good of past, present and future humanity." It is important to add that these individuals and other nonhuman animals are not treated by the 1994 Catholic claims as the equivalent to mere things (this being signaled by the reference to compassion). This important qualification is, however, expressly limited by paragraph 2418 in favor of another human species membership feature, namely, personhood: "It is contrary to human dignity to cause animals to suffer or die needlessly. It is likewise unworthy to spend money on them that should as a priority go to the relief of human misery. One can love animals; one should not direct to them the affection due only to persons."[3]

There are, of course, other important senses in which various human claims or views are "about" other animals. The most prominent of the other, competing senses of "claims about nonhuman animals" are those reliant upon empirical studies of specific populations of nonhuman animals (the studies cited in chapter 4 provide many paradigmatic examples). Such empirical studies are now cited regularly to challenge the relevance and thus cogency of "claims about animals" that do not countenance the realities of the animals themselves.

The difference between these two senses of a claim being "about animals" highlights yet another important feature of the 1994 Catholic claims. In the alternative, empirically based sense of speaking "about" something, the Catholic Church may be unable to speak about other animals, since its *evaluative* view is not closely attached to, in the sense of following from, structured exploration of these animals' factual realities. Importantly, those views most heavily committed to empirical investigation differ widely, as is evident in the widely divergent approaches and conclusions of sociobiology, behaviorism, and the cognitive revolution of modern psychology. While each of these empirically based approaches relies on a systematic exploration of *some* falsifiable features of other animals' lives, none is exhaustive as to those features. Common to the empirically based alternatives, however, is a commitment to exploration of some factual realities of nonhuman biological individuals in order to provide bases for comments "about" them. It is this feature in particular that distinguishes them from the 1994 Catholic claims, which are, arguably, neither information-intensive nor information-sensitive. For example, it is hard to imagine what kind of new information might change the Catholic Church's views, and this is one of the features that gives these claims the hallmarks of ideology discussed in chapter 2. These distinctions make it clear that the 1994 Catholic claims are but one option in a series of alternatives for seeing and talking "about" other animals. Competing alternatives also include other, more positively inclined, evaluative schemes (for example, the views of some indigenous peoples, which are often characterized by minute, observation-based knowledge of the activities of individual nonhuman animals).

The 1994 Catholic claims have one additional obvious feature. They include the element of exclusion (other animals' interests, relative to human interests, are eclipsed). It is this feature that makes these views potentially subject to the anti-speciesism critique. It would be misleading, however, to characterize the 1994 Catholic claims as exhaustive of the views of the entire Christian tradition, since the tradition features a continuum of views. The 1994 Catholic claims are, nonetheless, arguably very close to the views of the early Christians described in chapter 8. For example, the sole citation given as support for the claim that "[a]nimals, like plants and inanimate things, are by nature destined for the common good of past, present and future humanity" is the passage at Genesis 1:28–31 that has played such a central role in the history of Christian views of other animals. The 1994 Catholic claims, then, can be used to raise the centrally important role of the scriptural grant to humans of dominion over the rest of creation.

The Issues of Dominion and Stewardship

The story that the Christian tradition tells about the relationship between, on the one hand, members of the human species and, on the other hand, all other animals is part of a more encompassing story about how humans (1) are different, either ontologically or in some other, crucial way, and (2) ought to rise above and bring under control the realm of nature, including one's own animality as represented by bodily and egotistical desires. As noted in chapter 8 and particularly with reference to Augustine, as a historical matter this story, as it pertains to nonhuman animals, has relied heavily on the dominion provisions of Genesis 1:26 and 28. The RSV, following KJV (which uses "dominion" in both verses 26 and 28), uses the English word "dominion" in its translation, "fill the earth and subdue it; and have dominion over the fish of the sea and over the every living thing that moves upon the earth."

The English noun "dominion" is a free translation of the Hebrew original, which uses the verb *radâ*; this verb has many meanings on the order of "to rule" or "made him to rule," as a wise king rules over his subjects with care and respect.[4] Thus, the passage now traditionally translated with the English word "dominion" does not *necessarily* mean to tyrannize, subjugate, or exploit for one's own purposes. As a way of suggesting that exploitation is *not* the message of the passage, Westermann notes that *radâ* "can be compared with what is said in [Genesis] 1:16 about the sun and the moon, which are to 'govern' the day and night" and that "man would lose his 'royal' position in the realm of living things if the animals were to him an object of use or of prey" (quoted in Barr 1972, 23). B. Clark, noting that "dominion" has been equated with "domination," observes:

> There are nearly a dozen different Hebrew words which have been translated into English as "dominion" or "rule." In biblical Hebrew, however, each of these words has a meaning much more precise than merely the exercise of authority. Some words are used to characterize the rule of tyrants, while others refer to responsible stewardship, and yet other words denote the power of intellectual persuasion. (1990, 185)

He concludes that the passage imposes responsibilities for the well-being of everything that creeps on earth. Cohen argues that up until the Reformation, "the primary meaning of Gen. 1:28" was taken to be "an assurance of divine commitment and election and a corresponding challenge to overcome the ostensive contradiction between the terrestrial and the heavenly inherent in every human being" (1989, 313). Others, such as von Rad, read the passage as sending a "remarkably strong" message about the exercise of dominion, "especially over the animals" (1972, 60).

It is suggested here that the original Hebrew phrasing implies a respectful and caring attitude toward creation and a sense of responsibility. It is, in fact, now common to find qualified claims regarding the meaning of the biblical passages dealing with as "dominion" over the earth and other animals.[5] This, of course, gives the text a completely different meaning than some of the narrower interpretations, such as domination for humans' benefit alone, which are often read into the standard English translation as "dominion." This conclusion provides a basis for challenging the claim of paragraph 2415 that all other animals are meant for humans' use, especially the non sequitur reasoning of paragraph 2417 cited earlier (that is, the "hence" clause not strictly following from the earlier claims). In fact, paragraph 2415 is a good example of the common tendency to convert the dominion charge into a divinely sanctioned right to instrumental use of *any* nonhuman animals.

Linzey's Nondomination Notion of Dominion/Stewardship

Linzey, who maintains the "theological superiority" of members of the human species relative to other animals, interprets the traditional dominion/stewardship claim as a part of God's plan of creation.[6] His model is not, however, domination but, rather, "the Christ-given paradigm of lordship manifest in *service*" (Linzey 1994a, ix, emphasis added). Through his use of terms such as the "moral priority of the weak" (1991), "self-costly generous loving" (1994a, 71), and "servant species" (1994a, 57), Linzey makes the point that, because "God suffers in all suffering creatures" (1994a, 57), there are fundamental theological and moral issues involved in human interactions with other creatures. He concludes that humans have the special role of a "sacrificial priesthood": "The inner logic of Christ's lordship is the sacrifice of the higher for the lower; not the reverse. If the humility of God in Christ is costly and essential, why should ours be less?" (1994a, 71).

These *untraditional* arguments reflect that, for a Christian, there is no *necessary* connection between being a steward and having additional privileges or eclipsing others' interests.[7] The gulf between Linzey's views of dominion and the dominion interpretation explicit in the 1994 Catholic claims exemplifies some of the problems of attempting to state "the Christian view of other animals."

The Pervasiveness of the Basic Division

The dominant view holding that there is a basic division between humans and all other animals does not appear in only those passages explicitly separating humans from other animals. A review of Isaiah 11:6–9, a passage widely cited as reflecting a favorable view of human–other animal relations, suggests that the basic division can even appear as a part, albeit subtle, of those passages in the tradition's scriptures usually claimed to be the most "animal friendly." The Isaiah passage is, in Bauckham's words, "[t]he classic scriptural expression of hope and peace between humans and wild animals" (1994, 14). But consider the following challenge to the traditional view that the passage is unequivocally positive about nonhuman animals. The parallels in this passage between, on the one hand, the human and domestic animals (which are the extension or property of humans) and, on the other hand, those animals that competed with human interests, reveal that wild animals were *not* appreciated for their intrinsic value.[8] This can be shown by reference to the constant tension between unacceptable behavior of wild, nondomestic animals and the goal of humanizing, domesticating, or making nondomestic animals subservient to human needs. In the following, the bracketed, italicized comments are added for the purpose of identifying that tension:

The [*wild*] wolf shall lie down with the [*humans'*] lamb,
the [*wild*] leopard shall lie down with the [*humans'*] kid,
   the [*domestic*] calf and the [*wild*] lion and the [*domestic*] fatling together [*conducive to domestication's goals*],
and a little [*human*] child shall lead them.
The [*humans'*] cow and the [*wild*] bear shall graze [*an activity of the domestic animal, not this wild animal*],
   their young shall lie down together [*in the manner of the domestic animal*];
and the [*wild*] lion shall eat straw like the [*humans'*] ox.
The nursing child shall play over the hole of the [*wild*] asp,
and the weaned child shall put his hand in the [*wild*] adder's den.

The interests here are *all* human interests, and the perspective of the ideal world is an ideal human world. Bauckham notes, "[T]here is no mention of peace between the predatory wild animals and the prey *wild* animals (such as gazelles or antelope) which they usually hunt and kill, but only of peace between the predatory wild animals and the domestic animals which they sometimes attack" (1994, 15). Thus, the passage "depicts peace between the *human* world, with its domesticated animals . . . , and wild animals . . . which were normally perceived as threats to both human livelihood (dependent on the domestic animals) and to human life" (15, emphasis added). Children, Bauckham argues, are the representatives of humanity, as young domestics are of their kind, because they are particularly vulnerable to wild animals (15).

Arguably, then, the thrust of the passage is *humans'* peace with the nonhuman world and *not necessarily* generalized peace among all living things. It is thus possible that the traditional interpretation of this passage glosses over subtle anthropocentric, and perhaps even exclusivist, hints. Murray, noting that "in Isai[ah] 11:6–9 the picture does not yield easily to one line of interpretation," argues, "Those used to thinking of it simply as a messianic prophecy should realize that the tradition of reading the verbs with reference to a distant future belongs to the later messianic reinterpretation. The latter is 'classic' for Christians" (1992, 105, 103). He notes further that "prior to the messianic re-reading of the Isaian vision . . . the poem was a happy augury for a Davidic prince, new-born or soon expected" (106). These comments provide another basis for arguing that the passage may have been intended for purposes more exclusively human-oriented than is immediately apparent in the traditional interpretation of these comments as a vision of a natural and harmonious world where "the wolf shall lie down with the lamb" and other animals are valued on a *nonanthropocentric* basis.

Other Animals "in and of Themselves"

It was argued in part II that some other animals will not be seen well if they are not seen in their own historical contexts as individuals fully integrated into complex social and familial groupings where they have identifiable interests that moral agents can respect. This amounts to arguing that "in and of themselves" individuals of some other species can matter. This insight has been stated in numerous ways by "animal rights" advocates, such as the "moral individualism" of Rachels, the principle of equal consideration of interests advanced by Singer, and Regan's "subject of a life" criterion (Regan 1988, 243). Cobb, an environmentalist rather than an "animal rights" advocate, has noted, "Sooner or later Christians will have to recognize that the suffering of individual animals has its importance" (1993, 176).

In assessing whether other animals have been recognized "in and of themselves" by the Christian tradition, both the coarse generalizations used to describe them and the persistent refusal to notice them or take their lives seriously must be considered as highly relevant. Since in the tradition the dominance of the second- and third-level generalizations provided little, if any, preparation to take specific animals or their biological kinds seriously, Christians have, on the whole, made no really meaningful divisions among other animals that reflect either *their* distinctive interests and abilities or *their* moral significance related to *their* individuality. Formally, the "strings" inherited from the Hebrew Bible involve some division of other animals into generalizations more specific than second-level generalizations, but the categories of that method of division remain extremely generic. Strings of very broad third-level generalizations hardly allow the ordinary user of such distinctions to notice or take seriously the different kinds of animals within each division. The special, ethical legislation regarding domestic animals, cited in chapter 8, does countenance different kinds of animals and in some instances reflects recognition of the individuals' interests. Generally, however, as also noted in chapter 8, such concerns are confined to *domestic* animals, that is, the valued property of humans whose interests were greatly advanced by husbandry rules that protected these animals' lives and extended the period of their usefulness to their owners. On the altogether different subject of wild animals or those with regard to which good husbandry practices would not benefit human interests, Murray (1992, 119) counts the laws of the sabbatical year, at both Exodus 23:11 and Leviticus 25:4–7, as the single example from the Torah.

In general, then, the mainline tradition's views of other animals do not reflect that the tradition has seen other animals well nor "in and of themselves." Arguing in this manner, however, is not meant to suggest that *none* of the realities of other animals were seen, for the tradition clearly does display some sense of the obvious continuities with other animals. An eloquent statement of these continuities was inherited in the passage from Ecclesiastes 3:19–20 regarding the similar "fate of the sons of men and the fate of beasts." Such human–other animal commonalities could hardly be denied, for they are simply too obvious, and thus recognition of them understandably intrudes at times into descriptions and analyses of human realities. The larger issue of not seeing nonhuman biological individuals well remains, however, since as a general matter dominant mental habits of leading Christian thinkers played down other animals' moral significance by ignoring or obscuring their realities. Linzey, searching for "Jesus' actual attitude to animals," suggests that "we have to work largely from hints and guesses" (1987, 48). He goes on to say that the "hints" are positive, referring to the so-called sparrow sayings at Matthew 6:26 and 10:29, and Luke 12:6 and 12:24, as well as a comparison between Solomon and the glory of the created world at Matthew 6:28–29 and Luke 12:27; Linzey concludes that "we do have Jesus' support for the idea that God's providential care extends even to the most insignificant animals." But even if this interpretation is correct, it has been very little noticed, as the quotation from Linzey at the opening of this chapter suggests.

In fact, other animals, when they have been noticed in any detail, have on the whole been negatively conceived. As Foerster notes when writing about the Christians' use of the Greek second-level generalization *thēria*:

> Linked with man and yet distinct from him, the animal world with its domination of instincts seems to have in fallen creation the significance of a perversion of that whereto man is called as the image of God. This fact is evident throughout the animal kingdom, but is particularly clear in wild animals. Hence individual animals, and especially the Θηρία, can serve as a figure of the demonic which perverts the divine similitude of man into that which is sub-human. (1965, 135)

To be sure, there are instances of positive descriptions in many eras of the Christian tradition, but these have not been characteristic of the tradition's most central documents or interpretations. One might counter that the encompassing passages of Romans 8:19–23 ("the whole creation will be set free"), Colossians 1:20 ("reconcile to himself all things"), and Ephesians 1:10 ("unite all things in him"), suggest some value for other animals in the general scheme of things. While this interpretation is not on its face implausible, these passages in their original language versions do not use the generic terms discussed here that were typically employed when authors of the late first century C.E. were intent on specifically including nonhuman animals. In general, then, it is the case with the Christian materials that *specific* references which suggest that other animals as individuals were known and appreciated for *their* realities are hard to identify.

Mechanisms for Acceptance of New Information and Perspectives

Thomas shows that as accurate information became available, negative perceptions of the lives of other animals, particularly as reflected in language, began to change.[9] Such changes were not, however, the product of mechanisms inside the tradition or its churches, even though historically in later centuries the tradition did *promote* a certain level of inquiry into the realities of other animals.[10] Thomas suggests that developments by which the realities of other animals came to be seen better were *not* a product of the tradition: "Yet to suggest that concern for animals' rights developed logically out of elements latent in the Judaeo-Christian tradition is merely to beg the question. For, if the intellectual possibility had always been present, why was it only in the early modern period that it was realized?" (1983, 181). His answer as to why these developments occurred when they did (from the sixteenth century on) is *external social change*, that is, "the emergence of an industrial order in which animals became increasingly marginal to the processes of production" (181). In some ways, features and institutions of the tradition blocked such inquiries or ignored them altogether, as suggested by Linnaeus's expression of his fear of the ban of "ecclesiastics" cited previously.

The historical lack of institutionally sanctioned mechanisms for developing, reviewing, or incorporating counterfactual information that challenges the mainline tradition's subordination of all nonhuman animals is arguably a corollary of the inherently conservative claim that a definitive revelation regarding humans' relative importance occurred at an earlier time. Still, there have in fact been important changes in recent years. The 1994 Catholic claims are a minor example relative to movement in other portions of the tradition, such as the Annecy report to the World Council of Churches (Birch and others 1990, 273–90). and some denominational statements.[11] Obviously, then, change is possible.

Also worthy of note is the fact that acceptance of new information does not require repudiation of two historically important assumptions within the Christian tradition that apologists for the tradition have often associated with exclusivist views regarding nonhuman animals. First, acceptance of new information is possible even if one continues to believe that humans as a whole have a special role because of their special powers and ability to care about "others." These others can, of course, be human or otherwise, and the new information discussed earlier can be a basis on which some nonhuman animals are included. Second, recognition of the special abilities of some nonhuman animals does not entail a wholesale acceptance of recent biological theory's repudiation of essentialism. Integration of new information, as well as use of it to establish new perspectives on at least some nonhuman animals, can take place without acceptance of the modern biological claim that all members of a species do not share identical essences. One might, for example, continue to assert that each other kind of animal is typified by an "essence," the specifics of which one defines in a manner consistent with careful observation of the features of other animals' actual lives.

Relatedly, repudiation of an essentialist notion of membership in the human species need not entail the conclusion that only some humans matter, or that it is automatically wrong to premise inclusion in the moral circle on mere species membership. The anti-speciesism critique is a challenge to *exclusion* of all other animals, not the mere inclusion of humans on the grounds of species membership. Such inclusion could, as some have recognized, be premised on prudential grounds.[12] It is the peculiar tension between inclusion of *all* and *only* humans, and the corollary exclusion of *all* and *only* nonhuman animals, that is the target of the anti-speciesism critique. Recognition of some nonhuman animals' interests as within the moral circle would, under the definition of speciesism offered in chapter 2, be nonspeciesist. Such a broad inclusion can be accomplished with or without species essentialism.

The points here are simple. Stewardship and dominion notions and essentialism can come in nonspeciesist forms, and both can be devices by which new, accurate information about nonhuman animals is integrated into a Christian understanding of which lives matter. Further, recognition of the fact that other animals' abilities have been poorly known or even intentionally ignored does not require one to assume that humans are unimportant. As noted in chapter 2, the anti-speciesism critique includes a profound affirmation of humans' moral abilities, and it remains logically possible for Christians to assert the significance of membership in the human species even as they engage fully the abilities of any animal outside their own species.

The Limited Relevance of Sacrificial Practices

It is sometimes argued that the general practice of ritualized killing of animals for the purpose of worship, which was a cultural datum in the ancient Near East,[13] is confirmation of the importance of other animals.[14] There remains, however, an important sense in which the issue of sacrifice and cultically slaughtered animals, though very telling about (1) views of *some* other animals, (2) the Hebrews' sense of the importance of humans, and (3) the relationship of humans to God, is only tangentially relevant to the issues discussed here.[15]

Frear presents a mild version of this argument, observing that animal sacrifice "in its way represents respect for animal life, reverence for animal blood" (1993, 7). There is some plausibility in this argument. In Leviticus 21:6, for example, the sacrifices are called "the bread of their God." The Hebrew term for the cereal offering specified in Leviticus 2 also means "present" or "tribute," thus suggesting that the object given was valued in some way. The provisions allowing the poor to offer grains, while the rich are to offer live animals, suggest that the live animals were considered better sacrificial material. Linzey comments in a related way, "The tradition of sacrifice did not necessarily involve a low view of animal life" (1987, 41).

Frear's and Linzey's measured comments hint at the possibility of strong counterclaims, the most obvious of which is that sacrifice was a human-centered practice that ignored the needs of the individual animal which was killed. But positive views of sacrifice, and even the more reserved arguments of animal advocates like Frear and Linzey, are based on the argument that it is not the individually sacrificed animal whose interests matter. Rather, these views suggest that the whole process, and the implicit values of honoring God in traditional forms, have positive implications for the importance of other animals and life generally.

This is in some respects a peculiar argument, since it is unlikely that a parallel argument would be made regarding sacrifice of *humans*. For example, Frear most likely would not attempt to justify human sacrifice by arguing that such a practice represents "reverence for human blood," any more than Linzey would opine that a tradition of sacrificing humans "did not necessarily involve a low view of those humans' life." This is not to argue that Frear and Linzey are wrong, for they make sensible points about some of the implications of the ancient practice of sacrifice. But there are more obvious implications, such as the undeniably anthropocentric and instrumentalist features of the general practice.

In general, any argument that humans' sacrificing other animals is a confirmation of those animals' importance is parasitic on an underlying notion that humans are more important, and that their God affirms this by accepting the sacrifice of another living thing by humans. The argument, then, ignores, or at least obscures, the main feature of the practice, namely, that the animal dies for human interests, not for its own. To value the practice of the kinds of sacrifice at issue, then, requires an assertion that humans are paradigmatically important. This criticism is not meant to deny that there is consistent reasoning which suggests that the animals chosen for sacrifice must somehow be important (for why would they, and not others, be chosen as a gift to the divine?). But the value of the sacrificed animals remains eminently instrumental, since the sacrifice was not for the victim's interest but the sacrificer's (as evidenced by the use of animal sacrifices for atonement, ritual purification, and commemoration). Such a concentration on others' benefits is precisely why human sacrifice is abhorrent. Sacrifice of other animals raises precisely the same issue.

Additionally, the argument that sacrifice implies a positive view of animals *generally* suffers from the logical and practical problems described in chapter 5, for these few animals are not obviously representative of other animals generally. This is especially so in light of the *domestic* nature of the acceptable animals. Further, a certain anthropocentrism can be seen in the provisions governing which *individual* animals were acceptable for sacrifice: they had to be healthy, sometimes only male (as in the case of the burnt offering of Leviticus 1), and always a member of a biological kind useful to humans.[16] These provisions reflect what was valuable to the humans who dominated the society. To a limited extent, a similar argument can be made with regard to the provisions for clean and unclean found in Leviticus 11 and Deuteronomy 14. These provisions, allegedly reflecting which animals are pleasing to God, in fact reflect which animals were generally pleasing and useful to the *human community*.[17]

Further, to argue that the few animals on the list of acceptable animals were more pleasing to God is in tension with several important core features of the belief in an all-good, omnipotent creator. According to Genesis 1, all animals created were part of a good creation, not just those on the sacrifice list. Similarly, if an animal had been injured, under the Hebrew view of the world, God had chosen to allow the injury to happen. One can then ask why it should be concluded that God would be more pleased by the sacrifice of a noninjured animal. It is clear why humans value healthy domesticated animals more than injured ones, or wild ones, but it is not at all clear why God would.

Generally, once one has distinguished the status of cultically slaughtered animals from the separable issue of the status of all other animals, the implications of the practice of sacrifice discussed earlier point up its deficiencies as a hallmark of positive views of other animals generally.

Sacrifice in the Early Christian Tradition

Sacrifice was an issue early in the Christian tradition, as can be seen from passages in the Letter to the Hebrews which argue that there is no need to perform sacrifices because Jesus offered himself "once for all" (7:27), "taking not the blood of goats and calves but his own blood, thus securing redemption" (9:12). JB summarizes the message and indeed the core of the Christian position: "The ineffectual levitical sacrifices are replaced by the one uniquely efficacious sacrifice of Christ himself."[18]

That the Christian tradition from the very beginning repudiated animal sacrifice might suggest that it was open to new views of the value of other animals. Yet, as

Frear observes, "the strong negative voices against sacrifice or against a false reliance on sacrifice never make the point that it is cruel to animals" (1993, 7). Adams and Procter-Smith also suggest problems if one makes assumptions about the positive implications of the early tradition's rejection of sacrifice: "A sign of this cessation of all animal sacrifices is reflected in the fact that the foods used for the Christian eucharistic meal are vegetarian foods: bread and wine. The problem in this interpretation is to assume that animals are not being sacrificed in other, more quotidian, ways by our own unexamined actions" (1993, 306). Chapple argues similarly when comparing different traditions' views of other animals, stating, "[T]he one life orientation of the prophetic religious traditions regards animals in an entirely different light and has allowed for their sacrifice in the laboratory environment."[19]

In summary, the early Christians' repudiation of animal sacrifice is only tangentially relevant to an assessment of Christian views of other animals, and on the whole irrelevant to the standing of the other socially complex animals examined in part II.

The Narrowing of Hebrew Concerns for Other Animals

A wide range of scholars have made observations that suggest that a limitation or constriction of the Hebrew concerns occurred. For example, Passmore (1974, chap. 2) has argued that the tradition ignored the texts which required it to care for other animals. Tillich refers to "passages in which the animals are excluded from the divine care (Paul)" (1963, 405), alluding to the oft-cited 1 Corinthians 9:9–10, which reads: "For it is written in the Law of Moses: 'You shall not muzzle an ox when it is treading out the grain.' Is it for oxen that God is concerned? Does he not speak entirely for our sake?"[20]

It is not necessarily the case that Paul's comments reflect what is characterized here as the Christian tradition's narrowing of the Hebrew concern for all creation. The questions, Is it for oxen that God is concerned? and Does he not speak entirely for our sake? can be interpreted to mean only that God provided the Deuteronomy provision for human instruction, not that Paul took the apparent import of the Deuteronomy passage (God's concern for domesticated oxen and perhaps other nonhuman animals) to be false. Along these lines, Murray (1992, 131) argues that Paul had "mental furniture" not far from that of the Hebrew tradition. Clark argues similarly: "When Aquinas deduces from Paul (1 Corinthians 9:9) that God does not care for oxen, but that all the injunctions to the manifest contrary in the Old Testament are economic or symbolic in origin, he is taking the apostle far too literally. Paul, as a good Jew, knew well that God did care for oxen" (1977, 196–97). It is the case, however, that the Aquinas's *reading* of Paul does reflect narrower concerns for other animals than some of those found in the Old Testament. Paul's comment has thus been used to support the view that God's real concern is the membership of the human species, rather than all animals.

Barbour notes a different kind of narrowing "under the influence of late Greek thought" by which "the early Church increasingly viewed a human being as a separate soul temporarily inhabiting a body" (1996, 10). He suggests that humans are set apart, "but not in the absolute way which classical Christianity maintained. . . . The

Bible itself gives humanity a special status, but it also asserts our kinship with other forms of life" (10–11). Similarly, Ruether argues that, relative to the Hebrews' sense of salvation which included themselves as kin of earth and other animals, Christianity "[o]ver the first several centuries of its development . . . marginalized the Hebrew vision of salvation as a future time on earth of justice between humans and harmony with animals. Instead it focused its hopes on the escape of the soul from its encasement in the mortal body and its ascent above" (1993, 17). Midgley also argues that there was a regressive series of narrowings in the tradition:

> The belief that only human beings mattered—a belief which can be called Exclusive Humanism—has been very deeply rooted in our cultural tradition, and linked with much in it that was of the greatest value. From the start, it was present in Christianity, which went to some trouble to narrow down older Jewish ideas of community with a wider creation. Protestantism carried this process further, clearing the stage for a drama involving only man and God.[21]

Pertinent to the issue of whether the Christian tradition narrowed its inheritance on the issue of care for other animals is the argument of chapter 8 that the Hebrew tradition itself manifested a tension between (1) the more exclusivist claims regarding the special place of humans in creation and (2) affirmations of creation and the realities obviously shared by humans and other animals. The leading figures of the early Christian tradition without question maintained the heavy emphasis they inherited from the Hebrews regarding the special place and nature of members of the human species. This was accomplished, at least in part, by a heavy reliance on the Priestly writer's account of creation while de-emphasizing certain features of the Yahwist account that reflect more integration with the land. Arguably, however, the principal factor leading to such a pronounced emphasis on membership in the human species was the fact that as the Christian tradition was elaborated by the postbiblical theologians, it lost the counterbalancing emphasis on continuity with the rest of creation. Certainly by the time of Origen, but arguably as early as Justin, the developing Christian tradition's emphases on humans appear heavier and more stark than the Hebrew claim that humans are the most important among the earth's animals. Once the counterbalancing sense of continuity had been diminished, statements of a stark contrast between humans and other animals became more common and, arguably, eventually normative in the subsequent tradition.

Such a "narrowing" provides a way of accounting for the differences between the one-sidedness of the 1994 Catholic claims and the more encompassing vision of the Old Testament as it balanced the connectedness of humans and other animals with the conviction that human animals have a very special place in the broader creation.

The Basic Christian Understanding of Other Animals

The mainline Christian tradition has historically asserted, as part of its basic message, not only a fundamental, radical division between human animals and all other animals but also the *exclusion* of all other animals' interests when they are in conflict with even minor, unnecessary human interests. The exclusion has been premised not merely on the claim that membership in the human species entails that each human is made in the image of God and is "unique-better" relative to all animals outside the human species. It has also been based on claims that, if and when the realities of all animals (humans included) are measured relative to one another, it is *only* human realities that are morally considerable (in the sense specified in chapter 2) and thereby deserve advancement at the expense of the realities and even lives of all other animals.

An examination of the origin, expression, and development of Christian views of other animals suggests that they were integrally tied to background views that operated at the level of cultural datum. These ancient views are of great significance, for present views remain grounded in the tradition of interpretation that arose at the very beginning of the Christian tradition. Thus, the articulation of the relative standing of humans and all other animals described in chapter 8 continues to be the dominant one in mainline Christian circles.

Whether the dominant interpretation will remain immune to new factual information developed during careful inquiries into the lives and realities of other animals will be an important indicator of the quality and nature of Christian views "about" nonhuman animals. Continued insistence that the traditional view remains definitive, even if it was based on a persistent refusal to investigate, would signal, of course, that mainline Christian views on this subject are functioning as the kind of ideology described in chapter 2. If the historically dominant exclusions based on either (1) the pretense to have knowledge of all other animals, or at least those that might compete with humans, or (2) an implicit claim to understand other animals' lives, remain unchallenged, the problem of excluding the interests of the more complex nonhuman animals will have been assumed away by virtue of the lack of inquiry and an unpreparedness to notice the details of their actual lives.

The Argument That the Christian Tradition Has Been Speciesist

I suggest here that both the term "speciesism" and the gist of the anti-speciesism critique have valuable applications to the Christian tradition, particularly as it has sanctioned, and even promoted, practices and problems applicable to the key and other animals generally. I begin with a consideration of an important problem that arises in applying the speciesism notion bluntly.

First, the binary qualities of the question, Has Christianity been speciesist or not? mislead, in that they do not provide an adequate range for answering. The tradition is so complex that one can cite evidence that cuts both ways. The better question is, perhaps, Where are the speciesist elements relative to the nonspeciesist elements, and which, if any, predominate? It has already been suggested that both exclusivist and nonexclusivist elements are at the heart of the tradition, but that as the tradition developed the exclusivist elements came to dominate more and more.

Acknowledging the richness of the tradition, and speaking only generally about attitudes that predominate, one can ask whether the mainline Christian tradition's attitude toward other animals fits the description "inclusion of all human animals within, and exclusion of all other animals from, the moral circle."

In answering, it is emphasized again that the *two* elements of inclusion and exclusion must be met. The Christian tradition generally does include all humans, but it has been mixed on the exclusion issue. It has already been suggested that postbiblical theologians excluded all other animals from the three fundamental moral protections at issue, and that such an exclusion is a core feature of the 1994 Catholic claims. Thus, the description "exclusion of other animals from the moral circle" does fit the mainline tradition, given that the mainline Christian tradition has not advocated protection of any other animals' fundamental interests even when some *minor* human interests are involved (such as the "leisure" rationale cited in the 1994 Catholic claims). Since Linzey and others who advocate protection of nonhuman animals' fundamental interests are no less Christian for doing so, one can very forcefully argue that the tradition itself is not irretrievably speciesist. As a matter of history, however, the tradition has been overwhelmingly inclined to combine its fundamental anthropocentrism with a radical exclusion of other animals' interests, and thus to tolerate and at times promote the practices and problems that generated the anti-speciesism critique.

Further, regarding the justifications given by the mainline tradition regarding who should be included or excluded from the moral circle, there is little doubt that the principal explanations have been integrally tied to membership or nonmembership in the human species. Whether one concludes that, thereby, these decisions (that is, inclusion and exclusion) have been based *solely* on species membership factors is largely a matter of how one chooses to talk about biological beings, species membership, and their ethical dimensions. Again, however, as a historical matter, it is hard to deny that the basis of inclusion has often been mere membership in the human species or that the basis of exclusion was nonmembership. The discourse of contemporary mainline Christianity repeatedly confirms this, as exemplified by the common tendency to use the "image of God" notion for all and only members of the human species. Even though it is commonly asserted that Christian ethics starts with the injunction to love others as yourself, as Cobb says, "The others are, of course, human beings" (1993, 177).

The mainline Christian tradition, then, has values, emphases, and exclusions that fit within the definition of speciesism used here. The problem of anachronism, however, remains, such that application of the term to the early tradition, even if illuminating as to how concepts and words worked, is *different* than application of the term to *contemporary* views held *in spite of* newly generated perspectives and information.

For many centuries in the Christian tradition, exclusivism favoring humans on the basis of species membership considerations was held to be wisdom and the highest form of morality. There are signs that that may be changing, and these go considerably beyond the slight movement in the Catholic Church's position discussed earlier. Moltmann, for example, has argued, "An animal is not a person in the human sense, but it is not a 'thing' or a product either. It is a living being, with rights of it own, and it needs the protection of public law" (1990, 132). Moltmann maintains further that "the special destiny of human beings applies only *within* the community of all creatures, which they are intended to respect [citing Psalm 104]. We can talk about the special dignity of human beings on the presupposition that the dignity of other beings as creatures is recognized" (132). It may also be that the ecological concerns now found widely throughout parts of the tradition will turn the tradition's discourse away from the exclusivist features of the claims that historically have been associated with the inclusivist attitude toward all humans.[22]

In conclusion, three suggestions are made. First, the failure to consider the essential concerns of individuals outside the human species risks being arbitrary in that the criteria of inclusion and exclusion are based on species membership, are ideological in nature, and are based ultimately on a failure and refusal to inquire. Second, the term "speciesism" and the underlying anti-speciesism critique are useful tools in seeing the history, structure, and implications of the mainline tradition's view of the significance of all nonhuman animals. Third, the analysis does *not* exhaust the tradition's possibilities and resources for taking account of nonhuman animals. In other words, the tradition may not be irredeemably speciesist by virtue of unbreakable commitments that tie inclusion of all members of the human species to a related exclusion of all nonhuman animals. Nonetheless, the history of the tradition through its first two millennia suggests that speciesist values and orientations have been far more than a mere specter. Rather, on many occasions, in many places, and in many Christian hearts, speciesism has been a persistent reality, such that it is not misleading to suggest that, to date, the Christian tradition has not enabled its adherents to notice or take other animals seriously. In this regard, the mainline Christian tradition has, in a meaningful sense, been speciesist.

Conclusion

Parts III and IV concluded that the claims of, respectively, the early Buddhist and Christian traditions were characterized by exclusivist moral judgments about non-human animals, and that these judgments have an ideological dimension. This controversial characterization is based on several grounds. First, in each tradition the relevant discourse was dominated by coarse generalizations. Second, central documents in each tradition frequently exhibit confident assertions about other animals that have a broad sweep which is sometimes undiscriminating and often aggressive despite (1) the poor state of knowledge of other animals in each tradition, (2) a disinclination to seek systematically evidence contrary to the established view, and (3) the epistemological limitations discussed in the text.

This attempt to point out exclusivist features of the ways in which mainline interpretations of two major religious traditions have viewed other animals has only occasionally focused on the features of these traditions that adherents could use to challenge those mainline interpretations. Thus, to argue that the views found in these traditions involve insensitivity, particularly because the dominant views are the result of coarse analytical methods, is not to claim that the traditions are themselves fundamentally deficient. It is to claim, however, that views dominant in these traditions are characterized by an inability to capture the depth and complexity by which some animals beyond the human species line live their lives. It has been noted that "[o]ur understanding of the world is achieved more effectively by conceptual improvements than by the discovery of new facts, even though the two are not mutually exclusive" (Mayr 1982, 23). The notion of speciesism, particularly when it is defined in such a way as to reflect the substance of the anti-speciesism critique, is a valuable descriptive tool that sheds light on the manner in which valuation of animals, human and otherwise, has occurred. It can, especially if applied in conjunction with the kinds of factual information now being developed, encourage "conceptual improvements" and a willingness to engage new perspectives that will allow the dismantling of pervasive prejudices and exclusions regarding living beings who happen not to be members of the human species.

Appendix 1

Transliteration, Orthography, and Italicization

A. *Hebrew*

The transliteration of the Hebrew into English is, generally, in the style used by Weingreen 1959, with transliterated words being italicized. There are slight changes, as follows:

1. 'Aleph is indicated by ' and 'Ayin is indicated by ʿ
2. When Weingreen indicates that romanized, transliterated letters should be printed with a dot underneath (as with the letters .*Hêth*, .*Teth*, *Sādhê*, and .*Kôph*), this is indicated by the convention of a dot (".") appearing *before* the letter, rather than under it as in Weingreen.
3. The Hebrew letters are those of the font known as Hebrew7SSK found in the Key Fonts Pro 3003 software package. Generally, Hebrew words are unpointed.
4. The consonants known as the "bgdkpt" letters are, when soft or spirant, respectively, bh, gh, dh, kh, ph, and th. When hard, they are simply b, g, d, k, p, and t.
5. שׂ in Weingreen is š, whereas here it is *sh*.
6. Note that the ending *ah* (for example, the noun *'okhlâ* ["food"], ending מָה) in Weingreen is *â* (Weingreen 1959, 7, with examples on 13).

B. *Greek*

The alphabet is the system of transliteration used in The *Interpreter's Bible* (IB), and the accents are eliminated as in Hudson 1992. Transliteration uses only two additional signs for the long vowels η (ē) and ω (ō). Greek letters transliterated with compound Romanized letters are θ (th), φ (ph), χ (ch), and ψ (ps). The rough breathing is indicated by the letter "h".

"LXX" refers to the Septuagint, and the version used is the Rahlfs text listed in the bibliography.

The New Testament in Greek is the version appearing in Green 1986.

C. *Pali and Sanskrit*

Generally, terms from these languages are italicized. However, the following terms have *not* been italicized: Abhidhamma, Buddha, Vinaya. In some instances, Sanskrit terms which are better known than the corresponding Pali terms are used (for example, bodhisattva rather than bodhisatta).

Explanation of orthography: Pali and Sanskrit both require extensive use of diacritical marks. The following set of conventions, widely used on the Indological Forum (indology@liverpool.ac.uk) and by Buddha-L (buddha-l@ulkyvm.louisville.edu), have been adopted:

1. Long vowels are indicated by a macron.
2. Consonantal diacritics precede the consonants marked by them; thus retroflex consonants are written as .r .t .th .d .dh .n .m .s.
3. Visarga is written as .h.
4. The palatals that take diacritics are ~n and "s.
5. The guttural nasal is written "n.

Appendix 2

Defined Terms

The following terms are used in very specific, defined ways in this study. The following definitions or uses are given in the text; the chapter in which each is first used is indicated here in parentheses.

Complex individual   Biological individuals who have the following general characteristics: large brains, interindividual communications, prolonged periods of development in complex familial and social envelopes, and levels of both social integration and individuality that humans can recognize (chapter 4).

Essential concerns   Three distinguishable interests or concerns of each living animal: (1) an opportunity of continued life, unless a danger to others; (2) freedom from interruption of that life by captivity, enforced work, or any other form of harmful instrumental use; and (3) freedom from intentional infliction of negative consequences such as harm, pain, or suffering (chapter 2).

Ideology   A systematic scheme of ideas . . . regarded as justifying actions, especially one that is held implicitly or adopted as a whole and maintained *regardless of the course of events* (chapter 2).

Interests   The term used to designate the fact that lives can, from the standpoint of the individual, go better or worse. Each individual can then be said to have an "interest" in having its life go better rather than worse (chapter 2).

The key species or the key animals   The three groups of animals known in common parlance as apes, elephants, and whales and dolphins. The first group is more technically known as "great apes," and the third group is scientifically known as "cetaceans" (chapter 4).

Moral considerability   Used in the limited sense of designating *only* the notion of moral agents taking a biological individual to deserve three fundamental protections, namely, a right to life, freedom from captivity, and freedom from intentionally inflicted unnecessary harm. These three fundamental protections are also described as "essential concerns" (chapter 2).

Unnecessary   Said, for example, of an exclusion of interests when that exclusion is not needed for immediate biological survival; in other words, the excluding party can refuse the exclusion and still have a healthy life (chapter 2).

Notes

Introduction

1. Aristotle 1984, *Politics* I, 2, 1253a 9–11, p. 1988.
2. "Other great apes" is used because humans are, biologically speaking, great apes, there being "no natural category that includes chimpanzees, gorillas and orang-utans but excludes humans" (Dawkins 1993, 82).
3. For example, certain bodhisattva and Christological formulations.

Part I

1. Clarke and Linzey (1990, 7) cite the original passage from *Summa Contra Gentiles*. Aquinas reasoned that God was exhorting humans to refrain from harming nonhuman animals because doing so set a bad example that might lead humans to harm other *humans*.
2. MSBB 247; discussed in parts II and III.
3. A number of these claims are cited at the beginning of chapter 7.

Chapter 1

1. Smith 1962, 12. As for Buddhism specifically, Gombrich (1996, at 4 and 6, respectively) argues that Gotama took a nonessentialist view of his own teachings and that "Buddhism as a human phenomenon has no unchanging essence."
2. Sorabji (1993) deals with the debate in Western intellectual history. The important and distinctive views of the Indian subcontinent generally are discussed in part III.
3. Interesting examples appear in Wilbert and Simoneau 1970–92; Suzuki and Knudtson 1992; and Ingold 1994b.
4. Keown notes, "[The sources of] the canonical and commentarial literature of the Theravada school, . . . recorded in the Pali language, are the closest we are likely to get to the ethical teachings of the Buddha. . . . [While it is not certain that they record Gotama's statements, they are] among the most ancient and are at least as authoritative as any other" (1995, xi). See also Warder's comments (cited at DW 536 n. 10) and Lamotte 1958, 622 ff.
5. "Hebrew Bible" and "Old Testament" are not identical either in denotation or in connotation. This point, with supporting details, is made by Murray (1992, xv–xvi). The term "Old Testament" will be used when the reference is to the Christian tradition's collection, arrangement, and translations of works from the Hebrew Bible.
6. Found in Green 1976.
7. Found in Green 1976.
8. The two-word phrase "propositional, descriptive" will be used in quotes and it will have the simple, narrow sense of designating any claim purporting to be descriptive of specific features of the phenomenal world.
9. Unattributed author, *The Animals' Voice* 2, no. 4 (August 1989): 28.
10. Examples of such claims are Hick 1989 and Ward 1994.

Chapter 2

1. Ryder 1993, 222 n. 1, where he cites Ryder 1970; Ryder and Wood 1970 (see also Ryder 1979, 4, 219 n. 8).

2. The literature on this development is enormous; see, for example, Harrison 1964; Fiddes 1991; Mason and Singer 1993.

3. In the concluding section of this chapter, it is noted that "instrumental use" in this study *always* has the sense of *harmful* instrumental use.

4. M. II, 8. See also Pp. 77; A. II, 220.

5. Bentham 1970, 1. Singer (1979, 203) and Feinberg (1974, 55–56) make the same point regarding individuals, rather than species, being the locus of interests. Use of the term "interests" in this manner occurs widely in the animal rights movement as an alternative to "rights" language. Singer 1987 discusses these two alternatives.

6. Outside this study, the terms "moral considerability" and "morally considerable" have no one accepted meaning. Accordingly, it is essential in following the argument here to confine this term to a narrow range (this is elaborated on in the text). Note, also, that the defined terms used in this study appear in appendix 2.

7. The meaning of "necessary" here begs definition, and this is supplied in the next paragraph.

8. Chapter 9 addresses the minor limitations imposed by the 1994 Catholic Catechism.

9. White 1967 is the source of the claim. Cohen (1989) argues persuasively that White's claims are wrong in some important specifics, since the dominion charge of Genesis 1:28 (relied on heavily by White) was not taken by ancient and medieval readers as any sort of license "selfishly to exploit the environment or to undermine its pristine integrity" (1989, 309). Cohen does note, however, that the passage was consistently taken as a divine call to rule over other animals. This analysis provides an interesting example of the how "environmental" issues and "animal" issues are by no means coextensive.

10. Thomas 1983, 46. Feminist versions of this argument are Fisher (1979, 190, 197) and Ruether (1993, 14). Crosby 1986 cites harms to other animals that have had detrimental effects on *humans*.

11. This argument is analyzed in Pluhar 1995 (discussed later) and in the discussion of "natural kinds" in part II.

12. Many "marginal humans" cannot reach the necessary level of abstraction.

13. See, respectively, de Waal 1989, 78; Povinelli 1997, emphasis in the original.

14. The most influential use of "sentience" (alternatively, "sentiency") in this sense is Singer's definition: "a convenient if not strictly accurate shorthand for the capacity to suffer and/or experience enjoyment" (1976, 9).

15. This approach is found both inside religious traditions (as in the creation theologies discussed in chapter 3) and outside of them (see, for example, Diamond 1978, discussed in chapter 2).

16. See, for example, Bowler 1992, 504–32; Nash 1973.

17. Staddon (1989) comments on anthropocentrism in various scientific fields; Jonas (1984, 4) makes the argument that traditional ethics has been anthropocentric.

18. There are many histories; see, for example, Ryder 1975. Kalechofsky 1991 provides many relevant details.

19. Ryder 1975, 16. This passage goes on to include a parenthetical reference that includes sexism as well, noting that all three "overlook or underestimate the similarities between the discriminator and those discriminated against" and "show a selfish disregard for the interest of others, and for their suffering."

20. The proceedings of this conference were published as Patterson and Ryder 1979. The declaration appears at viii, with a list of signatories.

21. See, for example, Ryder 1974, 1975, 1979, 1989; Ryder 1992b explores the new term "painism."

22. Singer (1993b, 11), following Hare (see, for example, 1981, 10), argues that equal consideration is a formal requirement of morality. Singer goes on to state (1993b, 22) that the principle of equal consideration of interests "really amounts to this: an interest is an interest, whoever's interest it may be. . . . The principle of equal consideration of interests prohibits making our readiness to consider the interests of others depend on their abilities or other characteristics, apart from the characteristic of having interests."

23. See, for example, Collins 1991, 1484; Chambers 1993, 1656.

24. A negative evaluation appears in Henshaw 1989, a book-length journalistic piece criticizing radical elements in the post-1970 English "animal rights" movement. There are also five journalism entries included by the OED as examples of the noun and adjective.

25. Cohen 1986, 867. Cohen's argument (868) is that there are profound differences between human and nonhuman animals, such that the pain of other animals does not have as much moral weight as human pain.

26. Examples include Gill 1995, where Soskice (1995, 62) uses the term "anti-species-ists" without definition and only in passing to describe those among whom Singer's *Animal Liberation* found acceptance. See also Pinches and McDaniel 1993; only Pinches and Regan use the term in this collection, although at least four of the other contributors (McDaniel, Linzey, Adams, and Cobb) use it *elsewhere*.

27. Schmithausen (1991a, 3 n. 10) says of "anthropocentrism": "I use it in the sense that the guideline for man's behavior, or of ethical theory, is only or primarily man's interests."

28. Kalechofsky 1991, 55, 79; Pluhar 1995, whose views are described later. See also Seed 1985, 243.

29. Midgley 1986, 10; she also argues (1984, chap. 1) that the rationalist tradition and industrialization played significant roles in discouraging attention to nonhuman animals.

30. See Midgley 1984, especially chap. 1.

31. Regan 1988 contains several references (for example, 155). See also Regan 1979, 5; 1989, 104; 1991, 110–11.

32. For example, Naess 1980; Callicott 1980; Attfield 1983, 174; Taylor 1987, 19.

33. Adams and Donovan 1995, 1–3, summarize this argument. See also Dunayer 1995, 19; Kappeler 1995, 320; and Adams and Procter-Smith 1993, 297.

34. Some who challenge various features of the anti-speciesism critique use the term (Steinbock 1978, 255; Frey, a signatory of the 1977 declaration, at 1979, 108; 1980, 165; 1987, 51; and 1988, 196; and Carruthers 1992, 52, 82, 86, 96).

35. For example, Trusted (1992) uses it to mean merely a preference for members of one's own species in a crisis.

36. These two quotations are from the 1995 encyclical *Evangelium Vitae* (at 102).

37. Pluhar (1995) notes that there are several uses of the term "person." She uses the term "full-person" only for normal human adults with full, normal capacities. This category excludes many humans who are designated "persons" in either common parlance (such as infants and senile people) or some contemporary debates (such as antiabortionists' use of "person" for human fetuses).

38. Rachels (1993, 154–55) notes that Aristotle first formulated this principle.

39. Pluhar examines many kinds of arguments, including those of S. I. Benn, Alan White, Carl Cohen, Michael Ween, Peter Wenz, Michael Fox, A. I. Melden, and H. J. McCloskey.

40. Pluhar includes many references to abilities of nonhuman animals (particularly mammals), although her review is not systematic.

41. Her argument is in the last two chapters of her book, and it, of course, includes some nonhuman animals.

42. This latter option is chosen by some philosophers, such as the utilitarian Frey (1988, 197).

Chapter 3

1. Kappeler 1995, 320. Adams and Donovan 1995, 1–3, and Dunayer 1995, 19, provide examples and a summary of this argument.

2. Klug 1992. The page numbers are from a version of the essay obtained from the author.

3. Klug also challenges Singer's reliance on analogies to sexism.

4. Sapontzis (1988, 98) rejects the analogies not because they are inaccurate but because, in his view, they denigrate women, racial minorities, and nonhumans. Pluhar (1995, 129–31) rebuts this claim, arguing that the purpose of the analogies is to show that morally similar individuals are treated in morally different ways.

5. Abbagnano (1967) points out the diversity of themes and movements called "humanism" (listing communism, pragmatism, personalism, and existentialism). Ehrenfeld (1981, 5) notes the OED definition, "the religion of humanity," and generally critiques the exclusivist aspects of modern humanism which he characterizes as any "supreme faith in human reason—its ability . . . to rearrange both the world of Nature and the affairs of men and women so that human life will prosper."

6. Protagoras's dictum has been taken to mean many different things, as pointed out by Kerferd 1967.

7. Benton (1988) makes the opposite equation, arguing that humanism is speciesism and challenging the exclusiveness of humanistic assumptions.

8. For example, Linzey 1994a.

9. This is the second definition of "prejudice" in the OED.

10. This is the view in the *Timaeus*, Plato/Jowett II, 67–68, paragraphs 90 ff.

11. See, for example, George and Yapp 1991.

12. See N. K. Smith 1952, 136, 140; Cottingham (1978) argued that Descartes himself, as opposed to his followers, did not hold a view of other animals that included a denial of "consciousness and feelings (i.e., physical sensations—pain, pleasure, joy)." Regan (1988, 3–4) rebuts this.

13. Note, also, to whom the term "speciesist" might arguably apply most forcefully—not to the originators of traditional views but to *contemporary* moral agents who adhere to them in the face of contrary information.

14. This is *not* to say that favoritism of some kinds is never a justified practice, for it clearly is the case that many kinds of favoritism receive moral approval (an example is loyalty to family members and community, which is discussed later).

15. For example, it has been suggested that humans *can* treat some other animals as "persons" who must not be used as means to ends. Recent examples include Patterson and Gordon 1993 (regarding a gorilla); Miles 1993 (an orangutan named Chantek); Miller 1993 (nonhuman great apes); Francione 1993 (nonhuman great apes); and White 1991, 441–68; 1996 (dolphins). Perhaps the best known arguments are those of Singer (see, for example, 1993b, chaps. 4 and 5). There have been, of course, many human cultures that have viewed some nonhuman biological individuals as persons. See, for example, Malay-

sian and Dyak views of orangutans as "old person of the forest" (Kaplan and Rogers 1994; Galdikas 1995) and Ojibwa (Amerindian) views of other animals as persons (Hallowell 1960).

16. Part II provides examples.

17. Kant 1993, 66, 90–91: only humans have rational natures and thereby the abilities to (1) conceive of the idea of the law, (2) self-legislate, and (3) understand the supreme principle of morality. For Kant, then, members of the human species are the only biological members of the kingdom of ends ("persons"). Kant's specific claim that nonhuman animals are unable to be "self-aware" in this very specific sense is found in his lectures on ethics (Kant 1963, 239, where he claims, "Animals are not self-conscious and are there merely as a means to an end. That end is man").

18. Examples from Hare and Singer are cited in chapter 2. Williams discusses the issue at 1985, 60–61, 69–70.

19. Ward 1986, 54, regarding views of the moral significance of human fertilization.

20. Midgley 1994b, 33. Midgley uses "species-ist" to describe eighteenth-century language characterized by the absolute dichotomy "persons" and "things." She also uses the word (1987) favorably to mean "species-vanity or species-imperialism."

21. Midgley has in mind the complicated problems of defining racism, an undeniably negative word of moral condemnation, in such a way that it does not invalidate acts of reverse discrimination, which are often asserted to be moral.

22. Pluhar (1995, 131–34) offers a detailed rebuttal to Midgley's views, emphasizing that the analogy with speciesism shows that morally similar individuals are treated in morally different ways.

23. Note also that the critique does not address those discriminatory acts that exclude other animals' *nonessential* concerns from the moral circle, and that discriminations not involving the taking of life, captivity, or intentional infliction of avoidable suffering are not within the working definition of speciesism offered in chapter 2.

24. Dawkins 1989, 182; see also 112 ff. Dawkins adds in an electronic mail communication dated January 18, 1995, "There simply isn't any Darwinian support for species-favouring, in any sense whatsoever!"

25. de Waal's works listed in part II cite many examples of this phenomenon.

26. Arguing in this way is not meant to suggest that the effects are not real, for they surely often are. James notes, "[T]he reaction due to things of thought is notoriously in many as strong as that due to sensible presences. It may even be stronger" (1923, 53).

27. This is a favorite contention of sociobiologists. See, for example, Dawkins 1989; Wilson 1980.

28. See Dawkins 1989, 83–84.

29. Lecky 1884, 100–101. This is the theme of Singer 1981.

30. Crooke argued that "no savage fixes the boundary line between man and the lower forms of animal life so definitely as more civilised races are wont to do" (1894, 315). Similar observations can be found at Ingold 1994a, 11–12, regarding the worldviews of hunter-gatherers; Thomas 1908, 484, regarding natives of North and South America; and Tylor 1891, I, 381, regarding indigenous peoples of "the Indian Archipelago." Part II includes additional references.

31. On the issue of "natural" bonds, Wilson (1984) has suggested that certain tendencies in humans suggest a bond to other life generally.

32. Diamond 1978. A similar critique is that of Gaita 1991.

33. Diamond does not use Wittgenstein's term "form of life" in this essay, but it can be used to capture some of the nuances of her subtle arguments.

34. These are *not* Diamond's words.

35. The italicized "*the difference*" will be used when referring to Diamond's position that what we must see as fundamental is not "the differences between humans and animals" but "*the difference* between humans and animals."

Chapter 4

1. McGrew 1992, 215, citing Groves 1986. There is no consensus presently on this subject. Other sources that raise the issue are Diamond 1992; Yunis and Prakash 1982; Koop and others 1986.

2. See, for example, Mayr 1982, 147 ff. and 221 ff., for the history of taxonomic classifications and information on modern approaches.

3. Charts and some explanation of these relationships can be found in Byrne 1995, 17–27.

4. McGrew 1992, 42. Ruvolo (1994) suggests that all gorillas do not belong to the *same* species.

5. Diamond 1992. Byrne (1995, 26–27) discusses the issues but prefers, as does Dawkins (1993, 84), to extend the label "African great apes" to include humans as well, or to keep the term "great apes" with it signifying humans as well.

6. Reeves and Leatherwood (1994, v) give the number seventy-nine and list these at 4–6. See also Ellis 1991, 2; Watson 1981, 11. See Wilson, 1992, 148–49, regarding new species of this group being discovered at the rate of one per decade during the twentieth century.

7. The key species represent less than .00001 percent of existing species, based on Erwin 1983 (10 to 30 million insect species alone). In terms of the percentage of living beings, the number is obviously much smaller.

8. It cannot be said that *all* members of these species have these features, for as pointed out later, many of the species are so poorly known that any guess as to features of their lives would be pure speculation.

9. The concept of "complex individual" is an example of a principle of differentiated value, by which some forms of life are valued more than others. These principles are discussed in chapter 5.

10. The literature is endless. See, for example, Dennett 1996, for a discussion of the problem generally. On other animals, pioneering work appears in Griffin 1981, 1992; there are also interesting comments in Midgley 1994a, 41.

11. Diamond 1992, 14 ff., gives a general account of how this is done and what has been found.

12. First reported by Sibley and Ahlquist 1984. Subsequent work has suggested that the similarity in the active parts of the genetic coding mechanism is over 99 percent.

13. For example, according to Diamond (1992, 19), the principal hemoglobin of chimpanzees and humans is identical.

14. See, for example, Singer 1976 on "interests"; Regan 1988 on philosophically based "rights"; and Linzey 1987, 1994a on theologically based "rights."

15. There are many materials on the differing views. See, for example, Thomas 1908, especially 484, 523, and Willis 1990 on the widespread occurrence of beliefs that there is no definite line of demarcation between humans and other animals. Native American views are discussed in Grim 1994; Albanese 1990; and Erdoes and Ortiz 1984. Eliade (1978–85, 1:5–44) discusses Paleolithic humans. Smart 1976, 62; Mbiti 1991; and Opoku 1978 provide some information on African views. General information is available in Manning and Serpell 1994 (particularly Ingold 1994a, regarding the relationship between hunter-gatherer communities and the animals they hunted).

16. For example, "myopically anthropocentric" is the description Staddon (1989, 123, 133) gives of the history of astronomy, physics, biology, and psychology.

17. See, for example, Fox 1991; Linzey 1994a; and Ruether 1995.

18. See, for example, Linzey 1994a, 24–25.

19. See, for example, von Rad 1966; Wright 1952, at, for example, 38 and 45.

20. See, for example, Hiebert 1996, especially 4–12.

21. While there are many individual essays and collections for Buddhism (see, for example, Harris 1994; Batchelor and Brown 1992; Badiner 1990), the number of articles, collections, and books pertaining to Christianity is truly astonishing. An interesting recent collection is Hessel 1996.

22. The details of the overlap of the "animal movement" and the environmental movement are listed by Kinsley (1995, especially 180–83) in his comparative work dealing with the general overlap of spirituality and ecological awareness.

23. Savage-Rumbaugh and Lewin 1994, 260. Similarly, see Goodall 1971, 234.

24. Letter to J. G. Gmelin, February 14, 1747, at Seldes 1985, 247.

25. See, for example, Bond 1984; Orlans 1993. Among the earliest psychological uses of primates as human models are Darwin 1872; Yerkes 1916; and Köhler [1925] 1957.

26. Arguing that a relatively accurate picture has begun to emerge in *some* biological sciences is *not* to argue (1) that these sciences are the first place that such knowledge has been gained or (2) that "science" as a whole has been particularly good at developing this information. Both of these claims are surely wrong. The first fails to take into account the views of many indigenous peoples, and the second misleads because much of "science" has simply ignored such realities.

27. For the linguistic life cycle in humans, see Pinker 1994, chap. 9, and especially 290–96 on the decline in humans' ability to learn new languages.

28. Greenfield and Savage-Rumbaugh 1990, 543–44; in explanation, they state, "We use the term 'protogrammar' to indicate the very simple nature of the rules."

29. Savage-Rumbaugh and Lewin 1994, 91. Chapter 3 is a description of the work with Sherman and Austin.

30. Both Fouts 1997 and Savage-Rumbaugh and Lewin 1994 provide many relevant details, including responses to the Chomskian thesis that humans stand apart from all other animals because of their possession of a unique, brain-based foundation for using and learning the syntactical features of human language.

31. Greenfield and Savage-Rumbaugh 1990, 544. References to citations for related observations omitted.

32. Savage-Rumbaugh and Lewin 1994, 564. The rule is described as a "seemingly arbitrary" combination that "demanded extra motor steps" (564) which involved "combining agent gesture with action lexigram" (560).

33. See Sorabji 1993, 2, 81.

34. For example, *City of God* 1.20.

35. The ethological accounts of Goodall (1971, 1986, 1990) reflect, for example, the patent differences in strategy, temperament, determination, and intelligence among the common chimpanzees of Gombe.

36. Detailed studies of the wide variety of social realities found in primate groups appear in, for example, Hinde 1983, and Smuts and others 1987.

37. See, for example, de Waal 1982, 1989, 1996. The last work is a detailed analysis of the rudimentary concepts of reciprocity and obligation that exist in certain nonhuman primates. De Waal uses terms such as "moralistic aggression" (1996, 159) and "community concern" (205) and concludes that "many of the sentiments and cognitive abilities underlying human morality antedate the appearance of our species on this planet" (210).

38. Badrian and Badrian 1984, 325. One of the few detailed studies is Kano 1992.

39. Parker 1990b, 146. The relevance of brain size is discussed later.

40. It would be misleading to suggest that because bonobos display remarkable mental abilities, all other great apes also have these abilities. In fact, the social realities of the other great apes are different, as described in de Waal 1995, 61. See also Kano 1992; McGrew 1994; Goodall 1990; and Schaller 1995. Chimpanzee social structures have been the most thoroughly studied, but different groups are by no means identical in their features. A good example of how complex both the realities and argument over them can be appears in the lively debate over whether the notion of "culture" should be employed to account for the group differences among chimpanzees, as McGrew (1992) proposes and Tomasello (1990) opposes.

41. Fouts 1997 is a well-documented example of a long-term study. Greenfield and Savage-Rumbaugh (1990, 543) provide a list of studies and comment that "so many semiotic and symbolic capacities have been found in the great apes in the last 20 years."

42. See, for example, Miles 1990. Bard (1990, 368), using Piagetian techniques, concludes, "[T]hey [the gestures of orangutan infants] qualify as *intentional communication.*" See also Kaplan and Rogers 1994, on orangutans' spontaneous communicative and sign language abilities on a par with those of the other great apes.

43. See, for example, Patterson and Gordon 1993.

44. See, for example, Fouts 1993, 34, on instances of private signing; and Fouts, Fouts, and Cantfort 1989 (the young chimp Loulis is reported to have acquired a vocabulary of fifty signs solely from other chimps).

45. This quotation and the following are from Köhler [1925] 1957, 92, emphasis in the original.

46. Terrace 1985, 113. See, generally, Weiskrantz 1985.

47. See, for example, Poli 1988, 279; Parker 1990b, 129.

48. See, for example, Parker 1991a, 21; Parker and Baars 1990, 78. General descriptions can be found in Griffin 1992; Gardner 1985.

49. Dennett 1983. See, for example, Byrne 1995 for one prominent primatologist who uses this analysis.

50. There are additional levels as well. Dennett 1983, 345.

51. Some behaviorist theories, such as that of Skinner (1938), attempt this sort of an interpretation of human behavior as well.

52. For example, Miles 1990, 529.

53. Oakley 1972, 3. The first edition was published in 1949.

54. The history of the brain-intelligence association can be found in Lilly 1975, 86 ff. and in Jerison's many works, particularly 1982, 726 ff.

55. Ingold 1994b, xviii–xix. The figure 40,000 years is, of course, speculative. Regarding the evolution of human language, see Lieberman 1984, 1991, 1998. For a recent challenge to the figure of 40,000 years as the beginning date, see the archaeological finds described in Noble 1998.

56. See, for example, Deacon 1990, 691 ff.

57. There are many studies, some of which are mentioned in the following. The most complete collection of essays is Parker and others 1994. Kennedy offers a more parsimonious assumption that the experimental subject merely "forms a point-to-point association between the movements of the mirror image and his own movement" (1992, 107).

58. Griffin 1992, 249; see, generally, 245–52.

59. See Gallup 1970, 1977, 1982, 1983, and 1987; Suarez and Gallup 1981. As discussed later, there is some controversy over just what MSR means. De Waal has said unequivocally, "This experiment proved that chimpanzees have self-recognition" (1989, 85).

60. Miles 1990, 535 (orangutans); Hyatt and Hopkins 1994 (bonobos); Gallup 1970 (chimpanzees). There is disagreement over gorillas' MSR, with some claiming an affirmative finding (Patterson 1986; Patterson and Gordon 1993); different findings are set forth in Parker 1994, 5–6.

61. There are many studies on this topic; see, for example, Lewis and Brooks-Gunn 1979.

62. McGrew 1992, 58. Gergely (1994, 57) and Byrne (1995, 117) agree.

63. An excellent example occurs in Moss 1988, 124–25, regarding the communications and interactions of two groups and their respective matriarchs, Teresias and Slit Ear.

64. See, generally, Payne and others 1986.

65. He is not to the ordinary observer white in appearance but is rather merely lighter in color than most elephants. The key features are seven traditional marks that range from the lighter colored skin to gait, carriage, and overall shape (Chadwick 1994, 348).

66. Chadwick 1994, 346. Young ([1900] 1982, 388–99) describes the significance of "white elephants" in the Siamese kingdom. Veneration of white elephants is not an exclusively Buddhist phenomenon, for the legend of flying white elephants, usually supposed to have an affinity for clouds and rain, is found across Asia with local variations, and N. W. Thomas (1908, 514) and Crooke (1894) describe African peoples who venerate white elephants.

67. Chadwick 1994, 352. Young ([1900] 1982, 392–93), lists prayers and entreaties by Brahmins that reflect such beliefs.

68. Other examples appear in Chadwick 1994, 382, regarding a Suay blessing ritual at which Buddhist monks chant; and 383, where elephants are noted at Buddhist ordination ceremonies. See also Bock [1883] 1986, chap. 3, for a nineteenth-century description of Southeast Asian and Buddhist example strikingly similar to the circumstances of Pra Barom Nakkot.

69. The most detailed study of Indian elephants is Sukamar's (1994). Some of the more numerous studies of African elephants are cited in the following.

70. "Joint family" is Sukamar's term (1994, 90–91) for a group with several matriarchs. "Kin group" is the Douglas-Hamilton and Douglas-Hamilton term (1975), and "bond groups" is Moss's term (1988). During certain times of the year, there are even larger aggregations (Sukamar 1994, 91).

71. Much of what follows can be found in Moss and Poole 1983, 315.

72. The repertoire is described in Payne and Langbauer 1992.

73. The Mudevan people of Africa distinguished different elephant sounds as having different purposes. Borgese 1968, quoted at Williams 1989, 104.

74. Chadwick 1994, 69–70. Poole's earlier scientific report (Poole and others 1988) is more conservative.

75. Douglas-Hamilton (1975, 93) notes that a young elephant's ability to use its trunk even for simple tasks such as drinking is not innate but must be learned.

76. *Natural History*, 8.1 (p. 3); see Aristotle 1984, 630b19–22.

77. See Jerison 1973, 342 ff., and 359; Chadwick 1994, 77–78.

78. Rensch carried out studies for the purpose of assessing elephant "intelligence" and concluded, "Their performances suggest that elephants must be credited with true ideation, i.e., anticipating what will come of certain actions" (1957, 47).

79. See, for example, Moss 1992, 106–7, 112; Shoshani and Eisenberg 1992, 134–36; and Masson and McCarthy 1994, 148–49. Regarding play behavior as a foundation for development of cognitive and social abilities generally, see Fagen 1981 (178–79 regarding elephants specifically; Fagen also includes much on the nonhuman great apes, as well as a page on cetaceans).

80. Chadwick (1994, 18) reports that elephants who are in confinement and "being regularly fed and frequently bored, will work considerably harder for a reward of play than for food."

81. Griffin 1992, 209 ("clear evidence of elephant deceptive behavior").

82. Hart and Hart 1993, 70; Hyatt and others 1994 relying on Moss 1988.

83. Parbati Barua of northern India makes such a claim in Mark Shand's 1990s film *Queen of the Elephants*, which focuses on Barua's lifelong work with elephants.

84. The technical arguments for elephants' self-awareness based on experimental data are complicated. In experiments reported by Povinelli (1989), elephants learned to use mirrors to locate hidden food but showed no signs of MSR. While Gallup (1983) has argued that elephants can also monitor their own mental states, Gergely (1994, 55) argues that they show preconditions of MSR. Given that the eyesight of elephants is not as good as that of humans, and that their olfactory sense and hearing are the dominant senses, *visual* recognition might not be the only self-awareness medium.

85. This account is taken from page 2 of *Mālama Kai*, newsletter of the Kewalo Basin Marine Mammal Laboratory (Honolulu, 1995).

86. See, for example, Herman and others 1993a; Herman and others 1994.

87. See, for example, Bateson 1972, 276–78; Bateson 1979, 137–38; and Norris 1991, 47–48.

88. This passage is from the newsletter cited in note 85. The experiment is described in Braslau-Scheck 1994.

89. On the inevitable influence of experimental circumstances on the animals studied, see, generally, Davis and Balfour 1992.

90. For the fragmentary state of knowledge about mysticetes' social lives, see Evans 1990, 53 ff.

91. The relevance of this is, of course, that true *altruism* (rather than reciprocal or prudent altruism) is often thought to be a crucial ingredient of morality.

92. See, for example, Herzing 1993, 1994, 1995a, 1995b.

93. See, for example, Watkins and Schevill 1977.

94. See, for example, Morgan 1979.

95. All the mysticetes with the exception of the pygmy right whale have been studied, but unevenly. See, generally, C. Clark 1990 for an overview.

96. The humpbacks' vocalizations had been recorded as early as 1952 (Ellis 1991, 436), but the structure of the songs was not noticed until the Paynes, who began recordings in 1967, recognized in the early 1970s that the structure was changing from year to year. See Payne and McVay 1971; for recent evaluations, see Payne and Payne 1985; Helweg and others 1992.

97. See, for example, Cummings and Thompson 1971. The increasing sophistication is apparent in the recent evaluations appearing in Helweg and others 1992.

98. See Caldwell and Caldwell 1965, 1968; more recent work has shown that wild dolphins use mimicry of each other's signature whistle, although the purpose of doing so is not known. Tyack 1986; Caldwell, Caldwell and Tyack 1990, 204.

99. Caldwell and Caldwell 1965. Norris and Johnson 1994, 234–36, describes this in greater detail.

100. See Caldwell and Caldwell 1968.

101. See, generally, Deacon 1990, 691 ff. The relative position of mammals in terms of EQ are set forth in the chart at Jerison 1988a, 453.

102. Deacon 1990, 691. Deacon comments that this is the case in "presumably all cetacean brains" (691). He also presumes that the *microscopic* differences are shared by all cetaceans (693).

103. Deacon 1990, 694. He emphasizes the importance of refraining from attempts to compare the brains of cetaceans as "advanced or conservative"; rather, he emphasizes their distinct evolutionary origins.

104. For example, Klinowska (1988, 1992) relates large brain size to a lack of REM sleep.

105. See, for example, Passingham (1975); Masterton and Skeen (1972).

106. See, for example, Herman and others 1984, 1985; Herman 1986.

107. Possible by-products of some cetaceans' possession of large brains in social contexts are the widespread reports of humans and dolphins interacting cooperatively. Evans (1994, 85–86) lists seven geographically diverse instances, many of them long-established traditions.

108. Marten and Psarakos 1994. However, what "self" and "awareness" mean for a cetacean is difficult to say.

109. There are, of course, animal communication studies (for example, Sebeok 1968); the point is taking the richness of communication seriously.

110. An unstated assumption in this argument is one held by all major contemporary theories governing humans' moral considerability, namely, that in the area of essential concerns (as defined in chapter 2), pretechnology humans were as morally considerable as modern humans.

Chapter 5

1. These descriptions are in Whitaker 1959, 1969; see also Sebeok's summary (1994, 65). Lorenz (1952, 12) uses the terms "constructors," "consumers," and "decomposers."

2. Sam. III, 128 (Feer III, 152). Clement and Augustine provide examples of early Christians who recognized this phenomenon (see part IV).

3. Cited at Kalechofsky 1991, 78. Pius IX backed this up by opposing the establishment of a society for the protection of animals in Rome (Gaffney 1986, 149).

4. This is ~Na.namoli's translation (at MNB 445) of the passage that opens this chapter. Horner's is "For this . . . is a tangle, that is to say human beings. But this . . . is an open clearing, that is to say animals." M. II, 5.

5. This translation is at Linzey 1987, 48. The original is at Augustine 388/1992, 137–36 (2.17.54).

6. Linzey (1991, 48) argues that the story does not support the interpretation that Jesus *sent* the demons into the pigs.

7. "Third level generalizations" will also be referred to, and these will include narrower, but still broad, classifications such as "flying things" or "terrestrial animals" or "wild animals."

8. OED's second definition is "In common usage: one of the lower animals; a brute, or beast, as distinguished from man."

9. Berry refers to the "Enlightenment fallacy that knowledge automatically produces response" (1993, 33). A version of the fallacy relevant to morality would be a belief that knowledge *alone* is sufficient to create ethical awareness.

10. For example, of the key animals, elephants, and gorillas are.

11. Dunayer (1995, 12, 16–17). Note that the argument is not that *all* animal names offend, for they clearly do not. Dunayer argues only that "the vast majority offend" (1995, 17).

12. There are many descriptions of this movement. Recent ones are Gold 1995; Finsen and Finsen 1994; and Blum 1994.

13. Use of "animal" in this narrow sense has also been a long-standing tradition in scientific circles, as evidenced by titles of contemporary, technical scientific texts. See, for example, *Animal Biology* (Grove and others 1974; humans are not even listed in the index).

14. Mommsen and others 1985, vol. 1, xi, regarding the *Corpus Juris Civilis* of Justinian. It is equally true of earlier codes, such as the Theodosian Code. See Pharr 1952, 436, section 15.11.1. The distinction does not play nearly as prominent a role in the Laws of Hammurabi or other ancient Mesopotamian codes (Roth 1995 translates these with no references to all other animals as a group).

15. This distinction can be found at Gaius, *Institutes*, 1.8 (de Zulueta 1946, 5). Berger 1953, 356 and 628, provides definitions of, respectively, *animalia* and *persona* that reveal this fundamental distinction.

16. Berger 1953, 628. This is not to say that all humans were treated in the same way, for they clearly were not. Freemen and slaves, men and women, citizens and foreigners were treated quite differently from one another within the complex Roman legal system.

17. *Vocabularivm Ivrisprvdentiae Romanae*, I, 446, second definition. This is the *usual* sense in the Roman codes, which also use other generalizations such as "bestia." See, for example, Mommsen and others 1985, vol. 4, 487.

18. The "thinghood" status of all other animals in ancient and modern law is documented by Wise 1995, 1996.

19. See, for example, canons 96–112 in Code of Canon Law 1983, where, though not explicitly stated, the claim that only a member of the human species can be a "person" is fully assumed.

20. At, respectively, Wise 1996, 516 and 535. Schmidt and Schmidt 1995 provides detailed analyses of the property status of domestic animals in northern European countries. Francione (1995), who provides additional information regarding the United States and legal systems generally, argues that mere economic justification will *always* suffice to rebut the characterization of *any* action harmful to nonmembers of the human species as "unnecessary," "cruel," or "inhumane" (13).

21. Many of the traits that are unique to humans (such as anatomy of the pelvis, or spouse selection procedures) exemplify the potentially trivial nature of some claims that members of one species characteristically possesses unique-different traits. As Radner and Radner point out, "Every species is different from every other species: this much is plain biology" (1989, 33).

22. Diamond's list does *not* include characterizations of humans as the only beings who are moral, rational, or religious. For a challenge to the view that features of morality are found *only* among humans, see the detailed observations and arguments of de Waal (1996) regarding some other primates' social rules (these are mentioned in chapter 4). Relatedly, there are many arguments for the admittedly controversial conclusion that the capacity to be a moral agent is *not* a *necessary* condition of an individual being accorded moral considerability in the narrow sense of that term in this book (see, for example, Harré and Robinson 1995; this conclusion is also supported by the broad agreement on including marginal cases within the moral circle). "Rationality" is, as argued below in note 24, a vague enough notion that there have been prominent claims that it exists in some degree in some other animals (Sorabji 1993 details many of the ancient claims; M. Thomas's comments are mentioned in chapter 4). Religious sensibilities do appear, however, to be unique to humans, but, as suggested throughout this study, an individual's possession of this feature is only dubiously made a necessary condition of being "morally considerable."

23. See, for example, *City of God* 1.20 (discussed in the last section of chapter 8).

24. For example, there has been no general agreement in the history of ideas regarding what is meant by "rational." Sorabji (1993, 65–77) argues that the concept of reason itself often varied in ancient times. Especially difficult are claims that humans' "divine purpose" is the source of a critical difference between humans and other animals. While such a claim is formally like the claim "humans have language and other animals do not," verification procedures in each case are fundamentally different.

25. It is also worthy of note that, as a logical matter, saying that X is more valuable than Y in certain situations is *not* in any way the equivalent to saying that Y is not valuable in and of itself. One can thus validly assert a principle of differentiated value without implying in any way that the beings and entities not included in the highest category are without value.

26. "Animal rights," even its broadest forms, involves a concern for only *some* living things. These living things are typically the larger animals, commonly described as "higher" in the phylogenetic scale.

27. See, for example, Devall and Sessions 1985.

28. Chapple 1993 describes this in detail.

29. The fact that it can be used to *challenge* a narrower principle of differentiating value does not necessarily imply that it, as the new principle, is definitive or the only principle that could have been used to make that challenge. All that is necessarily implied is that the challenged principle is too limited.

30. See Ghiselin for the logical argument: "Biological species are, in the logical sense, individuals, and assertions to the contrary reflect mere verbal confusion" (1966, 208). See also Ghiselin 1974; Hull 1976.

31. See, for example, Ruse 1987.

32. The conceptual or categorical aspect of the term "species" has been, and still is, the source of many differences of opinion. Mayr notes that there is "almost as much difference of opinion as existed one hundred years ago" (1982, 251).

33. Ruse (1987, 232) also refers to "Aristotelian essentialism." Balme (1980) argues that (1) Aristotle's biology was not essentialist, (2) that interpretation has been aided by mistranslations of Aristotle, and (3) the tradition of equating essence and species began with Porphyry.

34. Mayr (1982, 254) notes as an example Albertus Magnus's description of five ways of transforming one plant into another.

35. These views are compared in Ayers 1981.

36. Ayers (1981, 253 ff.) provides a detailed analysis of Locke's reasoning. Dupré (1981, 67) cites the various sources in Locke, including the important observations in *An Essay Concerning Human Understanding*, vol. II, Book II, chaps. 6 and 8.

37. See Ruse 1987, 237–39; Dupré 1981, 89; Dupré 1993, chaps. 1, 2, for the conclusion that species taxa lack essential properties of the kind called for by the traditional natural kind notion.

38. Essentialism has been challenged in many contexts across intellectual history (for example, Popper [1974, 20] challenges it in science generally as "mistaken in suggesting that definitions can add to our *knowledge of facts*"). The validity of these broader challenges generally, however, does not control the validity of the very specific challenge described here to essentialist interpretations of what it means to be a member of a species taxon.

39. See Mayr 1976, 28–29.

40. See Dupré 1981.

41. One example given later (orangutans versus chimpanzees) is not, for most humans, an "everyday" example, but it exemplifies the principle that genetic endowment is often insufficient to determine which entity's interest in a particular fact situation might "justly" prevail. An extremely important qualification has already been suggested, namely, that in *some* cases (those where creatures' genetic endowment is vastly different, as with bacteria and mammals) species membership can be a relevant consideration. This is argued in more detail later.

42. For purposes of this argument, these words are interchangeable and include social relations as well as individual traits, and so forth. The word "features" will be used in the following.

43. The issue being raised in this section requires only that the first of these two be dealt with here.

44. There are important replies to arguments relying on unrealized potential. Ward (1986, 68) notes, "The argument from 'potential' is a difficult one. For some philosophers, to say

that x is a potential y is to say no more or less than that all or most x's tend to turn into, or to be contiguously succeeded by, y's." Feinberg (1986) holds that assigning moral significance on the basis of potential suffers from a fatal logical flaw because one cannot deduce actual rights from mere potential to hold those rights. Pluhar (1995, 107 ff.) suggests that this is too sweeping a dismissal of the potentiality argument.

45. For example, Singer 1990, 17–21; Glover 1990, 50–51; LaFollette and Shanks 1996, 43.

46. Lorenz 1966, 194, makes this and related points.

Chapter 6

1. *Tiracchānayoni* (at Trenckner 73) literally means "horizontals' womb." MNB 169 uses "animal realm"; and MSBB I, 49, uses "animal world." This is a common term; see, for example, D. I, 291 (Rhys Davids/Carpenter I, 228) where it is given the most typical translation, "animal womb."

2. This is an inflected form (the nominative), which, by convention, is the form cited in dictionaries and grammars (Warder 1991, 14). The plural is *sattā*.

3. For example, Vin. V, 149 (Oldenberg II, 110); A. II, 82 (Morris II, 73).

4. The saying is attributed to the leader of an important nonorthodox sect. Warder 1991, 176.

5. The Pali occurs at Rhys Davids/Carpenter I, 53; and Trenckner 407.

6. D. I, 71. This is an unusual translation in that it suggests "animals" for *sattā*.

7. For example, at Khp2. 143 and 156, the plural form *sattā* is first translated as "beings" and then only a few verses later as both "creatures" and "beings."

8. At Sn. 24, vv. 145, 147.

9. Chalmers's translation of Sn. 37.

10. See, for example, KhpA. 92.

11. As indicated in the PED definition already listed and as suggested by Mrs. Rhys Davids in her comments at A. II, ix.

12. At Khp2. 156–57, *sabbabhutesu*, "in creatures all."

13. At Khp2., 146–7, *bhūtāni*.

14. The term can also have more specific uses, such as something like "ghosts" or "goblins," as at D. II, 52 (Rhys Davids/Carpenter II, 57).

15. See Warder 1991, 396.

16. Schmithausen (1991c, 1 n. 7) notes that the early Buddhists largely avoided using *jīvo* in the sense of "living being" except when the view of "people" or non-Buddhists is referred to.

17. See, for example, Horner's comment at M. II, 76 n. 2.

18. Vin. III, 1 (Oldenberg IV, 124).

19. Vin. III, 2 (Oldenberg IV, 124). Importantly, "animal" here means *only* nonhuman animals. The word *tiracchānagata* will be explained later.

20. As in Pācittiya 20 and 62 at, respectively, Vin. II, 261–62, and Vin. III, 3–4.

21. As in Pārājika 2, at Vin. I, 87 (Oldenburg III, 152—*pā.no nāma manussapā.no vuccati*—Horner's translation is "Creature means: what is called a human creature").

22. Schmithausen (1991c, 19 n. 102) notes that this is also the sense the word has, at times, in Jain and Brahminical literature.

23. Schmithausen (1991c, 58, 64, 97, 106) argues that this reflects the earliest Buddhists' belief that living things did include plants as a borderline cases of *pā.nā*, and that use of *pā.no* for animate beings only is a departure from pre-Buddhist uses of "older, Vedic belief."

24. See, for example, A. III, 156 (Hardy III, 213); A. IV, 129 (Hardy IV, 188); and M. III, 250 (Chalmers 1896–99, 3:204).

25. See, for example, Sn. 20, v. 117; 35, v. 220; 66, v. 400; 104, v. 600.

26. Chalmers Sn. at 33, v. 117, and 148, v. 600, uses "living things," while he uses "life" at 53, v. 220. Pm. I, 245, 264–65 uses "living things."

27. See, for example, A. III, 156 (Hardy III, 213), and Khp2. 156–57. In the latter it is translated as "living things." At Sn. 24, v. 146, *pā.nabhūt'* is translated "living creatures"; Chalmers Sn., 37, uses simply "all."

28. Sam. III, 128 (Feer III, 152).

29. Sam. V, 203 (Feer V, 228) for the term *tiracchānagatā pā.nā*, of which the lion is reckoned king.

30. A. II, 36 (Morris II, 33).

31. Sam. III, 128 (Feer III, 152).

32. M. III, 213–14. An awareness of important differences among other animals is also reflected in the differentiation of the modes (the four *yonis*, or "wombs") in which living things are born (for example, M. I, 97). Under this classification scheme, humans and many other animals are understood to share the viviparous mode of birth (*jarāyu-ja*); many other animals are egg-born (*a.n.da-ja*) or moisture-born (*sa.mseda-ja*). The fourth category, that of spontaneously born (*opapātika*), contains gods, occasional human beings, and some underworld beings. M. I, 98 (Trenckner 73).

33. PED IV, 1. "Animal" here, of course, means "nonhuman animals."

34. D. I, 13. The term occurs often (see, for example, M. II, 192, 203, 223, 228, 230, 232–33).

35. Cited in DW 70 n. 33 at DW 539.

36. A. III, 217, *mige* (inflected plural form of *migo*) at Hardy III, 303.

37. A. II, 36 (Morris II, 33).

38. PED V, 156, explains that the term has a broader meaning, something like "wild animal" or "animal of the forest" when it is "characterised by another attribute" but "antelope" usually "when uncharacterised."

39. J. 175/50 (Fausbøll II, 73). Cowell translates it as "monkey."

40. A. III, 115; Hardy III, 149—this is an inflected form.

41. See, for example, A. II, 36 (Morris II, 33).

42. This is a breakdown of *sattā* at A. V, 16 (Hardy V, 21); see also A. II, 82 (Morris II, 72). The generic term *pā.na* is also broken down by footedness; see, for example, A. IV, 238 (Hardy IV, 360).

43. See, for example, A. II, 82, 122.

44. See, for example, D. II, 52 (Rhys Davids/Carpenter II, 57).

45. Such as *dehin*, which means "that which has a body, a creature" (PED IV, 166).

46. Additional passages that suggest awareness of diversity include Sam. I, 126; III, 123; V, 82; and V, 377.

47. The classic treatment of elephants in Indian iconography is Zimmer 1946, 102–9. Gonda (1965, 90 ff.) provides somewhat greater detail. Thomas (1908, 514) provides a summary of elephants in folklore generally, with comments relevant to India and Southeast Asia. Crooke (1894, 315–46) provides details as to the significant place that elephants and other animals have in the folklore of north India. Foucher (1963) provides some analysis of Buddhist art (some of which is discussed later).

48. See map in Chadwick 1991, 14–15.

49. Gibbons form a separate family, Hylobatidae, and are characterized by smaller brains and less complex social organization.

50. The areas where Buddhism predominated is part of orangutans' historic range, but they were very likely eliminated from eastern India well before fifth century B.C.E. Linden 1992, 31.

51. The date is argued for in great detail in Gombrich 1992.

52. The story numbers in Cowell 1895 are J. 5; 26; 27; 31; 37; 57; 58; 66; 70; 72; 73; 80; 105; 107; 122; 123; 140; 143; 148; 149; 161; 163; 182; 197; 202; 221; 227; 229; 230; 241; 249; 250; 259; 262; 267; 276; 284; 314; 322; 335; 357; 374; 380; 394; 404; 409; 410; 418; 419; 422; 423; 433; 454; 455; 463; 479; 482; 488; 490; 497–99; 506; 509; 510; 514; 519; 522; 525; 526; 530–33; 535–39; 542; 545–47.

53. See, for instance, J. 72, 357, 455, 514.

54. J. 80, 156, 229, 536, 546.

55. J. 70, 539.

56. J. 5, 105, 122, 140, 156, 197, 380, 409, 530, 542.

57. J. 26, 27, 73, 156, 463, 514, 547.

58. In the forest, J. 227.

59. J. 143, 227.

60. Killing of predators and dunging on them, J. 143.

61. J. 545.

62. J. 546/222.

63. J. 105, 182.

64. J. 510. The description of musth and other details can be found at Moss 1988, 108 ff.

65. See, for example, J. 161/28, where the Bodhisattva advises against keeping an elephant because kept elephants cause death; J. 26/67, where a captive elephant turns violent; and the story of Bhādavatikā at J. 409/233.

66. In, respectively, J. 409/233, 410/235, 533/175, and Dpda. 1990, 15, v. 330.

67. See DPPN I, 921, and Buddhaghosa's commentary on the *Majjhima* (MA. II, 25–26), which lists ten types or clans.

68. These are J. 20, 37, 46, 57, 58, 92, 173–77, 208, 219, 222, 224, 257, 268, 273, 278, 280, 304, 316, 321, 329, 342, 348, 365, 404, 407, 488, 516, 528, 546, and 547/263 and 278. Most of these, and perhaps all, are references to primates *other than* nonhuman great apes. For example, in J. 516/37 and 40, the primate has a tail, and only non–great ape primates have tails. Sometimes the word "ape" is used in translations (e.g., Mrs. Rhys Davids's Dpda. 1931, 334), but "monkey" occurs as well (e.g., Müller's Dpda. 1881/1968, 80).

69. See, for example, J. 58, 177, 219, 222, 404, 407, 516.

70. This is especially evident in Aarya "Sūra's *Jātakamālā* version. See the twenty-seventh story, at Khoroche 1989, 186–92.

71. J. 57, 58.

72. J. 219, 222.

73. See, for example, J. 157, 219.

74. For example, rats in J. 129.

75. J. 321/49. Fausbøll III, 73.

76. See, for example, J. 46 and 268, but also J. 173, 250, and 257, where monkeys are disguised as ascetics (perhaps suggesting, ironically, the intelligence-related ability to deceive discussed in chapter 4).

77. See, for example, J. 174, 176, 278, 299.

78. J. 348/98 and 435/311.

79. See, for example, Buddhadatta 1954, 155; PED V, 137–38.

80. J. 537/250. The Pali is at Fausbøll V, 462, lines 17–18.

81. Horner, in her translation of the *Milindapa~nha*, notes that the three words are "not necessarily to be taken together." Mil. II, 75–76, n. 4.

82. Similar passages also occur at Vin. V, 332–36; A. IV, 136; U. 96, 99 (USBB 65, 67); at Pm. 370, Mil. 118 and 247 are somewhat similar references to extraordinarily large marine creatures.

83. Footnote 1 in the text identifies the weed as the aquatic plant *vallisneria*; DPPN I, 1014 calls it seaweed.

84. It will be assumed below that this *is* a reference to cetaceans, but this assumption is admittedly speculative.

85. J. 545/136 (Fausbøll VI, 278, line 3).

86. PED VIII, 174; see, for example, J. 208, where it is translated as "crocodile" even though footnote 1 mentions a Russian folktale variant that does mention "whales." A slight variant, *sa.msumārena*, at Cp. 121 (the Pali is at Cp./Morris 97, v. 1) is translated "by a crocodile."

87. This is the translation at J. 296/302.

88. See, generally, Vin. I, 218–37.

89. Tin's introduction, Dpda. 1990, xiii. The Pali manuscripts of this widely used Buddhist scripture are representative of the other (Sanskrit and Prakrit) versions (Sangharakshita 1985, 46). The translation used is the Rhys Davids (Dpda. 1931) translation, although the translations by Müller (Dpda. 1881/1968), Easwaran (Dpda. 1987), and Tin (Dpda. 1990) are also mentioned.

90. Müller describes this as typical of Buddhists. See, for example, A. II, 43.

91. Dpda. 1987, 177. There is a description in chapter 7 of the harm caused by such tools of control. The pain-oriented treatment of elephants in captivity is also memorialized in descriptions such as "racked through and through like a goad-stricken elephant, poor wretch, he roars amain." J.530/134 and 138.

92. The English title is from Law 1938.

93. There are four key animal references, all to elephants. The first three are virtually identical references to going forth from the world riding on an elephant. Bv. 50, v. 21; 66, v. 17; virtually identical is Bv. 78, v. 20. The final reference is "having snapped his bonds like an elephant, he [the twenty-first buddha] obtained enlightenment" (Bv. 72, v. 2).

94. Each of these stories has a parallel story in the *Jātakas*.

95. This is the third story in the first group of ten, and appears at Cp. 97. The parallel in the *Jātakas* is J. 276.

96. The ninth story is almost identical. The same story is at J. 547 and is told more fully in Cone and Gombrich 1977.

97. Cp. 107; see also J. 72, 455.

98. Primates are mentioned in three of these stories, but these references are minor and very much have the tenor of the primate stories in the *Jātakas*. See, for example, the tenth story of the first chapter (J. 316 is similar); Cp. 110, v. 4 (similar to J. 278); and Cp. 121.

99. Gombrich (1991a, 9) comments, "The position of the monastic Order in Buddhism is even more dominant than that of the church in Christianity."

100. Vin. I, 87–88 (Oldenberg III, 52).

101. Many of these passages are listed in the following.

102. It is, of course, acceptable to act intentionally in self-defense. See, for example, Vin. III, 48.

103. Horner 1967, 24, regarding Vin. I, 183–85. See also, M. II, 55; M. III, 250; and A. V, 185–86. There is some irony in this claim, for while such formulae suggest that the lives of nonhumans are of value, the punishment, if a human kills them intentionally, is to be born *as one of them*.

104. See, Horner Vin. I, xxii–xxiii, which is a discussion of the *pārājika* offense of depriving things of life.

105. On plants, see, generally, Schmithausen 1991c.

106. See, for example, Vin. I, 38 ff.

107. Vin. II, 223. The prohibition includes burning the ground, breaking it, and causing these things to be done.

108. Vin. II, 261–62, and Vin. III, 3–4 (Oldenberg IV, 49, 125).

109. Vin. I, 1–2 (Oldenberg IV, 124–25).

110. Vin. IV, 183 (Oldenberg I, 137).

111. Vin. VI, 63 (Oldenberg V, 41).

112. Vin. I, 98 (Oldenberg III, 58).

113. The animals specified are lions, tigers, panthers, hyenas, wolves, and hawks. These are predators that can kill what humans want; an important gloss on this is that the taking cannot be for the benefit of oneself. See, for example, Vin. I, 105–6.

114. Vin. I, 92 (Oldenberg III, 55).

115. Vin. II, 178 (Oldenberg IV, 7). At Vin. II, 187, it is held that it is slander for an ordained person to use this "low mode of address" for another ordained person.

116. At, respectively, Vin. IV, 180; Vin. IV, 458, 480; and Vin. V, 375.

117. Vin. V, 273–74. In the story of the taming of the elephant Nālāgiri, Gotama is called "the elephant among men."

118. See, for example, Vin. IV, 292, Vin. V, 282.

119. Vin. IV, 504. The Pali word translated "sage" is nāga, which also is used for elephants and other animals and imaginary creatures but here is a reference to the wise human.

120. Vin. I, 38 ff., which involves a monk who kept a female monkey for intercourse. See also Vin. I, 51–52, where a monk's fornication with a monkey is confessed.

121. Vin. V, 226. Keown has noted, "The Cullavagga [a section of the Vinaya] is of the opinion that even animals who keep the five precepts will be reborn in heaven" (1992, 46). This is, however, an atypical viewpoint in the tradition, it being much more commonly argued that other animals cannot so progress. See, for example, Kv. 347.

122. Vin. V, 332–36. Timis, timingalas, and timitimingalas are the possible references to cetaceans; the others are imaginary beings.

123. See, generally, Walshe's exposition at DW 31 ff. and, more specifically, Jayatilleke 1963, 361 ff.

124. Counting species conservatively, these are (the numbers are the pages of the Pp.): serpent (51, 66–67); mice (60); ox (65); dog, flies, fish, antelope, cow, horse (76); owl, sheep, boar, deer, bird, fish, antelope, cow with a calf, bullocks, goats (77); rams (78); goat, sheep, fowl, pigs, elephants, cows, horses, mules, bird (80); cow (95).

125. This is true of the Dhammasa"nga.ni, the Discourse on Elements (Dhatu-Kathā), and the Pa.t.thāna. The Vibha"nga has a few nongeneric references (Vib. 109, birds; 325, "lion posture"; 415, lion's roar; and there are various references to "eel wriggling," a term of abuse for those who fail to argue properly in the Buddhists' view). The commentary on the Dhammasa"nga.ni in discussing the indriya.m or "faculty, potentiality of the female" does mention that female elephants lack tusks (correct natural history for most female Indian elephants). Cited by the translator at Dsan. 174 n. 3. The only specific animal regularly mentioned is, of course, humans.

126. For example, it is claimed of Gotama, "Even the mind of animals are known to him." J. 27/69; see also Vin. IV, 504, where it is claimed that Gotama knows the mind of an elephant.

127. See, for example, D. I, 172 ff., and II, 371. These antisacrifice diatribes appear throughout the canon. See, for example, A. II, 49–50; A. IV, 24; and Sam I, 102.

128. D. II, 14–16, and III, 134–38. This is a theme, like so many, taken over from the general culture; see Rhys Davids's comment in footnote 1 at D. I, 131.

129. Senart 1875, 25–27. See also D. II, 289. Elephants are among the five treasures at A. III, 126.

130. See, for example, D. I, 110; D. II, 204, 254; D. III, 137, 165; and M. III, 219.

131. D. II, 255. Buddhaghosa includes a description of the "elephant treasure" at KhpA. 187, which mentions that this elephant when "coming from the Uposatha Clan . . . is the

eldest of all (that clan), but when coming from the Chaddanta Clan he is the youngest of all (that clan)—fully trained and tamed." The clans are references to the ten "types" of elephants listed elsewhere in Buddhaghosa's commentaries (MA. II, 25–26). Most of these classifications are based on color differences.

132. D. II, 131 (*nāgapalokita.m*). Buddhaghosa notes Buddhas were accustomed when looking backward to turn the whole body around as an elephant does "because the bones in their neck were firmly fixed, more so than those of ordinary men!" See Rhys Davids's footnote 1 at D. II, 131; and see M. I, 400, and M. II, 323.

133. Cited by Rhys Davids in footnote 1 at D. I, 131.

134. This recurring material likely was a separate work, per Rhys Davids at D. I, 3. These are discussed in some detail at Keown 1992, 25 ff.

135. See, D. I, 6. The list includes elephants, sheep, goats, fowl, swine, cattle, horses, and mares; *and*, at D. I, 5, women, girls, and slaves (bondmen and bondwomen).

136. For example, D. I, 67 (caparisoned elephants); D. I, 177; D. II, 203 and 253.

137. See, for example, I, 53, 375; II, 26–27, 73, 168, 233, 248, 275 ff., 287, 342–43, 368, 370–71; and III, 71, 73, 85–86, 95, 117, 166, 209, 216, 249, 257, 298, 301.

138. The *Majjhima*, of course, contains the standard references to instrumental use of elephants as vehicles (M. II, 281; II, 297) or as gifts (M. II, 300). Cetaceans are not mentioned, and there is but one minor reference to a primate (M. II, 49–50).

139. M. I, 220 ff.; I, 230 ff.

140. M. I, 221, 224 (Trenckner 178).

141. See PED generally for these definitions. There are other words for elephant, such as *ku~njara*, which appear frequently in and outside the Pali canon; see, for example, Sam. I, 156; VvA. 309; 388; and Dpda. v. 322. At Vin. IV, 245, Horner cites a commentary passage dealing with the use of elephants in the army; the word for a group of six females and one bull is *anīka*.

142. M. III, 183; see also III, 176.

143. Vogel 1926, 281. At A. II, 43 n. 7, Woodward notes that Buddhaghosa gives a fanciful derivation of *nāga* unrelated to any other animals.

144. See, for example, Sam. IV, 131.

145. Sam. II, 66; Feer II, 95.

146. For example, Sam. I, 3; I, 119; III, 124; V, 395.

147. See, for example, Sam. V, 206; see also Sam. I, 111–12; V, 231; M. I, 229. Other incidental references to elephants occur at Sam. I, 172, 195 (*ku~njara*); and Sam. II, 146, 150.

148. Sam. II, 180; there is a similar story at Vin. V, 282.

149. Sam. II, 189; III, 70–72; see also A. II, 36.

150. Respectively, at Sam. I, 12, and II, 154 (tortoises); I, 186; I, 192; I, 241; II, 155; II, 170 (vultures, crows, falcons); II, 189 (swans, herons, peacocks, and "eke the dappled deer"); I, 185; and IV, 97–99 ("sharks"—the word at Feer IV, 157, is *sagāha.m*, which might also, per PED VIII, 120, be translated as "full of crocodiles").

151. See, respectively, Sam. I, 283 (bull), and IV, 64, 111, and 118 (lion-posture).

152. The domestic animals mentioned are cows (at Sn. 4—the numbers in parentheses in this note are page references to Sn.); bulls/bullocks (4); elephant (many); oxen (12); dogs (32, v. 201); and horses (50, v. 300). The larger wild animals mentioned are snake (1); rhinoceros (horn) (7); elephant (many); lion (10, vv. 71–72); antelope (27, v. 165); jackals and wolves (32, v. 201); tiger (69); monkey (133, v. 791; Chalmers at 190–91 translates this as "ape"—the Pali is *kapīva*; this is almost certainly not a great ape; and deer (skin, at 61, v. 1010). The birds include peacock and goose (35, v. 221; an alternative translation is swan); ravens, vultures, and crows (114, v. 675). The smaller, nonmammals include gadflies or

mosquitoes (4); worms (32, v. 201); beetles, moths, ants, and termites (104, v. 602); fish (104, v. 605). The twentieth-eighth species mentioned is the human species.

153. There are two *suttas* that include this word in their title, and many others use the notion as an image for proclamation of the Buddhist message.

154. M. II, 132. Trenckner 460 has both *kumbhīlabhaya.m* (*kumbhīla* in PED III, 50, is crocodile) and *susukābhaya.m* (PED VIII, 180, *susukā*—alligator); "fierce fishes" is the translation of *susukābhaya.m* by Horner; MNB 563 has "sharks"; MSBB 327 uses sharks as well. These references to these unusual animals are said to be images for other things, the latter being for women (M. II, 134).

155. At, respectively, Sam. IV, 67, and V, 356. There are many others, such as Osprey's Haunt (Sam. IV, 72), Crocodile Haunt (Sam. III, 1), Vulture Peak (many; e.g., Sam. I, 137), Boar's Cave (Sam. V, 209), Cock's Pleasuance (Sam. V, 14, 51). See also Squirrels' Feeding Ground (many; e.g., Vin. I, 271), Cock's Monastery (M. II, 14), Pigeons' Grotto (U. 47), "peacock's feeding place" (M. II, 203), and Kapinaccana (a place-name derived from the word for monkeys, *kapina.m* (Pv. 241).

156. Keown 1995, 49 ff. Keown notes at 45 that there is in the early Buddhist sources "no definitive statement as to which forms of life are valued and why."

157. This appears in very wide-ranging Buddhist sources, such as Sam. II, 128, and three *Mahāyāna* sources mentioned at Chapple 1993, 27, 29, 40.

158. See, for example, Sam. II, 171, discussing the fate of the deer hunters, pig butchers, sheep butchers, and fowlers. The animal tamer is also described as having the same fate, although the commentary limits this to one cruel in his or her methods. Cited by Mrs. Rhys Davids at Sam. II, 172 n. 1.

159. At, respectively, A. II, 222; V, 143; III, 229; (2) III, 216–17; (3) III, 282; (4) II, 37; III, 117; III, 243–45; and (5) II, 43.

160. See, for example, A. II, 120–21 (this section is titled "The Elephant"); and A. III, 117–19.

161. Schmithausen 1991a, 15, citing in footnote 84 a Mil. passage, Vasubandhu's *Abhidharmakosabhasya*, and Yasomitra's *Sphutartha Abhidharmakosabhasya* as further examples of the Buddhist insistence that liberation is possible for humans only. Schmithausen cites similar views in Vedic, classic Hindu, and Jain traditions, *and* a contrary view in the Tendai tradition of Buddhism.

162. Vetter 1988, 93, citing M. III, 215, and MNB 1021.

163. M. III, 215. Gotama notes that there is a risk that this "lucky" human could still, because of behaving badly in this new, low human station, then go "lower" to one of the hells.

164. See, for example, Fausbøll 1881, xii; Chalmers 1899, xiii; and Sangharakshita 1985, 49.

165. See, for example, the references to goads and oxen at Sn. 12; or the reference to elephants being part of the army at Sn. 70, v. 421.

166. See, for example, Sn. 7, v. 35; 21, v. 117; 35, v. 220; 66, v. 44.

167. Sn. 104, vv. 600 ff. This important passage also appears at M. II, 381, and the text used by Horner in her translation of the *Majjhima* is actually from the Sn. manuscript. The version cited in the following is the *Majjhima* version.

168. Horner's footnote 1 at M. II, 382.

169. Schmithausen 1991a, 14–15, citing the passages at A. III, 142, and DW 403.

170. U. 96, 99; USBB 65, 67. Dhammapāla's commentary on this passage provides no further hints as to knowledge of these animals. He mentions *mahata.m bhūtāna.m* (of great beings)—he calls them "three breeds of fish"—and says that it is reported that "*timi*"*ngalas*

are capable of swallowing the *timi*, *timitimi"ngalas* are capable of swallowing the *timi* and the *timi"ngalas.*" UA. 769. He appears to be, in essence, merely repeating the standard, rather vague claims about these animals. If so, he provides a good example of how purported knowledge of unfamiliar animals is passed on.

171. U. 72. The *Udāna* also includes a version of the classic story of the blind men and the elephant (U. 131–32).

172. Regarding the other books of the *Khuddaka-Nikāya*, the *Vimānavatthu* and the *Petavatthu* have imaginary beings as their principal subject matter and are not dealt with here. Similarly, the so-called minor anthologies (the *Itivuttaka*, the *Khuddaka-Pā.tha*, and the *Pa.tisambhidāmagga*) are good examples of texts in which other animals are, on the whole, a minor issue, and so are not dealt with here. The *Apadāna* and *Niddesa* are not yet translated.

173. Tag. 363, v. 1062.

174. Tag. 252, v. 539. Similar is Tīg. 150–51, v. 373.

175. At both Tag. 102, v. 113; and 267, v. 601.

176. Tag. 144 n. 1. See, for example, the recurring image of a monk who "would roam, like warrior-elephant in van of battle, mindful, diligent" at Tag, 36, v. 31; 167, v. 244; 287, v. 684. Similar images are at Tag. 144, v. 194; and Tag 373, v. 1105.

177. For example, Tag. 200, v. 355–56; and Tag. 378, v. 1130.

178. See also Tag. 364, v. 1070.

179. Tag. 112, v. 125–26; similar is Tag. 374, v. 1111—"unsteady is the heart like jigging ape."

180. Tag. 213, v. 399—a heedless man "hurries hankering from birth to birth / In quest of fruit like ape in forest tree."

181. Tag. 366, v. 1080—ape puffed up as were a monkey in lion's hide.

182. Tag. 226, v. 454—ape simile, deer, fish, all of which are caught by some device of humans—"so is the world ensnared."

Chapter 7

1. Singer 1993a, 221. Other statements of this kind include Keown 1995, 22 ("wider moral horizon"); Passmore 1974, 4 (more resources than in the "west"); and White 1967 (Zen Buddhism as a source for a new view of nature).

2. Because the Sanskrit terms are better known than their Pali equivalents, the Sanskrit forms are used here.

3. This is from a Korean *Mahāyāna* text entitled *The Bodhisattva Precepts*, cited by Batchelor 1992, 6, precept no. 20. As noted in the previous chapter, this reasoning appears in very wideranging Buddhist sources.

4. Again, the more familiar Sanskrit term is used.

5. Schmithausen 1991a, paragraph 4.2a. This is not necessarily Schmithausen's own position.

6. It is not, however, the oldest of beliefs in that general cultural milieu, since the most ancient of Indian scriptures, the *R.g Veda*, views humans as dying but once. Gombrich 1988, 41.

7. Keown 1995, 32, citing D. II, 99 (Rhys Davids/Carpenter II, 93), and M. III, 213 (Chalmers 1886–99, 3:167).

8. Gross (1993) argues that it was a development subsequent to the death of Gotama that *males* alone were held to be paradigmatic.

9. A Vinaya passage is cited in chapter 4. See also Vis. II, 239–40. These passages are interesting precisely because they go against the standard view.

10. Sangharakshita 1993, 210–12. See also statements attributed to the Buddha in the *Mahā-Parinibbana-Suttanta* ("The Book of the Great Decease," Rhys Davids 1881, 26–27).

11. Mil. 65. The translation here is by Warren (1970, 215). Technically, the results of action are mislabeled karma and should instead be understood as *vipāka* (ripening).

12. *Bodhicaryāvatāra* VI, vv. 45–47, in Matics 1970, 177.

13. Buddhist conceptualization of the composite nature of all beings does *not* often, if ever, come in forms that express the important sense of discontinuity asserted here.

14. See, for example, A. IV, 293.

15. Keown (1992, 75) cites A. I, 3 (the Pali is at Morris I, 4) on the issue of anger and Buddhaghosa's Vis. IX, 10, on the issue of hatred.

16. See, for example, Inada 1989, 233; Conze 1975, 126; Lamotte 1991b, 90; and Sangharakshita's claim (1993, 431) that the bodhisattva ideal not only is the central feature of *Mahāyāna*, but is also "the perfectly ripened fruit of the whole vast tree of Buddhism." Dayal (1932, 11) notes that the first name for the *Mahāyāna* tradition was *bodhisattvayāna* (*bodhisattva* vehicle).

17. Gombrich 1988, 141. The cite is from the *Mahāva.msa* XXV, 108–11.

18. Norman 1983, 32–33; Keown 1992, 26. Keown also notes that although there are many preceptual formulae, the prohibitions of the first four precepts are always found as core parts of those formulae.

19. See Rastogi 1990, in particular, Rock Edicts I–IV, VI, IX, XI, and XIII, and Pillar Edicts II, V, and VII.

20. *Visuddhimagga-A.t.thakathā* ii, 439, quoted in Keown 1995, 148.

21. Examples from prominent ethical theories are (1) the characteristic Greek concern for *eudaimonia*; (2) the pan-Indian concern for suffering; (3) utilitarianism's central notion of "utilities" epitomized by Bentham's 1789 dictum (already quoted); and (4) consequentialism, by virtue of its very definition, "the view that rightness or wrongness of all acts is determined solely by goodness or badness of consequences" (James Griffin, in lectures, 1994 Hillary Term, Oxford).

22. D. I, 3–4. Walshe translates slightly differently (DW, 68–69, sections 1.8, 1.10). In 1.8, the wording difference is "without stick or sword"; there is no roughness reference.

23. D. I, 6. The passage occurs many times in the Pali canon.

24. See Buddhadatta 1954, 239; PED VII, 190.

25. A related Pali word is (*vi*)*hi.msā*, which translates as "hurting, injuring, cruelty, injury" (PED VIII, 101).

26. *Sama.na* is a Pali term that means "ascetic" or "wanderer", but which in this context is a reference to the historical Buddha.

27. Chapple 1986, 221; Chapple cites Dayal 1931, 175.

28. Chapple (1986, 221) notes that this can be found in Dayal 1931.

29. Chapple (1986, 221) cites this passage, which is from Vinaya/Rhys Davids and Oldenberg I, 235 (I.78.4).

30. Chapple 1986, 221–22. This is J. 18; the version that Chapple relied on can be found in Francis and Thomas 1916, 20–22.

31. Schmithausen 1991a, 42; *pativirato* (PED V, 22) is "abstinence from."

32. "Occasional" is Schmithausen's word (1991a, 38 n. 233).

33. Scholars commonly note this. See, for example, Schmithausen 1991a, 21; Story 1964, 11; Law 1949, 12.

34. An account of patriarchy in the Buddhist tradition can be found in Gross 1993.

35. The monk should bear things as does the elephant. See, for example, A. II, 122.

36. See, for example, A. III, 228.

Chapter 8

1. נפש חיה is the unpointed text. Generally, only romanized spelling of Hebrew and Greek words will be included in this study.

2. These are not the first living things to be created, however, for Genesis 1:11 mentions a range of plants as having been created on the third day.

3. Green 1976, 1. Jastrow suggests translations of *tannîn* as "sea-monster, crocodile; large snake" (1950, 2:1682). Brown, Driver, and Briggs suggest "serpent, dragon, sea-monster" (1976, 1072).

4. LXX I, 2. This is the word used by Aristotle of "spouting cetaceans." Aristotle 1984, *Parts of Animals*, 669a8. Aristotle also mentions cetaceans in three other treatises, some (dolphins) in great detail.

5. The OED lists the first use as 1836.

6. See, generally, Klinowska 1991; Watson 1981.

7. Only monkeys have tails; Aristotle 1984, 502a19. The term "monkey" has not been used in this technical way. Rather, as noted by the OED, the widest use of the English term is for "any animal of the order *Primates* except man and the lemurs."

8. See, for example, Plato/Jowett II, 67–68, 78, paragraphs 114–15; and Aristotle's *History of Animals*, where there are many comments.

9. See, for example, Druce 1919.

10. Day (1985, 66 n. 19) notes this, citing *Studies of Job* (Leiden, 1939), 27–34.

11. Day 1985, 83. His reference is the Job 40–41 passages on Leviathan and Behemoth.

12. The OED lists examples from as early as the ninth century.

13. This is the title of Day 1985.

14. IB I, 480–81, is in accord.

15. HBD, 226, article on "dragon." Parker cites Ps. 104:26, Ps. 148:7, and Job 41:1 as other instances of *tannîn* where there is "certainly" no mythological allusion.

16. LXX, II, 283. HBD, 226, article on "dragon."

17. The first is at Eliade 1967, 97 ff.; the latter two are referred to at HBD, 226, in the article on "dragon." See also IB III, 964–65, references to *Enûma elish* IV, 138–40.

18. The Hebrew is at Green 1976, 512.

19. LXX, II, 162, *drakontes*; Vul I, 953, *dracones*.

20. Green 1976, 662. The transliteration actually is *tannîm*.

21. Vul II, 1311, *draconi*.

22. Some manuscripts have the word "jackal" here. NEB, footnote "c," at page 1222; Day 1985, 93 n. 20.

23. This, of course, does not mean that the KJV's translation "whale" has had no effect on the many readers who have taken *this translation* to be the "word of God."

24. Respectively, LXX, II, 78; and Vul I, 861 (Psalm 73).

25. While the more recent English translations differ from one another (NRSV, "dragons"; JB "monsters"; NEB "sea-serpent"), they do not use cetacean-referring words.

26. The word *tannîn* also occurs in Isaiah 51:9 (Green 1976, 571). LXX and Vulgate use dragon cognates (respectively, II, 636; II, 1150). The English translations, including KJV, use "dragon" as well. The context suggests that the reference is mythological.

27. RSV translates this word as "jackals" and KJV "dragons" at Isaiah 34:13, Jeremiah 9:11, 10:22, 49:33, and 51:37. RSV uses "monster" at Jeremiah 51:34. The word is translated by both the RSV and KJV as "serpent" at Exodus 7:9, 10, 12. At Deuteronomy 32:33, KJV uses "dragons," while RSV uses "serpents." There are other occurrences (for example, Job 20:14, 16) where the context makes it clear that no cetacean reference is possible.

28. The Hebrew is at Green 1976, 487.

29. For example, IB IV, 397; Day 1985, passim, but especially 179–86. Murray is in accord, commenting on Psalm 74:13–17 that "the passage on creation is one of the major witnesses for the myth of the conflict with Leviathan" (1992, 3).

30. There are six occurrences of the word, of which five are considered here. The sixth is in Job 3:8 and is clearly mythological in reference. All of the translations use the cognate, with the exception of KJV, which unaccountably uses "mourning." IB III, 926, notes the personification of this mythological use and draws parallels between *tannîn* and this and other uses of Leviathan.

31. Respectively, at LXX, II, 340; 40:25; and Vul I, 764; 40:20.

32. NEB's footnote "b" to 41:1 does give the alternative, "*Or* Leviathan."

33. See, respectively, Driver 1956, 1971.

34. Day 1985, 66–67. Day notes that Driver accepted the correct etymology elsewhere but in this passage used the new one to sustain the interpretation of the passage as referring to a whale.

35. Respectively, LXX, II, 112, in Psalm 103:26; and Vul I, 901; the first of the two Psalms numbered 104 in this edition.

36. Day (1985, 72) cites A. F. Kirkpatrick, *The Book of Psalms* (Cambridge, 1906), 612.

37. The word *livyāthān* also occurs in Isaiah 27:1 but is, by consensus, mythological. See, for example, Murray 1992, 1, who cites Day 1985, 13–17.

38. This story is found in other traditions as well. See, for example, Tylor 1891, 1:338 ff.

39. Found at Jonah 2:1; Green 1976, 709.

40. Day (1985, 111–12) does not mention any cetaceans in his discussion of this passage.

41. Emphasis added in each.

42. In English-speaking countries, Protestants generally omit these and other apocryphal works from Bible editions. Catholics consider 1 and 2 Maccabees "deuterocanonical" (canonical at a later date, and as compared to "protocanonical" books), whereas 3 and 4 Maccabees are considered "pseudepigrapha" (Jewish writings preserved and used by Christians but not incorporated into the Bible).

43. Charles 1913, 61, 128, for 1 and 2 Maccabees. 3 Maccabees appears to have been written in Greek (Charlesworth 1985, 510). There are no key animal references in 4 Maccabees.

44. Day (1985, 75 ff.) cites Bochart's *Hierozoicon* and gives the other interpretations of the passage, none of which suggests any connection to the key animals.

45. Green 1976, 308, 387. There is also a reference to an ivory throne at 1 Kings 10:18.

46. This is noted in the computerized program Bible Works.

47. In biblical Hebrew, a number of terms can be translated as "wilderness" or "desert," examples of which are *midbār* (Weingreen 1959, 305) and *.s.hî.hâ*, which Green 1976, 484, translates "dry place."

48. Nash, 1973, 14. Nash relies on the RSV translation and cites passages from Deuteronomy and Isaiah. He also cites numerous secondary sources, including Haldar 1950 and Williams 1962.

49. Williams 1962, 12–20; and Mauser 1963, chap. 2 (15–52), provide the range of symbolic associations.

50. There are many examples in the Psalms; see 10:9; 17:12; 22:12–13, 16, 21; 58:4–6; 118:12; and 140:3.

51. This is *not* to say, however, that they are not integrated at the conceptual level. Douglas 1966 is an influential analysis in the Durkheimian tradition that sees the structure of social regulations as the underlying basis of symbolic and religious phenomena. Douglas is not concerned primarily with the natural world animals themselves. Rather, she is interested in the

relation of nonhuman animal–referring symbolism (in particular pollution rules and food taboos) to both the Hebrews' total structure of thought and their group social structure.

52. Weingreen 1959, 297. Jastrow (1950, 2:927) gives many meanings, including soul, life, person, will, desire, disposition, and blood. Brown, Driver, and Briggs give "soul, living being, life, self, person, desire, appetite, emotion, and passion" (1976, 659). The word is related to the word for breath, and thus generically means that which breathes.

53. Weingreen 1959, 309. The adjective is in the feminine form.

54. The Yahwist-Priestly distinction is described fully in Hiebert 1996, whose breakdown of which passages belong to which tradition is used here. That breakdown appears at Hiebert 1996, 163–71.

55. Brown, Driver, and Briggs 1976, 659. See, for example, Deuteronomy 12:23–24, where it describes the life, as opposed to the meat, of the sacrificial victims.

56. Arguably a *first*-level generalization because both humans and other animals were destroyed. *The Dictionary of Classical Hebrew* (1996, vol. 3, 203, definition 3) lists dozens of first-level generalization uses. There are other common words in the Hebrew Bible that suggest concepts or notions which can operate as first-level generalizations. For example, *dām*, *bāśār*, and *rûa.h* have features in common with the *.hayâ*-related series, in that they are rooted in concrete biological realities and can thus act as generic terms that rely on obvious features of embodied, animal life.

57. On the general points about anthropocentrism and exclusion of other animals' interests being addressed in this study, there are at best minor differences between the Yahwist and Priestly accounts. Hiebert shows well, however, the ways in which discourse about other animals reveals their differences in worldview: "Whenever [the Yahwist] lists animals—whether those that were created (2:19), died in the flood (6:7, 7:23), found refuge in the ark (7:2–3), or were offered to the deity after the flood (8:20)—the Yahwist begins with the animals that live nearby in the field and that creep on the ground and concludes with the birds in the sky. This stance toward the world is just the opposite of the Priestly Writer's, which views nature from a divine, cosmic perspective. P's lists always proceed in the other direction, from cosmological space to the inhabited world, from the animals of the distant sky to those that live with humans on the land (1:20–27, 6:20, 7:21, 8:17, 9:10)" (1996, 51).

58. Examples can be found in 6:7, 20; 7:21, 23; 8:1,17, 19; 9:2, 10.

59. See, for example, Job 31:13–15.

60. I do not mean to imply that there have been no debates about this, for, as Cohen (1989) relates in detail, both ancient and medieval Christians and Jews wrestled with how inclusive the reproduction and dominion injunctions of Genesis 1:26 and 28 were meant to be. But that Genesis permitted, indeed enjoined, members of the *human* species to take "dominion" (whatever that be taken to mean) over all *other* animals seems never to have been doubted seriously.

61. Murray's breakdown of the complex features of biblical views of other animals appears at 1992, 95–96. "Rich" is Murray's description.

62. These are examined by Murray 1992, 114 ff.

63. Commonly cited expressions of concern for the welfare of domestic animals include Deuteronomy 25:4; Exodus 23:19 (also 34:26); and Leviticus 22:27–28. Examples from the *domestic* realm overwhelm the single example from the Torah that mentions wild animals. This can be found in the laws of the sabbatical year, at both Exodus 23:11 and Leviticus 25:4–7; Murray (1992, 119) counts this as the only occurrence of such concern.

64. See, for example, Linzey 1987, 9–36; 1994a, 34–35.

65. Murray 1992, 49. In some cases, later covenants are sealed by the sacrifice of other animals (see, for example, Genesis 15:1 ff.). Sacrifice is discussed more generally in the next chapter.

66. Murray 1992, 102. Regarding the reference in Job 5:22–23 to other animals as covenant partners, Murray dismisses the reference ("you will be in covenant with the 'stones' of the wild, and the wild beasts will be at peace with you") as an "isolated" statement that is "one of many opinions which are tabled for discussion and not necessarily recommended by anyone other than the characters who voice them" (1992,102–3).

67. Louw and Nida 1988, 37 ff. The English translations are not always certain, given that the native animals of the ancient Near East were not the same as those designated by the modern uses of these words.

68. Louw and Nida (1988, 39 ff.) list words for the following: (1) bull or ox/cow; (2) young of cattle; (3) young female of cattle; (4) kid; (5) he-goat/goat (several words); (6) sheep (several words designating young of sheep, lamb, and a collective for flock); (7) horse; (8) camel; (9) donkey/ass (several words); (10) dog (several words); and (11) pig/female pig.

69. Louw and Nida (1988, 44 ff.) list the occurrences.

70. Reptiles and other "creeping things" are *herpeton*, a third-level generic that can mean "creeping animal, reptile, or snake." Louw and Nida 1988, 46–47.

71. The assumption has been made, along with IB 14, 239, that Matthew used Greek. There is some possibility that he used Aramaic, although there is currently no Aramaic version extant.

72. Liddell and Scott 1968, 949–50. Jerome's Vulgate (Vul II, 1544) uses *ceti* in the Matthew passage, and while in Latin this term can mean "whale," it also has a generic quality suggestive of "any large sea-animal." See, Lewis/Freund 1993, 324. This phenomenon is sometimes referred to as "polysemy." Scalan (1996, 397) notes that the term was narrowed to whales and walruses by Albertus Magnus.

73. By no means are all images of Jonah expressed in terms of a cetacean image. For example, George and Yapp (1991, 95) note illustrations of the Jonah story in various bestiaries that portray *other*, obviously distinct, animals (a sea turtle, for example).

74. The contrast between these two cultures is the subject of many studies. Hatch 1914 is cited later. Another well-known differentiation between the two traditions is Niebuhr's (1964, I, 5 ff.). After commenting that "[a]ll modern views of human nature are adaptations, transformations and varying compounds" of the "Graeco-Roman" and "Biblical" views, Niebuhr remarks that these are "distinct and partly incompatible." It is argued here that the views are *not* incompatible in respects relevant to this study, since a central feature of each is the view that members of the human species are, by nature, qualitatively superior to and distinct from *all* other animals. Ruether (1994, 16–17) agrees on the issue of other animals but on the issue of humans suggests richer contrasts than does Niebuhr, relying heavily on the influence of gender differences in the resulting discrimination against female humans.

75. Both Liddell and Scott (1968, 760) and Lampe (1961, 597) list this as the first meaning. Liddell and Scott further note that the word is "post-Homeric, no generic word for *animal* being found till after the middle of the fifth cent. B.C."

76. The first definition is that of Liddell and Scott 1968, 759; the second is from Lampe 1961, 593. This word has many nonbiological uses that predominate, such as the very common meanings "eternal and spiritual life" or a life free from sin (Lampe gives many Patristic uses of this kind).

77. This is the first meaning given by Lampe for *psuchē*, which is as "polysemic" in meaning as virtually any other term in ancient Greek. See, generally, Lampe 1961, 1542–53, for the many possible meanings, almost all of which are nonbiological.

78. Liddell and Scott (1968) list the second meaning as "animal," which is its use in 2 Peter 2:12, discussed later.

79. Respectively, at Lampe 1961, 651; and Louw and Nida 1988, 37. Lampe (1961, 651–52) provides many instances of the wide use of this term and related adjectives in Patristic Greek, which are discussed later. See also Foerster 1965, 135.

80. This is a good example of a string of third-level generalizations operating as a second-level generalization.

81. Dierauer (1977, 33) gives many examples; this phrase was used heavily by the Stoics. After *thērion*, which occurs forty-six times (thirty-nine of which are in Revelation; Kohlenberger and others 1995, 2563–64), *zōon* is the most common second-level generalization in the New Testament. It occurs twenty-three times (twenty of which are in Revelation; Kohlenberger and others 1995, 2450). Other occurrences include Jude 1:10's reference to "irrational animals" (*aloga zōa*).

82. HBD 99 gives the latter interpretation.

83. The many definitions are given at Liddell and Scott 1968, 1964–65; the one given here is a combination of the first two meanings.

84. Cumont (1956) notes many examples of animal veneration from the Hellenistic and Hellenistic-Roman periods in Egypt, as well as Asia Minor (48 ff.) and Syria (116). In reviewing these or any reports of the "worship" of other animals, it is important to remember that the appearance of an animal image in rituals is not the truest test of what was thought about natural world animals. For example, Walens (1987, 293) points out some of the extreme shortcomings of interpretations by historians of religions and anthropologists with regard to the meaning of ritual identification with animals. Arguably it is, in the end, acts impacting other animals, rather than veneration or even mere knowledge claims, that betray the most fundamental beliefs about other animals.

85. This debate is described by Sorabji 1993 and is discussed later.

86. Lecky 1894, 1:244 (see also 2:166, where Lecky argues that "no adequate parallel [to Plutarch's emphasis on 'duty' and 'detail'] can be found in the Christian writings for at least seventeen hundred years"). Sorabji's detailed analysis suggests that Plutarch was not the *first* (see 1993, 46, for example, regarding Theophrastus's views).

87. Dombrowksi 1984 includes a history of vegetarianism, but it is not thorough. Haussleiter 1935 and Beckwith 1988 note the vegetarian options in various groups of early Christian centuries. See also Gruber and Kersten (1995, 179–86) on the Therapeutae community in Egypt; and Emmett 1994 on Empedocles' arguments, Plutarch's early arguments to the effect that minor interests of humans should not outweigh the major interests of other animals, and Porphyry's third-century arguments in *On Abstinence*. Berry 1998 deals with vegetarianism in most of the major religious traditions, but his treatment is neither systematic nor balanced. Rather, it is colored by his obvious desire to have religious traditions support his own vegetarian convictions.

88. Even though some "pagan" (non-Christian) philosophers advocated sexual restraint (Pagels 1988, 8, cites the work of Paul Veyne regarding the similarity of these proposals to what Christians advocated), Pagels 1988 and Brown 1988 show that lack of sexual restraint came to be deemed by Christians as one of the hallmarks of both pagans *and* other animals.

89. Carmody 1953. Carmody's reconstruction of the Greek text is not paginated. This comment occurs in the preface.

90. Janson 1952, 16. Apostolos-Cappadona's summary (1996) to the same effect has already been quoted in part II.

91. *2 Apology* 4 (Dods and others 1896, 75; Pautigny 1904, 156).

92. This point is made regularly by all of the secondary sources cited here: Osborn 1973; Barnard 1967; Hinson 1987b; Burnaby [1938] 1991; Pagels 1988; and Meeks 1993.

93. See, for example, 1 *Apology* 27. Goodspeed (1912, 188) lists more than a dozen occurrences of variants.

94. For example, 1 *Apology* 27, where Justin compares prostitutes to "herds of oxen, goats, or sheep" (Richardson and others 1953, 259).

95. While Sorabji comments (1993, 46) that *aloga* as the "conventional label" for other animals "on its own need not signify anything," it is clear that its use regarding other animals virtually always signaled the widespread belief that other animals could be classed together because they lacked the ability to think like humans. One exception, cited by Sorabji, is Plutarch's use in his treatise entitled *That Irrational Creatures Use Reason*. Liddell and Scott (1968, 72) provide many examples of principal thinkers (for example, Democritus and Plato) who used *aloga* by itself as a second-level generic term.

96. The Greek is at Pautigny 1904, 88; the English is at Richardson and others 1953, 269.

97. Barnard 1967, 117, makes this argument.

98. Williams 1971–72, 29. While the exposition of this doctrine "has produced universal difficulty" (Osborn 1973, 140), it is clear that one feature of the doctrine is that it is *species-based*, that is, every human has it by virtue of species membership, while other earthly, biological creatures that are *not* members of the human species do *not* have it.

99. *Against Heresies* 5.29.1; Roberts and Rambaut 1868–69, 2:133.

100. Roberts and Rambaut 1868–69, 1:xvii. The extant Greek, in Migne PG 7, is confined to the first twenty chapters and a part of chapter 21 of the first of five books.

101. *Proof* 12, at J. P. Smith 1952, 55.

102. See, for example, Wingren 1959, 91–94.

103. Wingren 1959, 91, citing *Against Heresies* 5.29.1.

104. See, for example, *Proof* 2, at J. P. Smith 1952, 48.

105. Santmire 1985, 42; the passage regarding Origen is at 1985, 53.

106. It may be true, however, that such differences in otherwise functionally equivalent anthropocentrisms can be quite significant. For example, general *negative* characterizations of the "inner logic" of mainline Christian theological claims about nature (such as the harsh judgment of Kaufman 1972 that Christianity *must* always be anthropocentric) do *not* apply as forcefully to Irenaeus's thinking as to the "ontologically anthropocentric" Origen.

107. Migne PG 7, 497 (Greek) and 498 (Latin).

108. *Against Heresies* 5.33.4; Roberts and Rambaut 1868–69, 2:146.

109. *Against Heresies* 2.2.4; Roberts and Rambaut 1868–69, 1:122–23.

110. *Proof* 61, at J. P. Smith 1952, 88.

111. In *Against Heresies* 2.28.7 (Roberts and Rambaut 1868–69, 1:225), Irenaeus comments that other animals were *not* affected by the cosmic fall or by Adam's deed, but instead "persevered, and still do persevere, in subjection to Him who formed them." Irenaeus's particular expression of this viewpoint was, as Santmire (1985, 48) rightly emphasizes, characterized by nuanced differences from his peers and much subsequent theology, which, unlike Irenaeus, for the most part tended to take creation for granted. See, for example, Santmire (1985, 49); Williams (1971–72, 125).

112. Tatian, a student of Justin who may have been Clement's teacher (Whitaker 1982, ix), wrote the influential *Oratio ad Graecos*, a "vitriolic denunciation" (Amundsen 1995, 377) and "a violent polemic against the whole of Greek culture" (Bolgiani 1992b, 815). His views, including those regarding other animals, were important influences on the subsequent tradition. See, additionally, Bolgiani 1992a.

113. Lilla 1971, 1–2. Lilla takes the latter view, whereas Völker 1952 holds the instrumental view.

114. *Stromata* 2.20; the inflected *alogois zōois* is at Migne PG 9, 1056; in the Latin version at 1055, *bruta*. See also *Protrepticus* 3.34 (Butterworth 1953, 84–85). At *Stromata* 3, 102 (Ferguson 1991, 320–21), the Greek is simply *alogōn* (acting as a noun; the Greek is at Migne PG 8, 1205; the Latin at 1206 is *animantium*).

115. *Stromata* also features *zōa* as a *first*-level generalization, as at 8.4 (Migne PG 9, 572–73; the Latin is at 574 *animalia, animantia*).

116. *Stromata* 2.20 also includes an example of *zōa* as a second-level generalization.

117. As Lilla (1971) repeatedly points out, Clement was in many important ways in agreement with certain Gnostics of his time.

118. See, for example, *Protrepticus* 3.37 (Butterworth 1953, 94–95); *Protrepticus* 10.82 (Butterworth 1953, 224–25).

119. *Stromata* 2.20;Wilson 1869, 2, 64; Migne PG 8, 1055 *pithēkou*; the Latin version at 1056 uses *simiae*.

120. See, for example, his views on women sharing the same basic human nature as men at *Stromata* 4.8.

121. Clark 1987, 533. Pagels (1988, 39) and Lilla (1971, 15) note that Clement derived his egalitarian views from Genesis 1.

122. *Against Celsus* 4.74 (Chadwick 1953, 243, at Migne PG 11, 1144–45). The works concentrated on in this study are *On First Principles* (Butterworth 1966) and *Against Celsus* (Chadwick 1953). The Greek and Latin appear in Migne PG 11.

123. Williams 1971–72, 22–23. Santmire calls Origen's human-centeredness "ontological anthropocentrism" (1985, 53).

124. Santmire 1985, 50, citing *Against Celsus* 4.81–89.

125. Tatian's influence also is evident. Bolgiani (1992b, 815) notes that *On First Principles* has "abundant traces" of Tatian's arguments.

126. Section 1.8.4, at Butterworth 1966, 74. The term that Butterworth translates as "bestial" is *apothērioutai*, which is related to *thērion* and means "change into a beast" or "make quite savage" (Liddell and Scott 1968, 199). The Latin is *bruti animalis* (Migne PG 11, 180–81), which Butterworth also translates as "irrational animals."

127. Sorabji (1993, 80) explains the difference between external *logos* (speech) and internal *logos*.

128. An example of Origen's use of the standard generic terms occurs in *Against Celsus* 4.86 (Chadwick 1953, 252), where the familiar contrast is stated between, on the one hand, members of the human species (*anthrōpōn*) and, on the other, all other animals (*alogois*). Migne PG 11, 1160; the Latin at 1159 is *humanum genus* versus *brutarum animantium*.

129. Celsus's claims are quoted at *Against Celsus* 4.23

130. Amundsen 1995, 386. This is not as preposterous as it sounds to modern ears. The field of zoopharmocognosy studies the ways in which some nonhuman animals use the medicinal properties of plants and other naturally occurring substances to cure various ills. For example, regarding the diversity and transmission of traditions of such knowledge among chimpanzees, see Huffman and Wrangham 1994.

131. At, respectively, Aristotle 1977, *Politics* 1256b17; Cicero 1979/*De Natura Deorum* II 14, 37.

132. Chadwick 1953, 243, at Migne PG 11, 1144–45. Chadwick's footnote 2 indicates that the language here echoes a passage from the Stoic Chrysippus, which Plutarch quotes.

133. In the subsequent Greek-speaking tradition in the East, there were significant developments regarding views of the natural world beyond humans, such that it is sometimes argued that the Eastern tradition has, relative to the Western tradition, a distinguishable, *positive* emphasis on nature. See, for example, Jung 1993; Linzey 1987, 32; Sorabji 1993, 199;

and Allchin 1974, 5. It is clear that, relative to the very exclusivist anthropocentrism of Origen and much of the contemporary Western tradition, the Eastern tradition sounds inclusivist. It retains, however, the same basic division that Origen used, holding that humans collectively are radically different than the rest of creation. This conclusion continues to produce exclusivist statements, as can be seen in some recent materials from a conference convened by the Patriarchate of Constantinople, in which Bishop Pop comments "The whole of creation, the heaven and earth were made our subjects to serve and work for us" (1992, 37). Thus, even though this side of the Christian tradition has at times exhibited what Attfield has called "a compassionate view of nonhuman species" (1983, 34) the standard dualism "humans/other animals" underlies its evaluation of the created world. See, for example, Oikonomou 1992, 34; Ekdokimov 1965 (where the conceptual scheme is "humans and nature"); and Gregorios 1978 (see page 18, for example, where the scheme is the typical "humans and nature," with the word "animals" meaning "all other animals").

134. The claim that this second use was more common occurs in Lewis and Short's definition of *animans* (1962, 122).

135. Lewis and Short 1962, 122. They note that the gender varies and that in its widest sense it is neuter. When it is feminine, it is a reference to "brutes," while when it is masculine it is a reference to humans.

136. Glare 1982, 229, supplies numerous examples.

137. Würthwein 1979, 91. In Gaul and northern Africa, Latin was dominant earlier.

138. *On Christian Doctrine* 2.11.16, quoted in Williams 1975, 38.

139. The text can be found in Sabatier 1743.

140. Roberts 1975, 24–25; Würthwein 1979, 87. In these texts, the Latin used in the Genesis and New Testament verses discussed in the following is not significantly different from the Vulgate's Latin on the issue of generics being used coarsely for all other animals. See, for example, Sabatier 1743, 1, 10–12, for the Genesis passages.

141. The Hebrew includes a *.hayâ*-related noun (at Green 1976, 1), and the LXX is *tetrapoda herpeta thēria*; RSV is "cattle and creeping things and beasts of the earth."

142. See Way 1963, the first nine homilies of which constitute Basil's *Hexaemeron*.

143. Springer (1931) lists approximately seventy kinds of animals (either species or closely related groups of species).

144. See, for example, at *Hexameron* 5.1 (Savage 1961, 160) his references to dolphins "frolicking" (*delphines praeludebant*, a word related to the infinitive *ludere*, "to play or sport"; Migne PL 14, 219). Basil also refers to dolphins more soberly; see Way 1963, 106–7 (Homily 7.1–2). Basil used *delphines*, and the Latin translation used the same word (Migne PG 29, 149–50). Basil also refers to elephants, although apparently not to primates, in the *Hexameron*.

145. Robbins 1912, 51. Robbins also notes the central place of Plato's *Timaeus*.

146. Sorabji 1993, 102; Sorabji notes that this argument appeared as early as Solon (c. 640–558 B.C.E.); was used by Peripatetics, Stoics, and Sextus Empiricus; and was rebutted in great detail by Theophrastus (as reported by Porphyry).

147. See, for example, *City of God* 5.11.

148. For example, (1) the jump from the fact of noncommunity (other animals not being "partners" in the faculty of reason) to the right to kill, which is either a non sequitur or an enthymeme; or (2) the category shifts referred to in the *a-logos* discussion earlier.

149. Serpell and Paul, citing Midgley 1984 and Thomas 1983, argue, "[S]everal recent authors have suggested that this gulf between the animal and the human domains is not simply a product of human vanity, but a practical construct designed to allow people to exploit animals with a clear conscience by placing them, so to speak, beyond the pale of moral concern" (1994, 129).

150. This passage has often been cited, as by Aquinas at *Summa Theologiae* 2a, 2ae, q. 64, art. 1, Reply to obj. 1.

151. Holman 1931. *Not* included in Holman's list are dolphins (*City of God* 1.14, *dorso delphini*); monkeys (*City of God* 16.8, *cercopithecos*); and apes (*De Genesis ad litteram duodecim* 3.11.16, *simiis*, Taylor 1982, 85–86, at Migne PL 34, 286; and at *City of God* 16.8, *simias*).

152. Pelland 1972 compares these five works. He presents helpful comparative tables at 231–38, and these reflect that Augustine used standard generic terms.

153. The second account (that of the Yahwist) is generally thought to be older (Hiebert 1996, chap. 2, provides a review of the arguments and lists some scholars who disagree). Hiebert also analyzes the relatively greater anthropocentrism of the Yahwist account, contrasting it with the Priestly writer's more cosmological account. On the issues discussed here, however, the anthropocentrisms are, like those of Irenaeus and Origin, functionally equivalent. In many ways, the Yahwist's rural and subsistence farming–based account reflects a closer relationship with nonhuman animals (see Hiebert 1996, passim but especially chap. 2).

154. Teske 1991, 47–141. The Latin is at Migne PL 34, 173–220. Taylor (1982, 1, 1) suggests it was written in 388; Teske (1991, 3) suggests 388 or 389.

155. The Watts translation of the *Confessions* is used in the following. Taylor (1982, 1, 3) gives 397–401 as the composition dates.

156. Teske 1991, 143–88. The Latin is at Migne PL 34, 219–46. Taylor (1982, 1, 2) says it was composed circa 391; Teske (1991, 3) suggests "around 393."

157. Taylor 1982 has the text; per Taylor 1982, 1, 4, it was begun in 401. The Latin is at Migne PL 34, 245–486.

158. Taylor (1982, 1, 4) notes that *City of God* was started in 413. There are other books in *City of God* dealing with Genesis 1 passages (for example, 15.27, which addresses which animals were in Noah's ark and is pertinent to an understanding of Genesis 1's lists of the kinds of animals created).

159. At, respectively, 1.15.24 and 1.16.25; Migne PL 34, 184–85.

160. Burnaby reminds, "It is never to be forgotten that the Augustinian 'intellect' is not the discursive reason but the mind at worship" ([1938] 1991, 155).

161. Some references of a more specific nature, such as the narrower category "whales" (as at 13.20, *coeti grandes*; 13.24, *coetos*; and 13.25 *coetis magnis*), can be accounted for by the references to large sea creatures in Genesis 1:21 discussed previously.

162. Teske argues, "[T]hat [the text] remains incomplete bears witness to Augustine's inability to offer a literal interpretation of the text" (1991, 3).

163. Taylor (1982, 242 n. 26) suggests the other authors whose views he is invoking are Pliny and Ambrose.

164. References to other animals in *City of God* are dealt with later.

165. Much has been made of Augustine's emphasis on the goodness of creation as a resource for contemporary thinkers who want to find in the Christian tradition support for environmental ethics; see, for example, Santmire 1985; Attfield 1983.

166. The tenor of the discussion, though, is evident in his standard insistence that high-level mental functions (that is, rationality) are not, indeed cannot be, the explanation of such phenomena. In 1.4.6, for example, he uses the terms *animalia* and *irrationale animal* when insisting that imitation is the explanation, rather than a higher mental function. Migne PL 32, 1086.

167. At page 120 of the English translation; Migne PL 42, 954.

168. Gary Matthews in a lecture at Saint Antony's College, Oxford, on February 20, 1995, argued that this important argument in the philosophy of mind was first made by Augustine.

169. See, for example, Lovejoy 1960, 67.

170. Brown 1967, 224; Brown cites *City of God* 12.28.

171. When dealing with the Jonah story, Augustine uses possible cetacean-referring words (at 18.44, *in ventre ceti*; at 1.14, the more generic *in visceribus beluae*).

172. A common issue in the intellectual milieu; see, for example, Pliny, *Natural History* 7.2.10–30.

173. *City of God* 18.2. Note how Augustine advances the unity claim but also backs away in his concluding qualification, since he clearly recognized the realities of conflict discussed in part II.

174. It should be noted here how poor, in some respects, the natural history is. Wolves and lions, as is well known now, are fundamentally social mammals.

Chapter 9

1. Linzey (1994b, 9) has noted that the 1994 Catholic claims are the first official Catholic statement that any moral agent owes a *direct* duty (of kindness) to any nonhuman animal.

2. In English the most common uses of the terms "steward" and "stewardship" involve management of *another's* household (this is the dominant thrust of the OED definitions). Such a feature is, arguably, part of the earliest view, the world being conceived as God's and not humans', and there are numerous scriptural passages which support the notion that other animals belong not to humans but to God. See, for example, Deuteronomy 10:14; Leviticus 25:23; and Psalms 24 and 50.

3. In much of the tradition, "person" and "human" are synonyms. See, for example, paragraph 1700 of the Catholic Catechism ("The dignity of the human person is rooted in his creation in the image and likeness of God"). Being "in the image and likeness of God" is explicitly tied to the right to benefit from dominion (paragraph 2417). Importantly, *each* member of the species, and even each *potential* human (as noted in chapter 2, the Catholic Church argues that any human fetus is "an innocent human being," "absolutely equal to all others"), is deemed to be in the image of God solely by virtue of conception as a human.

4. Brown, Driver, and Briggs 1976, 919–20, list the many variations.

5. See, for example, Wolterstorff 1987; Berry 1993; Adams 1994a; and Jacobson 1996.

6. At, respectively, Linzey 1994a, 48 (theological superiority), 25, 29.

7. The traditional response has been to refer to the post-Flood grant in Genesis 9:3 of the right to eat "every moving thing." See, for example, Calvin, *Commentaries on the First Book of Moses Called Genesis*, 291–93. Traditional interpretations have, of course, been based on the *human* species line (all humans can eat all nonhuman animals).

8. This analysis relies on Bauckham 1994, 14–17.

9. See, in particular, Thomas 1983, 48, 121–36, 166–91.

10. See, for example, Mayr's comments (1982, 308) regarding Albertus Magnus, and Bowler's comments on the tradition generally (1992, 16, 61).

11. Many relevant statements from various denominations are included in Linzey 1991, 150–58.

12. Pluhar 1995, for example, addresses many such arguments.

13. There were also sacrifices that did not involve other animals, such as the cereal offerings described in Leviticus 2.

14. See, for example, Smedes 1987, 145.

15. There were several kinds of sacrifices involving other animals (Rattray 1985 lists the different forms), but the subdivisions are not particularly germane to these general comments.

16. Not all useful kinds of animals were acceptable, of course, but all those that were acceptable were commonly used and deemed valuable items of property.

17. The argument here is "limited" because certain unclean animals were useful for benefits that were prohibited (for example, pigs as food).

18. JB, in the introduction to Hebrews, at 265. There had, of course, previously been some prophetic voices that questioned the practice (for example, Psalm 50).

19. Chapple 1993, 43. There are, to be sure, many Christians who have argued against such practices, but on the whole the mainline tradition and its institutions have not. See, for example, paragraph 2417 of the 1994 Catholic Catechism.

20. See also Raphael 1994, 17–18.

21. Midgley 1986, 10. Importantly, Midgley's passage goes on to stress that non-Christian developments have made matters worse.

22. See, for example, Nash 1991; Hessel 1992, 1996.

Bibliography

I. SCRIPTURAL SOURCES IN THE CHRISTIAN TRADITION

Note: Where multiple English translations are listed, the first translation is the one used as a matter of course in this study.

A. *Hebrew*

Green, J. P., Sr., trans, 1976. *The Interlinear Bible: Hebrew-Greek-English.* 2d ed., Peabody, Mass: Hendrickson.

B. *Greek*

Green, J. P. 1976 contains the text of the Greek New Testament.

Rahlfs, A., ed. 1935. *Septuaginta: Id est Vetus Testamentum Graece Iuxta LXX Interpretes.* Stuttgart: Privilegierte Württembergische Bibelanstalt. V 1, 2. Referred to generally as "LXX" but occasionally as "Septuagint" for stylistic reasons.

C. *Latin*

Weber, R. 1969. *Biblia Sacra: Iuxta Vulgatam Versionem* [Vul]. 2 vols. Stuttgart: Württembergischen Bibelanstalt. While the translation is largely the work of Jerome done between 390 and 405, many parts of the text were not translated by Jerome. The Vulgate through history has existed in many versions. For example, the official Catholic version is not that of Jerome but a version prepared after the Council of Trent in 1546 declared the Vulgate to be the authentic Bible of the Catholic Church, "i.e., authoritative in matters of faith and morals, without any implication of rejecting or forbidding either the Septuagint or the original Hebrew text, or in the New Testament the Greek text." Würthwein 1979, 94 n. 13, citing F. Stummer. The official Catholic edition was based on the Clementine editions done between 1592 and 1598. The edition used here is a compilation based on the best manuscripts available.

D. *English*

The Holy Bible containing the Old and New Testaments with Apocryphal/Deuterocanonical Books, New Revised Standard Version [NRSV]. New York and Oxford: Oxford University Press, 1989.

The Jerusalem Bible [JB]. London: Darton, Longman and Todd, 1966.

The New English Bible: The Old Testament [NEB]. Cambridge: Oxford University Press/Cambridge University Press, 1970.

The Revised Standard Version [RSV] is used here unless otherwise indicated; it appears, along with a copy of *The King James Bible* [KJV], first published in 1611, in *The Interpreter's Bible: The Holy Scriptures in the King James and Revised Standard Versions with General Articles*

257

and Introduction, Exegesis, Exposition for Each Book of the Bible [IB]. 12 vols. New York: Abingdon, 1952–57.

II. SCRIPTURAL AND COMMENTARIAL SOURCES IN THE BUDDHIST TRADITION

Note: Where multiple English translations are listed, the first translation is the one used as a matter of course in this study.

A. *The Pali Canon*

1. Abhidamma *Pi.taka*

   a. *Dhammasa"nga.ni* [Dsan.]. *A Buddhist Manual of Psychological Ethics*, 3d ed., translated by Caroline A. F. Rhys Davids, Pali Text Society Translation Series, no. 41, (London and Boston: Pali Text Society, 1974).

   b. *Dhātukathā* [Dk.]. *Discourse on Elements* (*Dhātu-Kathā*), translated by U Nārada Mūla Pa.t.thāna Syadaw, assisted by Thein Nyun, Pali Text Society Translation Series, no. 34 (London: Pali Text Society/Luzac, 1962).

   c. *Katthuvatthu* [Kv.]. *Points of Controversy or Subject of Discourse*, translated by Shwe Zan Aung and Mrs. Rhys Davids (London: Pali Text Society/Humphrey Milford, 1915).

   d. *Pa.t.thāna* [Pat.]. *Conditional Relations* (*Pa.t.thāna*), 2 vols., translated by U Nārada Mūla Pa.t.thāna Syadaw, assisted by Thein Nyun, Pali Text Society Translation Series, nos. 37 and 42 (London: Pali Text Society/Luzac, 1969 [vol. 1]; London: Pali Text Society/Routledge and Kegan Paul, 1981 [vol. 2]).

   e. *Puggalapa~n~natti* [Pp.]. *Designation of Human Types* (*Puggala-Pa~n~natti*), translated by Bimala Charan Law, Pali Text Society Translation Series, no. 12 (London: Pali Text Society/Oxford University Press, 1922).

   f. *Vibha"nga* [Vib.]. *The Book of Analysis* (*Vibha"nga*), translated by Pa.thamakyaw Ashin Thi.t.tila (Se.t.thila), Pali Text Society Translation Series, no. 39 (London: Pali Text Society/Luzac, 1969).

2. Sutta *Pi.taka*

   a. *Anguttara-Nikāya* [A.]. The English translation is *The Book of the Gradual Sayings* (*Anguttara-Nikāya*), 5 vols., translated by F. L. Woodward (vols. 1, 2, and 5) and E. M. Hare (vols. 3 and 4), Pali Text Society Translation Series, nos. 22 and 24–27 London: Oxford University Press, 1932–36).

   The romanized Pali is in *The A"nguttara-Nikaya*, pt. I edited by Richard Morris (London: Pali Text Society/Henry Frowde, 1885, 1888) [respectively, Morris I and II]; pts. III–V edited by E. Hardy (London: Pali Text Society/Henry Frowde, 1896, 1899, 1900) [Hardy (I–III)].

   b. *Dīgha-Nikāya* [D., DW]. Two English translations are cited in the text. Unless otherwise noted, the translation used is *The Dialogues of the Buddha: Translated from the Pali of the Dīgha Nikāya*, edited by T. W. Rhys Davids and, second and third volumes only, C. A. F. Rhys Davids, 3 vols., SBB, nos. 2–4 (London: Henry Frowde, 1899; 1910; London: Humphrey Milford, 1921) [references in the text to D. will be to this translation].

   The second English translation cited is Maurice Walshe, trans., *Thus Have I Heard: The Long Discourses of the Buddha* (*Dīgha Nikāya*) (London, Wisdom, 1987) [referred to as DW].

The romanized Pali is in *The Dīgha Nikāya,* edited by T. W. Rhys-Davids (vols. 1–3) and J. E. Carpenter (vol. 3) (London: Henry Frowde, 1890–1911) [referred to as Rhys Davids/Carpenter].

c. *Khuddaka-Nikaya.* References are the individual sections listed in the following. Not all of the sections of this *nikāya* have been translated. There are no translations of *Apadāna* and *Niddesa.*

    i. *Buddhava.msa* [Bv.] and *Cariyāpi.taka* [Cp.]. *The Minor Anthologies of the Pali Canon: Part III Buddhava.msa, The Lineage of the Buddhas, and Cariyā-pi.taka or The Collection of Ways of Conduct,* translated by Bimala Churn Law, SBB, no. 9 (London: Humphrey Milford/Oxford University Press, 1938).

        A second translation of Cp. is *The Cariyāpitaka* [Law 1949], edited by Bimal Churn Law, 2d ed. (Poona: Bhandarkar Oriental Research Institute, 1949).

    ii. *The Dhammapada* [Dpda.]. Several translations are quoted. The primary translation used is *The Minor Anthologies of the Pali Canon: Part I—Dhammapada: Verses on Dhamma, and Khuddaka-Pa.tha: The Text of the Minor Sayings,* reedited and translated by Mrs. Rhys Davids, SBB, no. 7 (London: Humphrey Milford/Oxford University Press, 1931) [Dpda. 1931].

        Three other translations are referred to as well.

        The Dhammapada: A Collection of Verses [Dpda. 1881/1968], translated by F. Max Müller, SBE, no. 10 (Delhi/Varanasi/Patna: Motilal Banarsidass, 1968). This is a reprint of the edition published by Oxford University Press, 1881.

        The Dhammapada [Dpda. 1987], translated by Eknath Easwaran (London: Routledge and Kegan Paul, 1987.

        The Dhammapada: Verses and Stories [Dpda. 1990], translated by Daw Mya Tin, Bibliotheca Indo-Tibetica Series, no. 20 (Sarnath, Varanasi: Central Institute of Higher Tibetan Studies, 1990). This is a reprint of the edition by Burma Pitaka Association Publication, 1986.

    iii. *Itivuttaka* [Itv.]. *The Minor Anthologies of the Pali Canon: Part II—Udāna: Verses of Uplift, and Itivuttaka: As It Was Said,* translated by F. L. Woodward, Pali Text Society Translation Series, no. 8 (London: Humphrey Milford, 1935).

    iv. *Jātaka* [J.]. These appear in several versions, some of which are simple and plain, while others, such as the thirty-four stories appearing in the Sanskrit version by Aarya "Sūra known as the *Jātakamālā* (Khoroche 1989), are considerably more elaborate. The only complete English translation of the Pali version of the stories is *The Jātaka or Stories of the Buddha's Former Births,* 6 vols., edited by E. B. Cowell (principal editor; there are different translators for each volume) (Cambridge: Cambridge University Press, 1895–1907). References to these stories are in the format "J. (story number)," which refers to the story number in Cowell 1895. Occasionally, a reference to a page number is included in the cite, and the format is then "J. (story number/page number)." Thus J. 16/35 means the sixteenth story in Cowell 1895, at page 35.

        References are also made to *Buddhist Birth Stories or Jātaka Tales* [Rhys Davids 1880], translated by T. W. Rhys Davids (London: Trübner, 1880). There is a version of some of these tales in H. T. Francis and E. J. Thomas, *Jataka Tales* [Francis and Thomas 1916] (Cambridge: Cambridge University Press, 1916).

        The Pali is in V. Fausbøll, *The Jātaka together with its Commentary being Tales of the Anterior Births of Gotama Buddha* [Fausbøll], 6 vols., with separate index in volume 7 (London: Trübner, 1877–96).

v. *Khuddakapā.tha* [Khp.]. *The Minor Readings* (*Khuddakapā.tha*), translated by Bhikkhu ~Nā.namoli, Pali Text Society Translation Series, no. 32 (London: The Pali Text Society/Luzac, 1960). This volume includes the commentary by Buddhaghosa called *Paramatthajotikā*, pt. I [KhpA.].

A second translation referred to is *The Minor Anthologies of the Pali Canon: Part I—Dhammapada: Verses on Dhamma, and Khuddaka-Pā.tha: The Text of the Minor Sayings* [Khp2.], reedited and translated by Mrs. Rhys Davids, SBB, no. 7 (London: Humphrey Milford/Oxford University Press, 1931).

vi. *Pa.tisambhidāmagga* [Pm.]. *The Path of Discrimination* (*Pa.tisambhidāmagga*), translated by Bhikkhu ~Nā.namoli, Pali Text Society Translation Series, no. 43 (London: Pali Text Society, 1982).

vii. *Suttanipata* [Sn.]. Four translations are cited, although only the first two are quoted in the text.

The Group of Discourses (*Sutta-Nipāta*) [Sn], translated by K. R. Norman, with alternative translations by I. B. Horner and Walpola Rahula, Pali Text Society Translation Series, no. 44 (London and Boston: Pali Text Society/ Routledge and Kegan Paul, 1984).

The Group of Discourses (*Sutta-Nipāta*) [Norman 1992], revised translation with introduction and notes by K. R. Norman, Pali Text Society Translation Series, no. 45 (Oxford: The Pali Text Society, 1992).

A third translation referred to is *Buddha's Teaching Being the Sutta-Nipata or Discourse-Collection* [Chalmers Sn], romanized Pali text and English translation by Lord Chalmers, Harvard Oriental Series, no. 37 (Cambridge, Mass: Harvard University Press, 1932).

A fourth translation is *The Sutta-Nipāta: A Collection of Discourses*, [Fausbøll 1881], translated by V. Fausbøll, SBE, no. 10 (Oxford: Clarendon, 1881).

viii. *Theragāthā* [Tag.] and *Therīgāthā* [Tig.]. *Psalms of the Early Buddhists*, translated by Mrs. Rhys Davids, Pali Text Society Translation Series, no. 1 (London: Pali Text Society, 1980).

ix. *Udāna* [U.]. *The Udāna*, translated by Peter Masefield, SBB, no. 42 (Oxford: Pali Text Society, 1994). A second translation referred to is *The Minor Anthologies of the Pali Canon: Part II—Udāna: Verses of Uplift, and Itivuttaka: As It Was Said* [USBB], translated by F. L. Woodward, Pali Text Society Translation Series, no. 8 (London: Humphrey Milford, 1935).

x. *Vimanavatthu* [Vv.] and *Petavatthu* [Pv.]. *The Minor Anthologies of the Pali Canon, Part IV* (*Vimāna Vatthu: Stories of the Mansions, and Peta Vatthu: Stories of the Departed*), SBB, no. 12 (London: Luzac, 1942). The Vv. was translated by Jean Kennedy; the Pv. was translated by Henry S. Gehman.

There is another, superior translation of Vv. in SBB, no. 30, by I. B. Horner. This has not been used because the translation improvements do not pertain to the passages cited.

d. *Majjhima-Nikāya* [M.]. The primary English translation used is *The Collection of the Middle Length Sayings* (*Majjhima-Nikāya*), translated by I. B. Horner, 3 vols., Pali Text Society Translation Series, nos. 29–31 (London: Luzac, 1954, 1957, and 1959).

A second English translation is *Further Dialogues of the Buddha* (*Translated from the Pali of The Majjhima Nikāya*) [MSBB], translated by R. Chalmers, 2 vols., SBB, nos. 5 and 6 (London: Humphrey Milford/Oxford University Press, 1926–27).

A third English translation referred to is *The Middle Length Discourses of the Buddha* [MNB] translated by Bhikkhu ~Nā.namoli (original translator) and Bhikkhu Bodhi, editor and revising translator (Boston: Wisdom Publications, 1995).

The romanized Pali is in *Majjhima-Nikaya*, vol. 1, edited by V. Trenckner (London: Henry Frowde, 1888) [Trenckner]; vol. 2, edited by Robert Chalmers (London: Henry Frowde, 1896) [Chalmers 1896]; vol. 3, edited by Robert Chalmers (London: Henry Frowde, 1899) [Chalmers 1899].

e. *Sa.myutta-Nikāya* [Sam.]. The English translation is *The Book of the Kindred Sayings (Sa.myutta-Nikāya) or Grouped Suttas*, translated by Mrs. Rhys Davids, (first two volumes, assisted on the first volume by Sūriyago.da Sumangala Thera, and on the second by F. L. Woodward), and F. L. Woodward (last three volumes). These five volumes appear in Pali Text Society's Translation Series as nos. 7, 10, 13, 14, and 16 (London: Oxford University Press). The first volume has no date, but the preface is dated 1917. There is no date on the second volume, but 1922 appears on the editorial notes. The same is true of the third and fourth volumes, with respective dates of 1924 and 1927. The fifth volume is dated 1930.

The romanized Pali is in *The Sa.myutta-Nikāya*, edited by L. Feer, 5 vols. (London: Henry Frowde, 1884–98) [referred to as Feer (I through V)].

3. *Vinaya Pi.taka* [Vin.]. *The Book of the Discipline (Vinaya-Pi.taka)*. Trans. I. B. Horner. 6 vols., SBB, nos. 10, 11, and 13 (London: Humphrey Milford, 1938–42); nos. 14, 20, and 25 (London: Luzac, 1951–66). This is the translation used in the text unless otherwise specified. The citation format is the following: "Vin. I" refers to SBB vol. 10, "Vin. II" refers to SBB vol. 11, and so on. The citation format will include volume and page; for example, Vin. V, 193, refers to the fifth volume of this translation series (no. 20), p. 193.

The romanized Pali is in H. Oldenberg, ed., *The Vinaya Pi.taka.m*. 5 vols. (London and Edinburgh: Williams and Norgate, 1879–83) [referred to as Oldenberg].

B. *Other Pali Sources*

1. Dhammapāla's *Elucidation of the Intrinsic Meaning, so named The Commentary on the Vimāna Stories: Paramattha-dīpanī nāma Vimānavatthu-a.t.thakathā* [VvA.], translated by Peter Masefield, SBB, no. 35 (Oxford: Pali Text Society, 1989).

2. Dhammapala's *The Udāna Commentary (Paramatthadīpanī nāma Udāna.t.thakathā)* [UA.], 2 vols., translated by Peter Masefield, SBB, nos. 43 and 45 (Oxford: Pali Text Society, 1994, 1995).

3. *Milindapa~nha* [Mil.]. *Milinda's Questions*, translated by I. B. Horner, SBB, nos. 22 and 23 (London: Luzac, 1963–64).

4. *Papan~ncasūdanī Majjhimannikāya.t.thakathā* [MA]. 2 vols. (London: Pali Text Society/Humphrey Milford, 1928).

5. *Visuddhimagga* [Vis.]. *The Path of Purity, being a translation of Buddhaghosa's Visuddhimagga*, translated by Pe Maung Tin, Pali Text Society Translation Series, nos. 11, 17, and 21 (London: Pali Text Society/Oxford University Press, 1922, 1930, 1931).

C. *Indian Mahayana Sources*

1. *Bodhicaryavatara*, translated by Marion L. Matics, *Entering the Path of Enlightenment: The Bodhicaryavatara of the Buddhist Poet Santideva* (London: Macmillan 1970).

2. *Saddharma-Pu.n.darīka or The Lotus of the True Law* [SP], translated by H. Kern (New York: Dover, 1963). This is an unabridged, unaltered reprint of the SBE edition, no. 21, first published in 1884 by Clarendon.

III. WORKS CITED

Aarya "Sūra. 1989. *Once the Buddha Was a Monkey: Aarya "Sūra's Jātakamālā*. Trans. P. Khoroche. London: University of Chicago Press.

Abbagnano, N. 1967. "Humanism." In *The Encyclopedia of Philosophy*, edited by Paul Edwards, 4:69–72. London: Collier Macmillan.

Adams, C. J. 1994. *Neither Man Nor Beast: Feminism and the Defense of Animals*. New York: Continuum.

———. 1990. *The Sexual Politics of Meat: A Feminist-Vegetarian Critical Theory*. New York: Continuum.

———, ed. 1993. *Ecofeminism and the Sacred*. New York: Continuum.

Adams, C. J., and Donovan, J., eds. 1995. *Animals and Women: Feminist Theoretical Explorations*. London: Duke University Press.

Adams, C. J., and Procter-Smith, M. 1993. "Taking Life or 'Taking on Life'?" In Adams 1993, 295–310.

Albanese, C. L. 1990. *Nature Religion in America: From the Algonkin Indians to the New Age*. London: University of Chicago Press.

Allchin, A. M. 1974. *Wholeness and Transfiguration Illustrated in the Lives of St. Francis of Assisi and St. Seraphim of Sarov*. N.p.: SLG Press.

Amundsen, D. W. 1995. "Tatian's 'Rejection' of Medicine in the Second Century." In van der Eijk and others 1995, 377–91.

Antinucci, F. 1990. "The Comparative Study of Cognitive Ontogeny in Four Primate Species." In Parker and Gibson 1990, 157–71.

Apostolos-Cappadona, D. 1996. *Encyclopedia of Women in Religious Art*. New York: Continuum.

Aquinas, T. 1964–81. *Summa Theologiae*. Latin text and English translated by T. Gilby and others. 60 vols. London: Blackfriars/Eyre and Spottiswoode; New York: McGraw-Hill.

Aristotle. 1965–91. *Historia Animalium*. 3 vols. (with both Greek and English text). Loeb Classical Library Series, nos. 438, and 439 (first volume is unnumbered in the series). Vols. 1 and 2 trans. A. L. Peck. Vol. 3 trans. D. M. Balme. London: Heinemann; Cambridge, Mass.: Harvard University Press.

———. 1968. *Parts of Animals* (with both Greek and English text). Loeb Classical Library Series, no. 323. Trans. A. L. Peck, London: Heinemann; Cambridge, Mass.: Harvard University Press.

———. 1977. *Politics* (with both Greek and English text). Trans. H. Rackham. Loeb Classical Library Series, no. 264. London: Heinemann; Cambridge, Mass.: Harvard University Press.

———. 1984. *The Complete Works of Aristotle: The Revised Oxford Translation*. Ed. J. Barnes. 2 vols. Princeton, N.J.: Princeton University Press.

Ariyaratne, A. T., and Macy, J. 1992. "The Island of Temple and Tank: Sarvodaya: Self-Help in Sri Lanka." In Batchelor and Brown 1992, 78–86.

Attfield, R. 1983. *The Ethics of Environmental Concern*. Oxford: Basil Blackwell.

Attfield, R., and Belsey, A., eds. 1994. *Philosophy and the Natural Environment*. Cambridge: Cambridge University Press.

Augustine. 1950–51. *Confessions*. 2 vols. Trans. William Watts. Loeb Classical Library Series, Nos. 26 and 27. London: Heinemann; Cambridge, Mass.: Harvard University Press.

————. 1966–88. *The City of God against the Pagans.* 7 vols. Trans. George E. McCracken. Loeb Classical Library Series, nos. 411–16. London: Heinemann; Cambridge, Mass.: Harvard University Press.

————. 388/1992. *De Moribus Ecclesiae Catholicae et de Moribus Manichaeorum Libri Duo.* Ed. Johannes B. Bauer. Corpus Scriptorum Ecclesiasticorum Latinorum Series, no. 90. Vienna: Hölder-Pichler Tempsky.

————. 1994 *De Trinitate.* In "Augustin [sic]: On the Holy Trinity, Doctrinal Treatises, Moral Treatises." Ed. Philip Schaff. Vol. 3. first series, of Nicene and Post-Nicene Fathers, vol. 3, Peabody, Mass.: Hendrickson.

Ayers, M. R. 1981. "Locke versus Aristotle on Natural Kinds." *Journal of Philosophy* 78:247–72.

Badiner, A. H., ed. 1990. *Dharma Gaia: A Harvest of Essays in Buddhism and Ecology.* Berkeley: Parallax Press.

Badrian, A., and Badrian, N. 1984. "Social Organization of *Pan paniscus* in the Lomako Forest, Zaire." In Susman 1984, 325–46.

Baird, R., and Rosenbaum, S., eds. 1991. *Animal Experimentation: The Moral Issues.* Buffalo, N.Y.: Prometheus.

Balme, D. M. 1980. "Aristotle's Biology Was Not Essentialist." *Archiv für Geschichte der Philosophie* 62:1–12.

Barber, R., trans. 1993. *Bestiary: Being an English Version of the Bodleian Library, Oxford M.S. Bodley 764 with all the Original Miniatures Reproduced in Facsimile.* Woodbridge, Suffolk: Boydell.

Barbour, I. G. 1996. "Three Paths from Nature to Religious Belief." Farmington Papers, No. SC8 (Science and Christianity 8). Oxford: Farmington Institute for Christian Studies.

Bard, K. A. 1990. "'Social Tool Use' by Free-Ranging Orangutans: A Piagetian and Developmental Perspective on the Manipulation of an Animate Object." In Parker and Gibson 1990, 356–78.

Barnard, L. W. 1967. *Justin Martyr: His Life and Thought.* London: Cambridge University Press.

Barr, J. 1963. "Revelation through History in the Old Testament and in Modern Theology." *Interpretation* 17:193–205.

————. 1972. "Man and Nature: The Ecological Controversy and the Old Testament." *Bulletin of the John Rylands University Library of Manchester* 54:9–32.

Batchelor, M. 1992. "Even the Stones Smile." In Batchelor and Brown 1992, 2–17.

Batchelor, M., and Brown, K., eds. 1992. *Buddhism and Ecology.* London: Cassell.

Bateson, G. 1972. *Steps to an Ecology of Mind.* London: Intertext.

————. 1979. *Mind and Nature: A Necessary Unity.* London: Wildwoodhouse.

Bateson, P. P. G., and Klopfer, P. H., eds. 1989. *Whither Ethology? Perspectives in Ethology.* New York: Plenum.

Bauckham, R. 1994. "Jesus and the Wild Animals (Mark 1:13): A Christological Image for an Ecological Age." In *Jesus of Nazareth: Lord and Christ (Festschrift for I. H. Marshall),* edited by J. B. Green and M. Turner, 3–21. Grand Rapids, Mich.: Erdmans, Carlisle/Paternoster.

Bechert, H., ed. 1992. *The Dating of the Historical Buddha.* 2 pts, Göttingen: Vandenhoeck & Ruprecht.

Bechert, H., and Gombrich, R., eds. 1991. *The World of Buddhism: Buddhist Monks and Nuns in Society and Culture.* London: Thames and Hudson.

Beckwith, R. T. 1988. "The Vegetarianism of the Therapeutae, and the Motives for Vegetarianism in Early Jewish and Christian Circles." *Revue de Qumran* 13, nos. 49–52, fascs. 1–4 (October): 407–10.

Bekoff, M. 1997. "'Do Dogs Ape?' or 'Do Apes Dog?' and Does It Matter? Broadening and Deepening Cognitive Ethology." *Animal Law* 3:11–21.

Benirschke, K. 1986. *Primates: The Road to Self-Sustaining Populations.* New York: Springer.

Bentham, J. 1970. *An Introduction to the Principles of Morals and Legislation.* Ed. J. H. Burns and H. L. A. Hart. London: Athlone.

Benton, T. 1988. "Humanism = Speciesism: Marx on Humans and Animals." *Radical Philosophy* 50:4–18.

Berger, A. 1953. *Encyclopedic Dictionary of Roman Law.* Transactions of the American Philosophical Society Series, n.s., vol. 43, pt. 2. Philadelphia: American Philosophical Society.

Berry, R. 1998. *Food for the Gods: Vegetarianism and the World's Religions.* Brooklyn, N.Y.: Pythagorean.

Berry, S. 1993. "Green Religion and Green Science." In *Explorations in Science and Theology,* 23–27. Templeton London Lectures at the RSA. London: Royal Society for the Encouragement of Arts, Manufacturers and Commerce.

Birch, C., and Cobb, J. B., Jr. 1981. *The Liberation of Life: From Cell to Community.* Cambridge: Cambridge University Press.

Birch, C., and others, eds. 1990. *Liberating Life: Contemporary Approaches to Ecological Theology.* Maryknoll, N.Y.: Orbis.

Blackburn, S. 1994. *The Oxford Dictionary of Philosophy.* Oxford: Oxford University Press.

Blackstone, W. T., ed. *Philosophy and Environmental Crisis.* Athens: University of Georgia Press.

Blum, D. 1994. *The Monkey Wars.* New York: Oxford University Press.

Bock, C. [1883] 1986. *Temples and Elephants: Travels in Siam in 1881–1882.* Oxford and Singapore: Oxford University Press.

Bolgiani, F. 1992a. "Diatessaron." In *Encyclopedia of the Early Church,* edited by Angelo Di Berardino, translated by Adrian Walford, vol. 1, 234. New York: Oxford University Press.

———. 1992b. "Tatian." In *Encyclopedia of the Early Church,* edited by Angelo Di Berardino, translated by Adrian Walford, vol. 2, 815. New York: Oxford University Press.

Bond, N. W., ed. 1984. *Animal Models in Psychopathology.* London: Academic Press.

Borgese, E. M. 1968. *The Language Barrier: Beast and Men.* New York: Holt, Rinehart and Winston.

Bowker, J. 1970. *Problems of Suffering in Religions of the World.* Cambridge: Cambridge University Press.

Bowler, P. J. 1992. *The Fontana History of the Environmental Sciences.* London: Fontana.

Braslau-Scheck, S. 1994. "Innovative Behaviors and Synchronization in Bottlenose Dolphins." Master's thesis, University of Hawaii, Honolulu, 1994.

Brown, F., Driver, S. R., and Briggs, C. A., eds. 1976. *A Hebrew and English Lexicon of the Old Testament.* Third printing, with corrections. Oxford: Clarendon.

Brown, P. 1967. *Augustine of Hippo: A Biography.* London: Faber and Faber.

———. 1988. *The Body and Society: Men, Women and Sexual Renunciation in Early Christianity.* New York: Columbia University Press.

Brownlee, S. M., and Norris, K. S. 1994. "The Acoustic Domain." In Norris and others 1994, 161–85.

Brumbaugh, R. S. 1978. "Of Man, Animals, and Morals." In Morris and Fox 1978, 6–25.

Buddhadatta Mahāthera, A. P. 1954. *English-Pali Dictionary.* Colombo, Ceylon: Pali Text Society/Colombo Apothecaries' Co.

Burnaby, J. [1938] 1991. *Amor Dei: A Study in the Religion of St. Augustine.* Norwich: Canterbury.

Butterworth, G. W., trans. 1953. *Clement of Alexandria.* Loeb Classical Library Series, no. 92. London: Heinemann; Cambridge, Mass.: Harvard University Press.

———. trans. 1966. *Origen: On First Principles.* New York: Harper.

Byrne, P., ed. 1986. *Rights and Wrongs in Medicine: King's College Studies 1985–6.* London: King Edward's Hospital Fund for London/Oxford University Press.

Byrne, R. 1995. *The Thinking Ape: Evolutionary Origins of Intelligence*. Oxford: Oxford University Press.

Caldwell, M. C., and Caldwell, D. K. 1965. "Individualized Whistle Contours in Bottlenose Dolphins (*Tursiops truncatus*)." *Nature* 207:434–35.

———. 1968. "Vocalizations of Native Captive Dolphins in Small Groups." *Science* 159: 1121–23.

Caldwell, M. C., Caldwell, D. K., and Tyack, P. 1990. "Review of the Signature Whistle Hypothesis for the Atlantic Bottlenose Dolphin." In Leatherwood and Reeves 1990, 199–234.

Callicott, J. B. 1980. "Animal Liberation: A Triangular Affair." *Environmental Ethics* 2:311–38. Also published, with a new preface, in Elliot 1995, 29–59.

Callicott, J. B., and Ames, R. T., eds. 1989. *Nature in Asian Traditions of Thought: Essays in Environmental Philosophy*. Albany: State University of New York Press.

Calvin, John. 1847 *Commentaries on the First Book of Moses called Genesis* ["Commentaries on Genesis"]. Vol. 1. Ed. and trans. John King. Edinburgh: Calvin Translation Society.

Carmody, F. J., trans. 1953. *Physiologus: The Very Ancient Book of Beasts, Plants and Stones, translated from Greek and Other Languages*. San Francisco: Book Club of California.

Carruthers, P. 1989. "Brute Experience." *The Journal of Philosophy* 86:258–69.

———. 1992. *The Animals Issue: Moral Theory in Practice*. Cambridge: Cambridge University Press.

Catechism of the Catholic Church. 1994. London: Geoffrey Chapman.

Cavalieri, P., and Singer, P., eds. 1993. *The Great Ape Project: Equality beyond Humanity*. London: Fourth Estate.

Chadwick, D. H. 1991. "Elephants: Out of Time, Out of Space." *National Geographic* 179, no. 5:2–49.

———. 1994. *The Fate of the Elephant*. San Francisco: Sierra Club.

Chadwick, H., 1966. *Early Christian Thought and the Classical Tradition*. New York: Oxford University Press.

———. trans. 1953. *Origen: Contra Celsum*. Cambridge: Cambridge University Press.

Chalmers, R., ed. 1896–99. *Majjhima-Nikāya*. Vols. 2 and 3. London: Henry Frowde.

———, trans. 1932. *Buddha's Teaching being the Sutta-Nipāta or Discourse-Collection*, ["Chalmers Sn."]. Romanized Pali text and English translation by Lord Chalmers. Harvard Oriental Series, no. 37. Cambridge, Mass.: Harvard University Press.

Chambers Dictionary. 1993 ["Chambers 1993"]. Edinburgh: Chambers Harrap.

Chapple, C. 1986. "Noninjury to Animals: Jaina and Buddhist Perspectives." In Regan 1986, 213–35.

———. 1993. *Nonviolence to Animals, Earth, and Self in Asian Traditions*. Albany: State University of New York Press.

Charles, R. H., ed. 1913. *The Apocrypha and Pseudepigrapha of the Old Testament in English*. Vol. 1, *Apocrypha*. Oxford: Clarendon.

Charlesworth, J. H., ed. 1983, 1985. *The Old Testament Pseudepigrapha*. 2 vols. London: Darton, Longman and Todd.

Cicero. 1979. *De Natura Deorum* [*and*] *Academica*, ["Cicero 1979/De Natura Deorum"]. Trans. H. Rackham. Loeb Classical Library Series, vol. 19 of the Cicero volumes and no. 268 overall. London: Heinemann; Cambridge, Mass.: Harvard University Press.

Clark, B. 1990. "'The Range of the Mountains Is His Pasture': Environmental Ethics in Israel." In Engel and Engel 1990, 183–88.

Clark, C. 1990. "Acoustic Behavior of Mysticete Whales." In Thomas and Kastelein 1990, 571–83.

Clark, E. A. 1987. "Clement of Alexandria." In *The Encyclopedia of Religion*, edited by Mircea Eliade, vol. 3, 533–34. London: Collier Macmillan; New York: Macmillan.

Clark, S. R. L. 1977. *The Moral Status of Animals*. Oxford: Clarendon.

———. 1993. *How to Think about the Earth: Philosophical and Theological Models for Ecology.* London: Mowbray.

———. 1995. "A View of Animals and How They Stand." In RSPCA 1995, 6–7.

Clark, W. M. 1968. "The Animal Series in the Primeval History." *Vetus Testamentum* 18:433–49.

Clarke, P. A. B., and Linzey, A., eds. 1990. *Political Theory and Animal Rights*. Winchester, Mass.: Pluto.

Clement of Alexandria. The extant works include, among others, (1) *The Exhortation to the Greeks* (referred to by its latinized title, *Protrepticus*; Butterworth 1953 has both the Greek and an English translation; Ferguson 1991 is used for book 3); (2) *The Pedagogue* (*Paedagogus*); and (3) *Miscellanies* (*Stromata*). English translations of the latter two are in Wilson 1869. The Greek and Latin texts for all three can be found at Migne PG, vols. 8 and 9.

Cobb, J. B., Jr. 1993. "Economics for Animals as Well as People." In Pinches and McDaniel 1993, 174–88.

The Code of Canon Law in English Translation. 1983. Trans. by the Canon Law Society Trust. London: Collins Liturgical Publications.

Cohen, C. 1986. "The Case for Biomedical Experimentation." *New England Journal of Medicine* 315, no. 14:865–70.

Cohen, J. 1989. *"Be Fertile and Increase, Fill the Earth and Master It": The Ancient and Medieval Career of a Biblical Text.* London and Ithaca, N.Y.: Cornell University Press.

Collins English Dictionary. 1991 ["Collins 1991"]. 3d ed., Glasgow: HarperCollins.

Cone, J. H. 1969. *Black Theology and Black Power.* New York: Seabury.

Cone, M., and Gombrich, R. 1977. *The Perfect Generosity of Prince Vessantara.* Oxford: Clarendon.

Connor, R. C., and Norris, K. S. 1982. "Are Dolphins Reciprocal Altruists?" *American Naturalist* 199:363.

Conze, E. 1975. *Buddhism: Its Essence and Development.* London: Harper and Row.

Cook, F. H. 1989. "The Jewel Net of Indra." In Callicott and Ames 1989, 213–29.

Cooper, D. E., and Palmer, J. A., eds. 1992. *The Environment in Question: Ethics and Global Issues.* New York: Routledge.

Copeland, H. F. 1956. *The Classification of Lower Organisms.* Palo Alto, Calif.: Pacific.

Cottingham, J. 1978. "A Brute to the Brutes? Descartes' Treatment of Animals." *Philosophy* 53:551–59.

Cowell, E. B., ed. 1895. *The Jātaka or Stories of the Buddha's Former Births.* 6 vols. Cambridge: Cambridge University Press.

Crooke, W. 1894. *Popular Religion and Folklore of Northern India.* Allahabad: Government Press, North-Western Provinces and Oudh.

Crosby, A. W. 1986. *Ecological Imperialism: The Biological Expansion of Europe, 900–1900.* Cambridge: Cambridge University Press.

Cummings, W. C., and Thompson, P. O. 1971. "Underwater Sounds from the Blue Whale." *Journal of the Acoustical Society of America* 50:1193–98.

Cumont, F. 1956. *The Oriental Religions in Roman Paganism.* New York: Dover.

Dagg, A. I., and Foster, J. B. 1976. *The Giraffe: Its Biology, Behavior and Ecology.* New York: Van Nostrand Reinhold.

Darwin, C. 1872. *The Expression of the Emotions in Man and Animals.* London: J. Murray.

Davis, H., and Balfour, D., eds. 1992. *The Inevitable Bond: Examining Scientist-Animal Interactions.* Cambridge: Cambridge University Press.

Dawkins, R. 1989. *The Selfish Gene.* Rev. ed. Oxford: Oxford University Press.

———. 1993. "Gaps in the Mind." In Cavalieri and Singer 1993, 80–87.

Day, J. 1985. *God's Conflict with the Dragon and the Sea*. Cambridge: Cambridge University Press.

Dayal, H. 1932. *The Bodhisattva Doctrine in Buddhist Sanskrit Literature*. London: Kegan Paul, Trench, Trübner.

de Lubac, H. 1966. "Introduction" to Butterworth 1966, vii–xxii.

de Waal, F. 1982. *Chimpanzee Politics: Power and Sex Among Apes*. London: Jonathan Cape.

———. 1989. *Peacemaking among Primates*. London: Harvard University Press.

———. 1995. "Bonobo Sex and Society." *Scientific American* 272, no. 3:58–64.

———. 1996. *Good Natured: The Origins of Right and Wrong in Humans and Other Animals*, London: Harvard University Press.

de Zulueta, F., trans. 1946. *The Institutes of Gaius: Part I (Text with Critical Notes and Translation)*. Oxford: Clarendon.

Deacon, T. W. 1990. "Rethinking Mammalian Brain Evolution." *American Zoologist* 30:629–705.

Dennett, D. C. 1983. "Intentional Systems in Cognitive Ethology: The 'Panglossian Paradigm' Defended." *Behavioural and Brain Sciences* 6:343–90.

———. 1996. *Kinds of Minds: Towards an Understanding of Consciousness*. London: Weidenfeld and Nicolson.

Descartes, R. 1952. *Discourse on the Method of Rightly Conducting the Reason and Seeking Truth in the Sciences*. Great Books of the Western World Series, vol. 31, 41–67. London: Encyclopaedia Britannica.

———. 1970. *Descartes: Philosophical Letters*. Trans. and ed. Anthony Kenny. Oxford: Clarendon.

Devall, Bill, and Sessions, G., eds. 1985. *Deep Ecology: Living as If Nature Mattered*. Salt Lake City: Peregrine Smith.

Dewart, L. 1966. *The Future of Belief: Theism in a World Come of Age*. New York: Herder and Herder.

Diamond, C. 1978. "Eating Meat and Eating People." *Philosophy* 53:465–79. Also published in C. Diamond, *The Realistic Spirit: Wittgenstein, Philosophy, and the Mind* (London: Bradford, 1991), 319–34.

Diamond, J. 1992. *The Rise and Fall of the Third Chimpanzee*. London: Vintage.

Diamond, S., ed. 1960. *Culture in History: Essays in Honor of Paul Radin*. New York: Columbia University Press.

The Dictionary of Classical Hebrew. 1996. Ed. D. J. A. Clines. vol. 3. Sheffield: Sheffield Academic Press.

Dierauer, U. 1977. *Tier und Mensch im Denken der Antike*. Amsterdam: Grüner.

Dods, M., and others, trans. 1868. *Justin Martyr and Athenagoras*. Ante-Nicene Christian Library, vol. 2. Ed. Alexander Roberts and James Donaldson. Edinburgh: T. and T. Clark.

Dombrowski, D. A. 1984. *The Philosophy of Vegetarianism*. Amherst: University of Massachusetts Press.

Douglas, M. 1966. *Purity and Danger*. London: Routledge.

Douglas-Hamilton, I., and Douglas-Hamilton, O. 1975. *Among the Elephants*. New York: Viking.

Douglas-Hamilton, O. 1980. "Africa's Elephants: Can They Survive?" *National Geographic* 158, no. 5:568–603.

Driver, G. R. 1956. "Mythical Monsters in the Old Testament." In *Studi orientalitici in onore di Giorgio Levi della Vida*, vol. 1, 238–42. Rome: Instituto per l'Oriente.

———. 1971. Review of H. H. Rowley's *Commentary on Job*. *Journal of Theological Studies* 22:177–78.

Druce, G. C. 1919. "The Elephant in the Medieval Legend and Art." *Archaeological Journal* 76 (Second Series, vol. 26), 1–73.

Dunayer, J. 1995. "Sexist Words, Speciesist Roots." In Adams and Donovan 1995, 11–31.

Dupré, J. 1981. "Natural Kinds and Biological Taxa." *Philosophical Review* 90:66–90.

———. 1993. *The Disorder of Things: Metaphysical Foundations of the Disunity of Science.* London: Harvard University Press.

Ehrenfeld, D. 1981. *The Arrogance of Humanism.* Oxford: Oxford University Press.

Ekdokimov, P. 1965. "Nature." *Scottish Journal of Theology* 18, no. 1:1–22.

Eliade, M., ed. 1967. *From Primitives to Zen: A Thematic Source Book of the History of Religions.* New York: Harper and Row.

———. 1978–85. *A History of Religious Ideas.* Vols. 1 and 2. Trans. Willard R. Trask. Vol. 3 trans. Alf Hiltebeitel and Diane Apostolos-Cappadona. London: University of Chicago Press.

Elliot, R., ed. 1995. *Environmental Ethics.* Oxford: Oxford University Press.

Ellis, R. 1991. *Men and Whales.* New York: Knopf.

Emmett, K. 1994. "Vegan Stirrings in the Ancient World." *Vegan,* winter, 6–7.

Engel, J. R., and Engel, J. G., eds. 1990. *Ethics of Environment and Development: Global Challenge, International Response.* London: Bellhaven.

Erdoes, R., and Ortiz, A., eds. 1984. *American Indian Myths and Legends.* New York: Pantheon.

Erwin, T. L. 1983. "Tropical Forest Canopies: The Last Biotic Frontier." *Bulletin of the Entomological Society of America* 29:14–19.

Ettlinger, G. 1984. "Humans, Apes and Monkeys: The Changing Neuropsychological Viewpoint." *Neuropsychologia* 22:685–96.

Evans, P. 1990. *Whales.* London: Whittet.

———. 1994. *Dolphins.* London: Whittet.

Fagen, R. 1981. *Animal Play Behaviour.* Oxford: Oxford University Press.

Fausbøll, V., ed. 1877–96. *The Jātaka together with its Commentary being Tales of the Anterior Births of Gotama Buddha.* 6 vols., with separate index in vol. 7. London: Trübner.

———, trans. 1881. *The Sutta-Nipāta: A Collection of Discourses.* SBE, no. 10. Oxford: Clarendon.

Feer, L., ed. 1884–98. *The Sa.myutta-Nikāya.* 5 vols. London: Henry Frowde.

Feinberg, J. 1974. "The Rights of Animals and Unborn Generations." In Blackstone 1974, 43–68.

———. 1986. "Abortion." In Regan 1986, 256–93.

Feliks, J. 1972. "Animals of the Bible and Talmud." In *Encyclopaedia Judaica.* vol. 3, 7–19. Jerusalem: Keter.

Ferguson, J., trans., 1991. *Clement of Alexandria: Stromateis—Books One to Three.* The Fathers of the Church: A New Translation, vol. 85. Washington, D.C.: Catholic University of America.

Ferré, F. 1986. "Moderation, Morals, and Meat." *Inquiry* 29:391–406.

Fiddes, N. 1991. *Meat: A Natural Symbol.* London: Routledge.

Finnis, John. 1980. *Natural Law and Natural Rights.* Oxford: Clarendon.

Finsen, Lawrence, and Finsen, Susan. 1994. *The Animal Rights Movement in America: From Compassion to Respect.* New York, Twayne.

Fisher, E. 1979. *Women's Creation: Sexual Evolution and the Shaping of Society.* Garden City, N.Y.: Anchor.

Foerster, W. 1965. "Θηρίον (Thērion)." In *Theological Dictionary of the New Testament,* edited by Gerhard Kittel, vol. 3, 133–35. Grand Rapids, Mich.: Eerdmans.

Ford, J. K. B. 1983. "Group-Specific Dialects of Killer Whales (*Orcinus orca*) in British Columbia." In Payne 1983, 129–61.

———. 1984. "Call Traditions and Dialects of Killer Whales (*Orcinus orca*) in British Columbia." Ph.D. diss., University of British Columbia.

Foucher, A. 1963. *The Life of Buddha According to the Ancient Texts and Monuments of India*. Trans. Simone Boas. Middletown, Conn.: Wesleyan University Press.

Fouts, Roger. 1997. *Next of Kin*. New York: William Morrow.

Fouts, R. S., and Fouts, D. H. 1993. "'Chimpanzees' Use of Sign Language." In Cavalieri and Singer 1993, 28–41.

Fouts, R. S., Fouts, D. H., and Cantfort, T. E. 1989. "The Infant Loulis Learns Signs from Cross-Fostered Chimpanzees." In Fouts and others 1989, 280–92.

Fouts, R., and others, eds. 1989. *Teaching Sign Language to Chimpanzees*. Albany: State University of New York Press.

Fox, M. 1991. *Creation Spirituality: Liberating Gifts for the Peoples of the Earth*. San Francisco: HarperCollins.

Fox, W. 1990. *Towards a Transpersonal Ecology: Developing New Foundations for Environmentalism*. Boston: Shambhala.

Francione, G. L. 1993. "Personhood, Property and Legal Competence." In Cavalieri and Singer 1993, 248–57.

———. 1995. *Animals, Property, and the Law*. Philadelphia: Temple University Press.

Francis, H. T., and Thomas, E. J. 1916. *Jataka Tales*. Cambridge: Cambridge University Press.

Francis, L., and Norman, R. 1978. "Some Animals Are More Equal Than Others." *Philosophy* 53:507–27.

Frear, G. L. 1993. "Caring for Animals: Biblical Stimulus for Ethical Reflection." In Pinches and McDaniel 1993, 3–11.

Freud, S. 1913. *Totem and Taboo: Some Points of Agreement between the Mental Lives of Savages and Neurotics*. Trans. J. Strachey. New York: Norton.

Frey, R. G. 1979. "What Has Sentiency to Do with the Possession of Animal Rights?" In Patterson and Ryder 1979, 106–11.

———. 1980. *Interests and Rights: The Case against Animals*. Oxford: Clarendon.

———. 1987. "Autonomy and the Value of Animal Life." *Monist* 70:50–63.

———. 1988. "Moral Standing, the Value of Lives, and Speciesism." *Between the Species* 4:191–201.

Gaffney, J. 1986. "The Relevance of Animal Experimentation to Roman Catholic Ethical Methodology." In Regan 1986, 149–70.

Gaita, R. 1991. *Good and Evil: An Absolute Conception*. London: Macmillan.

Galdikas, B. M. F. 1995. *Reflections of Eden: My Life with the Orangutans of Borneo*. London: Victor Gollancz.

Gallup, G. G., Jr. 1970. "Chimpanzees: Self-Recognition." *Science* 167:86–87.

———. 1977. "Self-Recognition in Primates: A Comparative Approach to the Bidirectional Properties of Consciousness." *American Psychologist* 32:329–38.

———. 1982. "Self-awareness and the Emergence of Mind in Primates." *American Journal of Primatology* 2:237–48.

———. 1983. "Toward a Comparative Psychology of Mind." In Mellgren 1983, 473–510.

———. 1987. "Self-Awareness." In Mitchell and Erwin 1987, 3–16.

Gardner, H. 1985. *The Mind's New Science: A History of the Cognitive Revolution*. New York: Basic Books.

George, W., and Yapp, B. 1991. *The Naming of the Beasts: Natural History in the Medieval Bestiary*. London: Duckworth.

Gergely, G. 1994. "From Self-Recognition to Theory of Mind." In Parker and others 1994, 51–60.

Ghiselin, M. T. 1966. "On Psychologism in the Logic of Taxonomic Controversies." *Systematic Zoology* 15:207–15.

———. 1974. "A Radical Solution to the Species Problem." *Systematic Zoology*, 23:536–44.

Gibson, K. R. 1986. "Cognition, Brain Size and the Extraction of Embedded Food Resources." In Else and Lee 1986, 93–105.

———. 1990. "New Perspectives on Instincts and Intelligence: Brain Size and the Emergence of Hierarchical Mental Constructional Skills." In Parker and Gibson 1990, 97–128.

Gill, R., ed. 1995. *Readings in Modern Theology: Britain and America*. London: SPCK.

Glare, P. G. W., ed. 1982. *Oxford Latin Dictionary*. Oxford: Clarendon.

Glover, J. 1990. *Causing Death and Saving Lives*. London: Penguin.

Gnuse, R. 1994. "New Directions in Biblical Theology: The Impact of Contemporary Scholarship in the Hebrew Bible." *Journal of the American Academy of Religion* 62:893–918.

Godlovitch, S., and others, eds. 1971. *Animals, Men and Morals: An Enquiry into the Maltreatment of Non-humans*. London: Victor Gollancz.

Gold, M. 1995. *Animal Rights: Extending the Circle of Compassion*. Oxford: Jon Carpenter.

Gombrich, R. F. 1971. *Precept and Practice: Traditional Buddhism in the Rural Highlands of Ceylon*. Oxford: Clarendon.

———. 1988. *Theravada Buddhism: A Social History from Ancient Benares to Modern Colombo*. London: Routledge.

———. 1991a. "The Buddhist Way." In Bechert and Gombrich 1991, 9–14.

———. 1991b. "The Evolution of the Sangha." In Bechert and Gombrich 1991, 77–89.

———. 1992. "Dating the Buddha: A Red Herring Revealed." In Bechert 1992, pt. 2, 237–59.

———. 1996. *How Buddhism Began: The Conditioned Genesis of the Early Teachings*. London: Athlone.

Gonda, J. 1965. *Change and Continuity in Indian Religion*. London: Mouton.

Goodall, J. 1971. *In the Shadow of Man*. Boston: Houghton Mifflin.

———. 1986. *The Chimpanzees of Gombe*. Cambridge, Mass.: Belknap Press of Harvard University Press.

———. 1990. *Through a Window: Thirty Years with the Chimpanzees of Gombe*. London: Penguin.

———. 1993. "Chimpanzees: Bridging the Gap." In Cavalieri and Singer 1993, 10–18.

Goodpaster, K. E., and Sayre, K. M., eds. 1979. *Ethics and Problems of the 21st Century*. Notre Dame, Ind.: University of Notre Dame Press.

Goodspeed, E. J. 1912. *Index Apologeticus, Sive Clavis: Iustini Martyris Operum*. Leipzig: J. C. Hinrichs.

Gould, S. J. 1995. "Animals and Us." *New York Review of Books*, 19 August, 20–25.

Grant, F. C., ed. 1953. *Hellenistic Religions: The Age of Syncretism*. New York: Liberal Arts Press/Bobbs-Merrill.

Green, J. P., Sr. 1976. *The Interlinear Bible*. Peabody, Mass.: Hendrickson.

Greenfield, P. M., and Savage-Rumbaugh, W. S. 1990. "Grammatical Combination in *Pan paniscus*: Processes of Learning and Invention in the Evolution and Development of Language." In Parker and Gibson 1990, 540–78.

Gregorios, P. 1978. *The Human Presence: An Orthodox View of Nature*. Geneva: World Council of Churches.

Griffin, D. R. 1981. *The Question of Animal Awareness: Evolutionary Continuity of Mental Experience*. New York: Rockefeller University Press.

———. 1992. *Animal Minds*. London: University of Chicago Press.

Griffiths, P. 1981. "Concentration or Insight: The Problematic of Theravāda Buddhist Meditation Theory." *Journal of the American Academy of Religion* 54:605–24.

Grim, J. A. 1994. "Native North American Worldviews and Ecology." In Tucker and Grim 1994, 41–54.

Gross, R. M. 1993. *Buddhism after Patriarchy: A Feminist History, Analysis, and Reconstruction of Buddhism*. Albany: State University of New York Press.

Grove, A. J., and others. 1974. *Animal Biology*. 9th ed. London: University Tutorial.

Groves, C. P. 1986. "Systematics of the Great Apes." In Mitchell and Erwin 1986, 187–217.

Gruber, E. R., and Kersten, H. 1995. *The Original Jesus: The Buddhist Sources of Christianity*. Shaftesbury, Dorset: Element.

Haldar, A. 1950. *The Notion of Desert in Sumero-Akkadian and West-Semitic Religions*. Uppsala: n.p.

Hall, J. 1996. *Illustrated Dictionary of Symbols in Eastern and Western Art*. New York: Icon Editions.

Hallowell, A. I. 1960. "Ojibwa Ontology, Behaviour and World View." In Diamond 1960, 19–52.

Hardy, E., ed. 1896–1900. *The A"nguttara-Nikāya*. Vols. 3–5. London: Pali Text Society/Henry Frowde.

Hare, R. M. 1981. *Moral Thinking*. Oxford: Clarendon.

Harper's Bible Dictionary. 1985. Ed. P. J. Achtmeier. London: Harper and Row.

Harré, R., and Robinson, D. 1995. "On the Primacy of Duties." *Philosophy* 70:513–32.

Harris, Ian. 1994. "Causation and Telos: The Problem of Buddhist Environmental Ethics." *Journal of Buddhist Ethics* 1:45–56.

Harrison, P. 1991. "Animal Pain." In Baird and Rosenbaum 1991, 129–39.

Harrison, R. 1964. *Animal Machines*. London: Vincent Stuart.

Hart, B., and Hart, L. 1993. "Biting Flies Flee Elephant Swatters." *Science News* 144:70.

Hatch, E. 1914. *The Influence of Greek Ideas and Usages upon the Christian Church*. London: Williams and Norgate.

Haussleiter, J. 1935. *Der Vegetarismus in der Antike*. Berlin: A. T. Pelman.

Häyry, H., and Häyry, M. 1993. "Who's Like Us?" In Cavalieri and Singer 1993, 174–82.

Haynes, G. 1993. *Mammoths, Mastodonts and Elephants: Biology, Behavior and the Fossil Record*. Cambridge: Cambridge University Press.

Helweg, D. A., and others. 1992. "Humpback Whale Song: Our Current Understanding." In Thomas and others 1992, 459–83.

Henshaw, D. 1989. *Animal Warfare: The Story of the Animal Liberation Front*. London: Fontana.

Herman, L. M., 1986. "Cognition and Language Competencies in Bottlenose Dolphins." In Schusterman and others 1986, 221–52.

———. ed. 1980. *Cetacean Behavior: Mechanisms and Functions*. New York: Wiley Interscience.

Herman, L. M., and others. 1994. "Bottlenose Dolphins Can Generalize Rules and Develop Abstract Concepts." *Marine Mammal Science* 10:70–80.

———. 1993. "Representational and Conceptual Skills in Dolphins." In Herman and others, eds. 1993, 403–42.

———. 1985. "Can Dolphins Understand Sentences?" *Science Teacher*, October, 20–25.

———. 1984. "Comprehension of Sentences by Bottlenosed Dolphins." *Cognition* 16:129–219.

———, eds. 1993. *Language and Communication: A Comparative Approach*. Hillsdale, N.J.: Erlbaum.

Herzing, D. L. 1993. "Dolphins in the Wild: An Eight-Year Field Study on Dolphin Communication and Interspecies Interaction." Ph.D. diss., Union Institute.

————. 1994. "The Contextual Nature of Underwater Behaviour and Vocalizations in Atlantic Spotted Dolphin (*Stenella frontalis*)." *European Research on Cetaceans* 8:156–58.

————. 1995a. "Dolphins: Focusing on an Understanding." *Ocean Realm: International Magazine of the Sea*, June, 22–29.

————. 1995b. "Reflections 1985–1995: What Have We Learned?" *Notes from the Field*, 4, 3–6, Jupiter, Florida: Wild Dolphin Project.

Hessel, D. T. 1992. *After Nature's Revolt: Eco-Justice and Theology*. Minneapolis: Fortress.

————, ed. 1996. *Theology for Earth Community: A Field Guide*. Maryknoll, N.Y.: Orbis.

Hick, J. 1978a. *Evil and the God of Love*. Rev. ed., San Francisco: Harper and Row.

————. 1978b. "Foreword" to Wilfred Cantwell Smith, *The Meaning and End of Religion: A New Approach to the Religious Traditions of Mankind*, ix–xviii. London: SPCK.

————. 1989. *An Interpretation of Religion*. New Haven, Conn.: Yale University Press.

Hiebert, T. 1996. *The Yahwist's Landscape: Nature and Religion in Early Israel*. New York: Oxford University Press.

Hinde, R. A., ed. 1983. *Primate Social Relationships: An Integrated Approach*. Oxford: Blackwell Scientific.

Hinson, E. G. 1987a. "Irenaeus." In *The Encyclopedia of Religion*, edited by Mircea Eliade, vol. 8, 280–83. London: Collier Macmillan; New York: Macmillan.

————. 1987b. "Justin Martyr." *The Encyclopedia of Religion*, edited by Mircea Eliade, vol. 8, 220–23. London: Collier Macmillan; and New York: Macmillan.

Holman, M. J. 1931. *Nature-Imagery in the Works of St. Augustine*. Catholic University of America Patristic Studies, vol. 33. Washington, D.C.: Catholic University of America.

Horner, I. B. 1967. *Early Buddhism and the Taking of Life*. The Wheel Publication, no. 104. Kandy, Ceylon: Buddhist Publication Society.

Hudson, D. F. 1992. *New Testament Greek*. London: Hodder and Stoughton.

Huffman, M. A., and Wrangham, R. W. 1994. "Diversity of Medicinal Plant Use by Chimpanzees in the Wild." In Wrangham and others 1994, 129–48.

Hughes, E. J. 1986. *Wilfred Cantwell Smith: A Theology for the World*. London: SCM.

Hull, D. L. 1976. "Are Species Really Individuals?" *Systematic Zoology* 25:174–91.

Hyatt, C. W., and Hopkins, W. D. 1994. "Self-Awareness in Bonobos and Chimpanzees: A Comparative Perspective." In Parker and others 1994, 248–53.

Hyatt, C. W., and others. 1994. "Ele-Type: An Automated Feeding and Testing Device for Elephants." *ISEE Transactions on Instrumentation and Measurement* 43:101.

Inada, K. K. 1989. "Environmental Problematics." In Callicott and Ames 1989, 231–45.

Ingold, T. 1994a. "From Trust to Domination: An Alternative History of Human-Animal Relations." In Manning and Serpell 1994, 1–22.

————, ed., 1994b. *What Is an Animal?* London: Routledge.

Irenaeus. *Against Heresies* (the actual title is, in English, *Refutation and Overthrow of Knowledge Falsely So-called*), in Roberts and Rambaut 1868–69. The Greek and Latin texts can be found in Migne PG 7.

————. *Proof of the Apostolic Preaching*. In Robinson 1920; and J. P. Smith 1952.

Ishigami, Z. 1965. "Animals." In *Encyclopaedia of Buddhism*, edited by G. O. Malalasekera, fasc. 4, 667–72. Colombo, Ceylon: Government Press.

Jacobson, D. 1996. "Biblical Bases for Eco-Justice Ethics." In Hessel 1996, 45–52.

James, W. 1923. *The Varieties in Religious Experience: A Study in Human Nature*. London: Longmans, Green.

Janson, H. W. 1952. *Apes and Ape Lore in the Middle Ages and Renaissance*. London: Warburg Institute, University of London.

Jastrow, M. 1950. *A Dictionary of the Targumim, the Talmud Babli and Yerushalmi, and the Midrashic Literature*. 2 vols. New York: Pardes.

Jayatilleke, K. N. 1963. *The Early Buddhist Theory of Knowledge*. London: Allen and Unwin.

———. 1975. *The Message of the Buddha*. New York: Free Press.

Jerison, H. J. 1973. *Evolution of the Brain and Intelligence*. London and New York: Academic Press.

———. 1982. "The evolution of biological intelligence." In Sternberg 1982, 723–91.

———. 1985. 'Animal Intelligence as Encephalization." In Weiskrantz 1985, 21–35.

———. 1988a. "The Evolutionary Biology of Intelligence: Afterthoughts." In Jerison and Jerison 1988, 447–66.

———. 1988b. "Evolutionary Biology of Intelligence: The Nature of the Problem." In Jerison and Jerison 1988, 1–11.

Jerison, H. J., and Jerison, I., eds. 1988. *Intelligence and Evolutionary Biology*. Heidelberg: Springer-Verlag.

John Paul II. 1993. *Veritatis Splendor*. London: Catholic Truth Society.

———. 1995. *Evangelium Vitae*. London: Catholic Truth Society.

Johnson, A. 1991. *Factory Farming*. Oxford: Basil Blackwell.

Jonas, H. 1963. *The Gnostic Religion: The Message of the Alien God and the Beginnings of Christianity*, 2d ed. Boston: Beacon.

———. 1984. *The Imperative of Responsibility: In Search of an Ethics for the Technological Age*. Chicago: University of Chicago Press.

Jung, S. 1993. "Strangers, Friends or Kin?" In Pinches and McDaniel 1993, 47–61.

Justin. Translations of the first and second *Apologies* and the *Dialogue with Trypho, a Jew* (referred to, respectively, as "1 *Apology*," "2 *Apology*," and "*Dialogue with Trypho*") can be found in Dods and others 1868. However, the translation of *1 Apology* referred to in the text is that of Richardson and others 1953. The Greek for both *Apologies* is in Pautigny 1904.

Kalechofsky, R. 1991. *Autobiography of a Revolutionary: Essays on Animal and Human Rights*. Marblehead, Mass.: Micah.

Kano, T. 1992. *The Last Ape*. Palo Alto, Calif.: Stanford University Press.

Kant, I. 1963. "Duties to Animals and Spirits." In *Lectures on Ethics*, translated by L. Infield, 239–41. New York: Harper and Row.

———. 1993. *Groundwork of the Metaphysic of Morals*. Trans. H. J. Patton. London: Routledge.

Kaplan, G., and Rogers, L. 1994. *Orangutans in Borneo*. Armidale, NSW, Australia: University of New England Press.

Kapleau, P. 1981. *To Cherish All Life: A Buddhist View of Animal Slaughter and Meat Eating*. Rochester, N.Y.: Zen Center.

Kappeler, S. 1995. "Speciesism, Racism, Nationalism . . . or the Power of Scientific Subjectivity." In Adams and Donovan 1995, 320–52.

Kaufman, G. 1972. "The Concept of Nature: A Problem for Theology." *Harvard Theological Review* 65:337–66.

Kennedy, J. S. 1992. *The New Anthropomorphism*. Cambridge: Cambridge University Press.

Keown, D. 1992. *The Nature of Buddhist Ethics*. London: Macmillan.

———. 1995. *Buddhism and Bioethics*. London: Macmillan.

Kerferd, G. B. 1967. "Protagoras of Abdera." In *The Encyclopedia of Philosophy*, edited by Paul Edwards, vol. 6, 505–7. London: Collier Macmillan.

Khoroche, P., trans. 1989. *Jātakamālā: Once the Buddha Was a Monkey: Aarya "Sūra's Jātakamālā*. London: University of Chicago Press.

Kinsley, David. 1995. *Ecology and Religion: Ecological Spirituality in Cross-Cultural Perspective*. Englewood Cliffs, N.J.: Prentice Hall.

Klinowska, M., 1988. "Are Cetaceans Especially Smart?" *New Scientist*, 29 October, 46–47.

———. ed. 1991. *Dolphins, Porpoises and Whales of the World: The IUCN Red Data Book*. Cambridge and Gland, Switzerland: IUCN.

————. 1992. "Brains, Behaviour and Intelligence in Cetaceans." In *Whales and Ethics*, edited by Orn D. Jonsson. Reykjavik: University of Iceland Press.

Klug, B. 1992. "Speciesism: Some Skeptical Remarks about 'Prejudice against Animals.'" Paper delivered at the International Conference on the Philosophy of Hans Jonas, Hebrew University, January 12–15, 1992.

Kohlenberger, J. R., III, and others. 1995. *The Exhaustive Concordance to the Greek New Testament*. Grand Rapids, Mich.: Zondervan.

Köhler, W. [1925] 1957. *The Mentality of Apes*. Translated from the second revised edition by Ella Winter. Harmondsworth, England: Penguin.

Koop, B. F., and others. 1986. "Primate (eta)-Globin DNA Sequences and Man's Place among the Great Apes." *Nature* 319:234–37.

Küng, H., and Kuschel, K.-J. 1993. *A Global Ethic: The Declaration of the Parliament of the World Religions*. Trans. John Bowden. London: SCM. Preface and commentary translated by John Bowden from *Erklärung zum Weltethos. Die Deklaration des Parlementes der Weltreligionen* (Munich: R. Piper, 1993).

Küng, H., and Moltmann, J., eds. 1990. *The Ethics of the World Religions and Human Rights*. London: Concilium/SCM.

LaFollette, H., and Shanks, N. 1996. "The Origin of Speciesism." *Philosophy* 71:41–61.

Lal, B. K. 1986. "Hindu Perspectives on the Use of Animals in Science." In Regan 1986, 199–212.

Lammers, S., and Verhey, A., eds. 1987. *On Moral Medicine: Theological Perspectives in Medical Ethics*. Grand Rapids, Mich.: Erdmans.

Lamotte, E. 1958. *Histoire du Bouddhisme indien*. Louvain: University of Louvain.

————. 1991a. "The Buddha, His Teachings and His Sangha." In Bechert and Gombrich 1991, 41–58.

————. 1991b. "Mahāyāna Buddhism." In Bechert and Gombrich 1991, 90–93.

Lampe, G. W. H., ed. 1961. *A Patristic Greek Lexicon*. Oxford: Clarendon.

Law, B. C., ed. 1949. *The Cariyāpi.taka*. 2d ed. Poona: Bhandarkar Oriental Research Institute.

————, trans. 1938. *The Minor Anthologies of the Pali Canon: Part III Buddhava.msa, the Lineage of the Buddhas, and Cariyā-pi.taka or the Collection of Ways of Conduct*. SBB, no. 9. London: Humphrey Milford/Oxford University Press.

Lawson, J. 1948. *The Biblical Theology of St. Irenaeus*. London: Eppworth.

Leatherwood, S., and Reeves, R. R., eds. 1990. *The Bottlenose Dolphin*. London: Academic.

Lecky, W. E. H. 1884. *History of European Morals: From Augustus to Charlemagne*. 2 vols, 6th rev. ed. London: Longmans Green.

Lethmate, J. 1982. "Tool-Using Skills of Orang-utans." *Journal of Human Evolution* 11:49–64.

Lewis, C. T. 1993 (referred to as "Lewis/Freund 1993"). *A Latin Dictionary founded on Andrews' Edition of Freund's Latin Dictionary: Revised, Enlarged, and in Great Part Rewritten*. Oxford: Clarendon.

Lewis, C. T., and Short, C. 1962. *A Latin Dictionary founded on Andrews' Edition of Freund's Latin Dictionary: Revised, Enlarged, and in Great Part Rewritten*. Oxford: Clarendon.

Lewis, M., and Brooks-Gunn, J. 1979. *Social Cognition and the Acquisition of Self*. New York: Plenum.

Liddell, H. G., and Scott, R. 1968. *A Greek-English Lexicon*. Revised by Henry Stuart Jones, with a supplement. Oxford: Clarendon.

Lieberman, P. 1984. *Biology and Evolution of Language*. Cambridge, Mass.: Harvard University Press.

————. 1991. *Uniquely Human: The Evolution of Speech, Thought, and Selfless Behavior*. Cambridge, Mass.: Harvard University Press.

————. 1998. *Eve Spoke: Human Language and Human Evolution*. New York: Norton.

Lilla, S. R. C. 1971. *Clement of Alexandria: A Study in Christian Platonism and Gnosticism.* Oxford and London: Oxford University Press.

Lilly, J. C. 1975. *Lilly on Dolphins: Humans of the Sea.* Garden City, N.Y.: Anchor Press/ Doubleday.

Linden, E. 1992. "A Curious Kinship: Apes and Humans." *National Geographic* 183, no. 3:2–45.

Linzey, A. 1987. *Christianity and the Rights of Animals.* London: SPCK.

———. 1991. "The Moral Priority of the Weak: The Theological Basis of Animal Liberation." In *The Animal Kingdom and the Kingdom of God,* 25–42. Occasional Paper Series, No. 26. Edinburgh: Church and Nation Committee for the Church of Scotland.

———. 1994a. *Animal Theology.* London: SCM.

———. 1994b. "Why Catholic Teaching Perpetuates Cruelty." *The AV Magazine: The Journal of the American Anti-Vivisection Society* 102, no. 9:8–11.

Linzey, A., and Regan, T. 1988. *Animals and Christianity: A Book of Readings.* New York: Crossroad.

The Living Bible Paraphrased: New Testament. 1971. Wheaton, Illinois: Tyndale House.

Lorenz, K. Z. 1952. *King Solomon's Ring.* Trans. M. Latzke. New York: Crowell.

———. 1966. *On Aggression.* Trans. Marjorie Kerr Wilson. London: Methuen.

Louw, J. P., and Nida, E. A., eds. 1988. *Greek-English Lexicon of the New Testament Based on Semantic Domains.* 2 vols. New York: United Bible Societies.

Lovejoy, A. O. 1960. *The Great Chain of Being.* New York: Harper Torchbooks.

Mālālāsekera, G. P. 1937–38. *Dictionary of Pali Proper Names.* 2 vols. London: John Murray.

Manning, A., and Serpell, J., eds. 1994. *Animals and Human Society: Changing Perspectives.* London: Routledge.

Marten, K., and Psarakos, S. 1994. "Evidence of Self-Awareness in the Bottlenose Dolphin (*Tursiops truncatus*)." In Parker and others 1994, 361–79.

Mason, J., and Singer, P. 1993. *Animal Factories.* New York: Crown.

Masson, J., and McCarthy, S. 1994. *When Elephants Weep: The Emotional Lives of Animals.* London: Jonathan Cape.

Masterton B., and Skeen, L. 1972. "Origins of Anthropoid Intelligence: Prefrontal System and Delayed Alternation in Hedgehog, Tree Shrew, and Bushbaby." *Journal of Comparative and Physiological Psychology* 81:423–33.

Matics, M. L., trans. 1970. *Entering the Path of Enlightenment: The Bodhicaryavatara of the Buddhist Poet Santideva.* London: Macmillan.

Mauser, U. 1963. *Christ in the Wilderness: The Wilderness Theme in the Second Gospel and Its Basis in the Biblical Tradition.* London: SCM.

Mayr, E. 1976. *Evolution and the Diversity of Life.* Cambridge, Mass.: Belknap Press of Harvard University Press.

———. 1982. *The Growth of Biological Thought: Diversity, Evolution, and Inheritance.* London: Belknap Press.

———. 1992. *One Long Argument: Charles Darwin and the Genesis of Modern Evolutionary Thought.* London: Allen Lane/Penguin.

Mbiti, J. S. 1991. *Introduction to African Religion.* 2d ed. Oxford: Heinemann International Literature and Textbooks.

McCracken, G. E. 1966. Introduction to Augustine, *City of God,* vi–lxxxii.

McCracken, G., trans. 1949. *Ancient Christian Writers.* vol. 1. Westminster, Md.: Catholic University of America.

McDaniel, J. B. 1989. *Of God and Pelicans: A Theology of Reverence for Life.* Louisville, Ky.: Westminster/John Knox.

———. 1994. *Earth, Sky, Gods, and Mortals: A Theology of Ecology for the Twenty-first Century.* N.p.: Twenty-third Publications.

McDermott, J. P. 1989. "Animals and Humans in Early Buddhism." *Indo-Iranian Journal* 32:269–80.

McDermott, W. C. 1938. *The Ape in Antiquity.* Johns Hopkins University Studies in Archaeology Series, No. 27. London: Humphrey Milford/Oxford University Press.

McFague, S. 1983. *Metaphorical Theology.* London: SCM.

McGrew, W. C. 1992. *Chimpanzee Material Culture: Implications for Human Evolution.* Cambridge: Cambridge University Press.

———. 1994. "Overview: Diversity in Social Relations." In Wrangham and others 1994, 151–54.

McKenna, V., and others, eds. 1987. *Beyond the Bars: The Zoo Dilemma.* Wellingborough, Northamptonshire: Thorsons.

Meeks, W. A. 1993. *The Origins of Christian Morality: The First Two Centuries.* London: Yale University Press.

Mellgren, R. L., ed. 1983. *Animal Cognition and Behavior.* Oxford: North Holland.

Midgley, M. 1973. "Concept of Beastliness." *Philosophy* 48:111–35.

———. 1984. *Animals and Why They Matter.* Athens: University of Georgia Press.

———. 1986. "Conflicts and Inconsistencies over Animal Welfare." The Fifth Hume Memorial Lecture. N.p.

———. 1987. "Keeping Species on Ice." In McKenna and others 1987, 55–65.

———. 1994a. "Beasts, Brutes and Monsters." In Ingold 1994b, 35–46.

———. 1994b. 'Born Free, but Everywhere in Zoos." Review of Cavalieri and Singer 1993, *New York Times Book Review,* 6 February, 33.

———. 1995. *"Beast and Man: The Roots of Human Nature.* Rev. ed. London: Routledge.

Migne, J. P. 1856–1866. *Patrologiae cursus completus, series graeca.* Vols. 1, 6, 7, 8, 9, 10, 11, 29, 40, Paris.

Migne, J. P. 1844–1875. *Patrologiae cursus completus, series latina,* vols. 14, 32, 34, 42, 91, Paris.

Miles, H. L. W. 1990. "The Cognitive Foundations for Reference in a Signing Orangutan." In Parker and Gibson 1990, 511–39.

———. 1993. "Language and the Orang-utan: The Old 'Person' of the Forest." In Cavalieri and Singer 1993, 42–57.

Miller, H. B. 1993. "The Wahokies." In Cavalieri and Singer 1993, 230–36.

Mitchell, G., and Erwin, J., eds. 1986. *Behavior, Cognition, and Motivation.* Comparative Primate Biology Series, vol. 1. New York: Alan R. Liss.

———. 1987. *Behavior, Cognition, and Motivation.* Comparative Primate Biology Series, vol. 2, pt. B. New York: Alan R. Liss.

Mitchell, R. W., and others, eds. 1997. *Anthropomorphism, Anecdotes and Animals.* Albany: State University of New York Press.

Moltmann, J. 1990. "Human Rights, the Rights of Humanity and the Rights of Nature." In Küng and Moltmann, 1990, 120–35.

Mommsen, T., and others, eds. and trans. 1985. *The Digest of Justinian.* 4 vols. Philadelphia: University of Pennsylvania Press.

Morris, R., ed. 1885–88. *The A"nguttara-Nikāya.* Vols. 1 and 2. London: Pali Text Society/ Henry Frowde.

Morris, R. K., and Fox, M. W., eds. 1978. *On the Fifth Day: Animal Rights and Human Ethics.* Washington, D.C.: Acropolis.

Morgan, D. W. 1979. "The Vocal and Behavioral Reactions of the Beluga to Playback of Its Sounds." In Winn and Olla 1979, 311–43.

Mörzer Bruyns, W. F. J. 1971. *Field Guide of Whales and Dolphins.* Amsterdam: C. A. Mees.

Moss, C. 1988. *Elephant Memories: Thirteen Years in the Life of an Elephant Family*. New York: William Morrow.

———. 1992. "Elephant Calves: The Story of Two Sexes." In Shoshani 1992, 106–15.

Moss, C. J., and Poole, J. H. 1983. "Relationships and Social Structure of African Elephants." In Hinde 1983, 315–25.

Moulton, J. H., and Milligan, G. 1930. *The Vocabulary of the Greek Testament*. London: Hodder and Stoughton.

Muddiman, J. 1995. "The Gospel and Environmentalism: Different Shades of Green." The Yvonne Workman Lecture at Mansfield College, Oxford, September 1995.

Murphy, M. G. 1941. *Nature Allusion in the Works of Clement of Alexandria*. Catholic University of America Patristic Studies, vol. 65. Washington, D.C.: Catholic University of America.

Murray, R. 1992. *The Cosmic Covenant: Biblical Themes of Justice, Peace and the Integrity of Creation*. London: Sheed and Ward.

Naess, A. 1980. "Environmental Ethics and Spinoza's Ethics." *Inquiry* 23:313–25.

Nash, J. 1991. *Loving Nature: Ecological Integrity and Christian Responsibility*. Nashville, Tenn.: Abingdon.

Nash, R. 1973. *Wilderness and the American Mind*. 3d ed. London: Yale University Press.

New International Version of the New Testament. 1973. Grand Rapids, Mich.: Zondervan Bible.

The New World Dictionary-Concordance to the New American Bible. 1970. New York: World Publishing/Times Mirror.

Niebuhr, R. 1964. *The Nature and Destiny of Man: A Christian Interpretation*. 2 vols. New York: Scribner's.

Nishida, T. 1968. "The Social Group of Wild Chimpanzees in the Mahale Mountains." *Primates* 9:167–224.

———. 1994. "Review of Recent Findings on Mahale Chimpanzees: Implications and Future Reseach Directions." In Wrangham and others 1994, 373–96.

Nitecki, M. H., and Nitecki, D. V., eds. 1993. *Evolutionary Ethics*. Albany: State University of New York Press.

Noble, J. W. 1998. "New Findings Suggest Neanderthals Had Gift of Speech." *New York Times*, April 28, 1998, p. 1.

Norman, K. R. 1983. *Pāli Literature, Including the Canonical Literature in Prakrit and Sanskrit of all the Hīnayāna Schools of Buddhism*. Wiesbaden: Otto Harrassowitz.

Norris, K. S. 1991. *Dolphin Days: The Life and Times of the Spinner Dolphin*. London and New York: Norton.

Norris, K. S., and Johnson, C. M. 1994. "Schools and Schooling." In Norris and others 1994, 232–42.

Norris, K. S., and others, eds. 1994. *The Hawaiian Spinner Dolphin*. London: University of California Press.

Oakley, K. P. 1972. *Man the Tool-Maker*. 6th ed. London: British Museum/Natural History.

Oikonomou, E. 1992. "Holy Scripture and the Natural Environment." In *So That God's Creation Might Live: The Orthodox Church Responds to the Ecological Crisis*, edited by Ecumenical Patriarchate of Constantinople, 31–36. N.p.: Ecumenical Patriarchate of Constantinople.

Oldenberg, H., ed. 1879–83. *The Vinaya Pi.taka.m*. 5 vols. London and Edinburgh: Williams and Norgate.

Opoku, K. A. 1978. *West African Traditional Religion*. Accra, Ghana: FEP International.

Origen. *On First Principles* is in Butterworth G. W., trans., *Origen: On First Principles*. New York: Harper Torchbooks, 1966; originally published in 1936 by the Society for Promoting Christian Knowledge, London. *Contra Celsum* (referred to in the text as "*Against Celsus*") can be found in Chadwick, H., trans., *Origen: Contra Celsum*, Cambridge: Cambridge University Press, 1953.

Orlans, F. B. 1993. *In the Name of Science*. Oxford: Oxford University Press.

Osborn, E. F. 1973. *Justin Martyr*. Tübingen: Mohr/Paul Siebeck.

Pagels, E. 1988. *Adam, Eve, and the Serpent*. New York: Random House.

Paley, W. 1788. *Principles of Moral and Political Philosophy*. 7th ed. Philadelphia: Dobson.

Parker, S. 1985. "Dragon." In *Harper's Bible Dictionary*, edited by Paul J. Achtmeier, 226. San Francisco and London: Harper and Row.

Parker, S. T. 1990a. "Origins of Comparative Developmental Evolutionary Studies of Primate Mental Abilities." In Parker and Gibson 1990, 3–64.

———. 1990b. 'Why Big Brains Are So Rare: Energy Costs of Intelligence and Brain Size in Anthropoid Primates." In Parker and Gibson 1990, 129–54.

Parker, S. T. and Baars, B. 1990. "How Scientific Usages Reflect Implicit Theories: Adaptation, Development, Instinct, Learning, Cognition, and Intelligence." In Parker and Gibson 1990, 65–96.

———. 1994. "Expanding Dimensions of the Self: Through the Looking Glass and Beyond." In Parker and others 1994, 3–19.

Parker, S. T., and Gibson, K. R., eds. 1990. *"Language" and Intelligence in Monkeys and Apes: Comparative Developmental Perspectives*. Cambridge: Cambridge University Press.

Parker, S. T., and others, eds. 1994. *Self-Awareness in Animals and Humans: Developmental Perspectives*. Cambridge: Cambridge University Press.

Passingham, R. E. 1975. "The Brain and Intelligence." In *Brain and Behavioral Evolution* 11:1–15.

Passmore, J. 1974. *Man's Responsibility for Nature*. London: Duckworth.

Patterson, D., and Ryder, R., eds. 1979. *Animal Rights: A Symposium*. London: Centaur Press.

Patterson, F. 1986. "The Mind of the Gorilla: Conversation and Conservation." In Benirschke 1986, 933–47.

Patterson, F., and Gordon, W. 1993. "The Case for the Personhood of Gorillas." In Cavalieri and Singer 1993, 58–77.

Patterson, F., and Linden, E. 1981. *The Education of Koko*. New York: Holt, Rinehart and Winston.

Pautigny, L. 1904. *Justin: Apologies: Texte Grec, Traduction Francaise, Introduction et Index*. Paris: Alphonse Picard et Fils.

Payne, K. 1989. "Elephant Talk." *National Geographic* 176, no. 2:265–77.

Payne, K. B., and Langbauer, W. R., Jr. 1992. "Elephant Communication." In Shoshani 1992, 116–23.

Payne, K., and Payne, R. 1985. "Large-Scale Changes over 19 Years in Songs of Humpback Whales in Bermuda." *Zietshcrift für Tierpsychologie/Journal of Comparative Ethology* 68:89–114.

Payne, K. and others. 1986. "Infrasonic Calls of the Asian Elephant (*Elephas Maximus*)." *Behavioral Ecology and Sociobiology* 18:297–301.

Payne, R., ed. 1983. *Communication and Behavior of Whales*. Boulder, Colo.: Westview.

Payne, R., and McVay, S. 1971. "Songs of Humpback Whales." *Science* 173:587–97.

Pelland, G. 1972. *Cinq études d'Augustin sur le début de la Genèse*. Paris and Tournai: Desclée.

Persson, I. 1993. "A Basis for (Interspecies) Equality." In Cavalieri and Singer 1993, 183–93.

Pharr, C., trans. 1952. *The Theodosian Code and Novels and the Sirmondian Constitutions*. Princeton, N.J.: Princeton University Press.

Philo. 1968. *De Praemiis et Poenis* (with both Greek and English text). Trans. F. H. Colson. Loeb Classical Library Series, no. 341. London: Heinemann; Cambridge, Mass.: Harvard University Press.

Pinches, C. 1993. "Each According to Its Kind: A Defense of Theological Speciesism." In Pinches and McDaniel 1993, 189–207.

Pinches, C., and McDaniel, J., eds. 1993. *Good News for Animals? Christian Approaches to Animal Well-Being*. Maryknoll, N.Y.: Orbis.

Pinker, S. 1994. *The Language Instinct: How the Mind Creates Language*. New York: William Morrow.

Plato. 1937. *The Dialogues of Plato* ["Plato/Jowett"]. Trans. B. Jowett. 2 vols. New York: Random House.

Pliny. 1940–63. *Natural History*. Vols. 3, 6 and 8. Vol. 3 trans. H. Rackham. Vols. 6 and 8 trans. W. H. S. Jones. Loeb Classical Library Series. London: Heinemann.

Pluhar, E. 1995. *Beyond Prejudice: The Moral Significance of Human and Nonhuman Animals*. London: Duke University Press.

Poli, M. D. 1988. "Species-Specific Differences in Learning." In Jerison and Jerison 1988, 277–97.

Poole, J. H., and others. 1988. "The Social Contexts of Some Very Low Frequency Calls of African Elephants." *Behavioral Ecology and Sociobiology* 22:385–92.

Pop, Bishop I. 1992. "The Care for Creation in Liturgical Theology." In *So That God's Creation Might Live: The Orthodox Church Responds to the Ecological Crisis*, edited by Ecumenical Patriarchate of Constantinople, 37–40. N.p.: Ecumenical Patriarchate of Constantinople.

Popper, K. 1974. *Conjectures and Refutations*. 5th ed. London: Routledge and Kegan Paul.

Post, S. 1993. "The Emergence of Species Impartiality: A Medical Critique of Biocentrism." *Perspectives in Biology and Medicine* 36, no. 2:289–300.

Povinelli, D. J. 1989. "Failure to Find Self-Recognition in Asian Elephants (*Elephas maximus*) in Contrast to Their Use of Mirror Cues to Discover Hidden Food." *Journal of Comparative Psychology* 103:122–31.

———. 1997. "Panmorphism." In Mitchell and others 1997, 92–103.

Rachels, J. 1991. *Created from Animals: The Moral Implications of Darwinism*. Oxford: Oxford University Press.

———. 1993. "Why Darwinians Should Support Equal Treatment for Other Great Apes." In Cavalieri and Singer 1993, 152–57.

Radner, D., and Radner, M. 1989. *Animal Consciousness*. Buffalo, N.Y.: Prometheus.

Raphael, D. D. 1994. *Moral Philosophy*. 2d ed. Oxford: Oxford University Press.

Rastogi, N. P. 1990. *Inscriptions of A"soka*. Varanasi: Chowkhamba Sanskrit Series Office.

Rattray, S. 1985. "Worship." In *Harper's Bible Dictionary*, edited by Paul J. Achtmeier, 1143–47. London: Harper and Row.

Reeves, R. R., and Leatherwood, S. 1994. *Dolphins, Porpoises and Whales: 1994–1998 Action Plan for the Conservation of Cetaceans*. Gland, Switzerland: IUCN.

Regan, T. 1979. "Exploring the Idea of Animal Rights." In Patterson and Ryder 1979, 73–86.

———. 1988. *The Case for Animal Rights*. 2d ed. London: Routledge.

———. 1989. "Religion and Animal Rights." *Animals' Voice* 2, no. 4:24–27, 104–6.

———. 1991. "The More Things Change." *Between the Species* 7:110–15.

———, ed. 1986. *Matters of Life and Death*. 2d ed. New York: Random House.

Regan, T., and Singer, P., eds. 1977. *Animal Rights and Human Obligations*. Englewood Cliffs, N.J.: Prentice-Hall.

Rensch, B. 1957. "The Intelligence of Elephants." *Scientific American* 196, no. 2:44–49.

Reynolds, V., and Reynolds, J. eds. 1995. *Poor Model Man: Experiments on Chimpanzees*. Nottingham: Fund for the Replacement of Animals in Medical Experiments.

Rhys Davids, T. W., trans. 1880. *Buddhist Birth Stories or Jātaka Tales*. London: Trübner.

———. [1881] 1969. *Buddhist Suttas*. New York: Dover.

Rhys-Davids, T. W., and Carpenter, J. E., eds. 1890–1911. *The Dīgha Nikāya*. London: Henry Frowde.

Rhys-Davids, T. W., and Stede, W., eds. [1921] 1952. *The Pali Text Society's Pali-English Dictionary*. London: Pali Text Society.

Richardson, C. C., and others, trans. and eds. 1953. *Early Christian Fathers*. Library of Christian Classics. Vol. 1. London: SCM.

Rickaby, J. 1888. *Moral Philosophy*. London: Longmans, Green.

Robbins, F. E. 1912. *The Hexaemeral Literature: A Study of the Greek and Latin Commentaries on Genesis*. Chicago: University of Chicago Press.

Roberts, A., and Rambaut, W. H. 1868–69. *The Writings of Irenaeus*. 2 vols. Ante-Nicene Christian Library: Translations of the Writings of the Fathers, vols. 5, 9. Edinburg: T. and T. Clark.

Roberts, A., and others, trans. 1867. *The Writings of the Apostolic Fathers*. Ante-Nicene Christian Library, Vol. 1. Edinburgh: T. and T. Clark.

Roberts, B. J. 1975. "The Old Testament: Manuscripts, Text and Versions." In *The Cambridge History of the Bible*. Vol. 2, *The West from the Fathers to the Reformation*, edited by G. W. H. Lampe, 1–26. Cambridge and New York: Cambridge University Press.

Robinson, D. N. 1985. *Philosophy of Psychology*. New York: Columbia University Press.

Robinson, J. A., trans. 1920. *The Demonstration of the Apostolic Preaching*. London: Society for Promoting Christian Knowledge.

Rollin, B. E. 1989. *The Unheeded Cry: Animal Consciousness, Animal Pain and Science*. Oxford: Oxford University Press.

———. 1992. *Animal Rights and Human Morality*. Rev. ed. Buffalo, N.Y.: Prometheus.

Rolston, H., III. 1988. *Environmental Ethics: Duties to and Values in the Natural World*. Philadelphia: Temple University Press.

———. 1994. "Value in Nature and the Nature of Value." In Attfield and Belsey 1994, 13–30.

Roth, M. T. 1995. *Law Collections from Mesopotamia and Asia Minor*. Atlanta: Scholars Press.

Routley, R., and Routley, V. 1995. "Against the Inevitability of Human Chauvinism." In Elliot 1995, 104–28.

RSPCA. 1994. *Ethical Concerns for Animals*. Ed. Maggy Jennings and Sheila Silcock. Horsham, West Sussex: RSPCA.

———. 1995. *On the Side of the Animals: Some Contemporary Philosophers' Views*. Ed. Maggy Jennings and Sheila Silcock.: Horsham, West Sussex: RSPCA.

Ruegg, D. S. 1980. "Ahi.msā and Vegetarianism in the History of Buddhism." In *Buddhist Studies in Honour of Walpola Rahula*, edited by Somaratna Balasooriya and others, 234–41. London: Gordon Fraser.

Ruether, R. R. 1993. "Men, Women and Beasts: Relations to Animals in Western Culture." In Pinches and McDaniel 1993, 12–23.

———. 1994. "Ecofeminism: Symbolic and Social Connections of the Oppression of Women and the Domination of Nature." In Adams 1994c, 13–23.

———. 1995. "Matthew Fox and Creation Spirituality: Strengths and Weaknesses." In *Green Christians: Journal of Christian Ecology Link* 24:10–13.

Ruse, M. 1987. "Biological Species: Natural Kinds, Individuals or What?" *British Journal of the Philosophy of Science* 38:225–42.

Russon, A. E. 1990. "The Development of Peer Social Interaction in Infant Chimpanzees: Comparative Social, Piagetian, and Brain Perspectives." In Parker and Gibson 1990, 379–419.

Ruvolo, M. 1994. "Proceedings of the National Academy of Sciences," 13 September 1994. In *Science* 265, 1661.

Ryder, R. D. 1970. *Speciesism*. Oxford: privately printed.

———. 1971. "Experiments on Animals." In Godlovitch and others 1971, 41–82.

———. 1974. "Speciesism: The Ethics of Vivisection." N.p.: Scottish Society for the Prevention of Vivisection.

———. 1975. *Victims of Science: The Use of Animals in Research*. London: Davis-Poynter.

———. 1979. "The Struggle against Speciesism." In Patterson and Ryder 1979, 3–14.

———. 1989. *Animal Revolution: Changing Attitudes towards Speciesism*. Oxford: Basil Blackwell.

———. 1992a. "An Autobiography." *Between the Species* 8:168–73.

———. 1992b. *Painism: Ethics, Animal Rights, and Environmentalism*. Cardiff: University of Wales, Centre for Applied Ethics.

———. 1993. "Sentientism." In Cavalieri and Singer 1993, 220–222.

———. 1995. "Speciesism." In RSPCA 1995, 14–15.

Ryder, R. D., and Wood, D. 1970. *Speciesism*. Oxford: printed leaflet.

Sabatier, P. D. [1743] 1976. *Bibliorum Sacrorum Latinae Versiones Antiquae, seu Vetus Italica et Caeterae quaecunquae in Codicibus Mss. & antiquorum libris reperiri potuerunt: quae com Vulgata Latina, & cum Textu Graeco comparantur*. 3 vols. Turnhout, Belgium: Brepolis.

Sagan, C. 1977. *Dragons of Eden*. New York: Random House.

Sagan, C., and Druyan, A. 1992. *Shadows of Forgotten Ancestors: A Search for Who We Are*. London: Century/Random House.

Sangharakshita. 1985. *The Eternal Legacy: An Introduction to the Canonical Literature of Buddhism*. London: Tharpa.

———. 1993. *A Survey of Buddhism: Its Doctrines and Methods through the Ages*. 7th ed. Glasgow: Windhorse.

Santmire, H. P. 1985. *The Travail of Nature*. Minneapolis: Fortress.

Sapontzis, S. 1987. *Morals, Reason and Animals*. Philadelphia: Temple University Press.

———. 1988. "Speciesism." *Between the Species* 4, no. 2:97–99.

Savage, J. J., trans. 1961. *Saint Ambrose: Hexameron, Paradise, and Cain and Abel*. The Fathers of the Church: A New Translation, vol. 42. New York: Fathers of the Church.

Savage-Rumbaugh, E. S. "*Pan paniscus* and *Pan troglodytes*: Contrasts in Preverbal Communicative Competence." In Susman 1984, 395–413.

Savage-Rumbaugh, E. S., and Wilkerson, Beverly J. 1978. "Socio-Sexual Behavior in *Pan paniscus* and *Pan troglodytes*: A Comparative Study." *Journal of Human Evolution* 7:327–44.

Savage-Rumbaugh, E. S., and others. 1986. "Spontaneous Symbol Acquisition and Communicative Use by Pygmy Chimpanzees (*Pan paniscus*)." *Journal of Experimental Psychology: General* 115:211–35.

Savage-Rumbaugh, S., and Lewin, R. 1994. *Kanzi: The Ape at the Brink of the Human Mind*. London: Doubleday.

Scalan, J. J. 1996. "Zoology and Physiology." In *Medieval Latin: An Introduction and Bibliographic Guide*, edited by F. A. C. Mantello and A. G. Rigg, 395–400. Washington, D.C.: Catholic University of America.

Schaller, G. B. 1995. "Mountain Gorillas of Africa: Threatened by War." *National Geographic* 188, no. 4:58–83.

Schmidt, G. H., and Schmidt, B. A. 1995. "Animal Welfare Legislation in Northern European Countries: A Study Tour." Report prepared for the American Farm Bureau Foundation for Agriculture.

Schmithausen, L. 1991a. *Buddhism and Nature: The Lecture Delivered on the Occasion of the EXPO 1990—An Enlarged Version with Notes*. Tokyo: International Institute for Buddhist Studies.

———. 1991b. *Buddhism and Nature: Proceedings of an International Symposium on the Occasion of EXPO 1990*. Tokyo: International Institute for Buddhist Studies.

———. 1991c. *The Problem of the Sentience of Plants in Earliest Buddhism*. Tokyo: International Institute for Buddhist Studies.

Schusterman, R. J., and others, eds. 1986. *Dolphin Cognition and Behavior: A Comparative Approach*. Hillsdale, N.J.: Erlbaum.

Scott, B. B., and others. 1995. *Reading New Testament Greek*. London: Society for Promoting Christian Knowledge.

Sebeok, T. A., ed. 1968. *Animal Communication: Techniques of Study and Results of Research*. Bloomington and London: Indiana University Press.

———. 1994. "'Animal' in Biological and Semiotic Perspective." In Ingold 1994b, 63–76.

———, ed., 1977. *How Animals Communicate*. Bloomington: Indiana University Press.

Seed, J. 1985. "Anthropocentrism." In Devall and Sessions 1985, 243–46.

Seldes, G. 1985. *The Great Thoughts*. New York: Ballantine.

Senart, E. 1875. *Essai sur La Légende du Bouddha, Son Caractère et Ses Origines*. Paris: Imprimerie Nationale.

Serpell, J. 1996. *In the Company of Animals: A Study in Human-Animal Relationships*. Cambridge: Cambridge University Press.

Serpell, J., and Paul, E. 1994. "Pets and the Development of Positive Attitudes to Animals." In Manning and Serpell 1994, 127–44.

Shoshani, J., ed. 1992. *Elephants*. London: Simon and Schuster.

Shoshani, J., and Eisenberg, J. F. 1992. "Intelligence and Survival." In Shoshani 1992, 134–37.

Shoshani, S. L. 1992. "Famous Elephants." In Shoshani 1992, 168–71.

Sibley, C. G., and Ahlquist, J. E. 1984. "The Phylogeny of the Hominoid Primates, as Indicated by DNA-DNA Hybridization." *Journal of Molecular Evolution* 20:2–15.

Sikes, S. K. 1971. *The Natural History of the African Elephant*. London: Weidenfeld and Nicolson.

Singer, P. 1976. *Animal Liberation: A New Ethics for Our Treatment of Animals*. London: Jonathan Cape.

———. 1979. "Not for Humans Only: The Place of Nonhumans in Environmental Issues." In Goodpaster and Sayre 1979, 191–206.

———. 1981. *The Expanding Circle: Ethics and Sociobiology*. Oxford: Clarendon.

———. 1987. "Animal Liberation or Animal Rights." *Monist*, 70:3–14.

———. 1990. *Animal Liberation: A New Ethics for Our Treatment of Animals*, 2d ed. New York: Avon.

———. 1993a. *How Are We to Live? Ethics in an Age of Self-Interest*. London: Mandarin Paperbacks.

———. 1993b. *Practical Ethics*. 2d ed. Cambridge: Cambridge University Press.

———. ed. 1993c. *A Companion to Ethics*. Oxford: Blackwell.

Skinner, B. F. 1938. *The Behavior of Organisms: An Experimental Analysis*. New York: Appleton-Century-Crofts.

Smart, N. 1976. *The Religious Experience of Mankind*. 2d ed. New York: Scribner's.

Smedes, Lewis B. 1987. "Respect for Human Life: 'Thou Shalt Not Kill.'" In Lammers and Verhey 1987, 143–49.

Smith, J. P., S. J., trans. 1952. *Proof of the Apostolic Preaching*. Ancient Christian Writers Series, vol. 16. London: Longmans, Green.

Smith, N. Kemp 1952. *New Studies in the Philosophy of Descartes*. London: Macmillan.

Smith, W. C. 1962. *The Meaning and End of Religion: A New Approach to the Religious Traditions of Mankind*. New York: Macmillan.

Smuts, B., and others. 1987. *Primate Societies*. London: University of Chicago Press.

Sorabji, R. 1993. *Animals Minds and Human Morals: The Origins of the Western Debate*. London: Duckworth.

Soskice, J. 1995. "Creation and Relation." In Gill 1995, 58–66.

Spiro, M. E. 1971. *Buddhism and Society: A Great Tradition and Its Burmese Vicissitudes*. London: Allen and Unwin.

Springer, M. T. 1931. *Nature-Imagery in the Works of Saint Ambrose*. Catholic University of America Patristic Studies, vol. 30. Washington, D.C.: Catholic University of America.

Staddon, J. E. R. 1989. "Animal Psychology: The Tyranny of Anthropocentrism." In Bateson and Klopfer 1989, 123–35.

Stark, W. 1967. "Sociology of Knowledge." In *The Encyclopedia of Philosophy*, edited by Paul Edwards, vol. 7, 475–78. London: Collier Macmillan.

Steinbock, B. 1978. "Speciesism and the Idea of Equality." *Philosophy* 53:247–56.

Sternberg, R. J., ed. 1982. *Handbook of Human Intelligence*. Cambridge: Cambridge University Press.

Story, F. 1964. *The Place of Animals in Buddhism*. Kandy, Ceylon: Buddhist Publication Society.

Suarez, S. D., and Gallup, G. G., Jr., 1981. "Self-Recognition in Chimpanzees and Orangutans, but Not Gorillas." *Journal of Human Evolution* 10:175–88.

Sukamar, R. 1989. *The Asian Elephant: Ecology and Management*. Cambridge: Cambridge University Press.

———. 1994. *Elephant Days and Nights*. Delhi: Oxford University Press.

Susman, R. L., ed. 1984. *The Pygmy Chimpanzee: Evolutionary Biology and Behavior*. New York: Plenum.

Suzuki, D., and Knudtson, P. 1992. *Wisdom of the Elders: Honoring Sacred Native Visions of Nature*. New York: Bantam.

Tatian. *Oratio ad Graecos*. In Whitaker 1992.

Taylor, J. H. 1982. *The Literal Meaning of Genesis*. Ancient Christian Writers Series, vols. 41, 42. New York: Newman.

Taylor, P. W. 1987. "Inherent Value and Moral Rights." *Monist* 70:15–30.

Terrace, H. 1985. "Animal Cognition: Thinking without Language." In Weiskrantz 1985, 113–28.

Terrace, H., and others. 1979. "Can an Ape Create a Sentence?" *Science* 206:892–902.

Teske, R. J. 1991. *Saint Augustine: On Genesis—Two Books on Genesis against the Manichees, and on the Literal Interpretation of Genesis: An Unfinished Book*. Washington, D.C.: Catholic University of America Press.

Thomas, J. A., and Kastelein, R. A. eds. 1990. *Sensory Abilities of Cetaceans: Laboratory and Field Evidence*. New York: Plenum.

Thomas, J. R., and others, eds. 1992. *Sensory Processes of Marine Mammals*. New York: Plenum.

Thomas, K. 1983. *Man and the Natural World: Changing Attitudes in England, 1500–1800*. New York: Pantheon.

Thomas, N. W. 1908. "Animals." In *Encyclopedia of Religion and Ethics*, edited by J. Hastings, vol. 1, 483–535. Edinburgh: T. and T. Clark.

Tillich, P. 1963. *Systematic Theology*. Vol. 3. Chicago: University of Chicago Press.

Today's English Version (the full title is *Good News for Modern Man: New Testament in Today's English Version*) 1966. 3d ed. New York: American Bible Society.

Tomasello, M. 1990. "Cultural Transmission in the Tool Use and Communicatory Signaling of Chimpanzees?" In Parker and Gibson 1990, 274–311.

Trenckner, V., ed. 1888. *Majjhima-Nikaya*. vol. 1. London: Henry Frowde.

Trusted, J. 1992. "The Problem of Absolute Poverty: What Are Our Moral Obligations to the Destitute?" In Cooper and Palmer 1992, 13–27.

Tucker, M. E., and Grim, J. A., eds. 1994. *Worldviews and Ecology: Religion, Philosophy, and the Environment*. Maryknoll, N.Y.: Orbis.

Tyack, P. 1986. "Whistle Repertoires of Two Bottlenose Dolphins, *Tursiops truncatus*: Mimicry of Signature Whistles?" *Behavioral Ecology and Sociobiology* 18:251–57.

Tylor, E. B. 1891. *Primitive Culture: Researches into the Development of Mythology, Philosophy, Religion Language, Art, and Custom*. 2 vols. London: John Murray.

van der Eijk, Ph. J., and others, eds. 1995. *Ancient Medicine in its Socio-cultural Context*. Vol. 2, Amsterdam and Atlanta: Rodopi.

van Hooff, Jan A. R. A. M. 1994. "Understanding Chimpanzee Understanding." In Wrangham and others 1994, 267–84.

Vetter, T. 1988. *The Ideas and Meditative Practices of Early Buddhism*. New York: E. J. Brill.

Vocabularivm Ivrisprvdentiae Romanae. 1903. Tomvs I (A–C). N.p.: Berolini.

Vogel, J. Ph. 1926. *Indian Serpent-Lore or the Nāgas in Hindu Legend and Art*. London: Arthur Probsthain.

Völker, W. 1952. *Der Wahre Gnostiker nach Clemens Alexandrinus*. Berlin: Akademie-Verlag.

von Glasenapp, H. 1970. *Buddhism: A Non-theistic Religion*. trans. Irmgard Schloegl. London: Allen and Unwin.

von Rad, G. 1966. "The Theological Problem of the Old Testament Doctrine of Creation." In *The Problem of the Hexateuch and Other Essays*, translated by E. W. T. Dicken, 131–43. New York: McGraw-Hill.

———. 1972. *Genesis: A Commentary*. Philadelphia: Westminster.

Walens, S. 1987. "Animals." In *The Encyclopedia of Religion*, edited by Mircea Eliade, vol. 1, 291–96. London: Collier Macmillan.

Wallace-Hadrill, D. S. 1968. *The Greek Patristic View of Nature*. Oxford: Manchester University Press.

Walshe, M., trans. 1987. *Thus Have I Heard: The Long Discourses of the Buddha (Dīgha Nikāya)*. London: Wisdom.

Ward, K. 1986. "Persons, Kinds and Capacities." In Byrne 1986, 53–79.

———. 1994. *Religion and Revelation: A Theology of Revelation in the World's Religions*. Oxford: Clarendon.

Warder, A. K. 1991. *Introduction to Pali*. 3d ed. Oxford: Pali Text Society.

Warren, H. C. 1970. *Buddhism in Translations*. New York: Atheneum.

Watkins, W. A., and Schevill, W. E. 1977. "Sperm Whale Codas." *Journal of Acoustical Society of America* 62:1485–90.

Watkins, W. A., and others. 1971. "Underwater Sounds of Monodon." *Journal of Acoustical Society of America* 49:595–99.

Watson, L. 1981. *Sea Guide to Whales of the World*, New York: E. P. Dutton.

Watts, W., trans. 1950. *Confessions* [of Augustine]. 2 vols. Loeb Classical Library Series. London: Heinemann.

Way, A. C., trans. 1963. *Saint Basil: Exegetic Homilies*. Fathers of the Church: A New Translation, vol. 46. Washington, D.C.: Catholic University Press of America.

Weingreen, J. 1959. *A Practical Grammar for Classical Hebrew*. 2nd ed. Oxford: Clarendon.

Weiskrantz, L., ed. 1985. *Animal Intelligence: Proceedings of a Royal Society Discussion Meeting Held on 6 and 7 June 1984*. Oxford Psychology Series, No. 7. Oxford: Clarendon.

Westermann, C. 1982. *Elements of Old Testament Theology*. Trans. Douglas W. Scott. Atlanta: John Knox.

Whitaker, M., ed. and trans. 1982. *Tatian: Oratio ad Graecos and Fragments*. Oxford: Clarendon.

Whitaker, R. H. 1959. "On the Broad Classification of Organisms." *Quarterly Review of Biology* 34:210–66.

———. 1969. "New Concepts of Kingdoms of Organisms." *Science* 163:150–60.

White, L., Jr. 1967. "The Historic Roots of Our Ecologic Crisis." *Science* 155:1203–7.

White, T. I. 1991. *Discovering Philosophy*. Englewood Cliffs, N.J.: Prentice Hall.

———. 1996. "Is a Dolphin a Person?" *Notes from the Field*. Jupiter, Florida: Wild Dolphin Project, 5.1, 10–11.

Wilbert, J., and Simoneau, K., eds. 1970–92. Folk Literature of (Various Tribes of South American Indians). 24 vols. Los Angeles: UCLA Latin American Center Publications.

Williams, B. 1985. *Ethics and the Limits of Philosophy*. London: Fontana.

———. 1993. *Shame and Necessity*. Berkeley: University of California Press.

Williams, C. S. C. 1975. "The History of the Text and Canon of the New Testament to Jerome." In *The Cambridge History of the Bible*. Vol. 2, *The West from the Fathers to the Reformation*, edited by G. W. H. Lampe, 27–53. Cambridge: Cambridge University Press.

Williams, G. H. 1962. *Wilderness and Paradise in Christian Thought*. New York: Harper.

———. 1971–72. "Christian Attitudes toward Nature." Parts 1 and 2. *Christian Scholar's Review* 2:3–35, 112–26.

Williams, H. 1989. *Sacred Elephant*. New York: Harmony.

Williams, P. 1994. *Mahayana Buddhism: The Doctrinal Foundations*. London: Routledge.

Willis, R. G. ed. 1990. *Signifying Animals: Human Meaning in the Natural World*. London: Unwin Hyman.

Wilson, E. O. 1980. *Sociobiology: The Abridged Edition*. London: Belknap Press.

———. 1984. *Biophilia*. London: Harvard University Press.

———. 1992. *The Diversity of Life*. Cambridge, Mass.: Belknap Press.

———, ed. 1988. *Biodiversity*. Washington, D.C.: National Academy.

Wilson, W. 1869. *The Writings of Clement of Alexandria*. Trans. William Wilson. Ante-Nicene Christian Library, vols 10, 12. Edinburgh: T. and T. Clark.

Wingren, G. 1959. *Man and the Incarnation: A Study in the Biblical Theology of Irenaeus*. Trans. Ross MacKenzie. Philadelphia: Muhlenberg.

Winn, H. E., and Olla, B. L. 1979. *Behavior of Marine Mammals*. Current Perspectives in Research Series, No. 3. New York: Plenum.

Wise, S. M. 1995. "How Nonhuman Animals Were Trapped in a Nonexistent Universe." *Animal Law* 1:15–43.

———. 1996. "The Legal Thinghood of Nonhuman Animals." *Boston College Environmental Affairs Law Review* 23:471–546.

Wolterstorff, N. 1987. "Why Animals Don't Speak." *Faith and Philosophy* 4:463–85.

Woodruff, G., and Premack, D. 1978. "Does the Chimpanzee Have a Theory of Mind?" *Behavioral and Brain Sciences* 4:515–26.

Wrangham, R. W., and others, eds. 1994. *Chimpanzee Cultures*. London: Harvard University Press.

Wright, G. E. 1952. *God Who Acts: Biblical Theology as Recital*. Studies in Biblical Theology, no. 2. London: SCM.

Würthwein, E. 1979. *The Text of the Old Testament: An Introduction to the Biblia Hebraica*. Trans. Erroll F. Rhodes. Grand Rapids, Mich.: Eerdmans.

Wynne-Tyson, Jon 1993. "The Subtleties of Speciesism." *Between the Species* 9:1, 45–47.

Yerkes, R. 1916. *The Mental Life of Monkeys and Apes*. Cambridge, Mass.: Holt.

Young, E. [1900] 1982. *The Kingdom of the Yellow Robe: Being Sketches of the Domestic and Religious Rites and Ceremonies of the Siamese*. Petaling Jaya, Selengor, Malaysia: Oxford University Press.

Yunis, J., and Prakash, O. 1982. "The Origins of Man: A Chromosomal Pictorial Legacy." *Science* 215:1525–29.

Zimmer, H. 1946. *Myths and Symbols in Indian Art and Civilization*. Ed. Joseph Campbell. New York: Bollingen Foundation.

Index

Abhidhamma, 16, 126, 141
Adams, Carol, 33, 213, 225 nn.26, 33,
    226 n.1, 254 n.5
ahi.msa, 146, 152
Albertus Magnus, 235 n.34, 248 n.72,
    254 n.10
anachronism, 11, 43, 216
analogies to speciesism, 28–30, 36, 47, 55,
    226 nn.3, 4, 227 n.22
    value and problems with analogies, 40–
    42, 55
    See also race and racism; sexism;
    speciesism
animal protection movements, 13, 28, 99–
    100, 108, 234–235 n.26
    Animal Liberation as bible of animal
    protection movement, 29
    compared to environmental issues, 63
    diverse movement, 62
    and principles of differentiated value,
    99
    use of "animal," 96
    use of species membership, 107–110
    See also animal rights; rights
animal rights, 13, 29
    individuals "in and of themselves" as
    focus, 208–209
    use of "interests" in place of "rights,"
    224 n.5
    See also animal protection movements;
    rights
animals, nonhuman
    animal-plant distinction as universal,
    88
    derogatory alternative terms, 21, 43, 68–
    69, 71, 89, 92, 93, 96, 142, 144
    diversity makes this category
    problematic, 88–89
    factors limiting human knowledge of,
    62

histories of views of, 62
meaning of "animals," 3–4, 22, 88–95,
    96, 110, 194, 233 n.8
traits in common, 93
use of poor representatives, 89–90, 92,
    93, 132, 180, 196, 247 n.63
as warring against humans, 92, 170,
    183
See also cetaceans; complex individuals;
    elephants; interests; language about
    other animals; natural history; great
    apes, nonhuman; principles of
    differentiated value
anthropocentrism
    in Buddhism, 124, 127, 153, 155
    in Christianity, 63, 177, 179–182, 184–
    188, 193, 198, 201, 206–208,
    247 n.57, 250 n.106, 251 n.123, 251–
    252 n.133, 253 n.153
    as common sense, 177
    in ethical traditions, 40, 44
    in Gnostic views, 181, 182, 251 n.117
    as hidden assumption, 93
    humans-centeredness as moral, 6, 216
    in interpretations of animal sacrifice,
    211–212
    in notions of individuality and
    rationality, 45
    in science, 28, 224 n.17, 229 n.16
    in search for language abilities in
    nonhuman animals, 68–69
    in Stoic views, 180
    in tension with Augustine's humility
    about humans, 197–199
    as term compared to "speciesism," 32,
    225 n.27
    in *Timaeus*, 190
    See also ethics; humans
anthropology, 14, 75, 63
anthropomorphism, 151

287